SECURING BORDERS, SECURING POWER

SECURING BORDERS, SECURING POWER

THE RISE AND DECLINE OF ARIZONA'S BORDER POLITICS

MIKE SLAVEN

Columbia University Press
New York

Columbia University Press

Publishers Since 1893

New York   Chichester, West Sussex

cup.columbia.edu

Copyright © 2022 Columbia University Press

All rights reserved

Library of Congress Cataloging-in-Publication Data
Names: Slaven, Mike, author.
Title: Securing borders, securing power : the rise and decline of Arizona's
border politics / Mike Slaven.
Description: New York : Columbia University Press, [2022] | Includes bibliographical
references and index.
Identifiers: LCCN 2022000670 (print) | LCCN 2022000671 (ebook) |
ISBN 9780231203760 (hardback) | ISBN 9780231203777 (trade paperback) |
ISBN 9780231555227 (ebook)
Subjects: LCSH: Border security—Political aspects—Arizona. | Arizona—
Emigration and immigration—Government policy. | Arizona—Politics and
government—1951– | United States—Boundaries—Mexico.
Classification: LCC JV6912 .S53 2022 (print) | LCC JV6912 (ebook) |
DDC 325.7910905—dc23
LC record available at https://lccn.loc.gov/2022000670
LC ebook record available at https://lccn.loc.gov/2022000671

Cover photo: IrinaK © Shutterstock
Cover design: Milenda Nan Ok Lee

CONTENTS

INTRODUCTION

Arizona and the Rise of Populist Border-Security Politics

There is no higher priority than protecting the citizens of Arizona. We cannot sacrifice our safety to the murderous greed of drug cartels. We cannot stand idly by as drop houses, kidnappings and violence compromise our quality of life. We cannot delay while the destruction happening south of our international border creeps its way north. We in Arizona have been more than patient waiting for Washington to act. But decades of federal inaction and misguided policy have created a dangerous and unacceptable situation.

—GOVERNOR JAN BREWER, APRIL 23, 2010

O n April 23, 2010, warning of a violent emergency creeping north from the Mexican border, Governor Jan Brewer of Arizona signed into law Senate Bill (SB) 1070. The event convulsed Arizona politics. Mandating, among other measures, that Arizona law enforcement officers inquire during lawful stops about the immigration status of anyone they reasonably suspected to be in the United States unlawfully, the bill shot the state to international headlines and fierce criticism. Within Arizona, incendiary debate seemed to expose deepening tension between Arizona's growing Hispanic minority and its politically dominant Anglo majority. Strident objections that the bill licensed racial profiling, compromised civil rights, and violated important constitutional principles had come to nothing. There was a crisis, it was argued—a gaping border-security hole, scandalously ignored for too long. "I will not back off until we solve the problem of this illegal invasion," Russell Pearce, the state senator who authored SB 1070, had vowed a couple of years earlier. "Invaders, that's what they are. Invaders of American sovereignty, and it can't be tolerated."[1]

The stroke of Brewer's pen was the kind of moment that seems to characterize much of early twenty-first-century politics, an event prefiguring the rise of Donald Trump.[2] Declaring a new kind of emergency and citing the fears of an ignored and betrayed people, a leader had enforced exclusion in the name of security, sweeping away constraints. It was an exceptional turn of events. But the paths that led to it and those that were paved afterward were full of unexpected turns: it was neither the beginning nor the end of the story.

A HARDENING LINE

Immigration is interpreted and represented in many ways in politics. Activists, citizens, experts, and officials portray migration variously as an economic phenomenon, a humanitarian concern, a matter of rights, and a natural part of an interconnected world. So why is it that governments so often come to treat immigration as a security issue? Immigration politics is hotly contested by both those who paint immigration as a threat and those who emphatically reject this claim. Public opinion on immigration in many Western democracies, not least the United States, is complex.[3] There are some areas of broad agreement as well as overlapping interpretations, sympathies, and concerns.[4] Yet in many democracies, security has seemed to exert an unusually strong pull over the politics of immigration, despite these muddled conditions.[5] Although it may not seem so in the context of world politics today, this development is not inevitable or obvious. Why, then, do policy makers choose to treat immigration as a matter of security when other interpretations are available?

Understanding this choice can perhaps help us imagine or pursue different possibilities for immigration politics or for other issues that are treated as security concerns. The task of this book is to address this question—to grasp why, given the circumstances of politics and the seeming workings of the immigration issue, it makes sense to policy makers to treat immigration in a "securitized" way. This book holds, in essence, that to trace the reasons for this development in our politics, we must understand how the purported presence of security in an issue shapes political competition. Rather than understanding security as a separate or exceptional species of social relations, as has been common, seeing the distinctive meanings that security brings to political life—while understanding how these meanings inflect the larger, competitive political game in twenty-first-century democratic processes—can give us crucial insight into why our politics treats issues such as immigration as matters of security.

Such a process unfolded gradually in the first decade of this century in Arizona, the frequent epicenter of the fractious immigration politics of the United States. In the early 2000s, Arizona's 389-mile-long border with Mexico had become the main site of unauthorized border crossing into the United States, the principal corridor for one of the world's most voluminous migrations. In the U.S. federal system, it had been settled that state governments such as Arizona's bore little responsibility related to the issue: the border and immigration had long been treated as federal domains.[6] Around 2004, however, immigration rose to become the dominant issue in Arizona state politics. The previous consensus—that there was no relevant action at the state level to take on these issues—was quickly abandoned. The policy-making system in Arizona began to yield immigration- and border-related policy proposals by the score. This policy outflow was remarkable in another key way. Nearly all of the proposed measures had a clear security orientation, despite the fact that Arizona's government was not dominated by "border hawks" who agitated for immigration enforcement as a matter of ideological priority. On the contrary, for much of this period, nonhawkish figures in both the Democratic and Republican Parties—including many who had previously tried to downplay the need for state action or had said they lacked proper authority to take it—held key positions.

As many of these proposals were enacted, immigration and the border in Arizona politics became markedly "securitized": they were increasingly treated as or became security issues. In a basic sense, the term *securitization*—which has developed an extensive body of academic theory and critique around it—simply describes this empirical phenomenon wherein other possible understandings of an issue are de-emphasized, defeated, or forgotten and security understandings predominate. To securitize immigration is not merely to restrict it. There are many potential reasons to want to reduce immigration and many potential mechanisms to pursue that goal. The issue progression on immigration that seems familiar to us today, however, is one that advances on images of threat and urgency and that proposes to suffuse immigration governance with security practices,[7] "integrating [the] issue into a security framework that emphasizes policing and defence."[8] In Arizona from 2003 to 2011, more than one hundred policies proposed or enacted clearly employed a security approach to these issues, seeking to integrate diverse areas of state policy into a burgeoning border-security governance. During this same time, only one politically viable proposal for a concrete state policy change saw immigration through a lens that was distinctly not one of security. SB 1070 was a remarkable development, recognized as a watershed moment in immigration politics in the United States.[9] But it unfolded only within a longer process in Arizona,[10] where security overwhelmed all alternatives when it came to addressing immigration and the border and where the state adopted a series of policies that had previously been broadly considered exclusionary, racist, or extreme.

In this way, Arizona presents a familiar story. At the time, SB 1070 was covered in the national media as a draconian and outlying measure. Today, it is perhaps more readily apparent that Arizona's experience mirrors a global phenomenon. Security-heavy treatment of immigration and the more exclusionary politics that accompanies that treatment have emerged strongly across the West. Where this trend has taken hold, it has often appeared to have the acquiescence of political figures who at first resisted more radical calls but who have bent as the issue has developed. Europe's response to movements of people from Africa and Asia across the Mediterranean Sea seemed to harden broadly according to such a pattern, and the Trump administration's "Muslim ban" and family-separation policies were brought forward as major Republican Party figures euphemized these securitizing measures and buried their formerly more moderate immigration positions.[11] Even as such a trajectory becomes familiar, though, it remains puzzling. These policies often do not seem to closely follow on-the-ground developments, as governments such as Italy's grew more hard-line about Mediterranean crossings even after the number of crossings plummeted.[12] Nor have these policies typically enjoyed an obvious consensus within the polities that adopt them; they have often unfolded amid passionate public dispute, even if many political elites are muted.

So it was in Arizona. The state's amplification of border-security politics intensified even as the purported problem of unauthorized border crossing greatly declined. U.S. Border Patrol apprehensions, the measure usually employed as a proxy for levels of unauthorized traffic, peaked in Arizona around 2000 and then again around 2005. But by the time of SB 1070 in 2010, this metric had been declining for years, reaching lows not seen in decades.[13] Perhaps even more puzzling, the dominance of a security approach to immigration in Arizona also occurred when other possible interpretations of the problem found substantial support. In public-opinion polls at this time, around two-thirds of Arizonans typically supported state immigration-enforcement provisions, such as allowing state and local law enforcement to check immigration status, requiring businesses to verify the legal status of workers, and barring the issue of a driver's license to those without legal status in the United States. However, similar majorities expressed support for expanding legal channels for work migration and for enacting a legalization program for millions of unauthorized immigrants.[14] In Arizona, the birthplace of the U.S. sanctuary movement in the 1980s,[15] activists and citizens continued to mobilize prominently for these kinds of policies and against a draconian, securitized view of immigration and the border.[16] One would imagine that this multifaceted quality of public opinion would provide the political material for a varied policy-making effort, featuring both security and nonsecurity approaches. In Arizona, however, the security approach dominated—even though it did not flow clearly from the "objective" policy problem or from a single obvious reading of the issue's politics.

Despite this securitization tendency deepening over the course of years, the Arizona case was to yield another striking development. Less than a year after Arizona's border hard-liners had won passage of SB 1070, their most notable achievement to date, the securitization trend in

Arizona state government came to a screeching halt. This process was therefore deflated in Arizona years before Donald Trump descended in his golden escalator to champion this kind of politics at a national level. By that time, Arizona had already seesawed from a relatively relaxed status quo ante to an extended period of intense border-security politics and then to the issue's decline from the top of the state's agenda—a progression that belies structural accounts of immigration policy, which indicate that vested interests work effectively against such wild swings in direction.[17]

To decipher this complex, dramatic issue trajectory in Arizona, this book makes several interrelated arguments from a starting point of analyzing how the association of security with immigration changes the political calculations surrounding immigration. At base, the book holds that we can illuminate these processes if we foreground this competitive political context around security—if we focus analysis on how politicians, by securing borders, are securing power. Explaining why political actors of many different ideologies may so quickly cluster around security approaches to immigration and seem loath to challenge them, this book traces how interactions between populist and security logics in political debate lead governing elites to adopt yielding strategies that "mainstream" more hard-line approaches. This book identifies how new party-competition dynamics, shaped by concepts of responsibility and accountability emerging from security meanings, can deepen the securitization process: where political actors trade on security politics toward differing political ends, their maneuvers against one another may entail assenting to security-heavy immigration policy as the price of power, thus deepening securitization even while relative moderates hold key offices. What is not necessary for this process to happen is any actual agreement on what, if any, threat the community faces. This book demonstrates how the formidable mobilizing power of securitizing immigration—starkly illustrated in the passage of SB 1070 and the subsequent consolidation of power by its champions—emerges not from a single coherent logic of security but from a combination of more contingent political circumstances, in this case rooted in Republican intraparty dynamics and polarized national politics in the United States. Finally, this book argues that the heat of security politics not only propels these securitizing trends but also can undo them. Backlash from those affected can activate a cosmopolitan countersecuritization logic among those in the Center Right, who are oriented toward being seen by important outsiders as reasonable and open rather than irrational and exclusionary. In Arizona, this logic emerged from the tempest of post–SB 1070 politics with enough force to halt a securitization juggernaut.

Other places that have witnessed similar immigration politics may not have experienced this kind of reversal, at least not yet. But the fact that a strong securitization trend in immigration politics can so quickly fall apart adds to both the puzzle and the urgency of understanding why. Whatever political dynamics propelled Arizona's securitization forward, they were not inexorable or even as strong as they seemed. To analyze securitizing trends as inherently fragile allows a better grasp of what sorts of politics can effectively counter them. We can understand how politicians typically read their political contexts and respond through securitization—and also how this could be otherwise.

First, however, we must think about why immigration is treated as security in some relatively new ways. In the following sections, this introduction makes some particular interventions in three areas of the scholarly literature to start decoding the Arizona puzzle and illuminate its larger significance. First, I establish why understanding these events requires challenging some typical ways of thinking about the politics of security and how this challenge can be achieved by more fully embracing a reading of securitization as "normal" politics. Second, I argue that there needs to be greater account of populism in securitization analyses and vice versa. Analyzing these two concepts' relationship may allow us greater purchase in addressing key questions in both literatures—why securitization processes advance and why nonpopulist political actors so often "mainstream" securitized approaches to immigration that they previously regarded as extreme. Third, I identify the need for new perspectives on how securitization processes might end, which could promise key insights on the process of rolling back populist border-security politics. I conclude the introduction with a discussion of the book's largely narrative form, its process-tracing approach, and its interview-based interpretive methods.

WHY SECURITIZE IMMIGRATION? THE PUZZLES OF SECURITY'S POLITICAL GAME

To analyze this securitized trajectory of immigration politics—in Arizona or wherever else it may occur—it seems critical to understand why policy makers choose to navigate immigration in such a securitized way even amid a political environment where diverse perspectives and multiple alternatives appear potentially viable. Despite the apparent importance of this question, however, we know quite little about why security interpretations so often win out in immigration-policy deliberations. This gap in our knowledge results in large part from blind spots in the security studies field caused by its origins as a branch of the international relations subdiscipline rather than of more generalist political science.[18] Security studies has employed starting points focused on survival, necessity, and sovereign prerogative—instead of on choice, contingency, and political competition.[19] The latter qualities are intrinsic to our substantive understanding of politics and, as this book explores, are frequently central to the politicians who make policy decisions about immigration. It is key to understand something that within the study of this field represents a relatively new topic: how security shapes the political game.

I start from the basic constructivist idea that the meaning of an event or thing—such as a group of people migrating—is not something inherent to it but rather an interpretation, something socially constructed by human actors.[20] It may seem natural for some people to see immigration as a threat, but this view rests on a number of interpretations that are not obvious: why these "others" are not part of "us" (Who is the community?), why we should be suspicious of rather than friendly to these others, just what it is they are threatening, why that thing is important, and, crucially, why such a view would be held as more significant in making immigration policy than other views. Scholars have tried to bring this kind of analytical perspective into understanding the emergence of "new" security-agenda items such as migration, which lie outside the "traditional" state-security concerns of war and peace. But these analyses have often obscured essential political dimensions—especially the political decision making—embedded in these processes. The original view in constructivist security studies, put forward by the Copenhagen School,[21] saw security not as an objective state of threat but as a speech act that has won over an audience—an utterance by a top leader arguing that a certain issue is a matter of survival for some important "referent object" (such as the state or society), which a relevant audience accepts. That issue, then, is taken as no longer being one of normal politics. It has become "securitized"—marked as a matter of survival and elevated above the rest of the agenda. A state of exception surrounding that issue emerges, separating the issue from the rest of the "merely political"[22] and allowing leaders to break normal rules about rights and due process in relation to the issue because of the life-or-death stakes.

This view connects the making of security claims about new issues such as migration with a vision of politics marked by a tendency toward reduced pluralism and narrowed political debate and by the acceptance of certain policies previously regarded as extreme.[23] As immigration has become securitized amid an illiberal and often populist wave, that connection has intuitive appeal. Even as other security scholars have disputed most parts of the original theory—especially the rigidness of this "grammar of security" that allows anything potentially to be security but only in a particular way[24]—this vision of sovereign decisionism in security has nonetheless deeply imprinted later views of the topic.[25] So long as that vision endures, what it describes does not, in many ways, resemble politics as we would recognize it. Rather, it adapts an image of authority emerging amid danger, borrowed from Thomas Hobbes's social contract theory, because when survival is at stake, there is no other choice.[26] Although these starting points, resting on the decisionism of the securitizing actor and the power of fear, are sometimes described as a more extreme form of politicization,[27] they lend themselves more to describing a state of antipolitics, brought into being by a need to survive and therefore, when it comes to a securitized issue, producing one overwhelming kind of political response.

Examining the reasons behind immigration-policy decisions in Arizona, however, exposes very different dynamics. In the interviews I conducted, policy makers do not describe a situation where their actions were guided by their own feelings of fear. Nor do they even paint a scene where officials worked from clear agreement that immigration constituted a stark danger in the ways alleged—the sort of "repressive consensus"[28] (or, less dismally, "extensive consensus")[29] that securitizing actors may aim to bring about under the heat of supposed threat.[30] These officials often do recall an intense political situation. Several independently liken it to a "gasoline fire." But their worries at the time were largely the ones we would normally expect of politicians. They sought to represent their publics in the ways they believed best, to achieve their policy goals in a wide array of areas, and, of course, to keep their power or perhaps gain more. The development of immigration as a security issue affected their strategies to achieve these aims—indeed, in ways that this book examines in detail. However, it did not fundamentally alter their aims into something other than normal political goals. The moves may have changed, but the objects of the political game remained the same.

As one interviewee put it regarding the fear surrounding the immigration issue, "People have fears that, I think, certainly the political strategists can hook into." What does it mean for fears to be a platform for varied political strategizing rather than simply an entrée into one kind of emergency treatment of an issue, led by those atop the existing political hierarchy? Jan Brewer's statement that serves as the epigraph to this introduction seems very much like the kind of "securitizing move" that the original theory would describe: an electrifying expression of emergency from a top leader, rallying support for urgent action that puts aside the niceties of rights or due procedure to ensure security and constitute a protected "people." But as this book explores, taking a longer and deeper view of the varied politics that arose around border security in Arizona shows that such a reading would massively oversimplify the event, to the point of fundamentally misunderstanding it. Rather, Brewer's move was but one link in a much longer political chain—one that was made up of many participants, was in no one person's particular control, and was inextricably intertwined with broader political struggles.

By taking this view, this book contributes to a diverse array of "sociological" securitization scholarship that has sought to uncover the thicker social relations that constitute processes such as the securitization of migration.[31] Even within this branch of scholarship, understanding the reasons why policy makers in a given context might pursue the securitization of an issue has not been a major focus.[32] This has left a gap in our understanding. "Sociological" approaches to securitization have come to form a substantial branch of research, but it has been a large task to recover these varied security-inflected social processes from a theoretical starting point where security's "grammar" works only in certain ways. In these sociological contributions, as in earlier ones, the dominant method in analyzing the emergence of "new" security issues has been discourse analysis—examining political discourses, usually public ones, to understand how security problems are socially constructed.[33]

As we have gained better understanding of the lower-grade forms of anxiety and unease in which security can manifest itself apart from emergency and imminent threat,[34] the complex variations on how new groups or phenomena can come to be painted as dangers,[35] and the multifaceted processes of threat construction that involve a wider variety of actors,[36] the focus has remained on how security issues are represented in discourse. Indeed, this is essential to the issue. Yet there remains a key distinction between political talk and policy action[37]—between a discursive form of securitization and an institutionalized securitization that occurs through changes in policy treatment.[38] Indeed, immigration scholars note how political talk and policy action on migration can often diverge.[39] Discourses shape but do not determine actions in politics, and, ultimately, they cannot reveal actors' motivations and strategies.[40] Understanding why political actors such as those in Arizona choose to securitize immigration policy, therefore, requires a different approach—one that accounts for how public discourses surrounding immigration, among many contextual factors, affect how policy makers decide to approach it.

Drawing from extensive interviews with policy makers key to Arizona's policy evolution, this book takes a view of securitization that is actor centered and interpretive,[41] focusing not just on what officials said and did but also on the officials and what they understood themselves to be saying and doing. This approach takes account of discourse as part of the context in which these actors operate but recognizes that political actors may have reasons for acting that they do not reveal in public discourses.[42] A clear possibility is that policy makers might choose securitization not out of belief in an objective threat but for the tacit purpose of retaining or accruing political power.[43]

Reasons for securitizing issues that are related to political power have been sketched before now but until recently only in a very rudimentary way. Even the earliest work on securitization suspected that political elites would try to securitize issues inappropriately in order to gain greater authority over them.[44] More recently, an examination of the ways in which securitization may evoke an intensified "politics of the extraordinary" that transforms understandings of political community has advanced a perhaps less categorically dismal interpretation of how political figures may use securitization to command uncommon levels of political mobilization.[45] But because these studies largely have not employed the kinds of methodological tools to explore these reasons empirically, they have not dealt in detail with political reasons for securitizing issues. They have instead tended to blend the substance of securitarian concepts (security's ideational core or "logic" of threat, necessity, and survival), the supposed political effects of securitization (if it is successful, either producing exceptionalism or reducing dissent), and presumptions about which political actors ("top leaders") might seek securitization, given that it yields those effects.[46] Yet conversations with policy makers in Arizona bear out the complexity and indeterminacy of the relationship between security and political power. Against the prevailing scholarly image of securitization as a straightforward tool for consolidating and marshaling power, Arizona politicians show the frequent defensiveness of such moves. One Arizona politician recalled a recurring theme in conversations with colleagues: "Sometimes they would even say it, you know, behind closed doors or what have you. They would say, 'I can't vote that way because I won't get reelected,' or 'I'm voting this way because this is the public, this is the popular thing to do.' And they changed." The reasons why politicians change in this way form a key part of the securitization phenomenon and require a robust explanation.

Although this book examines Arizona in particular to understand the securitization of migration, underlying the study is a curiosity about securitized politics in general. Does security affect politics in ways that are unique or at least distinguishing? Studies of migration have frequently been used to explore this question because the issue is not part of the "traditional" state-centered security agenda and thus can show how the meaning of security widens.[47] Nevertheless, what precisely security does to politics remains elusive, its distinct quality often difficult to pinpoint.[48] Scholars have identified at least a couple of troubling symptoms that appear to grow from the sowing of insecurity within politics: the evaporation of substantial contestation over whether an issue is truly one of security and, following from this, the adoption of policies that would have previously been regarded as unacceptable.[49] Amid the illiberal politics of securitizing migration, these observations resonate. In Arizona, a pattern repeated: the border-hawk agenda continuously unspooled, with every incremental victory representing some step previously regarded as far-fetched.[50] Would-be opponents heard this drumbeat grow louder and louder. As one interviewee recalled, "At first, the general kind of consensus was that these are extreme members proposing some extreme ideas that aren't gonna go anywhere. . . . Each year they kind of slowly gained more and more power, and those measures started gaining more and more traction in the legislature. So it was a growing, growing issue."

This pattern, where securitization progresses onward and onward with limited checks, has deepened scholars' concerns about securitization's perceived tendency to threaten democratic values.[51] The original theory held that for an issue to be "securitized," it must dominate political discussion for at least some time; empirical immigration politics seems to reflect this understanding to some extent as the issue's securitization coincides with increased saliency. In such a process, the political scene becomes dominated by issues discussed in terms of urgency, exclusion, and authority. Such developments inevitably color fundamental questions about freedom, citizenship, and belonging. As these discussions begin to inflect and often subsume other policy areas, it becomes clearer that the effects of securitization processes cannot be neatly confined to the discrete issue in a specific discussion. Given the clear importance of these tendencies for securitization to progress—in the quoted legislator's words, "to slowly gain more and more power"—it is a problem that we do not yet have a cohesive explanation for this progression, an explanation that could guide us in addressing it. The typical view has relied on the premise that security is different from "normal" politics in permitting normal rules to be broken as well as limiting deliberation and dissent.

However, many scholars, after examining an array of cases, have suggested that this sharp theoretical distinction is not viable.[52] In Arizona, for instance, the logics of securitizing employed by policy makers were replete with the calculations of "normal" politics. This questioning of the distinction has led to an increasing focus on how "security" issues become part of "normal," professional politics, debated and contested in typical domestic political arenas.[53] This focus has opened up a key space to examine security politics apart from the idea of exceptionalism, showing that "an issue can very well be about security and at the same time remain within the regular sphere of politics, without an automatic escalation into the extraordinary."[54]

Such efforts to understand the doing of "security politics" in a political-sociological sense offer the opportunity for a much richer understanding of why security emerges to policy makers as the seemingly sensible way, even amid other possibilities, to govern immigration. This literature is still emerging, however, and rather than offering strong propositions about how the purported presence of "security" affects politicians' strategy or tactics in engaging in political contestation, it has often focused mainly on dispelling the shadow of "exceptionalism" that has so frequently divided security analysis and political analysis. What might constitute the particular "rules of the (political) game" when security is invoked—how this invocation shifts politicians' approaches to achieving goals and gaining power—has emerged as a prominent question only recently,[55] despite its seemingly great importance to understanding securitization processes.

These emerging examinations of "security as politics" have often employed a historical turn, looking at classical national-security issues to analyze how they have moved into more contested, often legislative arenas and become "(re)politicized."[56] This sort of perspective has provided key purchase in examining the varied politics around security but perhaps offers only a partial view, focusing on instances where certain kinds of debates over security reemerge in certain arenas.[57] If it is clear that "normal" politics continues even when securitization is present, it has nonetheless remained somewhat unclear what exactly this politics is like. Given how thoroughly this theoretical boundary between "normal" politics and "exceptional" security has been criticized, this book proposes that we must in essence step beyond it, delving into the empirically evident fact that actors in political arenas maneuver politically around security. Our attention will then turn to whether on an issue that is seen as connected to security politicians may play the political game in different and distinctive ways.

By analyzing how policy makers approach security politically, this book offers a markedly different sort of explanation for why political debate often dissipates and extreme positions are adopted when security dominates the treatment of an issue. Rather than seeing competition as something put aside amid calls to safeguard the survival of the state or society, this book examines why politicians adopt security-heavy treatment of immigration precisely to preserve or enhance their power in a competitive political context. This is not to argue that there is nothing distinctive about the politics of security—far from it. But there is nothing inherently exceptional about that politics. The specific security meanings that shape political debates over issues do not necessarily determine how a given issue ends up being treated or mark an exceptionalist transformation. Nevertheless, security can—and indeed does—seem to shape politics in some distinct ways. In immigration politics, this would be the familiar pattern—such as that identified in Arizona—where the issue continually shifts, becoming increasingly imbued with urgency and mobilized increasingly through exclusion, whether exacted by center-left forces such as the French Socialists under François Hollande or by center-right forces such as the Austrian People's Party under Sebastian Kurz.[58] It is urgent, then, to identify the political logic that, rather than resisting demands that formerly seemed extreme, drives movement toward them.

In the heat of politics, such a development can be unmistakable to observers and participants even as its causes can remain murky. In an interview, one retired Arizona state legislator, sitting at his kitchen table, reflected on debate around SB 1070. Unthinkably extreme just years earlier, by 2010 SB 1070, despite being loudly decried as racist, was gliding toward enactment. He and his allies felt powerless to stop it. The interview dwelled on these questions: "Why do you think things got so extreme? . . . What happened in that process to move something that people thought was really beyond the pale to something that was getting endorsed?"

The former lawmaker paused for a long time. "That's a question I've thought a lot about," he finally said. "And my short answer is I don't know." In providing answers to this question, this book builds upon the concept of "security as politics"[59] rather than seeing securitization as distinct from competitive politics as we know and study it. When politicians deal with purported security issues in ways that produce seemingly extraordinary effects, we should hold to the basic observation that in order to realize their preferred policies, politicians must seek first to preserve their power in a competitive political context.[60] In securitizing an issue area such as immigration, what are politicians aiming to achieve? They may be acting against a perceived threat in order to secure a valued thing, but not necessarily the state or society. Rather, they are securing power.

POPULISM AND THE POLITICS OF SECURITY

To understand what happened in Arizona, we must embrace approaches beyond a specific securitization theory that separates security from "normal" politics. The resemblance of securitization to agenda politics has motivated attempts to merge securitization theory with political science concepts such as agenda setting and framing.[61] In connecting securitization concepts to analogous political science ideas that then perform the explanatory work, these efforts have shown that political science concepts can take a leading role in explaining securitization processes—rather than a secondary one where they merely patch gaps in a separate securitization theory that remains incommensurate to their "normal" political premises. Indeed, the explanatory potential of political science concepts in these cases deserves to be embraced more fully, which would illuminate the "rules of the game" of security politics through a new starting point by drawing on political science literatures that have already examined cases where security meanings are present in the competitive politics of immigration.

In the attempt to make such disciplinary links, a promising place to look is an area of political science that has long examined many of the same cases as the securitization literature, where immigration policies have become more hard-line and animated by images of threat. But rather than being analyzed as instances of securitization, these events have often been examined as studies of the party politics of migration, especially of the influence of radical right-wing populism.[62] Many of the most potent recent right-wing challenges to immigration-policy regimes have been characterized by populism, which may be understood as a "thin-centered ideology" that attaches itself to fuller substantive ideologies (such as those of the Right), importing an ideational core that portrays a corrupt elite as standing opposed to a pure people and arguing that the general will of the people must prevail.[63] Studies of migration politics and populism overlap substantially; scholars in both fields have noted in many cases across Europe and North America a hard-line progression in the political direction of the issue, a progression that is sometimes conceptualized as a "contagion" emanating from the Far Right or a "mainstreaming" of its immigration views.[64] Arizona represents such a case, albeit in a U.S. context in which there are clear populist radical-right (and far-right) forces but no separate party formed from them.[65] Indeed, in Arizona maximal immigration enforcement began as the pet issue of a populist radical-right faction of the state Republican Party, headed by Russell Pearce (the eventual SB 1070 author), who railed from the fringes of power against an inert elite. Soon, this issue became a major preoccupation for Arizona elites across the political spectrum: "a constant calculus," one interviewee described it.

Bringing these disciplinary views into greater conversation can shed light on the central questions of why immigration policy often becomes increasingly hard-line. Securitization studies has presumed that governing elites have strong control over this process and no impetus to let challengers in on it, so nuanced explanations for why politicians might shift their immigration stances in more hard-line directions have tended to come from the migration-politics scholarship. In these accounts, the radical Right might "tug moderate parties to the extreme right" by raising public concern about immigration.[66] Many cases show evidence of this process.[67] Yet there is no single settled explanation for why these shifts are so contagious across party systems—for example, affecting even center-left parties when the competition would seem to be for right-wing votes. Nonpopulist parties can adopt a number of different strategic responses to such a challenge, which include ignoring or confronting populist radical-right competitors.[68] Sometimes these responses work at locking the populists out of power or influence.[69] Thus, political strategizing in this policy area does not inherently point in a securitized direction.[70] Indeed, at first Arizona's political elites tried some of these other strategies before adopting positions that securitized immigration.

This "mainstreaming" process in Arizona is examined here through the eyes of the decision makers who navigated the issue, adopting and shifting policy positions. It becomes clear that it is impossible to fully explain this process without connecting it to security. Indeed, as one interviewee recalled of crafting positions on immigration issues, "Without that sense of security, it was abundantly clear that not only politically was it not going anywhere, but that the public was not going to buy into it." That sense of security carries particular meanings surrounding urgency and necessity that need to be accounted for analytically, which typical analyses of party positioning on immigration have not done explicitly. What these political actors are doing when they shift in such a way is not just "restricting" immigration but securitizing it, not simply modulating a position in one direction or another along a kind of elaborated number line[71] but rather helping to bring distinct meanings into the treatment of the issue. Explicitly considering security as a distinct set of meanings within politics might help make sense of why politicians adopt stances on immigration that in many ways seem puzzling because it can shed light on the differences they might see in the political dynamics when debate over an issue becomes inflected by security. Efforts to distill "logics of security"[72] have sought to pinpoint just what these core meanings are so that these meanings' effects on politics can be examined empirically. This book, in essence, proposes that the reason that security politics has recognizable patterns is that the introduction of security meanings changes the ways it makes sense to compete politically around an issue. In other words, security changes the political game.

Most migration-politics studies investigating "mainstreaming" have not considered specifically how the introduction of security meanings affects politicians' positioning on immigration; likewise, security scholarship has not systematically considered the fact that the shift toward the hard line on immigration often occurs amid mobilizations that are distinctly populist—a core observation in political science literatures on the topic. Indeed, following decades of intensifying academic attention to the concept, popular discussions about the advance of hard-line immigration positions in recent years—from Italy to Sweden, Germany, and the United States—have invariably been linked to a "rise of populism."[73] It appears that the particularly populist nature of such challenges, beyond being right wing, has to do both with their success and with the ways that nonpopulist policy makers respond.[74] The antielitism at the core of populism is especially important to consider when it comes to painting migration as a security issue.[75] Securitization accounts—even critical ones focused on resistance[76]—have tended to assume that elites hold strong authority over defining security as the purported stakes of the situation produce deference to top leaders.[77]

Therefore, we have lacked any kind of explanation for how insider political elites might be put on the defensive about security by outsiders—including populists who begin outside the most central circles of power and whose success in breaking in has depended in large part on their challenges over immigration.[78] Roxanne Lynn Doty's studies of border vigilantes in Arizona in the early 2000s show how outsiders made security claims with a distinctively populist angle—mobilizing a concept of popular sovereignty that is "aimed at the state, which they claim has failed 'the people.'"[79] But how do such security demands, voiced in the desert by "citizen border patrols" with no particular power or clout, come to sway the elite insiders who decide how the state deals with immigration and who are presumed to possess unmatchable authority over what is considered "security"?[80] To explain such cases, the relationship between populism and security—which seems evident in empirical immigration politics yet is often conceptually elusive—must be specified.

Populist logics can open a key avenue for outsiders to successfully challenge governing elites over security. This works in large part because the logic of populism and the (classical) logic of security share key affinities that have gone unrecognized,[81] both summoning the image of a homogenized—frequently racialized[82]—people facing powerlessness and abuse at enemies' hands. Through such an image, populism and security may converge powerfully in a political logic that champions a commonsense defense of a "people" against the corrosion of their autonomous power. Such images of asserting control may thereby accord with racism "as a mode of domination and form of power" frequently exercised through migration control and borders,[83] including in a Southwest border context where securitization is directed against Hispanic immigrants portrayed as a threat to the social and political order of (an at least implicitly) white America.[84] Despite these convergent logical elements, it is also clear that populism and securitization convey meanings that are distinct; they can be and often are mobilized separately. Especially where immigration is concerned, however, they often seem to complement each other, playing coresonant roles in advancing the political traction of hardline claims.

The distinctively populist formulation that elites and their corruption are a key source of a security problem introduces a twist that earlier concepts of securitization have not contemplated and that comprises a potentially major complication for policy elites. Even nonpopulist politicians' security-intensive interventions in immigration are prone to be dismissed: "It's just a ploy," Pearce explained in an interview for this book. "It's that doublespeak that they get away with, 'cause everybody wants border security. Not really, but everybody talks as if they do . . . they never vote for anything to really do it. The public has such a disdain for our politicians, and I understand that. I share that with them." How should a politician who is not predisposed to securitizing immigration but who is now put squarely in the crosshairs respond? As the populist attack unfolded in Arizona, the governing-elite response formed a pattern that moved immigration policy farther and farther in the direction of security, thus "mainstreaming" farther-right positions.

Together, these observations—about security, on the one hand, and about political maneuvering in the face of populist challenges, on the other—form an arc. In one way, what happened in Arizona suggests a departure from securitization theory. Models of politics, rather than a separate theory of securitization, can take the lead role in explaining the policy decisions that compose a securitization process such as Arizona's. Yet this does not at all mean that security as a category of analysis should be dismissed. Without determining how issues are treated, the particular meanings security brings forth might still shape in distinct ways these choices and thus the larger political game. The securitization of immigration in Arizona was, in many senses, mere politics, competitive and Machiavellian; while subject to strong patterns or regularities, like all political developments it was also contextual, contingent, and fragile.

ROLLING BACK POPULIST
BORDER-SECURITY POLITICS?

How does all of this end? With hard-line anti-immigration politics appearing on the march in so many places, rooted in seemingly durable forms of structural racism and exclusionary discourse, this question has grown all the more urgent for people on the move and for those who would stand with them. Illustrating how hemmed in policy makers can be by their own perceptions of how immigration plays politically, this book details just how straitened immigration politics can become. A collective acceptance of particular issue dynamics laid a path in Arizona where immigration was increasingly securitized. This pattern had become well established by 2009, when a new distribution of partisan power in state government lent populist border hawks greater opportunities than before. When virtually the whole state Republican Party joined this faction in enacting SB 1070, it seemed the border hawks' views had achieved total victory, with no alternative in sight.

But this perception proved wrong. Only a year later, the politics of immigration in Arizona had turned. The state's leading immigration hardliner, Russell Pearce, was even ejected from office. With this sudden shift away from hard-line action on the issue, an era of intense border-security politics came to a close. What happened?

Whereas scholars have often focused on how processes of securitization reorder social relations around images of insecurity,[85] this book highlights a different possibility: from the heat of such politics, new, perhaps unexpected political configurations may emerge. In particular, backlash and resistance to securitization measures are not self-contained but can activate concern about securitization—and even action against it—among disparate political groups, including a Center Right concerned with maintaining social conditions for growth and exchange. "Security politics" in Arizona indeed must be considered from both sides: securitization's energy and its vulnerability.

Against an image of securitization as a strong tool for political consolidation and repressive policy, the story of Arizona underscores securitization's indeterminate nature and the possibility of unintended consequences.[86] In illustrating a distinct and seldom explored phenomenon—the politically enacted end of a securitization process—this part of the story may also illuminate possibilities for immigration politics in places where populist, securitized approaches are currently on the march. To this day, Arizona border hawks still sound their calls, but the courts' invalidation of many of SB 1070's most controversial provisions has met with a new tendency among many Arizona political elites to dampen the kind of immigration politics that the act exemplified.

This development would be just as surprising to constructivist security scholars as to any observer of Arizona politics in 2010. The concept of "desecuritization"—returning an issue to "normal" from an exceptional status as a security matter—has long been explored theoretically.[87] Shifts in social discussions and understandings of racism may also make politicians hesitant to link minority groups to threat in ways that were previously politically opportune.[88] What largely has not been considered in any case is a sudden shift of elite orientations on a security issue. Both elite contestation of and subaltern resistance to security practices—to the extent they have been theorized—have been portrayed as slow and iterative in their effects.[89] What happened in Arizona, though, was a rapid resettlement of the issue, quite soon after populist anti-immigration figures had reached the apex of their power.

In a roiling environment of Hispanic resistance, activist backlash, and national media attention, pivotal center-right forces who previously had been squeamish about responding to the border hawks rediscovered their opposition. The Center Right was especially pivotal in Arizona because it held the balance of power in state government. It may also be evident that center-right politicians are not the usual suspects regarding who would aim to uproot or reshape the social relations conditioned by security, as desecuritization concepts would suppose.[90] After all, SB 1070 is still on the statute books. These circumstances render the end of this era a key, final puzzle in the case. What logics and strategies drove this unexpected effort that materialized seemingly from thin air? Perhaps it was a mobilization against the domineering and exclusionary nature of securitization—or for a different concept of security. In either case, the Arizona Center Right's rally in 2011 seems to represent a distinct species of opposition to hardline security measures that the scholarship has not much contemplated. Additional logics of security—beyond identified cousins such as resilience and risk[91]—may potentially have a decisive effect on our politics. The backlash against Arizona's border hawks may reveal such a powerful alternative logic.

Less abstractly, this episode points toward the political movements and forces in Arizona that were key to the turnabout of immigration politics. Hispanic, left-wing, and liberal groups protested and resisted, and over time a dormant center-right opposition to border-hawk politics reawakened. The Center Right's recalculation was multifaceted but was based on some sense that a shift in political dynamics around immigration had created a new possibility for action when its interests seemed newly threatened. Key players in encouraging this turn included not only the typical agents of resistance from the left, such as youth, civil rights, and labor activists, but also forces that had the ear of Republican policy makers, such as the Arizona Chamber of Commerce and Industry and the Church of Jesus Christ of Latter-day Saints. This book analyzes how a confluence of aims drove these motley forces to work in a functional if not closely cooperative fashion toward broadly shared objectives.

The ultimate importance of the Center Right's change in calculation in response to this shift in Arizona also underscores its importance in migration-politics analysis[92] and is a crucial part of the story—though perhaps an inauspicious one for those working to promote alternative approaches to immigration today. A once-divided national Republican Party now seems to definitively accommodate populist and far-right elements. But if the browbeaten immigration moderates in the Arizona Republican Party could be cajoled—with requisite political cover, of course—to swiftly turn against the state's border hawks in 2011, are such surprises still possible this decade? Or are today's Republicans so invested in white backlash politics that for them only a Trumpist line on immigration is viable?[93] Beyond the United States, could European center-right parties that have shifted rightward on immigration amid populist radical-right pressure—France's Republicans, Germany's Christian Democrats, Britain's Conservatives—restore lost moderation to the issue? Reasons for doubt abound. Yet the Arizona case does offer a counterexample to the idea that securitization and the exclusionary politics of border security, once unbound, ceaselessly march on. In the moment, the possibility of any alternative can seem far away. But Arizona, in the eight years from 2003 to 2011, shows the larger arc of politics. Somehow, some way, all politicians or parties, all ideas or approaches, can fall just as surely as they once rose.

ARIZONA IN NARRATIVE

To illustrate this arc, the story of what happened in Arizona unfolds as just that—a story, a narrative through time. In constructing this narrative, I conduct a process-tracing account wherein the deliberative processes behind major policy decisions are uncovered.[94] Only through a process-tracing narrative can the contingency of the political developments and judgments that formed the securitization process in Arizona be fully preserved and exposed. This approach also serves the broader inductive purpose of drawing out from events their contextual meanings and significance to political actors. Indeed, single-case studies like this one are important because they allow for this kind of induction in order to build "theoretically explicit narratives" that clarify the causal mechanisms that operate between political context and the securitized policy outcomes in question.[95] This research understands securitization in Arizona as a process composed of mechanisms.[96] An account like this does not aim to expose what can be generalized about securitization processes across all cases but responds to a need for new theoretical propositions to address gaps in our knowledge about the securitization of migration as politics. Exploring one such instance in depth can form new and useful theoretical propositions that can be tested in and illuminate other cases.[97]

Such a narrative permits an approach that in this introduction I have argued is key to understanding why policy makers advance securitization processes: interpretivist political science. Politicians face complex worlds that they must try to simplify in some way.[98] It is important as well to emphasize these actors' creative potential: all social actors depend on ideas that come from context, but they also have the ability to act in novel ways to modify that context.[99] Here, human beings' fundamental creative capability even in the face of strong social regularities—the distinctly human quality at the soul of social science[100]—animates how the emergence of a powerful trend is analyzed. Securitization scholarship has not adequately parsed this duality through its usual methodological approaches, which have relied upon analyzing developments in a discursive context.

We can instead see policy makers as "situated agents" who inevitably draw from a social background but who always can try to change that background and sometimes succeed.[101] Understanding these actors through a process-tracing study means taking particular interest in how they respond to dilemmas when existing ways of responding no longer seem viable.[102] We can understand the importance of contextual factors in decision-making processes through the eyes of participants.[103] Interpretive approaches can identify widely held beliefs that amount to "social facts"—beliefs that, even though they are socially constructed, are shared broadly enough to be considered a durable social reality.[104] This approach provides a rigorous, empirically grounded way to analyze how Arizona politicians read and navigated the political environment of immigration from 2003 to 2011. Indeed, this introduction has argued that we should presume that the policy actors who securitize immigration are acting less like Hobbes's Leviathan than like the kind of politician familiar to Machiavelli—if not always sinister, then reliably calculating. Grasping Arizona policy makers' contextual reasoning means understanding them as rational actors of a sort, following a view of rationality found in Max Weber's work as "the way actions make sense to the agents who carry them out."[105] In this account, how Arizona's policy actors applied this kind of subjective rationality amid the contingencies and ambiguities of politics constitutes their political rationalities,[106] the examination of which helps to construct a broader sociology of political decision making around security.

To zero in on these political rationalities, this book employs twenty-seven interviews with Arizona policy actors involved in immigration-related policy decisions in the period examined (see the appendix). I selected the interview subjects by identifying policy makers who were important to certain key policies.[107] This selection led naturally to these policy makers revealing other respondents who had participated in these episodes, sometimes in a less visible way—a process of "snowball sampling."[108] To understand the differing views and approaches among various political factions, I made a concerted effort to interview policy makers from differing ideological groups within parties. The interviews unfolded in a semistructured way,[109] which allowed the interviewees to introduce new aspects of the issues and the dilemmas they faced in immigration policy making in the period discussed.[110] Beyond interviews, consulting documents helped to ground essential facts—the who, what, and where of the case—fleshing out much of the context for understanding what interviewees revealed.[111] More than six hundred press and government documents were coded for this study. I drew the press accounts especially from the *Arizona Capitol Times*, an "insider" political publication; the mass-market newspaper the *Arizona Republic*; and the Associated Press news wire's reporting from the Phoenix political desk, in addition to many other media sources. Online state government archives provided access to key official documents and records. Beyond being rich original sources, these documents provided a way to

"triangulate" interview data and thus test it for accuracy or credibility.[112]
These methodological blocks built this book's narrative of Arizona's
immigration politics.

The story proceeds in four chapters—which, despite inevitable overlap,
divide the era of Arizona's intense border-security politics into four distinguishable phases. At the start, there was a broad consensus in Arizona
politics that the state government had little to no relevant role at the international border. From 2003 to 2005—as elaborated in chapter 1—this status quo ante rapidly collapsed. By the end of this period, a state-declared
emergency existed on Arizona's border with Mexico. Political elites of all
stripes changed their understandings of immigration as a political issue,
yielding an ostensible securitized consensus. The period from 2005 to
2008, discussed in chapter 2, saw intense, Machiavellian interparty border-
security politics, with frequent turnabout and arm-twisting. Amid the
apparent consensus that there was a security problem on the border, all
parties and factions sought to use a perceived popular clamor for greater
action on the security problem to their own advantage and against their
opponents. But even while moderates won major tactical victories to stay
in power, they continually ceded policy ground to border hawks. The regular patterns of contestation that this competitive period produced came
to a sudden end at the close of 2008. Chapter 3, which details developments
in 2009 and 2010, focuses on the intraparty politics that became pivotal
upon the advent of one-party Republican government in Arizona. It
explains the contingent intraparty dynamics and competitive strategies
that provided the conditions for Arizona border hawks' greatest triumph:
SB 1070. By the end of this period, border hawks had won sweeping
political victories, both within their own party and among the general
electorate, and held more formal power than ever before. But their tri-
umphal moment was cut short by the surprising events of 2011, examined
in chapter 4. Newly powerful opposition to the border-hawk movement
arose, bringing an era of intense immigration politics to a pronounced
close. Each of these chapters contains a discussion section that analyzes
their implications for theorizing the securitization of migration. Chapter 5
elaborates this theoretical contribution, tying together the strands from
the narrative to synthesize how the Arizona case sheds new theoretical
light on how we might understand populist border-security politics.
Concluding the book, chapter 6 explores the possible implications of

what happened in Arizona for other places experiencing similar politics, and in the appendix I provide an elaboration of my methodology.

Those interviewed sometimes asked about the point of this book (though less often than one might think). The answer, in one way, is that it will provide a scrupulous account of a political period that many Arizonans will long remember as both difficult and divisive and that is increasingly understood as a watershed in the state's politics.[113] This has not yet been done as exhaustively and so is important enough reason for the book. Beyond that, though, it is clear that what happened in Arizona may have relevance elsewhere. For all the theoretical discussion about what it means to understand securitization politics better, this is not just an academic question. The politics described here exacted consequences, often with great human costs; other places in the world have seen similar outcomes. How we understand the workings of these political processes has essential implications for how we might effectively intervene. The distinct view that this book offers may lead to new possibilities—some identified here, others yet to be seen. And it is with all of this in mind that the narrative of Arizona's immigration politics now unfolds.

1

A BORDER EMERGENCY IS BORN

In 2003, the State of Arizona had little history of border- or immigration-related policy making. Amid a continuing settlement of the state largely by white Americans, a growth-oriented political culture upheld a relaxed approach toward unauthorized immigrant labor, while a relatively small group of populist border hawks championed proposals that were broadly dismissed as extreme. By the end of 2005, though, a state of emergency had been declared across Arizona's border counties. How did this happen? How did such an apparently stable political settlement—where the border was not seen as a major state policy issue at all—so rapidly collapse? And why did the feverish political action that followed so thoroughly center on just one interpretation of a complex immigration issue—as a threat to security?

This shift constituted the first phase in the immigration issue's longer securitized arc in Arizona, setting in place new concepts of the issue's political dynamics that would guide the state's immigration politics in the coming years. This chapter identifies the new issue dynamics that began to surround immigration as it became widely acknowledged as possessing security meanings, which quickly began to reorient the way Arizona's political actors addressed the issue. In particular, the chapter identifies the process by which the coupling of these meanings with populist attacks on governing elites made strategies of downplaying or openly contesting the issue seem unviable to actors across the political spectrum.

The widespread acceptance that immigration issues were at least partly ones of security further entailed that voters must be able to see the problem somehow being urgently addressed and that, therefore, the issue could not be safely downplayed, pegged on jurisdictional issues, or challenged. These calculations followed from the anxiety and need for action associated with the issue and from the perception that many counterarguments in competition with populist border-hawk messages were too nuanced to succeed in a media environment favoring simple messaging.

This state of affairs moved governing elites from a position of dismissive underestimation of "extreme" efforts on immigration to one of reconfiguring their own stances on the issue. In general, against the assumption that a security threat elevates the authority of top leaders, populists working from outside the most decisive circles of power to securitize immigration—including in Arizona—often blame elites for the problem and articulate this blame as a betrayal of the people.[1] In Arizona, border-hawk populists mapped, to significant political effect, the Manichean dichotomy between lawbreaking and law keeping onto populism's moralized people/elite distinction. Such a dynamic creates a dilemma that securitization scholarship has not much contemplated and that disrupts the presumption that successful proclamations of security reinforce the authority of existing elites to address the problem. In fact, governing elites in Arizona began to perceive this populist challenge as a political danger on an issue where security meanings had already been successfully attached. This was especially true after border hawks successfully employed Arizona's institutions of direct democracy in 2004 to win passage of an anti-immigrant initiative at the ballot box, bypassing elite veto points. These dynamics prompted governing elites to move away from a dismissive posture and closer to a position on immigration they had earlier regarded as "extreme"—thus helping to "mainstream" a securitized approach to the issue.[2]

This period in Arizona therefore provides a window into some bigger questions about the politics of security. The shift seen in these two years represents a key kind of event in the process of immigration becoming "securitized": the moment elite politicians first conclude that immigration needed to be treated as a security matter instead of as a nonissue or something dealt with in a different way. Since there has been little thorough empirical examination of reasons why political elites make these decisions, some assumptions about them have become dominant in the way they are understood. The possibility of a true threat aside, securitizing elites have often been assumed to be trying to manipulate publics and consolidate power,[3] following an image of the securitization process where elites are firmly in control. But how much do policy makers' initial decision to treat an issue as security truly resemble such assumptions? The answer for Arizona was: not very closely. This decision did not occur rapidly and decisively but rather through a process of political learning about what issue positions appeared to suit politicians' larger political objectives. This learning process culminated with governing elites seeking to seize the immigration issue as a security one in order to prevent it from escaping their control. A greater similarity in positions therefore emerged despite a lack of actual consensus.

Indeed, a key aspect of this period in Arizona was the rapid consolidation of this new apparent consensus. The state's governing elites, in a quick about-face from the positions most of them held, began to profess that immigration was a security issue the state had to address—a process that culminated in the declaration of emergency in the summer of 2005, a new type of security response to by then long-standing issues. This shift opens up an avenue to explore a key symptom of securitized politics that has long troubled both scholars and observers: the apparently narrowed pluralism and limited political contestation over an issue's meaning that seem to accompany issues purported to be ones of security. Didier Bigo, in discussing security and policy elites, calls these narrowing factors "the homogeneity of their reaction"[4]—the all-too-familiar process whereby real dissent about an issue seems to disappear once securitization takes hold, yielding a "repressive consensus."[5] Indeed, the ability to diminish contestation around an issue is seen as a key benefit for elites in securitizing it,[6] and even when security issues are debated in democratic arenas, it frequently seems that politicians are reluctant to challenge these dominant security framings.[7]

This chapter offers a new perspective of why this so often appears to happen in security issues by identifying the competitive issue properties that encourage crowding around securitized issue framings and that, furthermore, lead politicians to think they need to produce not just sympathetic talk but policy action on a security issue. Over time, this crowding discourages other possible ways to address the issue: in Arizona, other possibilities became markedly de-emphasized in political

deliberations, and a deluge of security-oriented immigration policy proposals quickly followed.

In the course of a couple of years, a wide variety of Arizona's policy
actors came to regard the security nature of immigration issues as a political reality they had to accept and work with. The new reading of immigration issues adopted by Arizona's governing elites narrowed the range
of what seemed politically possible by establishing broadly shared perceptions of the political situation. Yet this new reading of what was politically possible did not entail a single shared view of the immigration
"problem," of the political approach most apt for dealing with it, or of the
policy agenda needed to address it.

The success of Proposition 200—a border-hawk-championed ballot initiative targeting two characteristic populist radical-right bugbears, unauthorized immigrants voting and receiving public benefits—at Arizona's
polls in 2004 prompted a broad rethinking of the politics of immigration
among Arizona's policy elites. Major changes resulted in how they perceived, strategized about, and made policy regarding immigration.
Border hawks, previously politically sidelined, were emboldened. Policy
actors outside of this ideological group saw a need to become increasingly
active on the border and immigration as a way of responding to a palpable public concern. Yet to those opposed to the border hawks' hard line,
how best to respond proved an increasingly urgent puzzle. They began to
perceive that a strategy of simple opposition to border-hawk proposals was
politically failing. With Arizona's politicians working from a shared perception of a restive and anxious public and seeing a paramount need to
take control of a quickly emerging and politically perilous issue, the placid
status quo ante became a faint memory. A new political game of border
security emerged.

GROWING PAINS

Understanding where Arizona's immigration politics stood in 2003
requires a brief step into the state's deeper past. As migration mainly from
Mexico came to dominate its political agenda, Arizona was continuing
to be transformed by a different migration—that of mostly Anglo Americans, who had been arriving at breakneck rates since the end of World

War II. In one of the last parts of the United States extensively settled by whites, the Sonoran Desert cities of Phoenix and Tucson boomed into Sun Belt metropolises. A state with fewer than 500,000 people in 1940 had 6.4 million by 2010, and in 2012 only 38 percent of people living in Arizona had been born there.[8] Explosive population growth has led some analysts to comment that it can be difficult to detect bedrock in Arizona's political culture.[9] At the same time, the image of Arizona as a *terra nullius*, a largely blank canvas free for imprinting by new arrivals, forms part of a settler-colonial narrative that has minimized groups living in the state before recent Anglo settlement.[10] In fact, several long veins in Arizona politics fed the border-security politics that emerged in the early twenty-first century.

The first vein is, indeed, Arizona's racial politics, which has developed amid a particular southwestern expression of American white supremacy. Southwestern politics has always been inflected by an Alamo-style mythology portraying "vigilant Anglo Americans fighting inferior Mexican bandits for the right to self-rule,"[11] with the American nation's promises of freedom and democracy considered the possessions of the country's white (genuine) citizenry. Many thousands of American Indians and Mexicans were already living in the lands that became Arizona when the United States acquired its modern-day territory through war and purchase in the mid–nineteenth century. The Arizona society that emerged was shot through with racial hierarchy and conflict. For much of the territorial period, the lynching of Mexicans was tolerated by local Anglo elites amid a generally permissive attitude toward vigilante justice.[12] As Arizonans agitated for statehood, they rejected a proposal for Arizona and New Mexico to become a single state largely because Arizona Anglos refused to incorporate within their polity New Mexico's large and powerful Hispanic population.[13] Following statehood in 1912, Mexican workers, with or without legal status or U.S. citizenship, were employed in Arizona's mines under a "dual-wage" system where they were kept in inferior jobs or paid less than whites for the same work.[14] Even during the period of clear labor-movement power in early statehood, one of Arizona's major initiatives was an "80 percent law" that aimed to restrict the mines' hiring of foreign workers.[15] Formal segregation existed in schools until the 1950s.[16] While the federal Bracero Program welcomed Mexican farm labor between World War II and 1964, major deportation efforts in the 1930s and 1950s underlined how

Mexicans' and Mexican Americans' "treatment by the dominant society as second-class citizens . . . extended well into the twentieth century."[17]

Belying the social construction of Arizona and its booming metropolises as Anglo places, their growth was underlain by a dependency on Mexican Americans and Mexicans to play essential economic roles—a clear Hispanic presence that was increasingly recognized and pronounced in the twenty-first century.[18] Alongside the longtime presence of Mexicans and Mexican Americans in Arizona, however, were long-running discourses that portrayed the (implicitly Anglo) nature of American society and politics as under threat. In such "Latino threat narratives," Hispanics, unlike other immigrant groups, are painted as "incapable of becoming part of the national community. Rather, they are part of an invading force from south of the border that is bent on reconquering."[19] The Hispanic population in the twentieth and twenty-first centuries—growing in great part through immigration—was therefore increasingly primed by such narratives as a potential object of concern for Anglo-dominated politics.

Although such threat narratives were often more implicitly present in state politics, Arizona saw a much more explicitly headline-grabbing struggle surrounding racial politics in the late 1980s and early 1990s: a six-year controversy over whether the state would follow the national norm in adopting a holiday honoring Martin Luther King Jr.[20] This episode unfolded at first following the election in 1986 of a far-right governor, Evan Mecham, who ardently opposed a King holiday and made racist statements portrayed across national media as buffoonish.[21] Even after Mecham was impeached and removed from office in 1988, voters still refused to approve the holiday in a referendum in 1990, despite an active boycott against Arizona. In response to this refusal, the National Football League canceled plans to hold the Super Bowl there in 1993.[22] Fearing greater damage to the state's image and economy, a coalition that included civil rights and business groups eventually won voter passage of a King holiday in 1992. However, the drama lingered in local and national memory,[23] nurturing impressions of Arizona as racist and acting as a warning to businesses that provocative forays into cultural politics carried possible negative and isolating repercussions.

Intertwined with this racial politics is a second key aspect of Arizona's political culture: the history of tension between Arizona and the federal government, which was long seen to possess exclusive authority over the border and immigration. Arizona's need to win outsider approval was frequently tied to cultural politics. Arizona was a non-self-governing federal territory from 1863 until 1912, aligned with the Democratic Party during the long post–Civil War period of Republican domination of federal politics. This alignment deepened political tensions and often cooled Congress's willingness to grant Arizona statehood. The statehood effort continually encountered the view that Arizona was not "civilized" enough for equal admission to the Union—insufficiently advanced by the standards of progressive development and racially compromised by too small a white settler population. Although this characterization provoked resentment, the territory's leaders also worked to portray Arizona to eastern political and economic elites as civilized and progressive.[24] After Arizona became in 1912 the last of the forty-eight contiguous states admitted to the Union, a pattern in state–federal relations generally unfolded where Arizona continually appealed to the federal government for crucial infrastructure resources while also resenting alleged federal intrusion into and ignorance of local affairs.[25]

A final key current is the long transformation that the post–World War II population growth worked upon Arizona's political culture. This growth simultaneously shifted the predominant posture of the state's Anglo political leadership on racial politics and patterns of partisan competition in the state. Despite a western tendency toward radical rethinking of political forms and the state's early embrace of the progressive movement,[26] Arizona during early statehood also had a paternalist, conservative political streak. Sporadically challenged one-party Democratic rule was closely connected to a closed economic elite based in extractive industries such as mining and agriculture. When new residents from other parts of the country arrived after World War II, they often brought their partisan allegiances with them. The Arizona Republican Party strengthened from the 1950s and clearly held the upper hand in Arizona politics by the 1990s. Ascendant Republicans championed a brand of conservatism, exemplified by Barry Goldwater, that, growing from the diverse southwestern context, sought to suppress class- and race-based conflict in favor of a facially color-blind and intensely individualist entrepreneurial conservatism.[27] These Republicans joined the decades-long push by Arizona's congressional delegation, often led by Democrats such as Carl Hayden, to secure federal funding for massive transportation and water infrastructure projects.[28] Together, this link amounted to a bipartisan growth consensus and a regime in which business interests were influential in nearly all areas of state policy.[29] This new business coalition favored low taxes, minimal regulation, and population growth. Its occasional interventions on social issues were guided by sensitivity to the trade implications of how outsiders viewed Arizona. It also supported a relaxed approach to unauthorized migrant labor, critical above all to the booming construction sector,[30] which every day transformed acres of desert into habitat for new Arizonans.

Amid the long, post–Civil Rights Act realignment of America's parties, Arizona Republicans in particular became increasingly beset by ideological division. By the 1990s, elite control over the state party's factions had deteriorated as the right wing became a more assertive force within Republican politics nationwide.[31] Replacing intraparty conflict between conservatives and the party's vanishing liberal wing, new battle lines emerged between right-wing activists, often drawing strength from the party's grass roots, and business-oriented Republicans, who within the new alignment were sometimes relative moderates. Simultaneously in the 1990s, Arizona's Hispanic population was growing quickly, with international migration playing a major role. In 1990, Arizona had 3.7 million residents, 18.8 percent of whom were Hispanic; by 2000, it had 5.1 million residents, 25.3 percent of whom were Hispanic. Both parties were mulling the political ramifications of the growth of this community, which in elections largely supported Democrats.[32]

THE BORDER BEFORE

In contrast to what was to come, Arizona's border and immigration politics were remarkably settled in the late twentieth century. Federal border policy had been continually shifting since at least the 1980s amid a growing focus on drug enforcement. With the promise of more border enforcement, Congress had enacted the Immigration and Reform and Control Act of 1986, which introduced penalties for hiring unauthorized workers and created legalization programs that eventually naturalized 3 million unauthorized U.S. residents.[33] The employment provisions, however, were rarely enforced, and promises of a more controlled border went unrealized, despite federal legislation in 1996 that ramped up border enforcement and escalated punitive approaches toward unauthorized immigrants.[34]

In Arizona at this time, the border was not an issue of state policy focus. To the extent state policy makers did consider the border, its economic and trade dimensions dominated. Backlash in response to a growing Hispanic population, however, began to appear in state politics. Proposition 106, a citizens' initiative passed narrowly by Arizona voters in 1988,[35] would have required all state government business to be conducted in English but was overturned by federal courts.[36] In 2000, voters passed Proposition 203, an initiative that required English-only instruction for English-language learners in Arizona schools.[37] With House Bill (HB) 2154 in 1996, Arizona was also one of the first states to prohibit unauthorized immigrants from obtaining a driver's license. Nevertheless, during the 1990s the politics of immigration in Arizona remained relatively muted compared to politics in neighboring California. There, Proposition 187, an anti-immigration measure eventually endorsed by the state's Republican establishment, aimed to restrict unauthorized immigrants' access to welfare benefits. This proposal reflected a discursive shift in the 1990s emphasizing the fiscal costs of unauthorized migration.[38] Though Arizona Republican officials made similar complaints about a state of affairs for which they blamed federal failures, they downplayed the need for such measures in Arizona and were cautious about damaging Arizona-Mexico trade relationships.[39] Though Proposition 187 won California voters' approval in 1994, by the end of the 1990s it was commonly cited as an albatross hanging from the Republican Party's neck in a state that was becoming increasingly diverse.[40]

An increase in the political salience of border security and unauthorized immigration in the mid-1990s brought on federal attempts to increase border security,[41] focusing on the urban areas that then saw the greatest unauthorized cross-border movement. Called Operation Hold the Line in Texas and Operation Gatekeeper in California, the relevant program was designated Operation Safeguard in Arizona.[42] These efforts failed to decrease overall unauthorized traffic across the border, however, instead driving this movement to become more clandestine. Main routes shifted to the remotest portions of the U.S.-Mexico border, largely in Arizona.[43]

Irregular crossings became much more dangerous.[44] Hardening enforcement—a trend unfolding simultaneously with increasing economic
integration—was continuing to generate further unanticipated feedback
loops that were structuring new policy problems;[45] for instance, it was also
discouraging the seasonal return migration in which many unauthorized
Mexican workers had previously engaged, and so greater numbers of them
began to settle in the United States permanently. In this time of shifting
enforcement approaches, federal and local agencies piloted new partner-
ships. One result, a joint operation in July 1997 between the U.S. Border
Patrol and police in the Phoenix suburb of Chandler, led to the arrest of
more than four hundred people who were racially profiled as suspected
unauthorized immigrants. The "Chandler Roundup" was vociferously
condemned, and in its wake future such operations appeared unlikely.[46]

By 2000, the Arizona section of the border had become the biggest
clandestine corridor into the United States for drugs and people. Apprehensions of unauthorized crossers in the Tucson sector, containing most
of the Arizona portion of the border, numbered more than 600,000 that
year, more than a third of all U.S. border apprehensions, also at an all-
time high.[47] The terrorist attacks of September 11, 2001 (9/11) led to the
Homeland Security Act of 2002, creating the U.S. Department of Homeland Security, which absorbed the main federal agencies dealing with the
border and immigration. Although lacking any connection to Mexico,
the 9/11 attacks amplified civilizationalist discourses that came to suffuse
discussions of border security, portraying Mexico as a "weak and disor-
derly state" from which violence may emanate.[48] This portrayal underlined the dehumanizing threat narratives that associated Mexican immigrants with a variety of social ills and resulted in an eventual acceleration
of border-security measures under the banner of homeland security.[49]
Yet though 9/11 rattled border policy instantly at the federal level,[50] it did
not trigger noticeable changes in state-level politics in Arizona immediately. Terry Goddard, a former Phoenix mayor who in 2002 was elected
state attorney general, said in a typical recollection: "You had this literal
highway of human beings coming from south to north. . . . I think it's
safe to say that in 2002, at least it was my impression, almost nobody
was paying attention. It had come to my attention in law enforcement
circles. The sheriffs on the border were significantly overwhelmed, mostly
by the drug aspects of this issue. But the general public wasn't paying

attention. Congress definitely wasn't paying attention."[51] Citizen border-guard groups were emerging in the early 2000s, conducting armed patrols and generating sporadic headlines, but with little embrace by political elites at the time.[52] One interviewee summarized the matter by saying that in Arizona's state-level politics of the early 2000s "immigration was not part of the conversation."

The elections of 2002 in Arizona produced divided government. Republicans won control of both chambers of the state legislature; Democrats faced continuing struggles, having not controlled either chamber outright since 1992.[53] Nonetheless, Democrats were riding high: Janet Napolitano became the first Democrat elected governor since 1982, winning the office by one percent of the vote. Napolitano had campaigned from the center in a state that Democrats then broadly considered, in the words of one interviewee, "usually red but sometimes purple." In a situation where "Democrats [are] always kind of struggling to gain traction on anything," as one Democratic state legislator described, party elites worked from the premise that Democrats would have to appeal to moderates in both parties as well as to independent voters to win and retain power. Napolitano sought to govern as a moderate with a "commonsense," take-charge approach, emphasizing education, the economy, and public safety. As Jeanine L'Ecuyer, Napolitano's communications director for most of her governorship, recalled, "Her brand, I always believed, was 'Janet has it under control so that you don't need to worry about it.'"

Confrontation between Napolitano and the Republican legislature began immediately. Napolitano set records for vetoes by an Arizona governor, which she often wore as a badge of honor for tempering a legislative majority she argued was out of touch with voters.[54] Mike Haener, Napolitano's chief liaison to the legislature, characterized a wide-ranging clash where on basic governing vision the Democratic governor and most Republican legislators "just weren't on the same page." Nevertheless, sufficient compromise emerged to pass some legislation, particularly on budgets. Already in 2003, the Republican caucus contained numerous divisions, which both facilitated Napolitano in finding legislative majorities for her budgets and threatened Republican unity generally. The Republicans' right wing, whose members tended to take the most hard-line stances on immigration, was a significant force within the party's legislative caucus but not a dominating faction. Most legislative Republicans, including the leadership of both chambers, were to varying extents more traditional conservatives. There was also a handful of true moderate Republicans with centrist ideologies.

Little legislative action occurred on immigration in 2003. Russell Pearce, a former sheriff's deputy serving his second House term from a conservative district in the city of Mesa, sponsored with legislative allies two bills (HB 2243, HB 2246) that presaged later proposals. Neither emerged from committee; supporting state-level immigration law enforcement at this time was widely considered extreme.[55] One bill the legislature did pass, however, was HB 2345, requiring voters to present identification (ID) at the polls. Pearce was one of fifty Republicans to cosponsor the legislation. Hispanic organizations opposed the bill as an attempt at voter suppression. Napolitano vetoed it in flamboyant fashion "before more than 900 cheering Hispanic elected officials attending a national convention in Phoenix."[56] Napolitano did not allege the bill was racist, arguing instead that it would inconvenience voters just to combat a nonexistent voting fraud problem.[57] Some of the bill's sponsors vowed that the issue was not over, but the declarative way in which Napolitano dismissed the proposal signified the times. Elites considered such issues only marginally relevant to the big picture of Arizona politics.

"IT STARTED A BATTLE": PROPOSITION 200

HB 2345's strongest legislative proponents, standing in the right wing of the Republican caucus, began to contemplate a strategy to advance what they saw as their broadly supported and commonsense proposals, which Napolitano and other elites stood in the way of. Pearce, the principal border-hawk legislator,[58] recounted:

Her mindset is she's not gonna support anything worthwhile. So let's go to the ballot. . . . The public wants something done. . . . Enough's enough. And so we said, "Okay, we'll do two things: proof of citizenship to register to vote"—kind of a good idea. . . . I think that's fair; it takes two forms of ID to get a Blockbuster movie, maybe we ought to require ID if you're gonna vote—and "no free public stuff." No free public benefits. You can't be in this country and get free stuff from the tax-payer. . . . And so I wrote the initiative, and we moved forward.

Pearce's description of this decision reflects several beliefs that would consistently guide border hawks. First, political elites, including Democrats and many Republicans, generally opposed action on these issues, but the public was clearly supportive of such action and was thus being betrayed by the elites. This moralizing antielitism and the border-hawk position's purported consonance with a general will constituted key populist elements in the border hawks' views and positioning.[59] As Pearce would allege, "Nobody's doing a dadgum thing—'cause you've got weak-kneed, simple politicians who are refusing to do their duty." Following from this positioning was a tactical willingness to use Arizona's institutions of direct democracy, including the citizens' initiative, to bypass elite veto points—a characteristic populist fondness for plebiscites.[60] But what Pearce described as "tremendous hurdles" in organizing and paying for initiative campaigns meant a preference for passing the border hawks' policies as normal legislation.

Beyond this populist angle—painting elites and "politicians" writ large as unwilling to fulfill the general will—the radical securitarian bent of this faction's arguments was unmistakable. Though at this time directed on face toward voting and welfare policy, border-hawk efforts were seeking to subsume these areas into a new, envelope-pushing governance of addressing an alleged border-security crisis through enforcement and exclusion. Indeed, demanding "law and order" when it comes to immigrants and the expansion of this logic to the welfare state are characteristic of the populist radical Right transnationally.[61] In Arizona, populist border hawks sought what they saw as a "commonsense" coherence between state policies and images of "illegality" in the immigration system. This particular form of lawbreaking was portrayed as a dire and self-evidently outrageous danger to society. As Pearce expounded, "Citizens have a constitutional right to the expectation of the enforcement and protection from those who break our laws. That's why we have laws. . . . And when I see us recklessly disregard those and, I believe, create a path to the destruction of this country, it offends me." Arizona's border hawks would, beginning in 2003, persistently portray immigration in a way that linked these populist and security logics: the threat of destruction, the flouting of common sense, and the betrayal of the people—all due to the weakness and corruption of governing elites in both parties.[62]

The initial paperwork for what would become Proposition 200 was filed in the summer of 2003 after the end of the main legislative session.[63] The main group promoting it came together under the name "Protect Arizona Now," reflecting the clear connection to border security. The proposal combined provisions of the vetoed voter-ID bill with further measures similar to California's Proposition 187, requiring proof of citizenship to obtain a number of benefits. National anti-immigration organizations supported the campaign,[64] but it proceeded without much state establishment support, relying on a band of dedicated activists and infusions of funds from individual donors and outside groups.[65] Although most elites considered the campaign a fringe effort,[66] the potential that the proposition could succeed was taken seriously. Among Hispanic policy makers especially, the prospect set off alarm. "I really believe it caught us all off guard," Steve Gallardo, a Democratic member of the state House and a Latino Caucus leader, recounted about the aftermath of the initiative's filing. "I mean, we knew about 187 in California. . . . [W]e decided to bring everyone [all Hispanic leaders] together, and we had [a meeting] at a union hall. . . . Everyone came in, probably forty people or so, to kind of, like, [ask,] 'What do we do?' And that was kind of the first of many meetings to try to figure [it] out—I mean, we were unprepared!"

Apart from within the Hispanic community, anti–Proposition 200 campaigning was slow to mobilize in a national election cycle where immigration was not a major issue. "The Democratic establishment, Democratic voters, they looked to us as Latinos, saying, 'This is your community, you guys are the Latino leaders—what are you gonna do?,'" recalled Martín Quezada, at that time a Democratic legislative staffer. Opponents of Proposition 200 initially aimed their arguments against its purported discriminatory intent. "Our response, our messaging, was so bad. The only response we had was, 'They're nothing but racists,'" Gallardo recalled. "That didn't fly."

For many elected Republicans, the Proposition 200 debate augured shifts in the political winds. Jennifer J. Burns, a centrist House Republican representing a vast and diverse border district, recounted an episode at a Republican Party event during the 2004 election: "A lot of the questions were about the border. . . . I don't remember the question, but I made a statement that people were not dying in our desert to vote in our elections. They were coming here for jobs, to feed their families. They were not coming here to vote. The crowd booed me. . . . And, you know, they weren't, though!"

Jonathan Paton, a traditional conservative Republican, was running for the House in 2004 from a southern Arizona district close to the border. To him, voter interest in immigration was clearly escalating. His district also saw a fierce Republican congressional primary election pitting Jim Kolbe, a centrist incumbent, against Randy Graf, a populist right-wing challenger who had helped to organize Proposition 200. "Prop 200 was kind of a litmus test in that election, and while Kolbe won, I think it sort of signaled the beginning of that era," Paton recounted.

As the November election drew nearer and polls suggested Proposition 200 would pass comfortably, its defeat became a greater priority for a broad group of political elites, including Democrats such as Napolitano and a number of Arizona Republicans, including the state's most prominent party member, U.S. senator John McCain.[67] The main opposition group was launched in September 2004 with the support of the business lobby and was chaired by Grant Woods, a centrist Republican and former state attorney general. Its campaign focused on the proposal's potential unintended consequences in obstructing delivery of vital services because of the ID requirements.[68] Leading up to the election, the proposition captured some national media attention, and Proposition 187's long-term damage to California Republicans was frequently noted.[69]

Proposition 200 won 56 percent of the vote. Despite its nebulous impact on fraud problems that its opponents argued scarcely existed, the political ramifications of its success were deep. To all, Proposition 200 represented a clear escalation in the salience of immigration issues in Arizona's political agenda. To the border hawks who had championed it, it not only vindicated their citizens' initiative strategy but also confirmed the public's support for the kind of tough policies toward unauthorized immigration that they felt governing elites stood unwilling to provide. Border hawks immediately grasped that such populist pressure might be used to push their bills through the state legislature.[70]

To other factions of political elites, the success of Proposition 200, alongside other events in the elections of 2004, triggered a longer process of reconsidering immigration's state of play. To everyone, the settlement that immigration and border issues had little to do with state-level politics seemed to be shifting. On the same election day, Andrew Thomas, a right-wing Republican, was elected as Maricopa County attorney—the chief public prosecutor for the Phoenix area, containing three-fifths of the state's population. Thomas had run on a platform of aggressively combatting unauthorized immigration. Jim Walsh, a lawyer and Democratic Party activist who later became the county attorney for neighboring Pinal County, recounted: "[Thomas's] signs included something about 'stop illegal immigration,' and we laughed! We said, 'What's he gonna do, subpoena them? What the hell does a county attorney have to do with illegal immigration? It's not your problem.' . . . Of course, the guy walks in 'cause it's a crowded primary field. He locks up the very conservative right-wing vote, and this is part of his deal. So this was, in a way, one of the first canaries in the mine."

While Democrats were reconsidering how they should understand and deal with the apparent politics of immigration, shifts in strategy proceeded slowly and unevenly. It was becoming apparent to all that the border hawks' intuitive, simple messages—rendered as "common sense"—were primed for political success. As Haener recounted, border hawks "don't really have to run a campaign on [their position] 'cause the messaging is 'Illegal means illegal.'" What constituted the best response, though, remained unclear. There was no organized rush to abandon the strategies used in the Proposition 200 battle, where final support levels for the measure were lower than polls had projected. As Gallardo recalled of the strategy to counter border-hawk efforts with accusations of racism, "It took us a while before we understood that we were losing more support with that messaging than earning it."

The immediate concern for elected Democrats after Proposition 200's passage was limiting implementation of both the voter-ID and public-benefits components. Such efforts by Napolitano and Goddard demonstrate the extent to which even in the aftermath of Proposition 200 apparent popular concern about immigration had yet not superseded interest-group politics when it came to making political calculations about immigration. Both parts of the proposition faced legal challenges. Joseph Kanefield, a lawyer who was the state's chief elections officer under Republican secretary of state Jan Brewer, recalled about the voter-ID provisions:[71]

The public was very supportive of this [proposition], obviously, from the vote itself. But even after that, I don't think the public ever understood what the issues were when they heard that there were lawsuits and problems. In our society, people are used to producing their ID everywhere. . . . So the people that were making the most noise were the [Hispanic and Native American] interest groups. . . . Secretary Brewer set forth from the very beginning to do this in a way that would address all the concerns. But it was like whack-a-mole. Every time we would address a concern . . . , [the attorney general and governor] would just come up with some other problem.

Public sparring over implementing Proposition 200 followed for months. The voting provisions were not agreed upon until July 2005.[72] The benefits provisions were eventually construed to apply to a small range of state-provided benefits in which the federal government played little or no funding role. A Napolitano aide only somewhat exaggerated in saying of Proposition 200, "We didn't implement it."

Republicans who had never felt disposed to focus on immigration issues saw Proposition 200 as signaling the issue's rising importance in their party's grass roots, where the most energetic activists tended to be the most right-wing. Nevertheless, elected Republicans took different views on what the problems at the border truly were. Some were more ideologically predisposed than others to support security-heavy policies. In this way, immigration and border issues highlighted existing ideological divisions. As Burns recounted about being booed by party activists, "For me, I probably said, 'You know what? These folks are extreme in their position, and they're not in touch with reality.'" Paton, taking a different view, identified immigration and the border as issues he would focus on, saying that he and Tim Bee, a fellow Republican who represented the same district in the Arizona Senate, "talked about 'What could we do about border issues for our district that would actually accomplish something?'"

The success of Proposition 200 thus began a process where various groups of policy makers in Arizona began to reinterpret their political context and how they should navigate the politics of immigration as a newly contentious field. Or, as Pearce recalled in his own style, "It started a battle."

CHANGING CALCULATIONS:
THE 2005 LEGISLATIVE SESSION

Arizona's border hawks began to push an expanded program as soon as the legislative session opened in 2005. "Anyone who entered the 2005 legislative session with the notion that, after claiming victory with Proposition 200 in the November elections, anti-illegal-immigration lawmakers would rest on their laurels was, in a word, wrong," one newspaper commented.[73] But many policy makers' readings of immigration politics were still in flux. Although most sensed the weakening of the consensus that the state had no substantive role to play regarding the border, assessments of the proposals put forward by Pearce and other border hawks had not brightened. "As Democrats," Quezada explained, "we were always aware of those [proposals], kind of keeping an eye on them. But we always kind of assumed also that they weren't gonna move very far." Or, as Kyrsten Sinema, at the time a Democratic legislator, put it, the border hawks "were so outlandish that no one took them seriously." Moderate Republicans took a similar view. Burns recounted this group as concluding, "Nobody's gonna believe [the border hawks], they're so far out there. . . . We're not gonna stand up and counter [Pearce]. We'll just keep it quiet, we'll vote when it matters, but we're not gonna confront him on the floor, speech versus speech."

Bills introduced in 2005 by the border hawks—a group that this time included Pearce as well as legislators Chuck Gray, Ron Gould, Jack Harper, Karen Johnson, and Rick Murphy—featured proposals on many issues that would become mainstays. They included creating state-level legal sanctions for employers who hired unauthorized labor (HB 2384); barring unauthorized migrants from accessing state financial aid for higher education or in-state university tuition rates (HB 2030); denying the validity of a Mexican-issued ID, the *matrícula consular*, for official state purposes (SB 1511); and denying bail to unauthorized immigrants (HB 2389) while admitting immigration status as a factor in criminal sentencing (HB 2259). House Concurrent Resolution (HCR) 2030 sought to refer to the ballot a measure that would make English the state's official language. Finally, SB 1306 aimed at the goal of "local enforcement," requiring local law enforcement departments to enter into agreements with federal agencies that would enable them to conduct enforcement of federal immigration laws.

Besides the border hawks, four other, broad groupings of actors within the legislative process were recalibrating their immigration positions.

TRADITIONAL REPUBLICANS

"Traditional" Republicans were by and large ideologically conservative and so were in neither the farther-right nor moderate wing of their party. Many had business-oriented sympathy for a more relaxed approach to immigration. In 2005, a number of politicians within this group began taking a dedicated interest in legislating about the border. Although they believed that their actions would be viewed favorably, they were generally moved by conceptions of these problems that were quite distinct from populist border hawks' accounts of danger, urgency, and betrayal.

Russ Jones was a Republican member of the House from Yuma, a community near the border with a major agriculture industry, large-scale cross-border work, and Hispanic and Anglo populations of roughly equal size. Jones, who considered himself a "conservative pragmatist," felt that although a district like his would not be supportive of hard-line legislation, the rise of the issue's salience posed real concern for his constituency: "I just didn't feel right sitting by. I felt I should defend agriculture, defend the community, and try to provide ways to address the real issue and not penalize one particular part of our community over the other. So I felt like I could have just sat back and done nothing, but I felt compelled." Demonstrating his approach, in the 2005 session Jones cosponsored a bill that would have had the state create a private prison in Mexico to house convicts who were unauthorized immigrants (HB 2709).

In the same session, Jonathan Paton, elected from a district that he described as feeling intense popular unease about the border, also took an entrepreneurial approach. Intending a contrast with Pearce and others, the freshman sought to take substantive steps against border-crime problems "rather than purely symbolic [ones]." The first bill resulting from this effort, SB 1372, criminalized human trafficking and smuggling under Arizona state law, forging a role for Arizona law enforcement to more actively combat human-smuggling networks, long considered a problem of federal concern.[74] Paton recalled: "Maybe I was naive at the time, but the challenge was, 'Okay, let's try to do something that goes at what they care about on the one hand but also actually accomplishes something on the other.' . . . And, quite frankly, something that the governor would sign. . . . It was the employers looking for cheap labor on the one hand and the traffickers who were becoming increasingly brutal in their own way. And we thought, well, who can really disagree with going after the traffickers?" Like the border hawks, these traditional Republicans worked from genuinely held problem conceptions about the issues that existed on the border and took salient public concern as a starting point. However, an approach toward enforcement like Paton's differed in important respects from the border hawks' approach, especially in trying to find consensus on which to base policy rather than simply supplanting a corrupted elite consensus. To Paton, human smuggling represented a "real" problem that could be substantively addressed in ways that would draw broad elite support.

Other immigration-related bills to emerge from the Republican caucus but from outside its far-right faction included a bill to ban municipal spending on day-labor centers (HB 2592), which cities including Phoenix had created as an alternative to the public places where largely undocumented laborers often gathered to look for work. Much of the increased attention that traditional Republicans paid to immigration, however, occurred in committees and in floor votes. The increase in the number of immigration-related bills the Arizona Legislature approved in 2005 was in large part a function of bills emerging from committee, where earlier they would have died due to insufficient Republican interest. More of these bills were being allowed to the floor by Republican leadership, and on the floor most Republicans were now voting for them.

MODERATE REPUBLICANS

A smaller group of ideologically centrist "moderate" Republicans often occupied pivotal middle ground in the legislature. On immigration, they took a distinct approach. Major fractures already existed by this point between this group and the rest of the Republican caucus. Pete Hershberger and Tom O'Halleran, two centrist Republicans then serving in the House, recalled an episode in 2003 when following a disagreement over a child-welfare bill, then Speaker Jake Flake stripped them of their committee chairmanships, major sources of power. Such episodes grew from and further entrenched the moderates' independent and somewhat defiant attitude toward their party. Hershberger explained:

> For me, I have to put [immigration] into context, the political context of being a moderate Republican in a conservative legislature. And my approach to that was that I was not gonna let leadership tell me how to vote and how to represent the citizens of my district. . . . Overall, whether it was immigration, education, child welfare, I studied those issues and to the best of my ability voted my conscience, what I thought was right. And I tried to take a practical approach rather than an ideological approach.

These Republican intraparty conflicts had grown significantly by 2005, but there were substantial attempts to preserve comity in the Republican caucus, often through procedural agreements, where leadership could rely on moderates to support Republican motions against the Democrats. Yet Republicans simply agreeing to vote in unity on the leadership's procedural measures—except when, on matters such as the budget, the issue was too important—highlighted the tenuousness of Republican harmony.

The moderate Republican response to immigration following the 2004 elections was aimed more at better understanding the issues and determining what kinds of efforts they would be prepared to support than at developing an entrepreneurial approach. O'Halleran recounted that he, Hershberger, and Burns decided,

> "You know, we need to know more about this." So we went to the federal government and sat down with the people at ICE [Immigration and Customs Enforcement] and the Border Patrol and people like that, and we didn't talk to them about how many people are coming across the border. We talked to them about, first, the law as it stood, what the state's involvement could or should be, and then why they were doing what they were doing. And what they would do if the state put certain types of statute in place.

O'Halleran's description of the nuances he saw in these issues was typical of this group:

As we saw it, immigration was having an impact on our crime rate. It was having an impact on our state's employment, not that a lot of these jobs were jobs that necessarily an Anglo or a citizen of the United States would want to have. . . . Our feeling, I think, was you weren't entitled to using taxpayer money to be able to live in the United States. But on the other hand, if somebody were to say that the federal government says these children can go to our schools in Arizona, you can't even ask them their citizenship, that's federal law. I have no problem with that. . . . We don't want families broken up. But on the other hand . . . we have consequences to people using our government services and not paying taxes.

While some Republicans looked to sponsor immigration legislation—including Bill Konopnicki, an eastern Arizona House member who sat between the party's moderate and conservative factions—moderate Republicans' activity in this area most often related to taking stances on others' proposals. The result was a mix of yes and no votes on immigration measures that varied from issue to issue and sometimes among the moderates themselves. Although this approach sometimes led to the moderates opposing bills supported by most of their own caucus, there were also substantial areas of common ground. An example was HCR 2028, which referred to voters the proposal to deny bail to unauthorized immigrants held on serious felonies and was written after a bill attempting to do this (HB 2389) had stalled.[75]

These moderate Republicans were developing another important function as the nucleus of a broader group of Republican legislators who frequently conferred on immigration and other issues. This group began to operate as an important forum for collective deliberation among Republicans who either publicly or privately identified themselves against the party's right wing. The membership of this informal group varied across the years, but interviewees described it in very similar terms. Jones recalled: "If you said something, you'd better be prepared in that group to back it up, not with just ideological sayings but [with] actual facts and stuff. . . . That was the group on the issue of immigration. . . . Pete [Hershberger], I would say, was a definite moderate . . . [b]ut the most part of the group . . . were just right-of-center, conservative Republicans [who] didn't follow the Ten Commandments of the Far Right."

LEGISLATIVE DEMOCRATS

Though legislative Democrats represented an ethnically diverse array of constituencies and were not homogeneous ideologically, they mostly had common ground on immigration issues. Despite being in the minority, they held some influence: their ally the governor controlled the veto pen, and they held enough votes to sustain its use. Among legislative Democrats, a shift in stances on immigration issues was beginning but was not uniformly embraced. Arguments against Proposition 200 had emphasized its unintended consequences and its racism as well as the skepticism that the problems that on face it sought to address really existed. In its aftermath, some legislative Democrats were starting to move toward expressly acknowledging the existence of immigration-related problems that demanded responses. "I think people are frustrated," Gallardo was quoted as saying at the start of the session, identifying state penalties for human trafficking as a possible area of action. "They want something done."[76]

Although acknowledging problems stemming from the border, these Democrats initially focused on calling for the federal government to fix them, citing the state's limited jurisdiction. Blaming the federal government became a consensus Democratic talking point. What met with less agreement was whether, beyond that argument, there was any true latitude for state action. Gallardo, for one, went further than some other Democrats at the time in finding state activity on border-crime issues to be supportable, while arguing both for the overarching need for federal action and against the concept that border-hawk proposals contained any real solutions. Gallardo recounted later: "We were hitting the drum on the need for a federal approach. We needed comprehensive immigration reform, and that was our message. We needed Congress to step up. . . . You cannot fix a federal problem in a state legislature. But what we could do from a state level is go after the criminals. . . . Hey, if you're a gangbanger, and you're doing bad things in our community, and you're undocumented, by all means. Let's go after them."

To Democrats who saw a need to shift to a different, more active stance on immigration, human smuggling was a real problem that state action could appropriately address. Taking a more proactive stance on that issue showed concern about the border and demonstrated action, in contrast to how Proposition 200 opponents had found it difficult to communicate their message in a way they saw as resonating with the public. "That was their [the border hawks'] message: 'We're trying to prevent voter fraud,'" Gallardo said, explaining what many Democrats described as a difficult messaging predicament. "As much as we stood and said, 'What voter fraud?' [and] 'We don't have cases of massive voter fraud,' we needed to be able to say, to an extent, 'We don't want voter fraud, neither!'"

Nevertheless, Democrats found most of the border-related bills presented in the legislature in 2005 to be unacceptable. Kyrsten Sinema, then a Democratic member of the House, called HB 2030, the bill to limit access to higher-education funding, "the worst bill I've ever seen . . . just nasty."[77] Democrats' reaction to other bills was only somewhat less hostile; they voted against them with near uniformity. But many legislative Democrats were beginning to believe that blanket opposition to these measures presented the same kind of problem that the anti–Proposition 200 efforts had raised. Democrats lent some support to antismuggling bills, including Paton and Bee's SB 1372. This support was not uniform, however: ten more left-wing House Democrats ultimately voted against that bill. The political difficulties of just saying no—which many political elites were starting to believe came across as a kind of denialism—were shown in a committee field visit Paton had requested for SB 1372 in a community that was experiencing substantial smuggling traffic.

> [Cynthia] Kolb, who lives in the Hereford area, has been an outspoken critic of what she sees as failed federal border policies. She held up a large poster board full of photos depicting what illegal immigrants have done to the environment, the trash they leave behind. . . . On the poster it stated, "Welcome to Cochise County, where we are invaded 24/7/365." . . . State Rep. Ben Miranda,[78] the only Democrat on the committee at the hearing, said all the photos in the world and emotions do not mean the proposed bill is a good one. He said it is far from it and intends to vote against it. That brought an angry outcry from Kolb.[79]

Paton recounted: "It was really entertaining to watch. Because you had people who, they had people going across their land, and you had Ben Miranda telling them, 'Well, this really is not even a problem, and it's none of your business. This should be the federal government.' . . . If you're defined by your opponents, it was a good thing to have them complaining about the bill at the time, politically."

Many Democrats were starting to agree that such an apparent political paradox did exist when it came to immigration and the border. Opposing any action related to the border appeared ineffectual at diminishing the public sense of a problem and instead seemed only to lend greater credibility to those who looked to be taking action. Yet although Democratic legislators started to move toward a position where they could contemplate some state actions on the border, there was not yet consensus among them either on the nature of the political problem or on how to counteract it. As an article from the end of the 2005 legislative session put it,

> Republicans and Democrats alike agree the clashes over how to deal with illegal immigration stem from the frustration of citizens and lawmakers—the two sides just don't agree on how to solve the problem. "None of us are soft on [illegal] immigration," Mr. Gallardo said. "We all oppose that—it's how we approach it." For many Democrats, this year felt like a constant uphill climb. Each time one immigration bill was heard, another was on the docket and awaiting a vote, when, in the past, there would only be a few immigrant-related bills. . . . Democrats don't want a solution to the immigration problem, Mr. Pearce said, because it hurts them politically. . . ."They're such hypocrites," he said. "They say we have a problem but they're never willing to do anything about it."[80]

THE GOVERNOR

Janet Napolitano had campaigned for governor on other matters and had little initial interest in making immigration or border security the signature issue for her administration. By 2005, however, the legislature was advancing immigration measures at a fast clip to a governor who presented herself as a moderate who tackled public-safety issues with a former prosecutor's mien. Napolitano, like most other Democrats, did consider the border to present significant problems to Arizona in terms of public safety (with regard to smuggling and border crime), state finances, and economic losses due to insufficient legal channels for labor migration. Tim Nelson,

Napolitano's general counsel until 2008, described this perspective: "To the extent that there were public-safety issues, both to the public at large and to individual immigrants, you certainly wanted to address that. You wanted to address the financial consequences to the state of what really was a failed federal policy."

Legislators in 2005 passed the bill restricting unauthorized immigrants' access to higher-education funding and in-state tuition rates (HB 2030), the bill allowing unauthorized status to be considered an aggravating factor in criminal sentencing (HB 2259), the bill prohibiting state officials from accepting the Mexican-issued *matrícula consular* (SB 1511), the bill prohibiting municipal funding for day-labor centers (HB 2592), the bill creating a private prison in Mexico (HB 2709), the bill requiring local law enforcement to enter into agreements with federal immigration authorities (SB 1306), and the bill entering human trafficking and smuggling into Arizona's criminal code (SB 1372). The bills met a mixed fate on Napolitano's desk. The governor showed a willingness in some areas to be more hawkish than legislative Democrats had yet decided to be but also drew battle lines with Republicans that would endure. She signed two bills that legislative Democrats had voted against in large numbers: the day-labor center bill (HB 2592) and the bill to allow unauthorized immigration status as an aggravating factor in criminal sentencing (HB 2259). She also signed the human-smuggling bill (SB 1372), on which legislative Democrats had been divided. She vetoed the rest.

Amid the unpredictability of a legislative session in which, according to aides, it was difficult to foresee what the legislature would pass, Napolitano took an approach to immigration-related bills that was animated by some larger concerns but substantially ad hoc. As Nelson described,

> I really do remember those decisions being very case-by-case oriented. You know, I think that she didn't want to default them, veto them just out of hand. But on the other hand there were some that just seemed so clearly unconstitutional or damaging to the state's ability to grow that they had to be [vetoed]. . . . I think she tried to strike a balance between recognizing that the impetus behind these bills was a clear public sentiment that something needed to be done and an effort to try to make sure that what did get done didn't do more damage than good.

Napolitano laid out what would become routine reasons for vetoing such legislation, faulting vetoed bills for being impractical or unfunded or for not addressing what she cited as the true problems on the border. "Our immigration system is broken and needs real solutions. . . . Senate Bill 1306, however, offers no new ideas or resources to fix the system and is little more than an unfunded mandate on state and local law enforcement officers,"[81] she wrote about the local-enforcement bill. "I have sent the federal government invoices totaling $195,668,017.46, representing Arizona's costs for incarcerating people who came here illegally and committed other crimes once they got here," she wrote in vetoing HB 2709 to create a prison in Mexico, which she said "will not reduce the number of criminal aliens Arizona must incarcerate [or] automatically reduce the per capita cost of incarcerating them" and would require a new international treaty.[82] The last point here reflected a frequent criticism of the constitutionality of immigration-related state legislation amid concerns over both civil rights and Arizona's powers vis-à-vis the federal system. While focusing on practical and legal barriers, Napolitano sometimes evinced humanitarian concern about border-related bills, as she did in vetoing HB 2030, regarding higher-education access. "While I agree that public programs should not be available to those who consciously decide to come here illegally, this bill goes too far by punishing even longtime residents of this state who were brought here as small children by their parents."[83] Her objection to this bill was narrower than the one expressed by Phil Lopes, the House Democratic leader: "[It's] disingenuous, it's stupid, it's ill-advised."[84]

State action against human smuggling emerged from the 2005 legislative session as the only border-related issue on which there existed any measure of bipartisan consensus. But that bipartisan support for SB 1372 as drafted did not last long. By September, Andrew Thomas, the Maricopa County attorney, announced that he would employ the law to indict unauthorized migrants as co-conspirators in their own smuggling. This move astonished the bill's Republican sponsors[85] and illustrated how some Arizona politicians were stretching the bounds of entrepreneurship on immigration issues. Such envelope-pushing moves accorded with a media environment increasingly saturated with border-security coverage, including border-vigilante spectacles in April 2005 that both commanded negative national media attention and began to attract support from right-wing state political figures.[86] The legislature closed its session in 2005 with immigration and the border occupying an unprecedentedly salient place on the agenda and an array of political actors altering their positions amid the issue's shifting politics.

A STATE OF EMERGENCY

In the summer of 2005, with the legislature out of regular session until January, Napolitano undertook a number of moves that employed her executive authority on immigration and the border. She had already done this to some extent previously, such as by invoicing the federal government for the costs of incarcerating unauthorized immigrants.[87] Napolitano's aides saw immigration issues as placing the governor in a bind that threatened to become a major political liability. Public concern pressed up against the fact that states were not main actors in this policy field. At the same time, voters saw citing jurisdictional reasons for not acting as dodging accountability. Dennis Burke, Napolitano's chief of staff for policy, explained later: "The difficulty was you had a problem that was created by the federal government because you had a system that wasn't working, and it was impacting the state. And so here's this hard-charging, active governor who wants to solve problems, and she doesn't have the authority to solve the problem within the federal government, and you've got this legislature coming up with these bills that she adamantly opposes 'cause they're bad policy. And so she's kind of stuck in the middle there."

Napolitano's executive authority as governor offered some tools to try to solve this predicament. In her veto of SB 1306, the local-enforcement bill, Napolitano said she would call for a statewide law enforcement summit to discuss dealing with immigration and border enforcement, which she did in July, heavily criticizing the federal government.[88] Later in the year, Napolitano directed state contractors to conduct work-authorization checks on people they hired,[89] which was described as a "step aimed at chipping away a small piece of the economic magnet for illicit border crossings."[90] In the autumn of 2005, ICE and the Arizona Department of Corrections began training that allowed some state prison personnel to identify possible unauthorized immigrants among state prisoners, traditionally a federal task.[91] Thus, the state entered into an early "287(g) agreement,"[92] though Napolitano had vetoed the bill requiring local police to do the same.

With this increasingly front-footed stance, Napolitano scored a political coup in August with her most salient executive action on the issue—a declaration of emergency for Arizona's four border counties.[93] Bill Richardson, the Democratic governor of neighboring New Mexico, had earlier issued a similar declaration, and Napolitano's staff "jumped on it immediately," Burke recalled, declaring Arizona's own emergency the next week. This action drew great attention from both national and local media.[94] Its policy effect in Arizona was modest, providing $1.5 million in emergency funds, divided among four counties. Napolitano's declaration was more forceful in its political symbolism, however. In her aides' view, the declaration traded on the border hawks' strident language of emergency to recenter the border-security debate on Napolitano's more moderate stance, to win credibility on the issue by communicating the view that the border was indeed an urgent problem, and to give her a more prominent and less reactive role in policy debates.

Tactically, the political resonance of declaring an emergency would garner the governor a level of attention that would make the issue easier to control and less politically dangerous to her. The general feeling that Napolitano and other Democrats were playing defense on immigration in response to continual accusations that they were ignoring border problems had become a major political concern. As Burke said,

> Part of what we wanted to do was allow her to be the voice of the issue because it would be not only more stable, but she could control it, right? You don't want to be always responding to someone. . . . We want us to be saying, "Here's the direction we should be going—pay attention to what we're doing." And [the declaration of emergency] allowed us to do that because now everyone was like, "Well, look at Napolitano." And, once again, it fits right into her profile, which is—talk about taking action. She declared an emergency!

Strategically, governing elites had come to believe that border-hawk positions would gain the upper hand if they couldn't provide a response that credibly treated immigration and the border as urgent security problems. Such a view contrasted directly with the earlier reading that the border hawks' position was so extreme as to not warrant rebuttal and that playing their game risked assuming accountability for an issue that was "a black hole that few elected officials wished to enter."[95] The new strategic reasoning instead depended on an alternative being presented with sufficient political force to gain attention and an upper hand. Burke elaborated: "It's not just like, 'Oh, great, we don't want the governor on [CNN].' No. You want the governor on the news, so she says, 'Look, this is what we do.' . . . The last thing you need is people out there saying, 'Jeez, Russell [Pearce] is the only guy doing stuff. This must be the only thing you can do because he's proposing it and no one's challenging it,' or they are just saying, 'No, no, no.'"

With Napolitano taking her declaration of emergency to the national airwaves, the political status of immigration in Arizona was now far from the placid political settlement just two years earlier. New political strategies were beginning to draw entirely new battle lines on immigration. Above all else, such battles were premised on the emphatic agreement that there was, indeed, an urgent problem on the border—a problem of security.

DISCUSSION: NAVIGATING THE POPULIST BORDER-SECURITY CHALLENGE

In 2003, a class of officials took office in Arizona who had scarcely campaigned on immigration and who were focused on other policy issues. By the end of 2005, a state-declared emergency existed on the Arizona border. Every political faction in state policy making had reconsidered the politics of these issues and had adopted a stance significantly more willing to take security action toward a purportedly insecure border. At the state level, immigration had started to become distinctly securitized. Of course, the sweep of this development sounds familiar. It is consistent with one of the classically observed aspects of the "securitization" of a political issue—the emergence of a consensus that a problem indeed is one of security and the fading away of any salient counterargument. In other words, the "normal haggling of politics" dissipates around the issue as it is "dealt with decisively by top leaders prior to other issues."[96]

Yet this new settlement in Arizona did not emerge from the kinds of considerations or processes that securitization theory has usually imagined, nor did it entail the sorts of political effects that this scholarship has often assumed. Clearly, the haggling went on. In one sense, genuine consensus about the problem's security nature did not actually exist in Arizona. Different figures and factions continued to diverge markedly on what exactly the security problem at the border was. Elites' agreement was not on the precise nature of the problem or its remedies but rather on the purported political realities upon which any workable response had to be based. A certain "homogeneity" was real:[97] a new, broadly shared starting point that immigration needed to be addressed as security. In another sense, though, this homogeneity was shallow, making for basic disagreements and clashing political interests. These differences continued to drive the development of immigration politics as it became a major political battlefield in Arizona. The field of contestation narrowed not under the weight of an exceptional politics elevating executive decisionism but due to new apparent issue dynamics that shaped elites' competitive calculations.

IDENTIFYING SECURITY, IDENTIFYING POPULISM

Arizona policy makers' reflections make evident that by 2005 they all understood themselves to be dealing with an issue that possessed crucial security dimensions. Indeed, for security scholars, pronouncements of emergency,[98] clampdowns against human smugglers or traffickers,[99] and metaphors of invasion[100] are routine topics for analysis. However, it is notable how in Arizona this process occurred without many of the political effects theorized to accompany it—effects that in past literature have been key to distinguishing securitization as a concept. Both emergency language and the immersion of immigration into a framework emphasizing policing and defense became increasingly pronounced in Arizona,[101] but this process clearly had not elevated the issue to exceptional treatment set above the merely political agenda. It is that kind of treatment that is the distinguishing characteristic of successful securitization efforts in the Copenhagen School's view, a view that has strongly imprinted later scholarship employing speech-act or discursive conceptualizations of securitization processes.[102] As the introduction noted, such perspectives have tended to tightly bind together securitization's "logic" (characterized by threat, urgency, and extraordinary response) with the political effects presumed to occur if that logic succeeds in affecting treatment of an issue (exceptionalism).[103]

As a consequence, it has been difficult for the field to conceive of effects of securitization that sit somewhere between a "failed" securitizing move and a state of exception.[104] So if not through exceptionalism, how do we identify the presence of this quality of "security" in Arizona's treatment of the border issue? The question "How do we know security when we see it"[105] has produced a number of notable responses by sociological securitization scholars. These responses are focused largely on identifying a transversal core of security claims that analysts can identify across different contexts in which security manifests[106] or on taking various approaches to interpreting how security is constituted by interrelated meanings in historically particular contexts.[107] Scholarship on the "politicization of security" has made some significant strides in terms of examining how security issues have been increasingly debated in "normal" democratic settings and not simply left to executive "top leaders," as classically expected in securitization analysis. Though helpful, this approach is somewhat limiting:[108] What if we want to understand how security emerged as the dominant understanding of an issue that had no previous policy-making system surrounding it—as in immigration and Arizona state government? "How do we know security when we see it" in such a case?

To gain purchase on this question, it is instructive to look first toward how we identify populism at play in these issue debates in Arizona; populism scholars have already responded to similar issues in their field, developing a productive "ideational" approach from which security scholars may learn. Populism, in the "ideational" definition Cas Mudde crystallizes, is "an ideology that considers society to be ultimately separated into two homogeneous and antagonistic groups, the 'pure people' versus 'the corrupt elite,' and which argues that politics should be an expression of the volonté générale (general will) of the people."[109] This definition establishes four "core concepts" in identifying or analyzing populism: ideology, the people, the elite, and the general will.[110] Populism represents a "thin ideology,"[111] a "looser set of ideas"[112] that maps politics and offers a general guide to how it should be conducted but, unlike thicker ideologies such as liberalism or conservatism, does not offer a full political program. For that program, populism attaches to "thicker" ideologies. One key benefit of the ideational approach to populism is that it offers a way to identify populism across cases where its context or related "host ideologies" may greatly differ.[113]

The essential aspect about the people/elite dichotomy in the ideational account of populism is that it is rendered as a moral distinction for which the "host ideology" provides substantive grounding. The developments described in this chapter make clear the moral starkness of Pearce and his allies' campaign against "the politicians" (the "elite") of both parties, who in this account refuse to enact policies that possess incontestable, enduring support (evoking a general will) from a "people" idealized as adamant about upholding the moral quality of the "law." Here, the morally superior character of the people against the "elite" is to be found in the insistence upon "law and order," which border hawks argue the people crave to uphold as foundational to the (secure) nation.

The "illegal" quality of the immigration at issue is crucial because this framing positions unauthorized immigration as self-apparently morally unacceptable as well as dangerous. A "Manichean moralism" about lawbreaking is mapped onto the border hawks' people/elite distinction,[114] positioning the people's moralized "common sense" against the elites' moral weakness. The people see clearly the imperative of upholding the law (which, after all, is the people's law), but elites refuse this imperative due to clientelistic corruption: they kowtow to interest groups (minority constituencies, business lobbies) at the expense of the "people" and their will. Indeed, these "law-and-order" arguments relating to immigration and beyond as well as these logics' connection to areas such as welfare provision are characteristic among the populist radical Right in many different contexts.[115] In the U.S. context, of course, exhortations of law and order are always replete with racial politics and with associations to non-white groups purportedly possessing less "deservingness" and greater criminality.[116] The implications of who would be targeted through "law and order" in immigration were therefore distinctly related to the racial context in which Arizona border hawks constructed the threat and "the people" in question in the early twenty-first century.[117]

How does distinguishing the populism of the Arizona border hawks within their larger ideology help us to "know security when we see it" in the events discussed in this chapter? It is worth stepping back to understand how this "ideational" approach to populism responded to conceptual barriers in populism scholarship that are strikingly similar to the ones related to the identification of security, discussed earlier. It is particularly instructive how populism scholars have enabled richer analysis of such phenomena in immigration governance by moving away from purely discursive conceptualizations of populism. This ideational view of populism draws from earlier discursive accounts of the concept, in particular Ernesto Laclau's,[118] but redresses some limitations that this discursive approach places on empirical analysis. It rigorously separates the empirical questions of whether the core populist logic is being mobilized in politics and what effects such a mobilization has. These effects can be significant yet short of those sought by the populist discourse, where in discursive accounts they are treated more determinatively. Whereas Laclau's discursive approach "blends the substance of populist ideas with how they actually play out in the political sphere" and limits populism to "movements that attract a numerical majority,"[119] the ideational approach does not take these two factors as litmus tests of a true case of populism and, indeed, is able to analyze populist mobilizations from the margins, which do not dominate political life.

This approach in populism scholarship resonates with key sociological critiques of securitization theory, which have similarly identified how discursive approaches toward the phenomenon have limited analysis by presuming particular effects—especially exceptionalism.[120] How would a parallel approach to security be applied? It would consider the potential systemic effects of the mobilization of security meanings or "logics," including from marginal places. This consideration permits a vantage point on security where the introduction of security does not necessarily imply either failure or exceptionalism but has indeterminate effects on politics that may still amount to "securitization" in terms of the increasing security practices around an issue.[121] Indeed, the idea that there are basic logical elements or claims to security, identifiable across cases where the securitization concept pertains, has been the usual view in securitization scholarship.[122] This idea allows analysts to identify invocations of such a logic to determine that an issue has become "about security" even if previously theorized consequences do not empirically accompany this fact.

So what are these core "logics" or meanings of security? This question articulates an ongoing topic for this book and, indeed, has been a major point of discussion among security scholars.[123] But the discussion might start, at a basic (though still contestable) level, with the elements the Copenhagen School proposed are essential parts of the "grammar of security": a threat that imperils some referent object, the aversion of irreparable harm ("the point of no return"), "and a possible way out,"[124] which is classically defined as exceptional measures but may instead be understood simply as security practices.[125] We can see how this grammar was uttered in Arizona—the "illegal invasion" of immigrants would "create a path to the destruction of this country," in Pearce's words. We can similarly see the increasing security policies that followed this utterance—new laws and resources against "border crime" but not a state of exception—and so understand the causal mechanisms in policy deliberations that connected public discourses to securitized policy decisions.[126] The impact of security on these decisions comes into view in parallel with the impact of populism. This viewpoint provides analytical purchase for identifying security and populism throughout this narrative and for understanding how these concepts shaped the emerging governing-elite strategies that led to securitization even amid "normal" politics.

LEARNING BORDER-SECURITY POLITICS

As this chapter has made clear, new political calculations by Arizona's leading policy makers—made in relation to both the growing security aspects of public contestation over immigration issues and the populist character of the challenge to governing elites—were essential to how a nonsecuritized status quo ante regarding the border in Arizona so quickly collapsed. In security studies, the typical explanation for this kind of rapid shift cites the power and authority of executive securitizing actors. This kind of quick change in tack is well conceptualized in general political science, but in a very different way. Literatures on how policy elites process information identify clearly that when policy makers who had perceived few demands on them related to a given issue sense a sudden intrusion of information to the contrary, rapid changes in policy orientation naturally follow in a process of "alarmed discovery."[127] Proposition 200's success against broad elite opposition seemed to trigger such a process. To all policy makers except those who had ardently supported Proposition 200 (and to some extent even to them as well), the whole politics of immigration—and its place in the broader political field—began to look entirely different with this new information.

It is no surprise that a successful challenge to an elite-supported status quo from the outside would amplify contention and reconfigure alliances.[128] However, less clear is the reason for the particular shape of the issue contestation that followed in Arizona: one overwhelmed by a security-oriented way of looking at the issue. This outcome is even more striking given the lack of previous inclination by most actors in Arizona's political system to treat immigration in this way. A change in patterns of policy-maker attention, after all, might be assumed to more naturally trigger "typical" contestation among accounts of the issue—a contest between security approaches and other interpretations. Indeed, when confronting hard-line challenges on immigration from populist competitors, other political strategies—including fully opposing or downplaying the challenge—might also work.[129]

Here, the simultaneously populist and security-based nature of the challenge in Arizona is key to understanding the shape of the evolving governing-elite approach. That populism is key here is unsurprising in a way: Bigo's "homogeneity" seems related to the "contagion" that anti-immigration populists are observed to spread to their political competitors.[130] The initial response from most of Arizona's mainstream elites to the populist border-security push was to ignore or downplay the importance of the issue. As Napolitano's communications director, Jeanine L'Ecuyer, recalled:

INTERVIEWER: Was there ever much of an appetite to try to calm people down by saying, "This isn't really a problem"?
JEANINE L'ECUYER: We tried.

ɪ: Did you?

ᴊʟ: In the very early stages, we tried. We tried saying, "Look, gang, nothing has really changed. These are long-standing issues that are getting
more attention, but nothing has fundamentally changed." And that
didn't get any traction with anybody. It didn't get traction with the
media, it didn't get traction with the public.

Or as Gallardo more colorfully put it, "I honestly think we were trying to
find a message that resonated 'cause we were getting our asses kicked."
As these recollections make clear, new political postures embracing
security came from a process of political learning or puzzling.[131] This
understanding of the situation contrasts with views of securitization
processes that tend to see them occurring rather quickly and totally
instead of iteratively or partially.[132] The search for a workable political
response in Arizona was guided by policy makers' observations of two
interlinked qualities of the immigration issue, both tied to the security
meanings that had been attached to the issue as well as to their specifically populist articulations.

First, a prevalent sense emerged that the public was demanding or at
least restless for action. Governing elites began to sense that citing jurisdictional (federal/state) problems was coming off as dismissive. Populist
border hawks lambasted such attempts as characteristic elite obfusca-
tion.[133] The success of Proposition 200 was a major indicator, signaling
both that immigration was becoming a more salient issue and that a
rejection of the previous elite consensus was quickly developing. Postmor-
tems identified the scale of this rejection as surprisingly comprehensive.
As Gallardo recounted, "If you look at the election results on Prop 200,
even Latinos voted for it," referring to exit polls that showed significant
support even among traditionally Democratic-voting groups.[134] As Paton
recalled, "I mean, [my] district wanted something to be done. Let's put it
that way. And I don't know how else to put it. People say, 'How could you
say that your district wanted that?' I walked to 10,000 doors in my district. I mean, we talked to a lot of people and a lot of Democrats, for that
matter. . . . [T]hat was the issue that they cared about the most."

Policy makers also read public demands about immigration through
the state's major media institutions, whose coverage—especially in the

days before extensive social media use—was a key shaper of policy makers' perceptions of how issue positions were playing. Although policy makers read the media in order to understand and monitor the political environment, they also saw its coverage as steering issue dynamics in problematic ways. Populist border hawks saw the mainstream media as party to an elite pro-immigration bias. To those on the other side of the issue, the problem was the opposite: the mainstream media simultaneously reflected and exacerbated public concern. As Haener, Napolitano's legislative liaison, recalled, "This was the issue that Russell Pearce and those guys were pushing, and the media, which needs to sell controversy to sell papers or sell ads or sell whatever they sell, that's what was driving all of this. . . . I mean, when you did polling at that time, immigration was at the top of the list almost every time, from 2005, probably, on." In such a context, citing jurisdictional problems or federalism as barriers to taking action was proving insufficient. Kyrsten Sinema, a Democratic state legislator at the time, recounted: "The early response was to say, 'This is not your job; this is the federal government's job.' Yeah, well. You know, voters don't care. Most people don't know the difference between state, local, and federal government. What they do know is that someone's not doing their job somewhere 'cause things are messed up."

The second interlinked characteristic of the immigration issue lay in how this public demand for governing elites to act was seen as closely tied to an indelible public anxiety about the issue. In tandem, these perceived qualities—public demands to act and public anxiety—strongly resemble essential aspects of the classical securitization grammar drawn from a Hobbesian logic: the sensation of danger, the urgency of response, and the sweeping aside of niceties such as jurisdiction amid the need to act. Populist border hawks persistently introduced this logic into the debate and were aided by media dynamics. Their success at pushing the issue was seen as requiring new strategies to respond to and compete adequately with it, notwithstanding real barriers to introducing a new policy approach.

STEVE GALLARDO: We couldn't fix a national problem before the state
    Senate.
INTERVIEWER: I mean, did that message work in your opinion?
SG: No!

ɪ: Why?

sɢ: Why? I think at that time, when you're talking about—that '04, '06 time, I think you're still dealing with fear that the Spanish and the Mexicans are taking over. That fear.

Admitting a problem but holding it out as one for others to solve will fall flat with an anxious public primed by pervasive threat narratives. In this account, border hawks' early success grew partially from their populist self-positioning as speaking to voters' worries, which governing elites were ignoring. Accusations of racism served to make opponents of the hawks' characterization of the border issue look like out-of-touch elites insensitive to public concern. Assigning others the responsibility for the problem deepened the appearance of unresponsiveness. In this vacuum, border hawks dominated. As Sinema summarized, "What we learned over the years in Arizona was that . . . when given no response versus a marginal response, people will usually choose a marginal response. And what Democrats were offering was no response. And that's how Mr. Pearce's ideas gained traction."

If this process of political learning led to the conclusion that a different response was necessary, what kind of new response was workable? Public anxiety was indelible—the demand to act could not be safely deflected. The security quality of the issue could not be effectively contested or downplayed. Such attempts would only play into extreme hands. But the debate might be steered through making layered arguments about immigration—though only within a framework that acknowledged anxiety and the necessity of action. Sinema had been one of the ten more left-wing Democrats who had voted against Arizona's smuggling bill in 2005. Her explanation of her evolving approach reflects the shift among the border hawks' opponents.

KYRSTEN SINEMA: What I started to do was a strategy that I felt was more effective, which was to, number one, recognize and acknowledge the brokenness of the system, because it is totally broken. And then try to speak truth to the frustration that ordinary Arizonans felt about the fallout from that broken system. Right? Changing neighborhoods, you know, job loss, difficulty figuring out how to navigate a neighborhood that looks different than it used to look. . . . [I]t's normal for them to worry about those things.

INTERVIEWER: And you didn't think you could just say, "Don't worry about it."

KS: No. Because they're worrying about it. What you have to say is, "I see that you're worried, it makes sense that you're worried, of course you're worried, that's normal and valid to be worried, and here are some ideas that could work better than the proposal that you've been offered." And so to try to offer better solutions, which is challenging since the state does have, in actuality, a very limited ability to influence immigration policy.

This response addressed the public's immigration anxiety as a political reality that had already proven a productive target of political mobilization and was, at least in the short run, indelible. Amid the pressures of competitive politics, why this situation had come to pass became secondary to elites' acceptance of it as a durable political reality. For any position on the border and immigration to be accepted by the public as valid, it had to address insecurity. As L'Ecuyer recalled about Napolitano's approach to the security quality of the immigration issue, "I don't think she wanted to challenge it. . . . Without that sense of security, it was abundantly clear that not only politically was it not going anywhere but that the public was not going to buy into it." Tim Nelson, Napolitano's general counsel, explained the eventually dominant reading of why a purely oppositional approach to the securitizing direction of the issue was bound to fail: "People realized that that wasn't going to be effective, and it wasn't gonna make the sentiment go away. . . . When there's a real sentiment, you've gotta be responsive to the sentiment in some fashion. I think [Napolitano] calculated correctly that, you know, just a 'veto, veto, veto, no, no, no' approach would be perceived as not responsive to the sentiment. So she did what she did." If the opposition's resonance is rooted in what seems to be a durable public sentiment that can be politically exploited, and no similarly strong countervailing sentiment seems available, then success depends on co-opting that initial sentiment.

As this understanding came to the forefront for Arizona's non-border-hawk policy makers in 2005, distinct patterns of party competition over the issue began to emerge. The next chapter explores those patterns in depth. However, it was already evident that securitization was advancing from a broad, gradual, iterative process of learning from experiences of political competition. A border emergency was declared in Arizona so a top leader could seize greater control over the issue—as the Copenhagen School might suppose and as a broad range of critical security theorists would fear.[135] But the declaration of emergency was not the power grab usually imagined. There was little perceived political benefit in such a move outside of waging a defense, amid shifting political sands, against attacks by populist radical-right forces demanding even more hard-line approaches. In pressing forward, border-hawk legislators were clearly not conforming to images of speakers and audiences negotiating demands.[136] They played a much fuller, complex part, catalyzing a broad securitizing shift and moving the executive—a reversal of the presumed power dynamics of securitization that are often based in observations of parliamentary systems with institutionally strong executives.[137] In Arizona, a wider range of political actors learned to speak security in their own manner and in pursuit of their own objectives. These objectives were clearly and "normally" political in character—aiming to secure power amid challenge—but escalating security politics entailed a marked shift in political tactics and strategies.

⸙

From 2003 to 2005, Arizona went from a state-level elite consensus—relatively unshaken even by 9/11—that Arizona had no role to play in border security and immigration to the declaration of a state of emergency in Arizona's border counties. All relevant sides in political debate now supported greater security action toward immigration and the border. The alarmed discovery of apparent popular demands about the issue following the success of Proposition 200 in 2004 had led to the issue's sudden rise to prominence on the state policy agenda, driven by the border hawks' securitarian and antielitist attacks. By 2005, policy makers of many different ideological stripes were working from key shared perceptions. Moderates concluded that a strategy of flatly opposing state action on the border would fail. Engaging in a process of political learning, they instead sought a position that "resonated." They saw the issue's purported

security character as imbuing it with distinct new qualities. These qualities altered the sorts of political strategies that it made sense to take
toward immigration and thus the shape of the political contest over the
issue. The public was seen as anxious and demanding action, contesting
this characterization was perilous amid populist attack, the issue was
impossible to flatly downplay, and the initiative had to be taken. Janet
Napolitano's declaration of emergency was the coda to this initial shift in
calculations. Across the political spectrum, policy makers embraced new
political strategies oriented around the treatment of immigration as a
security issue. Policies toward immigration that were once widely
regarded as on the fringe now had at least a hearing. The securitization
of immigration in Arizona was under way.

Arizona's border emergency was born not of any kind of deep agreement about a security problem for the state or of the sort of exceptional
politics that could accompany such consensus. Rather, it emerged out of
a perceived need to adapt to new political information, newly mobilized
demands, and a shifting state of play. Instead of yielding an anesthetized
politics where agreement about the existence of the security threat
quashed dispute, this shift brought forth new, intense patterns of competitive border-security politics. The web of beliefs that was woven
between 2003 and 2005 became an engrossing way in which Arizona's
policy makers understood the political possibilities of the immigration
issue in the coming years and resulted in patterns of fierce political competition over border security.

2

SECURING VICTORY

Policy makers across Arizona's political spectrum had concluded by the end of 2005 that, amid a populist border-hawk challenge, they needed a more active position on immigration and border issues than they had held before. Above all, such a position had to accept that the border presented a security problem and that the state needed to act. This shift unleashed a distinct period of competitive interparty border-security politics in Arizona. Within the apparently prevailing consensus that the state needed to take action on immigration, both border hawks and their opponents sought to use the perceived attributes of the issue's politics to their own political advantage and to confound their rivals. With the basic security nature of the issue no longer openly in dispute, this competitive period featured intense public sparring over what policy path constituted the best response to the purported security problem as political rivals jostled for power in the election year 2006 and beyond.

The unmistakably Machiavellian character of this period invites an examination of what kind of role such competitive political calculations may play in deepening the security treatment of contested issues. With security broadly accepted by competing political groups and figures as the basic premise of an issue, what happens when they employ securitization as a political tool against each other? This chapter identifies how party-competition dynamics can form a crucial factor in the success or failure of efforts to treat immigration as a security issue. This discussion extends on the theme of the narrowing of the range of debate and possible solutions when security meanings suffuse an issue, explored in chapter 1. This narrowing, however, is not an endpoint for contention over securitization but rather can produce intense competitive dynamics that deepen the phenomenon because the actors who pursue securitization do so in the service of clashing political objectives. The "ownership" strategies of relatively moderate governing elites play a crucial role in deepening securitization and in continuing to accept in part and thus to "mainstream" populist-right positions. These ownership maneuvers, aiming to neutralize the issue or capture control over it through triangulating responses, may frequently function at stabilizing moderates' general political positions.[1] However, they systematically lead to situations where securitized approaches to immigration are primed to advance beyond what moderates prefer.

Those kinds of political considerations have rarely been explored in a securitization literature focused on security's alleged difference from "normal" politics or on the social construction of threats that occurs at a higher, more abstract level than the designs of particular political actors.[2] Yet as the previous chapters make clear, those who make the essential decisions in securitizing immigration policy are, after all, politicians[3]— people whose "normal" approach is to survey the political landscape and aim accordingly to achieve goals that require legitimacy and power.[4] Only relatively recently have securitization scholars challenging the purported exceptionalism of security politics moved toward detailed investigations of whether there are distinctive rules of the competitive political game when security is present.[5] The events and patterns this chapter analyzes help to advance this discussion.

Beyond that, this chapter speaks to a pressing public debate regarding whether and how the political "mainstream" should address the growing influence of the populist radical Right, especially on immigration.[6] It examines how as this competition deepened in Arizona state politics, so did securitization of the immigration issue—despite moderate officials achieving larger political victories and continuing to hold key veto points in the policy-making process. This issue trajectory is one that examinations of the effects of the populist radical Right have frequently echoed.[7] What explains this apparent paradox? This chapter argues that such dynamics are especially likely because the latter political objective—maintaining power—is more important to governing nonpopulist elites than are particular outcomes in immigration policy. Yet in shoring up their political fortunes against a populist security challenge in this way, those in power lay a path for continued difficulties in controlling both the issue trajectory and the development of the political environment. This phenomenon seems deeply related to the kinds of troubling symptoms that securitization scholarship has identified—including a march toward amplified exclusion and narrowed possibilities that issues seem to follow once security takes hold following the "mainstreaming" of more extreme views.

As Arizona entered an election year in 2006, border-security politics held major implications for those who sought to keep or win power in a general sense, interweaving the politics of border security with diverse political struggles. The security nature of immigration exerted profound influence over the issue's development not because it exceptionally stood outside normal politics but because it was inextricably shot through with that politics. The extent to which border security was enmeshed with goals across the political agenda came to the fore. Populist border hawks moved to box in their opponents, while nonpopulist politicians maneuvered to try to capture the issue from the border hawks by means of centrist triangulation. Democrats in particular machinated to deepen rifts between border hard-liners and their partisan allies in the business community. The issues of deploying the National Guard to assist at the border and of applying employer sanctions—that is, punishing employers who hire unauthorized labor—emerged as key issues in Arizona politics. Although Governor Janet Napolitano's centrist positioning met with considerable electoral success, the securitization of immigration continued to engulf more and more facets of public policy. The issue of local enforcement of immigration laws arose as the dominant aspect of the immigration controversy in Arizona when Joe Arpaio, the Maricopa County sheriff, undertook high-profile sweeps that were barely disguised immigration-enforcement actions, scorned as racial profiling. It looked in 2008 as if border-security contestation might be evolving again with the rise of local-enforcement issues to new prominence, but this period of pitched, partisan competition came to an abrupt end.

THE MODERATE'S DILEMMA

By the start of 2006, it had basically been accepted across Arizona's political spectrum that anxiety and concern gripped the public regarding immigration—a fact that was, at least in the short run, essentially unalterable. Fear therefore needed to be addressed for any position on the border and immigration to be accepted by the public as valid. For political elites, however, this did not necessarily mean a conscious, headlong plunge into the politics of fear. Working in a seemingly fearful environment, opponents of the border hawks hoped to ease it, avoid fearmongering, and leverage sympathy with voter worries toward alternative policy ends that nonpopulist governing elites viewed as reasonable. As Dennis Burke, Napolitano's chief of staff for policy, explained in relation to the governor,

> I think she agreed there was a problem. I don't think she would disagree with that at all. . . . But the solution isn't, "Let's go figure out a way to scare the crap out of everybody who's here." Let's figure out a more rational way to deal with it. I think she accepted their premise 'cause she said [border hawks] don't own that premise. I think her point was that's an objective premise—I'm just gonna not come up with fearmongering solutions to it, and I'm not gonna frame it in a fearmongering way.

As Napolitano explained her position in a media interview at the time, "My challenge is to devise a policy that makes Arizonans confident that some things are being done without going overboard and just throwing money at the problem to make it look like I'm 'tough,' whatever that means."[8] The particular emphasis on "something being done" underlined how the element of anxiety seemed to make it politically unworkable to resist a broad generalization of responsibility where "doing something" is more important than who does it. This dynamic ratcheted up pressure for action at all levels of government.

In trying to differentiate her own approach within a seeming securitized consensus, Napolitano sought to assert ownership over the issue, recentering the debate around her preferred policy path. This strategy, of course, grew from a sense that political maneuverability on immigration was constrained. Elites very broadly shared the conception that the border hawks' populist invocations were primed to win a message war where voters had limited attention and simplistic soundbites resonated in the media. Mike Haener, Napolitano's chief legislative liaison, recalled: "The advantage that the other side had is they can say, 'Illegal means illegal. Do you agree that illegal means illegal?' 'Well, yeah, of course I agree with that.' You know, their arguments and their rhetoric were designed and better than the [argument] 'Well, what are you going to do with the people who are already here?' 'Well, deport 'em!' 'Well, how do you deport 12 million people or whatever the number is? You can't do it.' 'Well, you should 'cause what part of illegal don't you understand?'"

Jeanine L'Ecuyer, the governor's communications director, reflected on the importance of resonating with the political symbolism of security amid a constrained scope for advocacy: "If there is a problem and you send a cop, you can put it in the category in your mind of 'problem solved.' . . . I think people aren't willing to invest the time to understand these issues because they've got too many other things that they're trying to understand in their own life. . . . I don't recall that we had a conversation along the lines of 'What will people really understand?' I do think that was implicit, though, in all the other conversations we had."

Given this limited conception of what messages might "work" politically at effectively signaling action, Napolitano and other border-hawk opponents were, in their minds, walking a tightrope in trying to add nuance to border-security policy. The effort to steer policy in a preferable direction while sensing tight constraints in potential political range heavily shaped the emerging response.

A NEW COMPETITION

With Napolitano's declaration of emergency in 2005 culminating the creation of a novel, ostensible securitized consensus on immigration in Arizona, the election year 2006 became characterized by a new kind of political competition over the issue. This struggle did not equate to a simple argument about who could secure the border better. Rather, it was a much more complex contest, where each side represented its own solution as the better one to address what all accepted as a serious problem and where all sides sought to subvert, strong-arm, and outmaneuver their opponents based on newly accepted understandings of the political terrain.

In the context of an election year when all of the state's elected executive and legislative offices were contested, immigration and border politics were inherently interlinked with all other items on the political agenda to a great extent. Burke offered a typical view: "It's not an issue that we wanted to drive the debate. It was not, from our perspective, the most important issue. It wasn't a policy priority of ours. But it was what was most interesting to voters. So the idea of just sitting there and saying, 'Yeah, thanks a lot, voters—you're interested in border security and the impact of immigration on the economy. I'm not. I'm interested in all-day kindergarten,[9] so I really don't want to talk about that.' I mean, you've got to be able to respond to them." Looking toward the elections, a credible stance on immigration was viewed as a necessity for a successful candidate in many races in Arizona in 2006. In a telling recollection, Burke described focus groups held by researchers working for Napolitano's reelection campaign: "There came a time where immigrants became a scapegoat for everything. I mean, you literally would go into a focus group and [ask], 'What are your top issues?' 'Well, illegal immigration's out of control.' 'Okay, give me another one.' 'Transportation.' 'Okay, what's your problem with transportation?' 'There's too many illegal immigrants on the road, and they're dangerous.' 'Okay, what's another top issue?' 'Education.' 'What do you think's the problem with education?' 'Too many illegals in our schools.' I mean, it was just bizarre."

Immigration's place as the most salient issue in Arizona politics meant that, for politicians, achieving any sort of agenda required an acute consciousness of positioning on immigration and the border lest it become a political liability. Doing so presented particular dilemmas to those who did not necessarily favor strong enforcement ideologically. Many of these officials saw a need to figure out how to adjust their positions in light of what seemed to be a prevailing public belief about the issue. Immigration also seemed to be a possible stumbling block within elite politics as well, threatening to derail the rest of an actor's political agenda by complicating broader compromises and agreements. As Haener explained in relation to the legislature's border-related bills, "How do you get other things done if the standoff is over immigration, and now the other side's unwilling to work with you?"

Despite these concerns, entering 2006 Napolitano's position seemed quite secure. As an admiring profile in *Time* magazine put it in late 2005, "The one issue Republicans think they can use against the popular Napolitano is illegal immigration, because the huge number of border crossings have left many Arizonans feeling overwhelmed and powerless. Her critics claim she came to the problem late, but she seems to have navigated it deftly."[10] Napolitano was also staking out a position vocally supportive of federal comprehensive immigration-reform proposals that would combine increased border security, a conditional legalization program for many unauthorized immigrants, and increased channels for authorized labor migration. She used her position as chair of the Western Governors Association to develop a bipartisan immigration-reform plan, released in February.[11] While Napolitano received criticism from left and right—"too-tough for some, not-tough-enough for others"[12]—she held consistently high approval ratings.[13] Throughout 2006, potential top-tier Republican opponents demurred on challenging her for reelection.

BROADENING THE FRONT, BRINGING IN THE GUARD

Border hawks picked up in 2006 where they had left off the previous year, reviving legislative efforts to restrict unauthorized immigrants' access to higher-education scholarships and in-state university tuition rates (HB 2068, HB 2069, HB 2599, HB 2597, and HB 2598), which Napolitano had blocked in 2005. However, in line with a consistent expansion of their agenda, border hawks also proposed legislation to dedicate millions of dollars in state funding to radar and camera technology at the border (HB 2578), an area where agreement with more moderate Republicans seemed possible.[14]

Policy posturing reflected a sharpening competition over securing the border. In her annual State of the State Address at the opening of the Arizona State Legislature's session, Napolitano painted herself as Arizona's leading figure of action at the border and placed the impetus for further action at the feet of Republican legislators and the federal government: "Last August I declared an emergency at the Arizona-Mexico border. That finally got the federal government's attention. And I applaud them for beginning to move equipment and manpower to Arizona. Until that movement is complete, however, the state of Arizona is going to step in because the situation demands it and our citizens deserve it. Today, I am proposing a four-part plan to crack down on illegal immigration. My plan is tough. It's realistic. And my budget includes $100 million to fund it."[15]

Republican legislative leaders immediately groused that Napolitano had stolen the idea of a $100 million border-security plan from them.[16] The Machiavellian flavor of Arizona's immigration politics grew stronger in debates that year about the deployment of the National Guard to the border. The National Guard, a reserve military force under joint state and federal control, had in small numbers assisted federal law enforcement at the U.S.-Mexico border since the 1980s.[17] Although guardsmen at the border did not carry out armed patrols, the symbolism of sending military personnel to the border was unmistakable. Hispanic groups and civil liberties organizations objected that increasing the presence of the National Guard would militarize the border. Napolitano, in her State of the State Address, called for the U.S. Department of Defense "to allow for us to station the National Guard at our border" until promised increases in Border Patrol manpower were fulfilled, intending those costs to be borne by Washington.[18] HB 2701 emerged from the legislature as the Republican response to such calls and to Napolitano's declaration of emergency in 2005. The bill "specifie[d] that if the Governor declares a state of emergency for the protection of the lives and property of citizens of this state resulting from an increase in unauthorized border crossings and the related increase in deaths, crime and property damage, the Governor shall mobilize the National Guard to address the emergency," providing a $5 million appropriation.[19] Sponsored by Rep. John Allen, a conservative Republican, the bill attracted ideologically diverse Republican cosponsors. Democrats objected that the bill would mandate that the governor deploy the National Guard in response to a border emergency. Allen maintained he was merely "trying to untie [the governor's] hands."[20]

The National Guard bill advanced relatively quickly through the legislature on party-line votes, drawing even Republican centrist support. With the bill about to receive a final legislative vote, Napolitano issued an executive order mobilizing the Arizona National Guard to provide assistance to law enforcement "immediately upon approval of funding by the federal government or the Arizona legislature."[21] "Despite my efforts," she continued, "Arizona can no longer continue to wait for such federal assistance and must begin doing what it can." The next day, Napolitano vetoed HB 2701: "As I made clear to the bill's sponsor, it contains a blatantly unconstitutional provision calling for automatic Guard mobilization any time a governor declares an emergency along the border . . . , an obvious violation of the separation of powers doctrine. . . . It is time to stop playing political games and get serious about our border."[22]

Allen, the bill's main sponsor, commented tellingly on the issue's symbolism, noting that in the deployment of guardsmen to the border to perform an assisting role, "I don't think this is what the public expected when she said, 'I'm sending the Guard to the border.' "[23] Addressing supporters to her left, Napolitano argued that although this deployment meant more manpower at the border, there was little significance to their being military personnel: "They are not there to militarize the border. We are not at war with Mexico."[24] Nevertheless, Napolitano championed her action on the issue. Later that year, the first television advertisement for her reelection campaign featured the cowboy-hat-wearing sheriff of a border county calling her "the first to send in the National Guard."[25] Napolitano's allies represented June's announcement of Operation Jump Start—a Bush administration program providing National Guard personnel to assist federal border agencies—as the result of her agitation.

Republicans' unanimity on the National Guard extended to few other immigration-related items in the legislature in 2006, though. Republicans in the mainstream of the party's caucus—between the right wing and the center—continued to become more active on the issue, proposing some measures that made moderates uncomfortable. Soon the legislature was considering a bill sponsored by the conservative Republican senator Barbara Leff that contained a proposal to hold unauthorized immigrants in Arizona to be criminally trespassing (SB 1157). Cosponsored by relatively moderate Republicans such as Sen. Tim Bee and border hawks such as Rep. Russell Pearce, SB 1157 attracted significant dissent from Republican moderates in floor votes. When the bill reached her desk, Napolitano vetoed it: "I cannot agree with the basic premise of this bill that all persons here in violation of 8 U.S.C. § 1325 should automatically be deemed criminal trespassers under state law. Among other things, this provision of the bill is likely unconstitutional. . . . It is unwise, to say the least, to divert Arizona's law enforcement resources away from the investigation and prosecution of violent felonies in order to pursue misdemeanor cases."[26] Presaging later proposals, the bill would also have barred local governments from prohibiting their peace officers from inquiring about the immigration status of individuals whom police had lawfully stopped. Leff also sponsored, with the support of an ideological array of fellow Senate Republicans, another bill to provide $75 million in grants to local law enforcement agencies to fund the apprehension of unauthorized aliens wanted for drug, weapons, or smuggling crimes (SB 1158). Although this bill passed the Senate with the support of a number of Democrats, it was held in committees in the House.

Much more divisive among Republicans was a bill proposed by Pearce taking aim against what border hawks called "sanctuary cities" (HB 2837). Border hawks had long criticized cities and counties whose police and sheriffs' departments declined to cooperate extensively with federal immigration authorities. HB 2837 would have prevented "a city, town or county that has any sanctuary policy involving any form of aid to illegal immigrants or any reduced or restricted enforcement of illegal immigration" from receiving funding from state tax receipts marked for redistribution to municipalities.[27] Such a move clearly endangered major revenue sources for communities that the state treasurer deemed not fully cooperative with immigration enforcement. HB 2837 failed to pass the House on two separate votes when it drew opposition from the moderate Republican bloc and from a number of conservatives: eight Republicans voted no in the second ballot, where the bill failed 26–28. Pearce's pushing of the envelope—bringing forth a controversial bill when victory was not assured—demonstrated his willingness to endure high-profile losses if increased controversy mounted pressure on hesitant Republicans to support more hawkish measures. Another local-enforcement proposal, establishing a fund to assist local police in conducting immigration enforcement (HB 2582), passed the House but was held in the Senate.

HB 2837 represented an enduring border-hawk vision of "local enforcement," which sought to involve state and local police in immigration enforcement through a number of mechanisms over time. The bill highlighted how deepening internecine conflict among Arizona Republicans was increasingly centering on immigration. Immigration was again the marquee issue in a fierce Republican congressional primary to replace the retiring Republican centrist Jim Kolbe.[28] Right-wing activists were behaving more confrontationally toward politicians they deemed "RINOs"—"Republicans in name only." Some moderates were concluding there was little point in trying to find common ground. Pete Hershberger, a centrist House Republican, recounted later:

> Jim Kolbe, our congressman . . . was invited to [a] District 30 [party meeting], . . . and he asked me to go represent him, and I went, and I talked about [immigration], and a guy in the third row stood up and said, "You're a liar!" Screamed it at me! Whoa! What do you do? Those audiences, you could see, they became more and more conservative all the time. It got so conservative that the moderates, the centrist Republicans, dropped out. They didn't want to go to those district meetings and have a shouting match.

Pressure was continually growing for all Republicans to accommodate a broad right-wing agenda, prominently including a much more assertive state role in immigration and border enforcement. Jennifer J. Burns, another centrist House Republican, recalled the atmosphere among many of her Republican colleagues: "Sometimes they would even say it, you know, behind closed doors or what have you: they would say, 'I can't vote that way because I won't get reelected,' or 'I'm voting this way because this is the public, this is the popular thing to do.' And they changed. . . . [T]he moderates were dwindling. . . . [T]hey were getting the message that if you vote this way, [if] you vote moderate Republican, then you're not gonna win your primary."

Despite this pressure and the decline in their number in the legislature, those moderate Republicans still sometimes held significant influence. In some votes, they held the balance of the legislature, and on immigration in particular moderates were acting as the core of the wider group of Republican lawmakers, mentioned in the previous chapter, who favored a more relaxed approach. That informal group at this time included centrists such as Hershberger, Burns, and Tom O'Halleran as well as more traditional business-oriented Republicans such as Bill Konopnicki, Russ Jones, Nancy Barto, Lucy Mason, Michelle Reagan, and later Kirk Adams, who entered the House in 2007. By 2006, this group was becoming more concerted in trying to prevent the passage of some border-hawk legislation that they considered extreme, especially local-enforcement legislation. The group would also play a significant role in the ascendant politics of employer sanctions. However, both for the purposes of intra-caucus harmony and because of Republicans' sharpening fear of being painted as moderate, their willingness to oppose other Republicans either publicly or behind closed doors had its limits. "You do pick your battles, and you can't vote no on absolutely everything, and you can't go against the Republicans every single time," Burns recalled.

While hesitant Republicans focused on legislative politics, Hispanic groups increasingly looked to demonstrate their prowess as a growing voting bloc and to stake claims to a rightful place in Arizona and U.S. politics.[29] A series of large marches in the spring of 2006 aimed to show these goals and were coordinated by activist and community groups with the involvement of elected Hispanic Democrats.[30] The marches accorded with a growing belief among many Hispanic politicians that countering the hostile popular politics of immigration required some show of counter-vailing popular political force. Demonstrations sponsored by Hispanic organizations occurred in Arizona in tandem with a national effort to march against a new immigration bill proposed by congressional Republicans led by Rep. James Sensenbrenner of Wisconsin and in support of bipartisan federal immigration-reform efforts.[31] The Arizona marches were especially prominent.[32] Despite bipartisan support, comprehensive immigration reform faced an uncertain fate in Congress. Martín Quezada, a former legislative staffer who was later elected as a Democrat to the Arizona Legislature, recalled: "The big strategy at that point was you put boots on the ground and make a show of force. . . . I think there were multiple expectations. One was to show the size of the community that was affected by this, both directly and indirectly, and two to show that because of that enormity of that size of our population here, that that can translate into votes. And it was supposed to be an expression of a flexing of political muscle."

Although highly visible in the media, these marches did not have an immediate apparent impact on patterns of contestation in Arizona. As the 2006 legislative session wore on, border hawks increasingly sought to work around Napolitano's veto by getting the legislature to refer policy proposals directly to the ballot. Senate Concurrent Resolution (SCR) 1031 revived proposals to prohibit unauthorized residents from accessing higher-education financial aid and in-state tuition rates, which Napolitano had vetoed in 2005. Passing both chambers, it was placed on the November ballot as Proposition 300. Late in the session, an attempt to shield border militia groups from civil judgments, SCR 1001, took the place of a stalled bill (SB 1057), proposing to bar unauthorized immigrants from collecting punitive damages in civil cases in Arizona courts.[33] This proposal was placed on the ballot as Proposition 102. A proposal to make English the official language of Arizona, narrower than a measure in 1988 overturned by courts, passed as HCR 2036 and was placed on the ballot as Proposition 103. These three propositions joined Proposition 100, which had already been referred to the ballot the year before through HCR 2028 and sought to bar bail to unauthorized immigrants accused of felonies. However, late-session efforts to advance local-enforcement and criminal-trespassing measures to the ballot failed.[34]

Outside of budgeting provisions, the only area of bipartisan cooperation on immigration- and border-related issues in the 2006 legislative session was an effort (HB 2580) to define what types of felonies Proposition 100 would apply to if passed. Similarly, the only successful legislative effort to refer to immigration from a perspective that was distinctly not one of security was a nonbinding legislative resolution, sponsored by the Yuma Republican Russ Jones, regarding federal cross-border agricultural-work commuting programs (House Concurrent Memorial [HCM] 2018). Loose ends from the debates in that legislative session were either referred to the ballot or were tied in to the ascendant issue of employer sanctions.

"QUEEN'S GAMBIT": EMPLOYER SANCTIONS

Arizona's increasingly competitive interparty border-security politics was clearly on display in tussles over issues such as deploying the National Guard. However, its strongest expression emerged in the politics regarding employer sanctions—the idea of punishing employers who hired unauthorized labor. This topic emerged for a time as the biggest single facet in Arizona's immigration politics.

It had been illegal under federal law to hire unauthorized immigrants since 1986, but federal agencies had enforced those rules only seldomly. Despite continued elite divergence over what exactly the border-security problem in Arizona comprised, all political elites clearly conceived of unauthorized immigration as driven by economic factors. Opponents of the border hawks often noted this economic aspect as part of an argument that real solutions would go beyond security measures. Border hawks largely shared this causal concept: as Pearce recalled, employment "was the magnet for drawing people here." Attempting to deactivate this "jobs magnet," employer-sanctions measures represented an attempt to bring the labor market under the aegis of border-security governance. Decrying the business community's alleged valuing of "profits over patriotism," border hawks encountered tension with business groups that constituted an important part of the Republican coalition. Democrats, in turn, sensed opportunity.

A STALEMATE BY DESIGN: EMPLOYER SANCTIONS AND THE ELECTION OF 2006

The issue of employer sanctions came truly to the fore in 2006 after Pearce and his allies had been floating proposals without success for several years. However, Democrats had first taken an interest in employer-sanctions proposals in 2005 amid the general search for a new strategy on immigration. Bill Brotherton, a lawyer then serving in the state Senate as a Democrat, recalled of border hawks' proposals:

> Those of us who were attorneys or whatever were saying, "Lookit, a lot of this stuff is not constitutional. You're stepping into a federal area where they have exclusive authority." And so we would oppose on that basis. And that's the lawyer part of me talking. But, you know, the public has very little knowledge, really, about laws or really very little understanding in general about it. So they don't like to hear somebody just saying, "Well, you can't do that. We can't do this, we can't do that." And I got to the point where I didn't like the fact that all we had was kind of a defensive strategy.

A Democratic employer-sanctions strategy emerged amid this perceived need for a less defensive stance and from the realization of a particular political opportunity. Brotherton recalled:

I had some conversations with Russell Pearce. . . . And he had mentioned, I guess, he had run in the House some kind of employer-sanction thing. The Chamber [of Commerce] guys, who were their big supporters for the Republicans, had come unglued with all this stuff about doing employer sanctions. And so he'd ended up backing off of it. . . . I'm not one who has a problem with stealing a good idea. . . . [W]hen their [the border hawks'] bills came forward which went after the immigrants, I started. And there could have been as many as twenty amendments on a bill, all about employer sanctions.

On HB 2030 in 2005, the bill to deny in-state tuition rates and higher-education benefits to unauthorized immigrants, Brotherton proposed a number of surprise amendments on the Senate floor. One of his employer-sanctions measures carried twenty votes in the thirty-member Senate on the strength of Democrats and right-wing Republicans, thus isolating the chamber's more moderate and business-oriented Republicans.[35] Twisting the dagger in the House, Democrat Steve Gallardo motioned to bypass a conference committee and agree to the Senate's changes, complete with employer sanctions. With business lobbies now engaged, a number of Republicans effectively voted against the version containing employer sanctions, so that when the bill was sent to conference, those provisions were stripped away.

A larger employer-sanctions strategy grew from this episode, its political rationale multifaceted and evolving. At the outset, although it was expected that the employer-sanctions amendments would ultimately fail, introducing them was an attempt to stall right-wing immigration bills while making Democrats look tough on the border in contrast. Threatening to force Republicans to vote against either their grassroots base and a supportive public on one hand or their key business allies on the other put pressure on Republican leaders to ease off immigration issues. Democrats had been frustrated that the business community, in particular the Arizona Chamber of Commerce and Industry (the main statewide business lobby group, often referred to simply as the "Chamber of Commerce"), was not working hard enough to tamp down Republicans' border-security enthusiasm. "They're kind of letting everybody sit back," Amanda Aguirre, then the Democrats' Senate leader, said about the business lobby at the time. "The sanction thing was saying, 'Get involved.'"[36]

Democrats also adopted the strategy in response to their perceived need to strengthen their own position on immigration. "I was driving a wedge. And at the same time, I was showing, okay, we're doing something on this issue of undocumented workers," Brotherton explained. To unhappy Republicans, Brotherton would say, "Well, you know, if these bills don't come up, I guess we won't need to do that anymore. . . . Use your influence to keep these things off the Board of Truth"—the electronic wall display in each legislative chamber that records members' votes for all to see.

Democrats were largely pleased with the discord their amendments sowed. In 2005, such efforts on employer sanctions had been largely a legislative strategy because the issue did not reach the governor's desk and Napolitano had staked out her own positions on immigration. However, in this new election year Democrats sought the larger goal of "neutralizing" the immigration issue—if not exactly winning on it, then at least getting it to go away as a perceived advantage for Republicans. "Basically, you have to lay down some cover, especially for the governor. I mean, we needed her, she needed us," Brotherton recalled. The "cover" to be laid down for Napolitano, Terry Goddard (the Democratic attorney general running for reelection), and vulnerable legislative Democrats was designed to have two elements. The first element was the political logic aimed at prevention, where Democrats would use employer-sanctions amendments to activate business pressure on Republican leadership to ease off the issue. Further than that, the second element was, as Brotherton explained, that "it gave Napolitano, when she vetoed some of this legislation, cover. . . . You say, . . . '[W]e're gonna go after both ends of the hose—the people coming in and the jobs. And they're not doing that—they're in the pockets of the Chamber of Commerce.' . . . That has a lot more gravitas when it comes to a message to the public, I think." This positioning essentially sought to resonate with the populism running through the issue but also to deflect its antielitism toward business elites whom Democrats saw as inexcusably inert on immigration rather than toward liberal political elites and their alleged "illegal immigrant" clients.[37]

There was one unresolved question, though: Was it better to raise the immigration issue assertively and highlight Democrats' ostensible and united willingness to take action in contrast to the Republicans' division? Or was it better to keep quiet on the issue and use it later as a foil in rejecting Republicans' legislative efforts? At the beginning of 2006, Democrats made a few moves in line with the first objective. Hispanic legislators highlighted it in the media as an area of focus,[38] and Napolitano discussed employer sanctions in her State of the State Address to legislators:

> We are going to get real about one of the root causes of this problem. People come here because they want work. And employers here are willing to hire them. If we want to stop illegal immigration we've got to stop the demand. Last year, I issued an executive order to make clear that the state will not contract with employers who hire people who are here illegally. Now, I ask you to expand that effort. Those who continue to intentionally hire illegal immigrants should face substantial fines and also penalties.[39]

In the Senate, Democrats Brotherton and Ann Kirkpatrick sponsored a stand-alone employer-sanctions bill at the beginning of the 2006 session (SB 1216). Though it passed one committee ballot, it never saw a floor vote.

To some extent, the Democratic employer-sanctions strategy was a bluff. Democrats' private attitudes about the acceptability of employer sanctions as policy were generally lukewarm at most. All Democrats viewed the border as presenting some real problems, and, for many of them, holding employers accountable was preferable to directly punishing individual labor migrants. Although some viewed the consequences of the bluff being called as quite bad, to others a realized employer-sanctions bill could still be tolerable. But, overall, the Democratic appetite for employer sanctions as policy was limited. As Brotherton said later about the reasons for his own employer-sanctions amendments, "I'd say it's about 90 percent to find a rebuttal, 10 percent [to address] the issue. I mean, I think it's a federal issue. . . . So I didn't think there was really much, if anything, we could do on the issue here. . . . So it was more an issue that we were just getting beaten up on it. And we needed to have a response. It was a popular response; it was one that got good press. It was one that a lot of voters liked." As Gallardo put it, "Our support for the employer sanctions was not because we thought it was a good bill. We wanted the Chamber of Commerce to get off their ass and get involved in this thing. The Chamber of Commerce every year would promote their success. They would walk around as if they could pass or defeat any bill at the legislature. And we wanted them involved. That's what it was. At least for me, I didn't really support it."

The perception that this sort of legislation was indeed popular among voters and could in the future be driven successfully by Russell Pearce and his allies prompted some business-oriented Republicans into action. Rather than simply try to block Pearce, these Republicans in 2006 introduced measures that they regarded as less draconian than earlier Pearce proposals, in this way aiming to head off the issue. Bill Konopnicki, a Republican businessman in the House representing an eastern Arizona district, was particularly active on this front, often working with Russ Jones, the Yuma Republican, and the rest of the behind-closed-doors group of Republicans who met to strategize their response on immigration. Jones recounted the much more business-friendly employer-sanctions proposal they devised (HB 2823), which offered indemnity for employers making good-faith efforts to verify employees' legal status:

> You could not be prosecuted in-state for any reason unless it was proven you were doing it fraudulently. . . . And if the federal government went after you, the state would defend you. . . . And on the other hand, we actually increased the fines substantially and split the fines with law enforcement so there was an incentive for the sheriff's departments and [police] to actually investigate. . . . We ran this bill, and what it provided was a safe haven for all of the closet Republicans . . . who wanted to look more to the right.

HB 2823 was never heard on the legislative floor, but Pearce's own efforts on employer sanctions also foundered. His proposal to refer an employer-sanctions measure to the ballot (HCR 2044) passed the House on a 31–29 vote but was never heard in the Senate. A regular bill Peace sponsored that was similar to his referendum proposal passed the House (HB 2577), but it was later amended in the Senate Appropriations Committee to include a concept of employer indemnity, though different from Jones and Konopnicki's proposal.[40] This bill passed the committee with some Democratic support. However, by the time HB 2577 had passed the entire Senate, a number of previously unsuccessful measures had been appended: it now contained provisions related to the National Guard, the application of criminal-trespassing offenses to unauthorized people in Arizona, and other issues. When the bill passed the House again, it was without Konopnicki's, Jones's, or Republican centrists' votes.

As Republican legislators both inside and outside the core group of border hawks were making HB 2577 into a more encompassing "omnibus" bill, noting they were working with the Chamber of Commerce on its employer-sanctions provisions, Napolitano suggested that the legislature hold off, citing increased Bush administration action on the border.[41] When the legislature passed the measure to Napolitano's desk, she vetoed it. This was unsurprising: HB 2577 contained a number of previously vetoed ideas. However, Napolitano dealt its employer-sanctions elements particularly sharp criticism, calling the legislation "a weak and ineffective illegal immigration bill": "Your unilateral decision to stock this bill full of provisions you know are opposed by our border communities, law enforcement agencies, and me, confirms that you view this bill more as a political game than as a serious effort to protect the border. . . . Despite my repeated calls for employer sanctions, House Bill 2577 offers full amnesty to any employer who hires an illegal immigrant and gets caught."[42] "Amnesty" was a notable turn of phrase because it had become a right-wing buzzword against regularization proposals. After the legislature left session, Napolitano lamented, "I was disappointed that they didn't really want to deal with employer sanctions."[43]

As the elections approached, the prevailing sense was that Napolitano's position on immigration had succeeded at neutralizing border issues as an electoral threat to her. Federal attention to the Arizona border was increasing, and by 2006 Border Patrol apprehensions were beginning to fall from a mid-decade peak in what would turn out to be a long-term decline in unauthorized cross-border traffic.[44] Politically, the employer-sanctions strategy was seen as having helped the governor. As Brotherton said, "It put that stalemate in place really for the election year of 2006."

In November, Napolitano was reelected with 63 percent of the vote. Goddard, the Democratic attorney general, was reelected with 60 percent, and Jan Brewer, the Republican secretary of state who was first in the line of succession to the governorship, was reelected with 57 percent. Democrats had relatively strong results in state legislative races, winning 27 of the 60 seats in the House of Representatives, though Republicans still held clear control of both chambers. Thus, the election of 2006 seemed to lock in place the existing dynamics of elite contestation over immigration.

However, also on the ballot were the four proposals Pearce and his allies had pushed to refer to voters. All passed overwhelmingly. Proposition 300, which over an earlier Napolitano veto excluded unauthorized immigrants from higher-education financial aid and in-state tuition rates, was the least broadly supported but nevertheless passed with 71 percent of the vote. Napolitano's reelection evidenced firm political footing in her approach to immigration, but it was more questionable whether her and other Democrats' policy priorities were the ones prevailing.

GAMBIT ACCEPTED: HB 2779

The immigration-related referenda of 2006 performed even more strongly than Proposition 200 in 2004. Border hawks had shown in successive elections that they could employ Arizona's institutions of direct democracy effectively to bypass elite opposition in what they represented as clear demonstrations of the will of the people. As Pearce put it, "We did a poll called an election. These things passed overwhelmingly. They passed by an average of 75 percent!" Opponents also noted their easy passage, though elite campaigning against them had been notably weaker than against Proposition 200 two years earlier. As Tim Nelson, Napolitano's general counsel, recalled, "It definitely weighs because you know that if you veto something, that they're just going to go around and turn it and run [it] as a referendum, and it's gonna get passed. Then you haven't addressed what the public wants, and it's just gonna come back in ways that you can't control." The concern that Arizonans had not yet seen an immigration-enforcement ballot measure they would refuse and that the success of these measures would strip the governor of control over those policies affected strategy. Haener, Napolitano's legislative liaison, recalled: "What can we do? Again, is it say, 'We'll sign that—fix these three things, and we'll sign it'? Go to the business community and say, 'You need to get these couple of things fixed, and then we can sign it, and it won't go on the ballot'? So I didn't look at it as an 'Oh, my God!' But it was more of 'anything they're gonna put on [the ballot] is gonna pass,' so we might as well try and figure out what we can veto, what we can't veto."

The 2007 legislative session continued to see a large number of proposals related to the border and immigration. They included revivals of previously stalled issues, such as local enforcement of immigration law (HCR 2049) and the tying of revenue sharing to it (HB 2461); prohibition of the acceptance of the *matrícula consular* as ID (HB 2460); and the application of trespassing law to unauthorized immigrants (HCR 2022). Border hawks also made new attempts to apply trespassing laws to day laborers on public streets (HB 2589), to encourage a federal constitutional amendment to end birthright citizenship for the children of unauthorized immigrants (HCM 2005), and to eliminate public-benefits eligibility for children of unauthorized immigrants (HB 2471). They also made efforts on other measures conforming to previously passed referenda on eligibility for public benefits (HB 2467) and bail (SB 1265). Napolitano signed the latter two and also signed a bill sponsored by Rep. Jonathan Paton that permitted the detention of a material witness to a criminal proceeding if there was reason to believe that person might not respond to a subpoena due to his or her immigration status (HB 2018). She vetoed HB 2589, the day-labor trespassing bill. Manifesting the increased procedural power accruing to him with seniority, Pearce used his new position as House Appropriations Committee chair to resurrect the contents of a previously defeated *matrícula consular* bill, HB 2460, bringing the proposal back as SB 1236.[45] SB 1236 eventually passed the legislature and then became the second *matrícula consular* bill vetoed by Napolitano as a hindrance to law enforcement.[46] Democratic proposals (HB 2270, HB 2271) to amend the smuggling law of 2005—to limit its application only to smugglers rather than to apply it to all unauthorized immigrants, which would have restored the law to the original intent of its Republican sponsors—were ignored. Notwithstanding these efforts, legislative action on immigration in 2007 focused intently on employer sanctions.

Whereas in 2006 employer sanctions were presented to the governor within an "omnibus" bill, in 2007 border hawks opted to try a stand-alone bill, in part because of a sense that many Democrats had been expressing support for employer sanctions with less than full sincerity. Pearce recalled: "I'll use one name: Ben Miranda. . . . [H]e used to always come up to me and say, 'Russell, if you'd just go after the employers that are bribing them to get here' instead of the illegal alien, 'I'd be with you!' I said, 'I've tried to do that!' He said, 'But single it out,' so I did. House Bill

2779." Although this exchange must be taken with a grain of salt since Miranda is no longer alive to present his side of it, the back-and-forth Pearce described still reflects a turn of ambivalence on employer sanctions among some legislative Democrats when the issue was raised again in 2007: "He comes to me, and I said, 'Ben, I'm going after the employer.' 'Ooh, Russell, I don't know if I can vote with you.' I said, 'Ben, you told me you would!' . . . I said, 'Because here's what I'm gonna do, Ben: I've got an initiative running. . . . I'll get it on the ballot—it'll pass. It's much tougher than the one I'm running through the legislature.'"

One of the main differences between these proposals was the number of "strikes" needed for a company to lose its state business license: in the normal legislation proposed, the number was two, whereas in the initiative it was only one. Competing employer-sanctions bills arose as attempts to head off Pearce's proposals. In HB 2386 and HB 2523, Konopnicki revived a proposal that modified the employer-sanctions provisions in the omnibus immigration bill vetoed the previous year, but it was ignored, so that only Pearce's initial draft bill and a Democratic counterproposal were granted hearings.[47] The strategy to forestall action on Pearce's bills by proposing a more moderate "counterbill" appeared to be failing.

All the while, tensions were escalating within the Republican Party as right-wing activists confronted more moderate figures with growing tenacity. Pearce often rallied activists, encouraging them to increase pressure on other lawmakers. A speech Konopnicki delivered on the House floor in February 2007, universally understood as aimed at Pearce, raised eyebrows among legislators and exemplified many Republicans' growing unease:

> In a recent committee hearing I voted against a bill that I thought was flawed. . . . After my vote, information began to circulate as to my motives for voting the way I did—false information. . . . [T]his petty attempt at misinformation has since escalated from several emails into threats against my family and against me. . . . How sad is the idea that by simply voting against another member's bill we may be exposing ourselves to baseless innuendo or, even worse, to threats against our loved ones? We find this most often when the subject of illegal immigration emerges. The passionate debate that seems to follow this issue is becoming reminiscent of the tactics of Joe McCarthy. . . . I can't help but recall the now

famous words of the attorney, Joe Welch, when he asked Senator McCarthy: "Have you no sense of decency, sir, at long last? Have you left no sense of honor?"[48]

Konopnicki's accusing Pearce of McCarthyism on the House floor was merely an especially open manifestation of mounting Republican tension. Within the Republican Party, opposing the border hawks was seeming to become more and more politically costly. The political pressure to fully support Pearce's proposals was intensifying not so much because of the kinds of threats against legislators Konopnicki mentioned but because of the apparent energy and power of a febrile party grass roots. Behind closed doors, Republicans seeking a more moderate path on immigration were calculating how to try to blunt Pearce, whose threats to resort to a citizens' initiative on employer sanctions were treated very seriously.

> JENNIFER J. BURNS: There were seven or eight legislators in the House that routinely met, saying, "How are we gonna fix this? And what are we gonna do to make this better?" Because [there was] the proposition out there collecting signatures, but then Russell had a similar bill, or a corresponding bill in the House and in the Senate. And we didn't like employer sanctions, and we didn't like what it was, but on the other hand we were almost held hostage by the threat of a proposition because if a proposition passes, it's now voter protected.[49]
>
> INTERVIEWER: And you thought it was likely to pass?
>
> JJB: It seemed that the sense of the—yes.

Pearce's opponents turned to two strategies, though not completely in tandem. The first was to see if employer-sanction legislation could be blockaded by Democrats and disinclined Republicans despite the political pressures on both: Democrats generally being on the record as supporting some kind of employer sanctions, Republicans facing a party grass roots that vocally supported sanctions, and both looking to a general public that they saw as broadly enthusiastic about the idea. Gallardo recounted:

> If you looked at any poll, sure enough, people felt that employers should obey the federal laws and make sure that they're hiring folks

that should be hired. . . . The Chamber of Commerce was working real hard, working with Bill Konopnicki at the time, and they created a small coalition of moderates. I was the [House Democratic] whip at that time, and we had the Democrats solid—we were all opposed to it. . . . And we would meet on a regular basis, just like, "What are they saying?" 'Cause they were being hammered by Russell Pearce and some of the far-right conservatives. And we held that bill off for a good three weeks.

The prospect of a citizens' initiative that all believed would be difficult to defeat complicated matters greatly. Republican opponents of employer sanctions in particular pursued a second strategy: to see if Pearce would accept enough amendments to his employer-sanctions bill to make it broadly acceptable to them, allowing them to support the bill in exchange for Pearce dropping his parallel initiative drive. Republican opponents' main objections focused on the severity of the sanctions—including how many infractions would be necessary for a business to lose its license—and on evidentiary standards, such as the need to prove that a business violated the law knowingly.

Pearce played hardball to drive his agenda, but as a legislator he could be open to at least some compromise. Despite seeming to have the wind in his sails after the referenda successes in 2006, Pearce saw the prospect that opponents could unify to defeat his bill as a potentially serious setback: as he recalled, "We could fail." Although confident that the public would support a tough sanctions measure, he retained reservations about the major organizational efforts needed to surmount signature-gathering hurdles to file a citizens' initiative. Amending his bill was therefore relatively acceptable. "I didn't need one strike," he said. "I wanted the law enforced."

Moderate Republicans regarded some of the modifications to HB 2779 as greatly limiting the law's downside for businesses. As Burns recalled, "The Chamber [of Commerce] knew what we were doing—they helped us, actually, with it, behind the scenes, putting this together to get these things in there that Russell then agreed to. We would often basically high-five each other, like, 'I can't believe he just agreed to that.'" Nevertheless, when the hesitant Republican bloc had negotiated as much as they believed possible, the result was a measure about which they nonetheless felt unenthusiastic. Burns summarized their calculation:

> [We] had a conversation saying, "We don't like this employer-sanctions bill. We don't like the things that are associated with it." . . . [T]his is where we felt almost blackmailed or held hostage. This proposition might pass, and it's likely to get on the ballot, and a better than 50 percent chance it's gonna pass. If we do that, then it's voter protected. . . . And so, at that point, we actually had the conversation and the discussion, "Are we gonna vote for a bad bill because we're afraid of a worse law?" And we actually looked each other in the eye and said, "Yes, we are."

The last Republican opposition to Pearce's employer-sanctions push thereby stood down. "I remember Bill Konopnicki coming in my office and saying that they'd peeled off enough votes that this thing is going through," Gallardo recounted. "And we went to the Democrats and said, 'Okay, just vote your conscience.'"

HB 2779 passed 47–11 in the House and 20–4 in the Senate. Although legislative Democrats were split, fewer than half in each chamber voted no. Not only were many Democrats on the record as supporting employer sanctions, but they were also looking to some of the same political forces as the Republican moderates: the possibility of a ballot initiative, which they saw as worse, and a restive public that overwhelmingly supported employer sanctions. As lawmakers in Phoenix were finishing their session and sending the employer-sanctions bill to Napolitano, in Washington much-touted bipartisan comprehensive immigration reform efforts collapsed under right-wing opposition and defections from politically vulnerable Democrats.[50] On top of the many dynamics already in play, definitive federal action had become, after a time of promise, more remote than it had been in years.

Napolitano's staff had been communicating with legislators during their HB 2779 negotiations, but the possibility of a veto was still discussed internally. The governor was concerned generally about the state's economy, but a veto was viewed as likely to damage her political standing and her ability to pursue the rest of her agenda. To a governor who had sought to position herself as a centrist on immigration, who had expressed support for tough employer sanctions, and who had long sought to preempt more hawkish figures in immigration politics, the prospect of vetoing the broadly supported HB 2779 was not inviting, even though a business community she worked with on other issues remained opposed to it. "It was pretty complex," Burke said of Napolitano's calculations on HB 2779. "Was this the best version? . . . [W]ould it take the issue off for a period of time?" Napolitano and her advisers considered negotiations to have created a bill that was relatively friendly to business and did not find the remaining business argument for a veto compelling. Burke recalled:

> She believed, politically, the business community had a big obligation in this area, and they were just expecting her just to veto bills, and they weren't really playing a role in it. . . . I mean, if you go back and look at the Republicans like Pearce and so forth, they were all getting max [campaign donations] from the business community and the Chamber and all them . . . they've created the environment in which a lot of these guys get elected. . . . It wasn't the overriding reason—it wasn't like a little spite. . . . [S]he said, "Look, this is the least harmful version. I'm willing to sign it and move forward on it."

With Napolitano's signature, HB 2779 became the highest-profile legislative action on immigration yet in Arizona or on the state level anywhere in the United States. The governor issued an uncommon signing letter, enacting the bill while identifying issues she hoped the legislature would address:

> With my signature on this bill, Arizona has taken the most aggressive action in the country against employers who knowingly or intentionally hire undocumented workers. Unlike House Bill 2577 from last session, which I vetoed because it offered employer amnesty and indemnification, this bill imposes tough consequences on those who knowingly employ undocumented workers. . . . Because of Congress' failure to act, states like Arizona have no choice but to take strong action to discourage the further flow of illegal immigration through our borders. I renew my call to Congress to enact comprehensive immigration reform legislation.[51]

Despite the tenor of media coverage and claims by all who supported HB 2779 that its employer sanctions were "tough," many more quietly regarded them as having been crucially mellowed. As Jeanine L'Ecuyer, Napolitano's communications director, recalled of her signing HB 2779, "Candidly, that was a political calculation. We need to pass an employer-sanctions bill for the public to appreciate that we've done something, but we also need to construct it in such a way that businesses have an option that makes it a little bit easier to comply. And that's exactly what we did."

For Pearce, the passage of employer sanctions amounted to his biggest legislative victory yet. The often-tacit feeling among elites that negotiations had softened the proposal seemed to affect neither Pearce's perceived political power nor his feelings about the law. "I'm hoping employers will self-comply. That's the purpose of law," he said on television shortly after his bill was signed.[52]

The employer-sanctions episode unearthed frustrations that policy makers in many different quarters felt toward a powerful business lobby that many saw as incoherent on immigration issues. These perceptions of the business lobby would become increasingly significant from this point because a wedge had been noticeably driven between it and some right-wing Republicans. As Burns recounted, "We didn't think the money that would be put in from the Chamber of Commerce or others was enough to argue against [an employer-sanctions ballot initiative] or defeat it. We couldn't trust that. . . . [I]n fact they were one of our frustrations because they went back and forth: 'We want a bill; we don't want a bill; well, we want a bill this way, we don't want a bill this way.'"

Overall, Democrats succeeded at magnifying tension within the Republican coalition. On face, they had also painted themselves as both active on immigration and enforcement-friendly. However, their original success in forcing a stalemate had been only temporary, and their goal of motivating powerful interest groups to force a stop to the border-hawk agenda had failed. Their bluff had been called, and the political results were mixed. Brotherton reflected on an analysis of employer sanctions written by the conservative former legislator Greg Patterson. "He wrote a little thing called 'Queen's Gambit' on it, where he actually said . . . that this was a political thing and that Napolitano wasn't forced into doing this." Patterson wrote:

> I've asserted that the Democrats overplayed their hand and ended up supporting the toughest sanctions bill in the nation. That's clearly the case for the Latino Caucus. . . . But what about Napolitano? . . . She didn't lose

this battle. . . . This was classic triangulation; it was Bill Clinton on welfare reform. . . . She drove a wedge between Republicans and the business community, signed a bill that is widely supported but opposed by her base, teamed up with Russell Pearce on a controversial issue and managed to call for the bill and sign the bill without really having her fingerprints on the bill. . . . Checkmate.[53]

Democrats championed employer sanctions in a piece of populist posturing to use its apparently huge popularity as a tool against their partisan opponents. The same issue, for the same reasons, became ripe for countermaneuvering by border hawks, which resulted in an offer that many Democrats felt they could not refuse:

INTERVIEWER: The Democrats did come around partially on some stuff—
RUSSELL PEARCE: Like what?
I: Like employer sanctions, in the legislature. How would you view that?
RP: [Laughs.] They had no choice.

NEW FRONTIERS OF CONTENTION: 2008

By 2008, immigration politics in Arizona was being waged on recognizable competitive battle lines. At the same time, the boundaries of the issue continued to expand. Legislative border hawks moved on from each victory to emphasize further points in an unspooling agenda, and the salience of the issue attracted attention from public officials at all levels of government. The issue's dominance represented a challenge to the agenda-setting ability of those who were uneasy with its continually creeping security orientation. Haener recounted:

There are certain times—the economic crisis, the immigration issue—where it becomes so pervasive in everything . . . that you are doing your best to continue to have that vision, have that agenda, while you're trying to manage this ride that you're on over here. . . . In this immigration issue, you had the legislature talking about it, you had the governor talking about it, you had outside groups talking about it. You had, you know, congressmen talking about it. You had U.S. senators talking about it. You had sheriffs talking about it. So everybody was kind of piling onto it, which, again, just makes it bigger.

Meanwhile, preceding the financial crisis of 2008, the Arizona housing market was in freefall by 2007.[54] The corresponding decline in household wealth, increase in foreclosures, and slowdown of the state's construction industry and growth-oriented economy meant that Arizona was entering an already pronounced recession.[55] In interviewees' eyes, this state of economic affairs only sharpened anxiety about immigrants.

LOCAL ENFORCEMENT, THE NEW BATTLEGROUND

With the issues of employer sanctions and the National Guard apparently settled, immigration politics began to refocus, this time on local-enforcement questions. Joe Arpaio, the Maricopa County sheriff, thrust local enforcement to prominence through his "crime-suppression sweeps," conducted so his deputies could hand over suspected unauthorized immigrants to federal custody.

Arpaio occupied a place of his own in Arizona public life. Self-appointed as "America's toughest sheriff" since his first election in 1992, he had risen to an uncommon level of national celebrity for a local law enforcement official through "tough on crime" posturing and publicity stunts in the "performative act of the lawman and the careful construction of the modern day Wild West."[56] Other political elites in Arizona regarded Arpaio as replete with uncanny instincts for penal-populist showmanship while completely bereft of shame.[57] Some of Arpaio's more notable policies to this point were the massive expansion of a "Tent City" jail to house mostly pretrial inmates, the issuing of pink underwear to male inmates to combat the purported problem of it being stolen, and the reintroduction of chain gangs. By many measures Arizona's most popular elected official and a constant object of media attention, Arpaio had been a frequent target of civil liberties groups. However, Arizona politicians had treaded around him very lightly due to his popularity and his record of opening spurious investigations into political opponents:[58] "There were few local or state politicians willing to criticize him publicly."[59] Critics of Arpaio claimed that Napolitano, as U.S. attorney for Arizona in the 1990s, had soft-pedaled federal investigations into alleged abuses in Arpaio's jails because of the sheriff's political clout and that she therefore enjoyed an accommodating if not close relationship with the sheriff.[60] Arpaio's appearance in an election advertisement with Napolitano in 2002 was seen as significant in her narrow victory in the governor's race that year.[61]

Arpaio had successfully ridden a "tough on crime" current in the 1990s that had mobilized punitive social attitudes and amplified racialized aspects of law enforcement,[62] but up to this point he had shown little interest in immigration issues. When the border hawk Andrew Thomas was elected in 2004 as Maricopa County attorney—an office that works closely with the sheriff—he and Arpaio quickly clashed over the case of Patrick Haab, a man who had held at gunpoint seven people whom he encountered and suspected of being unauthorized immigrants. Arpaio declared during that dispute, "Being illegal is not a serious crime."[63] By late 2007, though, something had changed.[64] As Jim Walsh, a Democrat who became county attorney for neighboring Pinal County in 2007, recounted later, "All of a sudden they [Arpaio and Thomas] got on the same page, and Joe realized there's more to this stuff about illegals."

Though Napolitano had nixed proposals to require them to do so, many law enforcement agencies in Arizona had entered into 287(g) agreements that, in cooperation with federal authorities, allowed local law enforcement to check the immigration status of people they encountered. Arpaio had engaged in immigration-related enforcement from the advent of the state's antismuggling law of 2005, but by mid-2007 he "was fully engaged as a self-made anti–illegal immigration tempest."[65] Arpaio began to make particularly aggressive use of his office's 287(g) powers; at one point, the Maricopa County Sheriff's Office (MCSO) had the most 287(g)-trained personnel in the United States.[66] The MCSO undertook what it termed "crime-suppression sweeps" in neighborhoods with large numbers of Hispanic immigrants, in which sheriff's deputies used pretexts to check the immigration status of people they encountered. By the spring of 2008, the sweeps were highly visible political spectacles that drew the outrage of activists,[67] producing arrests normally numbering in the dozens. Arpaio showed no doubts about their propriety: "We will continue to perform our duties of locking up illegal aliens," he declared.[68] Arpaio's splashy emergence as one of the most active players in Arizona immigration politics attracted him tremendous attention, including from national media.[69] The sweeps earned him star status among right-wing activists who had not before considered him an ally on immigration but a villainous reputation among others.

By 2008, Arizona political elites fell into two main camps on local enforcement. On the one hand, border hawks such as Pearce and later Arpaio championed the use of 287(g) agreements by local police to conduct immigration enforcement in expansive and envelope-pushing ways. On the other hand, the consensus around smuggling and "border crime" in Arizona meant that almost all political elites agreed with the use of state and local law enforcement to combat these problems and usually agreed with using 287(g) powers to check the immigration status of those arrested for serious crimes. 287(g) was supposed to play a supplementary role, allowing local police to determine the immigration status of those they encountered while performing routine duties such as booking suspects into jail. This presumed supplementary character of 287(g) activities underlay how voluntary local use of 287(g) agreements had been an early alternative position to border hawks' desire to maximize local police involvement in immigration enforcement. Sweeps like Arpaio's, done without evidence of serious crimes in the areas they targeted, were not allowed under 287(g) rules, but federal authorities in charge of the program did not take measures against the sheriff.[70] Local police departments that declined to use 287(g) powers extensively drew scorn from border hawks for creating alleged "sanctuary." Law enforcement leaders who opposed Arpaio's tactics became increasingly vocal throughout 2008, though, especially George Gascón, the police chief of Pearce's home city, Mesa.[71]

Reflecting consensus about some level of border- and smuggling-related enforcement, Arizona state budgets had been dedicating increasing funding to these purposes. Though the Gang Intelligence Team Enforcement Mission, evocatively styled "GITEM," had long existed within the Arizona Department of Public Safety as a state-led multiagency task force, Napolitano and the legislature had reinvigorated it. State budgets began to balloon funding for this task force, which took on an antismuggling focus and had an extra "I" for "immigration" added to its name by statute in 2006. Between fiscal year 2004 and fiscal year 2008, GIITEM's funding grew from $4.3 million to $31.8 million.[72] These measures met with the approval of border hawks, moderates, and liberals, representing a point of bipartisan consensus in a local-enforcement debate that was becoming more salient and fractious.

Even with local-enforcement issues roiling, the legislative session of 2008 saw substantial cooperation on state antismuggling efforts. By now, this was a comfortable political position for Democrats and an area of significant interest for several entrepreneurial Republican legislators. Napolitano addressed the topic extensively in her State of the State Address on January 14, 2008: "Let's keep working to take away the tools of the smuggling trade. We went after fake IDs with the Fraudulent ID Task Force, and that's working. We went after wire transfers of illegal profits, and that's working. We went after stolen vehicles used to bring people into the country illegally, and—guess what?—that's working, too. The next step is to target the drop houses located in family neighborhoods all over Arizona."[73]

A bill expanding who could be held legally accountable for smugglers' use of these "drop houses"—properties where smugglers would detain often scores of migrants simultaneously—was sponsored by Republicans Jonathan Paton and Adam Driggs (HB 2842), passed the legislature unanimously, and was signed. A proposal by Republican senator Thayer Verschoor to stiffen penalties for smuggling activities committed by using deadly weapons (HB 2486) also was signed after passing unanimously. The legislature also passed and the governor signed a bill (HB 2785) with numerous clarifications to the previous year's employer-sanctions law.

But a broader confrontation over local enforcement of immigration law was brewing amid Arpaio's aggressive tactics and headline grabbing. A bill sponsored by Republican representative John Nelson[74] would have required local police agencies to implement a plan to deal with violations of immigration law (HB 2807), mandating that they form working relationships with ICE but stopping short of requiring 287(g) agreements. The bill offered a contrast in language, at least, to earlier border-hawk bills to mandate full-throttle use of 287(g), and Nelson worked with the legislative Democrat Tom Prezelski, who called the bill a preferable alternative to mooted ballot measures.[75] The bill passed the House unanimously before encountering some opposition in the Senate. Activist groups belatedly began to raise the alarm about the measure. A number of Democrats who had voted for HB 2807 backtracked, publicly asking Napolitano to veto it.[76] Napolitano acquiesced, calling the bill an "unnecessary, unfunded mandate to law enforcement" and noting that nothing in state law prohibited local law enforcement from making such arrangements with federal authorities.[77] Nelson said after the vote, "What I saw and heard was basically a small group of zealots who were making a lot of noise, when in fact 70 percent of the state wants something like this."[78] Pearce, not a sponsor of the bill, brought forth a veto override motion that predictably failed but twisted the dagger by forcing Democratic backtracking onto the legislative record. Assertive local-enforcement champions wasted little time declaring that the governor's veto necessitated a local-enforcement ballot proposition. Pearce argued this, Arpaio and Thomas accompanying him, in a May event at the state capitol,[79] but no referendum followed.

DUELING AGENDAS: BORDER HAWKS AND TEMPORARY LABOR REFORMERS

In 2008, the legislative successes of border hawks noticeably declined. This weakening can partially be attributed to rising fiscal problems at the state capitol as the recession opened a chasm in state finances. The Republican leadership of the Senate, more moderate than the House leadership, had a clear tendency not to act on House border-hawk legislation. But a number of border-hawk proposals died in the House as well. Resurrecting the Napolitano-thwarted effort to apply trespassing law to unauthorized immigrants, Pearce proposed a referendum on the question (HCR 2039), but that bill was held awaiting a vote in the House. Rep. John Kavanagh's proposal to define day laborers on public streets as trespassers (HB 2412) passed in the House but failed in a Senate vote. A Pearce-sponsored proposal requiring proof of citizenship to be granted a marriage license (HB 2631) was not given a committee hearing, nor was a separate proposal to exclude unauthorized immigrants from worker's compensation (HB 2750). A proposed referendum to require proof of citizenship or legal status to attend any public educational institution (HCR 2043) was also held in committee. A Pearce proposal to bar the renting of property to unauthorized immigrants (HB 2625) was voted out of multiple committees but never received a House floor vote. A proposed referendum mirroring the vetoed local-enforcement bill (HCR 2064) was also held in the House.

While border-hawk measures were failing to rise up the legislative agenda, lawmakers were considering what amounted to the only serious state-level legislative proposal of this period to clearly view immigration through something other than a security lens. This bill, HB 2791, sought to create a state guest-worker system, the Arizona Temporary Workers Program, pending requisite federal permission. Aimed mainly at addressing chronic labor shortages in Arizona agriculture, the program would have enrolled only Mexican nationals who were sponsored by a valid Arizona employer. Proposed by Konopnicki and Marsha Arzberger, a cattle rancher who was leader of the Senate Democrats, the bill enjoyed significant support in both parties.[80] Expanding the channels for temporary low-skill immigration was also seen as possessing public support. Meanwhile, state officials, including Napolitano, pressed for Arizona to be able to pilot changes that the U.S. Department of Labor proposed to the existing federal agricultural worker program, H-2A, which businesses considered unwieldy.[81] Napolitano offered her notional support to HB 2791. By March, the adoption of such a program seemed likely as business groups and Republican leadership in the House and Senate publicly got on board with the bills. "With the leadership sponsoring, I expect the bills to fast track through," Arzberger predicted.[82]

Negotiations between Pearce and House Speaker Jim Weiers resulted in changes and new bills (SB 1508, HB 2863), but Pearce still withheld his support.[83] As HB 2791 was coming to floor consideration, Ron Gould, a Senate border-hawk ally of Pearce, announced his intention to propose amendments to require a certification that the border was secure for the program to go into effect and a prohibition on pregnant women taking part out of concern that children born to them would be U.S. citizens.[84] The amendments were explicitly hostile, aiming to kill the bill. "I will not be a party to selling out the Arizona worker," Gould was quoted as saying at the time. Having negotiated with Arzberger, Pearce pooh-poohed the resulting bill: "It's business as usual."[85]

Some on the left were cool to guest-worker programs, viewing them as exploitative, while others aimed to keep business as part of the constituency for comprehensive immigration reform, which separately addressing one of the business lobby's main concerns might harm. This made passage of the bill trickier because it could not rely on monolithic Democratic support.[86] With Gould's amendments looming and budget considerations consuming the Senate calendar, Arzberger held the bill, unsure that the measure could pass with incomplete attendance on the Senate floor.[87]

Despite promises to bring forward the proposal later, the only serious state-level policy-making effort since 2004 to explicitly address an Arizona immigration issue through an economic lens died.

Despite anti-border-hawk forces' failure on guest workers, by 2008 it appeared that Arpaio's sweeps had become antagonizing enough that otherwise hesitant opponents might emerge to sharply contest him. On March 28, following Arpaio's provocative move to conduct a sweep in Phoenix without first notifying the Phoenix Police Department, Phil Gordon, the city's Democratic mayor, denounced Arpaio at an event in remembrance of the labor leader Cesar Chavez: "These made-for-TV stunts of his are putting Phoenix and federal undercover agents, who are working that same area, at risk. And his own volunteer posse faces serious risks from serious criminals. All in the name of broken tail lights—on the cars of brown drivers. . . . I call upon everyone in this room—especially the non-Hispanic members of this audience—to speak out. Make our voices heard."[88]

The following week Gordon wrote to the U.S. attorney general to request that Arpaio be investigated for civil rights violations, saying the sweeps amounted to "a pattern and practice of conduct that includes discriminatory harassment, improper stops, searches, and arrests. I understand these are serious allegations."[89] This level of open opposition to Arpaio was at the time striking. Yet although Gordon continued to denounce Arpaio and was cheered on by many Hispanic leaders,[90] his voice was not joined by a chorus of others.[91] Gordon had nevertheless tapped into a latent criticism of Arpaio, whose office was responsible for serving warrants: "There are thousands of outstanding felony warrants in this county. How long are those going to stay piled up on his desk?"[92]

It came as a surprise when in May Napolitano's office announced it was shifting $1.6 million in funding from the MCSO to a new state task force dedicated to serving warrants to felony fugitives.[93] Arpaio smelled a rat. "A felony-warrant task force . . . is a cover-up for taking away grant money, my money given to me by the Legislature, to fight illegal immigration."[94] Although Napolitano's move was universally seen as having to do with Arpaio's sweeps, her staff represented it as a bureaucratic resource-allocation decision made by the state Department of Public Safety.[95] Arpaio continued with his sweeps and later appealed to the Republican-controlled Maricopa County Board of Supervisors to restore the funding. It obliged.[96]

ELECTIONS HAVE CONSEQUENCES

The established pattern of contestation over immigration politics in Arizona, in which many actors were seeking to employ the attributes of the issue's politics to secure their own victories, might have been witnessing an emerging line of contestation over Arpaio-style enforcement. However, elections in 2008 shook the state's power structure with two major developments.

First, battles within the Republican Party continued to broaden in state-level elections to the disadvantage of alleged RINOs. In the legislature, the centrist Tom O'Halleran, who had been serving in the Senate, lost his Republican primary to a conservative challenger. As Hershberger recalled, developments in 2008 fulfilled a "real trend where moderates started losing. Jennifer [J. Burns] didn't run again. . . . And I ran [for the Senate] and lost." Often with recourse to campaign funding under Clean Elections, Arizona's system of public election financing, right-wing candidates were able to run relatively unbeholden to Republican Party powerbrokers with business ties. A number of Republican legislators with moderate sympathies on immigration remained, but those who stood out as moderates had been hunted virtually to extinction or at least into hiding. Even with Republicans fielding more right-wing candidates, though, Democrats did not capitalize on the divisions in the opposing party. With some of their earlier gains reversed, Democrats remained squarely in the minority in the legislature after 2008.

Second, national politics was dominated in 2008 by the presidential election. Napolitano backed Barack Obama in the Democratic primaries at a time when the race seemed in the balance.[97] On the Republican side, the nomination was won by Arizona's John McCain. The election, fought against a backdrop of economic deterioration, barely featured immigration because the two candidates held broadly similar positions supporting federal comprehensive immigration reform.[98]

Obama's victory rattled Arizona politics when Napolitano accepted Obama's nomination to serve as U.S. secretary of homeland security. Obama's choice related in no small part to what was broadly seen as Napolitano's successful navigation of politically perilous immigration issues.[99] Her resignation as governor in January 2009 abruptly changed the distribution of power in Arizona state politics.[100] Jan Brewer, a Republican with little previous track record on border and immigration issues, now sat in the Governor's Office. Policy decision making over immigration issues had been shaped by several years of partisan security-politics competition. Now, Arizona immigration politics was entering a new period in which the tensions, disputes, and factional politics of the newly dominant Republican Party would determine the direction of policy. The border hawks looked upon their greatest window of opportunity yet.

DISCUSSION: PARTY COMPETITION, ISSUE OWNERSHIP, AND THE CREEP OF SECURITIZATION

By 2006, Arizona politicians of all stripes were trying to use the seeming attributes of securitized border politics as tools to their advantage in a competitive political contest. As discussed in chapter 1, the attributes that policy makers saw in Arizona's immigration politics had led most to rule out what we might see as "typical" competition over the issue—where they would seek to win a debate by advocating something close to their naturally most preferred position. By 2005, opponents of the border hawks had sensed that this mode of contestation was failing. Policy makers' understanding of the distinct politics of immigration, emerging from its security qualities and its populist articulation, instead led to a form of opposition premised on ostensible partial agreement. This altered approach relied tactically not just on argumentation about which policy path toward addressing the security problem was better but also on one-upmanship, wedge driving, turnabout, and arm-twisting. This mode of competition had a key effect on the issue's trajectory: it continually opened opportunities for securitization, which consumed new facets of policy beyond what most policy makers preferred, despite the fact that moderates continued to hold key veto points. Previously beyond-the-pale policies were increasingly considered in legislation and, indeed, enacted. What had earlier been extreme positions advocated by the Far Right were becoming "mainstreamed."

How did this work? The previous chapter explored many of the particular attributes that Arizona policy makers had begun to believe immigration issues possessed. Events between 2006 and 2008 further show the ways in which these securitarian and populist qualities affected strategies of political competition. An anxiety underlying public attitudes about the issue seemed to impart a generalized sense of responsibility to act among Arizona policy makers. Arizona politicians of all sorts frequently criticized Washington, as subnational policy makers often find national authorities useful foils on these issues.[101] Nevertheless, to opponents of the border hawks, the populist attacks against elites seemed to corrode elite authority over whether the issue was one of security, while the security quality of the purported problem made it urgent and politically impossible to ignore—an interaction that comprised a key mechanism driving the opponents' shifting positions.[102]

These features made action incumbent upon governing elites in a way that it seemed to them could not be successfully avoided. Terry Goddard, the Democratic state attorney general during this time, later explained the implications of accepting the characterization of the border as a security issue: It "plays into Russell [Pearce]'s hands, who says, 'Well, if the feds are missing, and they aren't protecting the border, and they aren't seriously engaged in reforming the immigration system, then we in the state have to take action.' And frankly I see why that's such a powerful statement because the feds had failed! The system was a mess. The problem was a broken border. So now, as somebody who thinks there are other, better, more humane, and economically viable solutions, you start in a hole." A security understanding of the issue was accepted in large part because alternative conceptions were seen as likely to be painted by populists as evasive or corrupt or as too complex to succeed politically. Following from this, the effort to work a way out of this "hole" was characterized by attempts to seize "ownership" over immigration *as* a security issue.

The immigration positioning of Democrats—specifically Napolitano, whom aides describe explicitly as endeavoring to "own" the issue over the border hawks—aimed to recenter the debate on preferable, though still securitized, ground. This goal is a notable challenge for center-left figures because voters across Western democracies consistently associate immigration control with conservative parties, who "own" it alongside other social control issues.[103] Ownership of immigration has frequently been discussed in scholarship on party competition over the issue, often working from the premise that traditional governing parties in Western democracies have converged in their issue positions. "Ownership" discourses, based on competence instead of on policy trajectory, allow parties to compete over issues where there is no substantial difference in policy vision between them.[104] On face, this might have seemed to occur in Arizona, except that the extent to which major differences in policy preferences on immigration persisted was clear, even if policy makers felt the politics of the issue pushing them toward a dominant problem conception. "Ownership" of immigration appealed in part instead because policy makers read it as offering an opportunity, albeit limited, to pursue such an alternative policy direction. Ownership strategies on immigration may also be read as driven by intraparty politics: because such strategies do not strike fundamentally at policy vision, they provide parties with ways of campaigning on immigration but without exacerbating existing internal divisions about it.[105]

What is striking in Arizona is exactly how this did not happen. Democrats initially pursued their employer-sanctions strategy precisely to turn different wings of the Republican Party against each other, imagining that Republican elites would be cornered into enforcing the kind of muted immigration positioning much ownership literature describes. This never occurred. U.S. political parties are organizationally weaker than most of their European counterparts, and in Arizona establishment of control encountered a particular set of further difficulties. The Republican Party contained an increasingly recalcitrant right wing, amply represented in the party grass roots, which wanted much more an ideologically pure party than a heterogeneous, unified one. To this end, they waged an intensifying "RINO" hunt. Border hawks' credible threat to use the mechanisms of direct democracy on employer sanctions—and thus entirely to subvert elite opposition within their own party—turned the tables, making negotiation preferable to a critical mass of Republican elites. Nonetheless, the negotiated nature of the employer-sanctions compromise showed that the non–border hawks within the Republican Party still held some sway.

The particular "ownership" strategy that legislative Democrats, business-oriented Republicans, and Napolitano attempted with respect to the securitized immigration issue more resembles the concept as modeled in political science outside of the migration-politics subfield.[106] In this sense, "ownership" is employed as a competitive strategy seeking to neutralize—or perhaps even capture—an issue where the other side appears

to have some entrenched advantage. In Arizona, beyond the general association between immigration control and right-wing parties, the border
hawks' entrenched advantage on immigration was that their security conceptualization appeared unable to be effectively rebutted: the public was
fearful and restive, opponents did not think they could successfully articulate an alternative approach given the perceived limitations of the public and the media, and downplaying the issue played into the hands of
populist antielitists. An ownership attempt thus comprises two moves.
The first is to try to gain credibility in line with the dominant issue conceptualization. Here, security is flamboyantly adopted as an approach.
Napolitano's declaration of a border emergency in November 2005 was a
momentous instance of this move, as was Democrats' enthusiastic positioning of themselves as champions of tough employer sanctions. The second move is a pivot, where one adds a new framing or understanding of
the issue in an attempt to partially reorient the politics of the issue. The
layer that the pivot adds is what gives voters a reason to support the pivoting politician rather than the issue's original owner. This ownership
maneuver is thus a strategy of "yes, but."[107]

In Arizona, this pivot was reflected in efforts by Napolitano, Democrats, and more moderate Republicans to argue for comprehensive immigration reform or to articulate that securing the border meant going
after smuggling networks or unscrupulous employers, not individual
labor migrants. Although this pivot aimed to shift the conversation to
more preferable ground, the initial move in the strategy, to gain credibility, was also seen as a weapon against the border hawks' excesses. This
move gave Napolitano the political capital to veto some border-hawk bills
from a position of strength. One perceived promise of "owning" the issue
was to lead policy in what nonpopulist governing elites considered to be
a better and more reasonable—if, admittedly, less than ideal—direction.
Dennis Burke, Napolitano's chief of staff for policy, described it this way:

> If you look at Napolitano, she said that border security's key, the federal
> government's fucked up, they're dysfunctional, here's what we're gonna
> do. Then look at what she proposed, as opposed to [what] Pearce pro-
> posed, which was driven by racism and fearmongering and bad, bad
> economics. And Napolitano's was: I'll take your premise of there's a prob-
> lem and we need to fix it and we have a role, but here's our role. . . .

[Voters] lacked someone like a Napolitano who can say, "Here's a rational way—I'm not gonna say you don't have a right to be afraid. I'm not gonna question the fact that you have a right to be concerned that things aren't getting done. But here's the solution."

In practical terms, this ownership maneuver aimed to steer political energy behind the securitized problem conception toward preferable areas such as "border crime," while pointing also to solutions beyond security. But a tension developed between the two parts of the move, the "yes" and the "but." Napolitano was seen as quickly establishing credibility by emphatically choosing security as a policy approach. However, the task of establishing this credibility had no self-apparent endpoint, especially when pitted against energetic opponents with a long wish list of securitized policies—opponents who, in populist fashion, were poised to paint any hesitancy as outrageous and corrupt. Even if the ownership strategy succeeds, the turn it executes regarding the issue is only partial. The liability, therefore, is that the "yes" devours the "but."

Indeed, when it came to immigration and border security, almost all sides in Arizona—except, notably, the border hawks—at times felt boxed in to awkward positions by their ostensible acceptance of the issue's security nature and their fears of appearing to shirk the generalized sense of responsibility in responding to threat that followed from this definition of the issue. Democrats tried to box in moderate and business-friendly Republicans with employer sanctions; border hawks boxed in both of those groups with the same issue; Republicans sought to box in Napolitano with the National Guard, which she then used to box them in; and so on. Beyond political sparring, however, the policy consequence of these moves was stark: every one of them advanced the securitization of immigration in state policy beyond where it had been before. Even as non-border-hawk figures added their "buts"—including stressing a need to focus on economic aspects of the issue—the security-heavy policy evolution provided little purchase for something even as apparently widely supported as the Arizona Temporary Workers Program. Securitization crept along.

In this way, because credibility was perceived as a crucial condition for success, this security-politics competition created continual opportunities for hawkish elements to advance securitization further than more moderate figures preferred—even after those moderates seemed, to a considerable degree, to have successfully captured ownership of the issue. Although that ownership approach preserves some potential for acting on other aspects of the issue, in Arizona, at least, that potential was much less manifest than the potential for further security action. Whether this halting creep of security is preferable to an unrealized, even more hawkish counterfactual became a key question for political actors, activists, and citizens. With the political rationalities of hawks and moderates interlocked in this way, securitization proceeded along despite contestation, acquiring an apparently irrepressible quality.

It is essential to recall, however, that exacting preferred immigration or border policy is rarely, if ever, a politician's only goal. Rather, politicians most often keep in mind both policy goals across whichever fields compel them as well as the maintenance of sufficient political power to possibly exact such goals in the future.[108] If the ownership maneuver seems to be mixed at accomplishing the former, in the Arizona case, at least, it proved to its users much better at accomplishing the latter. The two-step on immigration, even if it meant creeping securitization beyond what was preferred, was seen as a way to ensure that the issue did not endanger one's hold on power generally. Indeed, this latter consideration was arguably the paramount one in Arizona—where, except for border hawks, few had started out seeing immigration as a policy priority. As Tim Nelson put it regarding Napolitano, "If she were to get labeled as being totally pro-immigrant and not responsive to this sense that immigration was creating real problems in Arizona, it would have significantly compromised her ability to pursue agenda items that were important to her, like education. I'm not sure she would have ever gotten all-day kindergarten. I'm not sure she could ever have done the types of things that she did."

It has long been apparent to securitization theorists that political leaders, rather than fully believing in the security nature of an issue, might try to securitize that issue to make it easier to take preferred action on it, bolstering its prominence to consolidate power.[109] Rarely has it been explored how such leaders may agree defensively to securitization largely to preserve their power in order to pursue preferred outcomes in entirely separate issues on the political agenda. Such political uses of securitization are relatively self-apparent in examining cases such as Arizona's. Yet they are difficult to discern unless security is conceived as being deeply contextualized within—and, indeed, deeply a part of—the web of normal political competition, interwoven with larger political struggles.

⸎

This period of competitive interparty border-security politics in Arizona from 2005 to 2008 shows how immigration became increasingly securitized due to patterns of party competition and interacting political strategies, which were shaped by the distinct political meanings of security. What policy makers had accepted by the end of 2005 as the realities of the issue shaped new approaches to it and thus new patterns of competition, based on a strategically adopted ostensible agreement that a security problem existed at the border. The disputes that followed—over the National Guard, local enforcement, and especially employer sanctions—show how this securitized agreement led to competition over the issue that was intense but narrow, remaining focused on security despite moderates' attempts to pivot toward more complex issue conceptualizations. These relative moderates often met with considerable success in capturing "ownership" over these issues. Democrats, especially, shielded their political power quite successfully in these years. But such a strategy meant that these moderates were continually boxed into giving ground toward the further securitization of immigration. New facets of state policy were continually pulled into the border-hawk orbit. Securitization crept along.

By the end of this period, interparty border-security politics was proceeding on recognizable battle lines, though ones that continued to expand as border hawks cornered their opponents into negotiated settlements while refocusing on further elements of their agenda. Republican intraparty competition was also clearly escalating. Whereas powerful Democrats such as Napolitano had found political safety through triangulating issue-ownership moves, Republican immigration moderates felt their positions become increasingly tenuous. With a sudden shift in the distribution of political power in 2008, however, the battle lines demarcated by an era of divided government were washed away. With the Republican Party now dominant in state policy making, its intraparty disputes were poised to become the immigration issue's new battle lines as Arizona's border-security politics moved toward a climactic moment.

3

THE TOUGHEST MEASURE

Arizona's border hawks looked out upon major opportunities with the advent of one-party Republican control over state government in 2009. Their main adversary, Janet Napolitano, had decamped to Washington, while right-wing activists had so vigorously contested Republican centrists that almost no Republican elected officials still stood outwardly as moderates. But the terrain was not completely clear. The difficulties of passing the employer-sanctions bill in 2007 showed that, despite the near extinction of Republican centrists, many Republicans remaining in the legislature were cool on the border-hawk push in quieter ways. Harboring business-sensitive doubts about a populist radical-right anti-immigration agenda, this group's decisions about how to navigate the issue were primed to be pivotal. And although a Republican, Jan Brewer, was entering the state's highest office, her positions on immigration could not easily be predicted. Brewer had little track record on the border. Besides, she had a major preoccupation: the deepening Great Recession and the resulting crisis in the State of Arizona's finances.

Despite uncertain terrain and major controversy, this potential opposition was ultimately moved toward an even fuller embrace of security as the state's approach toward immigration. This progression culminated in Senate Bill 1070, a proposal sponsored by the border hawk Russell Pearce that mandated unprecedented levels of involvement by Arizona's local police in enforcing immigration laws.

SB 1070 electrified Arizona politics. The feverish atmosphere surrounding the bill seemed to rapidly reshape Arizona's political landscape. More starkly than ever before, this period in Arizona brought forth the firm shift toward the hard line that has become frequently associated with twenty-first-century immigration politics—underscoring the invocation of threat as an extremely strong tool for political mobilization. In such moments, a change unfolds, striking at the very core of community and citizenship, seeming to render politics different than before. As securitization elevates issues that are increasingly defined by purported danger, the unbinding of authority, and the imperative to fortify the community against those outside it, these qualities cannot be neatly confined in the narrow securitized issue at hand but take on a greater, looming— even extraordinary[1]—significance. This sensation—leading many to wonder, as security grips politics, what has become of liberal and tolerant polities—is one reason why the idea that securitization produces a "state of exception" has resonated so fully with respect to these moments.[2]

However, the previous chapters have argued that reading such events as transformative of political life overstates the matter, with important implications for how we understand what is going on.[3] The presence of security in immigration politics increasingly centers policy responses on an alleged security problem. Yet, as we see in Arizona, there may be little sincere consensus on just what the problem is. The typical machinations of politics proceed apace, though now with an unmistakable security flavor. This continues to be the case even as the securitization trend enters its starkest and apparently most transformative moments, when political tensions are magnified and the exclusionary nature of this form of politics is most starkly exposed and feverishly contested. But given how less changes than it might appear, what precisely is occurring when security politics brings us—so seemingly swiftly—to such extreme states?

This chapter argues that the momentous shifts of 2009 and 2010 in Arizona—the enactment of hard-line and even exceptionalist policies in a fevered atmosphere, followed by the consolidation of power of those who championed the hard line—emerged not from a single cohesive securitization logic but from two distinct, contingent developments in competitive politics. The first was the further amplification of intraparty tension among Republicans even at a moment when a new distribution of power in state government had removed earlier veto players in border-security politics. With Pearce's policies becoming an increasingly exclusive litmus test for supporting border security, possible primary-election consequences if Republican stood in the way became even more palpable, eventually clearing the path for SB 1070's passage. But the subsequent dramatic consolidation of power by pro–SB 1070 figures in the elections of 2010—Jan Brewer, Russell Pearce, and Arizona Republicans in general—grew from a distinct dynamic: the rapid nationalization of Arizona's immigration conflicts, which mapped them on to existing partisan polarization, and the cultivation of a backlash within the state against the local and national criticism that Arizona received in SB 1070's aftermath. These two phenomena were driven by politicians' readings of two overlapping but distinct key constituencies: Republican primary voters in the first half of 2010 and Arizona general-election voters in the second half. While SB 1070 culminated the trends the previous two chapters outlined, the politics that surrounded it also extended these trends to new and more extreme degrees.

The period in which Arizona seemed to enter such a state offers a particularly important window into the effects of populist border-security politics within a big-tent party of the Right: how immigration can grow from a factional fixation to a consuming issue. Most scholarship on the populist radical Right has focused on Europe, where this political tendency has often occupied a distinct party family that competes directly with historically larger and more dominant center-right parties,[4] in contrast to the United States, where such tendencies have been historically more incorporated within two-party politics.[5] A longer historical view underscores how center-right parties play key roles in shaping the fate of radical right-wing movements amid the Center Right's temptation to accommodate these movements.[6] What happens, though, when the radical Right is growing in power and already on the inside? The ongoing discussion about the extent to which the Republican Party has become the "party of Trump"[7] illustrates the key role these intraparty dynamics will play, at least to the future of immigration policy in the United States.

By the end of 2010, efforts in Arizona to treat immigration as a security threat had reached a new zenith. Full support for border-hawk policy was seeming to become new Republican orthodoxy. Voters appeared to endorse these stances in that autumn's elections. And by the close of that year, Pearce himself was poised to possess more formal power than ever before. It seemed that Arizona's most controversial immigration measure to date would be merely a first step.

NO SANCTUARY

Arizona's new Republican governor, Jan Brewer, took office in January 2009 without a lengthy record on border issues and facing a looming problem: dire state budget shortfalls that the unfolding global financial crisis was deepening even further.[8] Brewer's inaugural address conveyed an overpowering sense of the fiscal problem: "At a government's new hour we normally find ourselves uplifted by possibility. But today, we find ourselves weighed down with obligation—overdue obligation." Brewer devoted the theme of her inaugural address to freedom: "In every way we can, we must make our people free. Free to work and earn a living, to build a business, to build a life. . . . Free from crime and violence and lawlessness of all kinds."[9] That skirting reference was Brewer's entire discussion of law enforcement or security in her first address as governor before her attention turned to the budget.

Despite dismal fiscal talk, there was a sense of possibility among Republicans in that they again held complete initiative in shaping state policy. Some observed hopefully that one-party control "may reduce gridlock and aid state officials in navigating a bleak budget."[10] Democrats saw their power evaporate in this new arrangement as they held neither the House nor the Senate nor the governorship. Among legislative Republicans, an intraparty coup in late 2008 had made Kirk Adams, who had often worked behind the scenes with immigration moderates, the Speaker of the House.[11]

Notwithstanding these developments, there was no impression that border and immigration politics had disappeared from the political scene, either as a concern for voters or as an awkward issue for the Republican coalition. Chuck Coughlin, a Republican consultant and close adviser to Brewer whose firm consistently conducted polls in Arizona, reflected that by the time Brewer took office, the issue was "full-blown":

We ask people what the number-one issue is, and we do a series of prompts. They all stay the same over time. Immigration and border security is always one of them since the beginning of the 2000s. And you can watch the thing just sort of spike, go to the number-one issue. You know, it dies down, and education and state budget issues will come back up . . . but it's always, in Arizona, and continues to be to this day [2015] the number-one issue with the electorate. And vast majorities of the electorate.

As had been clear for years, the salience of immigration—along with the apparent public popularity of border and immigration-enforcement provisions championed by figures such as Russell Pearce—presented a dilemma to less enforcement-inclined Republicans. Coughlin recalled a Republican office seeker whom he was advising around this time:

He was not inclined to the enforcement-first approach—or [enforcement]-only approach, I should say. Which I got. But we did a poll, and one of the questions was . . . if you get pulled over for a broken taillight, and you do not have proof of citizenship, should you be ticketed? And, you know, we went through a series of responses, one of which was "deported." Sixty-five percent, "send 'em home." For a broken taillight. I showed him that. I go, "This is how people look at this out here, man. This is how frustrated this part of the electorate is." . . . And I said, you know, "You have to handle this differently."

While the immigration drumbeat continued, the state's political elites were in 2009 devoting their primary attention to the budget. "Budget, budget, budget" is how Joseph Kanefield, a longtime Brewer aide whom she had appointed general counsel in the Governor's Office, described 2009. "It occupied 99 percent of our time."

Tax revenues were down, people were unemployed—I mean, the stock market—everything. It was just a very bad situation. So we spent the first few months of the administration trying to work with the legislature to put in place a workable budget, and at some point we realized the only way to do it—because in Arizona you can't go into a deficit, the Constitution doesn't allow it—the only way to fix the problem without dramatic cuts in public safety, education, health care, was to raise the [sales] tax. So Governor Brewer—as a fiscal conservative for three decades, a staunch fiscal conservative—had to go out and advocate for a temporary one-cent [per dollar] sales tax increase to get us through the recession. And that was bitter. A bitterly fought battle to get that question presented to the voters.[12]

This stance exposed divisions between Brewer and farther-right portions of her own party—among legislators, activists, and primary voters—to whom raising taxes was anathema. The emergent Tea Party movement was dialing up pressure on purported exponents of big government. Despite hopes for harmony in a one-party state lawmaking process, relations between the Governor's Office and the legislature quickly became, in Kanefield's words, "very bad." The veto pen's change of hands from Napolitano to Brewer also held potentially serious ramifications for Republican moderates on a wide range of issues. During Napolitano's tenure, squeamish Republicans frequently voted for legislation they saw as too right-wing if they were confident that Napolitano would veto the measure. It was unclear to what extent Brewer, subject to the same intraparty pressures as Republican legislators, would provide the same cover.

Though ongoing fiscal disputes eclipsed immigration as the legislature's major preoccupation, border issues continued to swirl. By early 2009, Mexico's campaign against drug cartels had resulted in a wave of violence in Mexican border areas, raising concerns in the United States built from long-standing narratives of Mexico as a weak state emanating violence.[13] The dubious claim that because of drug cartel operations Phoenix ranked second in kidnappings in the world became ubiquitous in the media, though it was later debunked.[14] Nonetheless, although unauthorized border crossing dipped to longtime lows as the recession reduced demand for workers, "spillover violence" emerged as a rekindled facet of border-security concern. The border hawks' usual opponents offered a mixed response, by now familiar in its outlines. At a congressional field hearing in Phoenix about border-related violence, Phil Gordon, the Phoenix mayor who had inveighed against the border hawk Sheriff Joe Arpaio, testified: "There can be no doubt that a crisis exists at our border with Mexico. . . . Phoenix finds itself at the center of this Perfect Storm—a storm that is growing increasingly violent, threatening and resource-consuming. . . . I would point out that the extreme violence we are seeing on the Mexico side of our border—including beheadings—has not yet spilled over to the

American side."[15] This was a less crystalline interpretation of the situation than the one offered by border hawks such as Pearce, who wrote in the *Arizona Republic* when arguing for his major immigration bill that year, HB 2280: "Phoenix runs second in the world in kidnappings and third in the United States for violence. Arizona has become the home-invasion, carjacking, identity-theft capital of the nation. These are not statistics Arizona should be famous for. Enough is enough. The laws must be enforced."[16]

Pearce and his allies in 2009 reintroduced many measures that had failed under Napolitano as well as some newer proposals. However, these proposals were clearly sidelined amid a particularly contentious budget negotiation, with most of the bills introduced only late in the session and few seeing floor votes. Rep. John Kavanagh's early-session bills relating to the Fourteenth Amendment and birthright citizenship (HB 2561, HB 2562; discussed further in chapter 4) were held before they reached the floor of the House. Pearce, newly elected to the Senate, also saw most of his legislation wither. A bill to require public schools to gather data on the numbers of unauthorized immigrant children they enrolled (SB 1172) was held in committee, as was a bill to make it a misdemeanor for unauthorized immigrants to solicit work (SB 1177). Two bills and a referendum proposal to apply state trespassing law to unauthorized immigrants (SB 1159, SB 1162, SCR 1010) were held in committees, along with a bill to exclude unauthorized immigrants from worker's compensation (SB 1334). A bill sponsored by Rep. Tom Boone to prohibit municipalities from adopting ordinances that inhibited local immigration enforcement (HB 2331) and to require police to ask about immigration status, but with many exceptions, passed a party-line floor vote in the House in June but was not supported by Pearce,[17] was held in the Senate, and was eventually withdrawn by its sponsor. A different bill to define day laborers as trespassers (HB 2533) passed a party-line floor vote in the House in June but was held in the Senate before a floor vote. A bill to create a new felony for concealing undocumented people (SB 1280) was held in the House after passing the Senate.

The most contentious immigration episode of the year occurred in the final moments of the regular legislative session on July 1. The first day of the new fiscal year, July 1 was the deadline to pass a budget without a state government shutdown as well as the date that the legislature would adjourn its regular session. Though eclipsed in the media at the time, the death of HB 2280, Pearce's major immigration bill, at the regular session's twilight intensified Republican intraparty dynamics favoring hard-line immigration politics.

For border hawks, the year 2009 seemed almost completely unproductive. SB 1175, proposed by Pearce and his Senate ally Jack Harper, sought to prohibit any local law enforcement agency from adopting policies that inhibited their enforcement of immigration law, to require officers or officials to attempt to check the immigration status of anyone of whom they were suspicious, and to create a trespassing offense.[18] This bill passed the Senate in a 16–12 vote on June 15, with only Carolyn Allen, perhaps legislative Republicans' last remaining open centrist, straying from the party line. However, it was not granted a hearing in the House Judiciary Committee—chaired by Adam Driggs, an immigration lawyer who often sided with a more moderate immigration approach. Pearce, who chaired the Senate Appropriations Committee, resuscitated the measure in that committee through a strike-everything amendment to HB 2280. The reintroduced measure drew the attention of activist groups, and hearings about it were unusually contentious: in one hearing, Pearce ejected clergy who attended to oppose the bill, and the committee's Democrats walked out in protest.[19] After the committee sent the bill to the Senate floor, it passed with the same sixteen votes as earlier and was sent to the House for consideration in the early morning hours of July 1.

The House was just concluding its budget business and wrapping up a contentious session that had gone throughout the night and would end at 7:30 that morning. Many Democrats had already left the chamber, and few members had an appetite for the quick consideration of a substantial immigration measure. Some Republicans who were normally cool to border-hawk efforts perceived tactically that they could also leave. Rich Crandall, a House Republican with largely traditional, business-oriented views who represented a district in Mesa, described HB 2280 and his departure from the chamber along with noted Pearce foe Bill Konopnicki: "It is everything and the kitchen sink. It's so unconstitutional it isn't funny. . . . I drove Bill Konopnicki to the airport, or he drove me to the airport, at like one in the morning, when the vote was being taken. So we weren't there. But it's the same thing as a no vote. . . . It was late, it had been cantankerous, everybody was mad at each other."

HB 2280 failed on a 26–15 vote, falling short of the 31 votes needed to pass. Three House Republicans—Russ Jones, John McComish, and Andy Tobin—were present and voted no. Six Republicans had left the floor before the vote: Doug Quelland, Driggs, Lucy Mason, Nancy Barto, Crandall, and Konopnicki. The latter five had participated in the informal Republican group mentioned in previous chapters that aimed to slow or defeat border-hawk legislation. Pearce quickly made clear in the media that he saw no difference between those who voted no and the absentees. "Though absenteeism likely was a factor in the bill's defeat, Pearce said he wasn't surprised that the measure failed in the House. 'Some people support law breakers over law keepers,' he said. 'How many more officers are we going to have killed?' He said he would keep trying to get the bill to become law and might gather signatures to take it to the ballot."[20]

In a special session immediately following the regular session, the legislature passed bills sponsored by then senator Jonathan Paton and related to smuggling and sex trafficking (SB 1281, SB 1282), in addition to a measure sponsored by Paton, Driggs, and Mason to create a new felony for human smuggling that involves the use of a deadly weapon (HB 2569). The legislature also passed a proposal by Rep. Michele Reagan (HB 2306) clarifying issues related to the employer-sanctions bill of 2007. Consistent with what were by then long-standing consensuses over this type of legislation, these bills passed with few votes against them and were signed by the governor. To border hawks, however, these efforts were quite apart from what they considered the truly important agenda.

By 2009, Republican lawmakers clearly saw resisting border-hawk proposals as an act of sticking their necks out politically. Outwardly moderate Republicans were nearly extinct, routed by more conservative primary challengers, and anti-immigration politics was becoming increasingly intertwined with the emergent Tea Party movement.[21] The aftermath of the HB 2280 vote embodied the kind of reaction that Republican policy makers had begun to fear. It emerged partially from the right-wing grassroots but was also encouraged by officeholders such as Pearce, who urged activists to contact the six Republicans absent for the HB 2280 vote as part of a concerted campaign to communicate potential political consequences.[22] The response to their absence was particularly sharp from conservative activist groups online. "They called us the 'Sanctuary Six,'" Crandall recalled.

One milder example, for instance, said, "Rep. Nancy Barto was one of six legislators (aka the 'Sanctuary Six') who walked out during the vote on HB2280, a bill to ban sanctuary cities, resulting in its defeat. . . . Barto ran on a platform sounding tough on illegal immigration. Turns out her fellow five walkers also have made statements in the past indicating they would be tough on illegal immigration. They can't have it both ways."[23]

In an email the week after the vote, its subject line "Blast Arizona State Reps. That Helped Derail Anti-sanctuary Bill," a national anti-immigration organization included legislators' office phone numbers and recommended talking points such as "I can't believe you voted no/didn't vote on HB 2280, Sen. Pearce's antisanctuary bill. How dare you! You were elected to help Americans, not illegal aliens. . . . How many citizens, including officers of the law, have to die or be maimed before you will stand up and fight back?"[24] Right-wing communications targeted hesitant Republicans but ignored Democrats who had also voted to kill the legislation. "RINO"-targeting sights were now turned to those who had passively failed to show full support for border-hawk measures.

To the Republican politicians caught within this storm, it seemed to rage on all sides. Crandall recalled: "That was the beginning of the end, kind of. Started with the [Republican] district meeting. All normal people stopped going to the district meeting, . . . and the only ones who went were the Far, Far Right. . . . I bet I went one more time after that. . . . They [right-wing grassroots Republican activists] started looking for someone to run against me at that point. And so they recruited a guy. . . . Literally, the backlash is they go and find someone to run against me."

The defeat of HB 2280 prompted what was, in both Pearce's account and others', a more concerted and organized push than in the past to build support for the next year's major immigration-enforcement proposal and to clear away opposition.[25] The vituperative tone of right-wing forums was putting possible repercussions at the front of would-be opponents' minds. The effect was simultaneously alienating and chastising. Many targeted policy makers felt frustrated with a portion of the Republican electorate who favored more moderate policies but who seemed unlikely to get involved in this issue. Crandall described how he read his larger political environment:

Everybody in the anonymity of the internet is just going off. Going off on Rich Crandall, the Sanctuary Six, any of us who have an opinion that's contrary to theirs. We're just getting trashed daily to where, you know, you don't read the blogs. . . . But 99 percent of people that favor my position won't speak up and say a word. . . . They have kids, they have jobs, they have lives, and politics means nothing to them. Whoever wins, they couldn't care less. They'll vote. They all vote. And I can tell they all vote because I won. . . . It was very frustrating because they would not go to a district meeting.

While the legislature continued in 2009 to meet in intermittent special sessions to plug widening budget holes, Pearce spotlighted local enforcement as the issue he was priming for action in 2010. One press account from October 2009 summarized Pearce's push:

His capstone proposal would end what illegal immigration opponents call "sanctuary city" policies, where local governments or law enforcement agencies have policies that prevent workers and police officers from questioning someone's immigration status. . . . Although the state is facing a $1.5 billion budget deficit this fiscal year, as well as forecasts for deficits greater than $2 billion in future years, Pearce said illegal immigration should still be a priority for lawmakers. . . . Pearce said he was initially hoping for a special legislative session [in 2009] to address the immigration issues, but backed off of that after speaking with Gov. Jan Brewer's office.[26]

As before, Pearce referred to the threat of a ballot initiative. "I'd rather get it done in the Legislature, but I'll go to the ballot with it if I have to," he said at the time. "And if it gets there, it'll pass by 75 or 80 percent."[27] All the while, the state budget continued to plunge into deeper revenue shortfalls, and Brewer continued to press the case for a sales-tax increase, which the legislature that summer narrowly refused to refer to voters.[28]

SB 1070

At the dawn of 2010, the consensus among Arizona political observers was that the budget would continue to dominate the state agenda but that immigration would also make an appearance as Pearce continued his push against "sanctuary cities." At the start of this gubernatorial election year, Brewer's path to reelection looked very rocky. Her polling numbers lagged, weighed down by unending bad budget news. Many Republicans were not only cool on her tax-hike proposal but also skeptical of her political acumen.[29] Rivals smelled blood in the water. Polls showed Brewer with negative approval ratings among Republicans and vulnerable to losing the Republican primary in August, while her presumed Democratic challenger, the state attorney general Terry Goddard, ran even with or slightly ahead of her.[30] As Coughlin recalled, "The CEO crowd had dismissed her. The national RGA [Republican Governors' Association] had dismissed her. She was not gonna be reelected. [But] I guaranteed people we would win. It was gonna be a hard fight on the fiscal issues."

Brewer's State of the State Address in January 2010 focused intently on those issues, calling for the sales-tax referendum while also attempting to cover her right flank. "If you have a better plan, produce it," she told legislators. "There is no one here, and no one elsewhere, who has fought any longer or harder than I have for lower taxes, job growth and economic freedom in Arizona. So, spare us the profiles in courage; it's time for a little less profile and a little more courage." Immigration briefly registered, with Brewer saying she would "work with the Legislature to enact common-sense reforms to deter illegal immigration in our state."[31] The border, though, was clearly a sideshow to the main event of balancing the budget.

Although contentious, budget discussions in 2010 moved much more quickly than in 2009. The legislature passed the referral for the sales-tax increase in February, scheduling a voter referendum for May 18, and by mid-March passed spending bills with major cuts to public programs.[32] Relieved to have at last won in the legislature on the revenue issue, Brewer's aides pivoted to the referendum campaign and to shoring up her election candidacy. Coughlin recalled: "She had five Republican [election] opponents who were all pillorying her for being a tax-and-spend liberal and a big-spending Republican governor. . . . [O]ur focus was 100 percent on the budget, delivering a fiscal package so we could demonstrate that we were governing and that we could govern as a party. We talked about that ad infinitum." With the most pressing budget work done in mid-March, the legislative agenda was cleared for other items, especially those concerning immigration issues. A Pearce bill relating to a pilot project for seismic sensors to detect aircraft landings by drug cartels (SB 1027) and a Paton-sponsored bill to expand the number of sex-trafficking violations defined as felonies (SB 1059) were passed and signed. An opening also emerged for action on Pearce's main immigration bill, SB 1070.[33]

Originally introduced in January and later amended significantly in committee in late March, SB 1070 contained echoes of many previous proposals and was represented as an "immigration omnibus bill." In part, it reiterated earlier "sanctuary city" proposals that would prohibit municipalities from adopting policies that would inhibit local enforcement of immigration laws. It also created new laws against day-labor practices, making it unlawful for people to hire or be hired from a vehicle impeding traffic, and it introduced new provisions against aiding or harboring unauthorized immigrants. In what would become the bill's most controversial provision, it directed local law enforcement officers to determine during lawful stops the immigration status of individuals they reasonably suspected of being unauthorized immigrants and of all people they arrested. To opponents, that provision in particular represented a recipe for racial profiling. The bill in its eventual form also created penalties under Arizona law for noncitizens who failed to follow federal rules requiring them at all times to carry their documents. The overall purpose of the bill was to make "attrition through enforcement" state policy—that is, to spur unauthorized immigrants to leave or not enter the country by the creation of a hostile everyday environment.[34]

Opponents viewed these proposals as odious but largely typical in the ongoing drumbeat of Russell Pearce's immigration bills. Pearce arrived at that year's session seeking to build support for SB 1070 in an unusually intensive way, though:

> RUSSELL PEARCE: I had stronger law enforcement support that I purposefully went out and got. . . . I had the Arizona Police Association endorse the bill. It makes up twenty-five agencies, 14,000 police officers. I had the Cops Arizona and other law enforcement organizations support the bill. I had a couple of unions support the bill. I had the [Republican] Party, who passed resolutions to support the bill. I mean, the momentum was huge in 2010, and I purposefully built that momentum.
>
> INTERVIEWER: Because of what had happened the previous year.

RP: Yeah. So that people couldn't run away from it and not be held accountable.

As a press report put it, Pearce "worked with special interest groups to keep them out of his way. He tapped law enforcement organizations, business groups and others to get them on his side, or at least to keep them quiet."[35]

Other policy makers took notice of what seemed to be mounting momentum behind Pearce's effort, especially since pressure for Republicans to support border-hawk measures had only increased following the Sanctuary Six episode. Although Pearce often criticized squeamish fellow Republicans and encouraged supporters to confront and work against them, he would alternately accept some changes to his bills to assuage the hesitant. Crandall, who had come under heavy political fire over his absence from the HB 2280 vote in 2009, recalled: "So then we go to the next year, and they tell us from the very beginning, 'Hey, we're going to bring that back.' And we're young enough and naive enough to think, 'Okay, but let's work together.' And to their credit, both to Russell's credit and to [then state representative] Andy Biggs's, they would say, 'Hey, read through it. What are your problems?'" Crandall, for instance, identified as his major qualm a provision that troubled many Republicans, which would have defined extremely broadly the legal standing to bring cases in state courts against Arizona municipalities that were alleged not to be enforcing immigration law to the greatest degree possible. "They said, 'Okay, we'll take that out,'" Crandall recalled. "And they did."[36]

Pearce's partial concessions hardly meant a pause in the grassroots radical-right push against skittish Republicans, however. Chad Campbell, a House Democrat then in the minority leadership, recalled that amid the legislature's consideration of SB 1070 "Russell Pearce would drum up the supporters, drum up his troops, so to speak, and start have them emailing, calling offices, going to the Republican district meetings." Democrats, with a keen sense of their limited formal power, had changed their own strategic outlook when it came to legislation they opposed. "Our role down there . . . [was] more about being a watchdog almost, to let the public know what's going on," Campbell said. "We got some things passed. We killed things. But we really [were] trying to frame the narrative." As SB 1070 proceeded through the legislative process, Democrats endeavored to work with hesitant Republicans to slow the bill, providing them with possible cover to oppose it because the legislation could only be killed with Republican votes against it. Although momentum was building for SB 1070, as had been the case with earlier Pearce proposals, "there were a lot of people that didn't want [it] to go to the floor," Campbell recounted.

Amid this growing political pressure behind SB 1070, on March 27 an Arizona rancher, Robert Krentz, was found murdered on his ranch near the border. Killings by suspected unauthorized immigrants or drug smugglers had featured heavily in Arizona news coverage for years. But the murder of Krentz—a figure from a long-established ranching family who was locally regarded as a Good Samaritan who would aid distressed border crossers[37]—seemed to take on a different dimension. Paton, then running for a southern Arizona seat in Congress, recalled that the aftermath "was like a gasoline fire": "You have a symbol of a rancher. What could be more American than that? And supposedly he was going out to see to somebody that was needing his help . . . 'cause he had done humanitarian-type things many times before, and he was revered in the ranching community, and that was just—it was like nothing I've ever seen before, the reaction to that." With Krentz's death resonating deeply in borderland ranching communities and featuring quickly in the local press and in national right-wing media,[38] border-area politicians of both parties swiftly called for the redeployment of the National Guard among other security measures.[39] In this context, the coming debate about SB 1070 would take on an especially incendiary character.

The Governor's Office, while holding the legislature at arm's length as usual, had already begun to engage with Pearce on SB 1070, in particular through Richard Bark, a Brewer aide whom Pearce knew from earlier roles. "We knew that that bill was moving, and we saw it coming," Kanefield said. "The governor and her staff very rarely engaged in the legislative process. . . . [But] on that one . . . , through our team, we did express some concerns." Pearce allowed a number of changes to SB 1070 in response. Media coverage of SB 1070 up to this point, although relatively scant, had often focused on it as being a "sanctuary cities" bill or as creating a trespassing offense for unauthorized immigrants.[40] Both of these angles emphasized the bill as a retread of earlier proposals. To accommodate the Governor's Office, however, Pearce agreed to remove the new trespassing offense and replace it with a provision that created a new state-level offense for failing to carry federally required immigration documents. "The bill's sponsor, Sen. Russell Pearce . . . said the substance of the bill has not changed, but that the new language was offered to pacify concerns expressed in meetings he had with Richard Bark, the governor's deputy chief of staff for policy. 'They had some concerns. None of them were legitimate. All I did was allow them to change this title,' Pearce said."[41]

The Governor's Office and some other Republicans were also eager that SB 1070's provision regarding aid to suspected unauthorized immigrants include clear exceptions for first responders and family members as well as nondiscrimination clauses. This amount of input was unusual from a governor whose relationship with the legislature was strained, but the signs that by this stage pointed toward legislative passage of the bill were prompting Brewer to engage. By late March, "It was clear that bill was gonna be on her desk," Coughlin recounted. "We were like, 'Okay. This is a major, major deal, and it could potentially have enormous consequences.' . . . So we started doing amendments. . . . It goes over here, you put an amendment on, then it's gotta go back over to the other chamber. So we're buying time. . . . [Governor Brewer] wanted to ensure that [the bill] was a defensible mechanism. While we looked at this from a practical standpoint of the law, we were also acutely aware of the politics."

A number of changes that the Governor's Office and legislative Republicans had identified as significant were rolled into the bill through an amendment in the House Committee on Military Affairs and Public Safety on March 31.[42] However, Republican ambivalence still potentially endangered the bill inasmuch as leadership could derail SB 1070 without leaving clear fingerprints. Adams, the Speaker of the House, was no border hawk, having worked quietly with other Republicans against Pearce's bills. John Kavanagh, a border-hawk House member, recalled:

> I was helping push it [SB 1070 in the House]. . . . The major opposition comes from the Chamber Republicans, the business community Republicans, who basically are worried about the state's image. You know, what the late-night TV talk-show jokes are about and things like that. Which didn't make much sense to me because, again, the polls showed overwhelming support for anti-illegal-immigration action. . . . It was mostly legislative leadership that were concerned. They were being

pressured by the chambers of commerce. So it was really more a matter of getting the bills on the floor and heard.

Amid a general atmosphere of growing pressure, though, even those who might have tried in the past to subvert such bills now seemed uninclined. "I'm not saying [leadership was] resistant to it," Kavanagh explained, "but they probably had more concerns than we had about the Chamber [of Commerce] influence." By this point, however, even the Arizona Chamber of Commerce and Industry publicly represented itself as neutral on the bill.[43]

Moving toward a final vote in the House, SB 1070 had captured the attention of opposing activists and was beginning to generate huge controversy, even by the standards of Arizona's already inflamed immigration politics. The prospect of local police inquiring about immigration status and demanding paperwork—which, to opponents, opened the door to widespread racial profiling and the expansion of a police-state atmosphere epitomized by Sheriff Arpaio's sweeps—caused alarm among civil libertarians, many people in the state's wider Hispanic community, as well as immigrant advocates. The broad implications of the police practices required by the bill seemed to summon front and center the racial politics of immigration issues in Arizona, which had often been buried beneath discourses that painted the targets of immigration-enforcement measures on face as border insecurity and "illegality." Steve Gallardo, a Democrat who was out of the legislature during this time but who had long organized opposition to Pearce's measures, recounted: "It now had U.S. citizen Latinos saying, 'Wait a minute, time out—this can hurt me. This can affect me. I can be pulled over just based on the color of my skin. It's no longer just about the undocumented—it's about us.' I think Russell Pearce and them crossed a line. Now it's no longer about the undocumenteds—it's about brown people."

With the murder of Krentz, amid the sense that an anxious public was demanding action on immigration and that a highly impassioned opposition—pro-immigration activists, many Hispanics, liberals, and (usually more quietly) some in the business community—was in play, SB 1070 was emerging as exceptionally explosive.[44] Despite the growing controversy, the bill's proponents were highly confident that if it did reach the legislative floor, it would be successful. With the bill's passage in the legislature now a matter of Republican intraparty politics, the border hawks were certain they had captured the conditions for success. Kavanagh summarized the impression at the time: "Any Republican who voted no on SB 1070 was doomed to death."

Many would-be opponents calculated that the measure would pass regardless of their opposition. Rep. Russ Jones cosponsored a separate bill (HB 2384) that addressed the same local-enforcement issues but in what he considered a more acceptable manner, as he had attempted to do earlier regarding employer sanctions. One of only three Republicans to stay in the House chamber and vote against HB 2280 the previous year, Jones calculated that the pressure behind SB 1070 was too strong to be combated effectively. "When I counted noses, real noses, . . . about two-thirds of the same group that walked on [HB 2280 in 2009] weren't gonna be able to walk on the 1070 vote," Jones said later. The only option that seemed available was compromise. Jones explained that he pledged his vote to SB 1070 in an effort to secure changes to it: "I'll vote for it . . . so that certain aspects that I felt strongly needed to be in there, that changed and moderated 1070, would get in. . . . I still didn't like the bill, and I was opposed to it, but I didn't have enough votes to stop it. . . . And so sometimes in politics, you have to hold your nose, you know, and do what's best for everyone. Knowing that 1070 was a juggernaut that I was not gonna be able to stop but I could mitigate or modify, I chose to do that rather than fall on my sword."

Jones eventually agreed to vote for the bill and drop his efforts against it if his concerns were addressed in later legislation.[45] Pearce recalled that with floor votes upcoming, he left privately protesting colleagues to their own calculus:

> I had legislators up to the last minute come in on the floor as they were getting ready to vote. . . . And they came up—and I won't name names, to protect the guilty—but knelt down by my desk and said, "Russell, you're gonna lose the bill in the House. If you just make two or three changes, I can get you the votes." And I said, "It's a good bill. It's written very carefully. I've had some of the best attorneys in the nation look at it to make sure that it was constitutional."[46] . . . I said, "Vote your conscience."

Despite a sense of futility, Democrats used floor debates on SB 1070—first in the House on April 13 and then in the Senate on April 19—to criticize the bill as socially and economically poisonous, overreaching, and unconstitutional. Republican representative Cecil Ash, explaining his vote for SB 1070, touched on a number of points raised regularly by other Republicans:

> For me, this has been a very difficult decision. There are reasonable arguments on both sides of this issue. I think some of the genuine concerns that have been expressed by the opposition to the bill have merit. . . . When I ran for office, approximately 70 percent of the people who signed my petition, the first question they asked me is, "What is your position on illegal immigration?" And they wanted to know if I was going to do everything I could do to fight it. And so I believe this is a step in the right direction. I believe there's more fear and alarm in the anticipation of this bill than there will be in its implementation.[47]

Much of the discussion from Republicans surrounded how various changes had made SB 1070 into a bill they could support. As Rep. Tom Chabin, a Democrat, noted ironically during the debate, "I've heard a great deal of discussion about the weakness of this bill from my colleagues that are voting for it."[48] Many Democrats, in explaining their own votes, dwelled on these same weaknesses. In her speech explaining her no vote, Rep. Kyrsten Sinema concluded: "This legislation does not solve our problems. It will not make us safer. It will not allow us to stop the drug runners, the gun runners, the human traffickers. But it will cost us not only our civil liberties, but costly litigation at all levels of government in Arizona."[49] This vocal opposition to the bill "was just not to let [Pearce] get by without somebody challenging that," Democratic representative Phil Lopes said of the Democrats' floor opposition. "We weren't gonna win."

Nevertheless, the self-acknowledged futility of Democrats' protests did not mean these criticisms failed completely to register either in media coverage of the bill or among fellow lawmakers. Crandall, who delivered a brief speech about how Biggs and Pearce had addressed his concerns, reflected in an interview on his decision to vote for SB 1070: "If you were the one or two Republicans that voted no on 1070, you weren't coming back."

> This is me reading it to myself, you know, going through—"I hope it doesn't allow that." And in my mind I'm saying, "This bill doesn't do any

of those things that people think it does. And so I'm gonna vote yes on it, and I'll go explain my vote." You don't stop to think, "Okay, is there more to it, though, than this? Is there an unintended social consequence? Is there an unintended message being sent with this?" You try to make it black-and-white. . . . Kyrsten [Sinema] had a special talent for making the Republicans look like idiots on several things. Because she would say, "This bill will do this," and you knew deep down she's right. And yet you still voted [for it].

As usual, Democrats' discussion of their opposition to the bill almost always noted what they represented as the real security issues the state faced due to the border. "We need armed forces on our borders. We need to be able to return fire when fired upon. We need to keep out those elements that make our neighborhoods unsafe by securing that border," Rep. Barbara McGuire, a Democrat from a rural district, said by way of voting against the bill.[50] Though most Democrats represented safely Democratic seats, the apparent popularity of enforcement legislation was such that the party worried that many members might be better off voting for SB 1070. "It was tough. There was a lot of pressure from all sides to vote yes on it. And I was encouraged to vote yes politically, because of my district, by the [Democratic] Party," recalled Eric Meyer, one of the few House Democrats who represented a district with a Republican voter-registration advantage. "The legislative leadership, they said I needed to vote yes. I told them I'm not voting yes. . . . They felt like I couldn't win in my district unless I did."[51]

SB 1070 passed the House 35–21 in a party-line vote. Republican opposition to previous local-enforcement bills, which had been crucial to their defeat, had, per Pearce and his allies' design, completely collapsed. The bill moved to the Senate, which had passed an earlier version in February. On April 19, the amended version passed on a 17–11 vote. "I do not want to live in the police state that Russell Pearce, Joe Arpaio and Andy Thomas are spearheading," Sen. Carolyn Allen, a moderate Republican who was retiring from the legislature, said in a media interview. "I really believe this bill is racist. And my whole district is tourism. I know this will strike a blow."[52] Allen's was the only Republican no vote in either chamber.

SB 1070 arrived on Brewer's desk, and the national media arrived in Arizona to cover the fate of "the toughest bill in the country which [activists] say [is] aimed at forcing out hundreds of thousands of Latinos living illegally in the state."[53] Despite the contentiousness of the issue, the suddenly massive amount of attention from major media organizations caught all sides off guard. "We had no idea of the national exposure that it would get and the national uproar it [would] cause," Campbell recalled. "We knew there was a reaction—I don't want to understate that. But we didn't know [there'd be] an overwhelming response." As Gallardo recounted, "We fought this bill last year, and we didn't have a CNN truck parked in front of the capitol! . . . It did catch us by surprise." Terry Goddard, the sitting state attorney general who was the Democrats' leading candidate for governor, recalled of the days before Brewer's action on SB 1070, "Except for the Super Bowl, I don't think we've ever seen that kind of national focus [on Arizona]. . . . So it was very quickly, you know, way out of our grasp locally."

Almost all Republicans in the legislature had supported SB 1070, but as it sat on Brewer's desk, no one seemed certain of its fate. Pearce recalled: "She never once promised me to sign that. . . . I burned up telephone lines to the [Governor's] Office to get a commitment. And I was fearful she wouldn't sign it. . . . I never got any word that she was against it, either. But with Richard [Bark] working with me, I had some hope that the governor would sign it 'cause he knows the governor as well as anybody."

"We thought she'd veto it," Campbell recalled. "And she thought long and hard about it." As the days wore on following the bill's legislative passage, the prominence of anti–SB 1070 protests increased. Kanefield recalled: "[We didn't] know what a big deal it was going to become. I mean, every bill is important and has interest groups. I think what was probably the most surprising thing about Senate Bill 1070, at least from my memory, was that there was pretty fierce opposition to it, with rallies and protest and everything else, staged at the legislature itself. . . . [A]nd they were very good at organizing themselves to get their people down [to the capitol], and they were very good about generating media."

With protesters speaking of economic boycotts, resonant of the economically damaging King holiday controversy and the state's pariah status twenty years earlier, the business community seemed to grow increasingly concerned as the bill sat on the governor's desk. Fears of a boycott sharpened when Raúl Grijalva, one of Arizona's members of Congress, added his voice to calls for a boycott while Brewer was deciding on the bill.[54] The business lobby's response still seemed scattered, though. As Kanefield recalled, "I don't think they [business interests] saw this coming. By the time they figured it out, it was too late to mobilize their forces. And they probably were in a little bit of a conflict because they generally align themselves with Republican interests." Brewer continued to hold her cards close to her chest. On April 22, she appeared at an event hosted by the Hispanic social service organization Chicanos por la Causa, where attendees cried out at her for a veto as she left. "I have heard your concern about immigration reform," she told attendees. "While I'm not prepared to announce a decision on Senate Bill 1070 this evening, I can tell you what I decide will be based on what is right for Arizona."[55]

With objections to the bill piling up from both within the Republican coalition and outside it, the governor weighed her options. "We had a robust conversation," Coughlin recalls, "which she entertained. . . . There were a lot of people in the room. She heard the debate. It was a full-on debate." Some participants, including Grant Woods, the former Republican state attorney general, encouraged Brewer to veto the bill because if enacted it would prompt racial profiling and expensive litigation.[56] Notwithstanding the loud opposition to the bill, the governor maintained a sense that it was broadly supported—perhaps even more than it would have been without the prominent protests against it and the increasing immersion of the bill within the contentious framework of national media coverage and politics. Coughlin recalled how, looking toward polls of Republican voters who would decide if Brewer would be renominated, "we knew how important the issue was to the electorate, to the Republican electorate. . . . We had tested the bill amongst Republican voters. I mean, we knew the passion that people had on this issue, which was not being assisted at all from the other side of the aisle, either. They just kept throwing gas on the debate." In the issue's politics, the general public's apparent overwhelming frustration with unauthorized immigration seemed to fuse with the particular grassroots Republican anxiety about the border. As Kanefield put it, "I think [Brewer] had a pretty good sense that most Arizonans were concerned and frustrated by this and . . . knew who the players were who were opposing this [bill], and of course the minority interest groups have their reasons, and that's understandable. The business community had its reasons."

This impression of the general public's angst was connected closely to the expectation by Brewer's inner circle that a veto would mean certain defeat in the upcoming primary election, where the governor was already being painted as insufficiently conservative. Moreover, she also faced the loss of what aides saw as her entire gubernatorial legacy.

CHUCK COUGHLIN: From my perspective, where I just completely hemorrhaged, was we've done all this work to right the state's fiscal ship, and you're telling me we're gonna hand the governorship over in this next election to one of these guys who's not worked or come up with one credible idea how to solve the state's fiscal problems? And we're gonna hand the boat, our party's nomination, over to one of these clowns?

INTERVIEWER: And that was your view—

CC: Absolutely.

INTERVIEWER: That if she vetoed it, that would be it.

CC: Absolutely. We're done.

Brewer signed SB 1070 on April 23 after four days of consideration, announcing her decision at a press conference, where she conferred her signature with representatives of law enforcement looking on:

For weeks, this legislation has been the subject of vigorous debate and intense criticism. . . . Though many people disagree, I firmly believe it represents what's best for Arizona. . . . There is no higher priority than protecting the citizens of Arizona. We cannot sacrifice our safety to the murderous greed of drug cartels. We cannot stand idly by as drop houses, kidnappings and violence compromise our quality of life. We cannot delay while the destruction happening south of our international border creeps its way north. We in Arizona have been more than patient waiting for Washington to act. But decades of federal inaction and misguided policy have created a dangerous and unacceptable situation.[57]

Brewer took exception to the notion that the bill licensed racial profiling. She addressed this issue extensively in her public statement upon signing SB 1070, saying that she had worked with legislators to strengthen its civil rights protections, while also issuing an executive order to institute law enforcement training for the implementation of the law.[58] "My signature today represents my steadfast support for enforcing the law—both *against* illegal immigration *and* against racial profiling."[59] But the divisive die of SB 1070 had been solidly cast.

DEFENDING ARIZONA

As denunciations of the new law began instantly at the local, national, and even international level with the government of Mexico registering its protests,[60] Brewer insisted upon signing the bill that she would not be cowed by what she portrayed as outside pressure: "We must acknowledge the truth—people across America are watching Arizona, seeing how we implement this law, ready to jump on even the slightest misstep. Some of those people from outside our state have an interest in seeing us fail. . . . We cannot give them that chance. . . . We must prove the alarmists and the cynics wrong."[61] That day, at a previously scheduled appearance at a naturalization ceremony for active-duty members of the U.S. military, President Barack Obama commented: "Our failure to act responsibly at the federal level will only open the door to irresponsibility by others. And that includes, for example, the recent efforts in Arizona, which threaten to undermine basic notions of fairness that we cherish as Americans, as well as the trust between police and their communities that is so crucial to keeping us safe. In fact, I've instructed members of my administration to closely monitor the situation and examine the civil rights and other implications of this legislation."[62]

With SB 1070 occupying obviously contestable legal ground, particularly regarding federal preemption of state laws about immigration, Obama's suggestion of possible lawsuits constituted no revelation. The president's intervention, however, illustrated how in the days surrounding Brewer's signing of SB 1070 Arizona's border politics seemed suddenly unsettled. Politicians of both parties in Arizona had long assumed the general popularity of hawkish state-level immigration legislation, and this assumption had been a major factor in the decisions of all policy makers who had decided to support SB 1070. But now highly visible opposition was emerging from rare and outsize visitors to Arizona politics, up to the president of the United States. National media attention, which had accelerated while Brewer mulled her options on SB 1070, exploded in the aftermath of its signing.[63] Observing this response within the Governor's Office, Kanefield later recalled that "the publications and rhetoric seemed to suggest that the public was hostile to Senate Bill 1070. And that was what these folks wanted everyone to believe, and you had to begrudgingly respect their political savvy."

As the first private civil rights lawsuits were filed and the bill continued to be a fixture in national media coverage, SB 1070 was recognized as having "thrust the dormant issue of immigration reform back into the national spotlight, energizing groups on both sides."[64] Soon a bill was working its way through the Arizona House (HB 2162) to make several clarifications to the law: it more explicitly prohibited racial profiling and narrowed the instances in which officers were required to ask about immigration status. Brewer signed this bill within the week,[65] but it did little to dim the controversy. On April 27, while answering a question about immigration reform at a town hall meeting in Iowa, Obama again personally weighed in on SB 1070: "One of the things that the law says is local officials are allowed to ask somebody who they have a suspicion might be an illegal immigrant for their papers. But you can imagine, if you are a Hispanic American in Arizona—your great-grandparents may have been there before Arizona was even a state. But now, suddenly, if you don't have your papers and you took your kid out to get ice cream, you're going to be harassed. That's something that could potentially happen. That's not the right way to go."[66]

As the weeks following the bill's passage wore on, though, public polls showed majority support for SB 1070 not just among Arizonans but also generally among Americans.[67] The overall public popularity of this type of policy once again emerged as Arizona immigration politics' guiding star—despite it being unclear to policy makers whether the public really grasped the substance of the bill. "Once it was signed, it slowly became clear to us that there was tremendous support for it, even if folks didn't exactly know what it did," Kanefield said. "I think it represented and embodied a frustration, a pent-up frustration among the public." Crandall, who had qualms about the bill despite voting for it, still saw the debate over SB 1070 as disconnected from the reality of the bill's provisions: "To this day, I still believe that 1070 didn't do 80 percent of the things people thought it was going to. The hysteria that enveloped around it . . . was more just opinion than it was fact." Kavanagh recalled:

> I'll tell you something even more amazing about the polls for SB 1070. And this maybe doesn't really speak that well of the people, but when the press had, in my opinion, either recklessly or purposely misrepresented 1070, where most people thought that 1070 would allow a cop to stop somebody merely because they looked Hispanic—in fact, that's what President Obama said about it—[and] even though many people had the perception that 1070 allowed cops to stop people just because they were Hispanic, which it didn't, they still overwhelmingly supported the law.

The issue's immersion in the polarized context of national politics had thrust Brewer, rather than Pearce, front and center as the law's main defender against national elites painting Arizonans in a critical light. Within weeks of Brewer's signing of SB 1070, her political position seemed to improve dramatically among both Republicans and general-election voters as she stepped into the role of champion for the state's frustrated residents against outsiders' accusations of racism. Meanwhile, Republicans led by Rep. Steve Montenegro, a Salvadoran immigrant, advanced another law, all the more controversial for the political context, aimed at ending an ethnic studies class offered in a Tucson high school (HB 2281). Republicans argued that such classes encouraged ethnic division and even sedition. Brewer signed the bill on May 11.[68] On May 18, Brewer's long-sought referendum for a temporary sales-tax increase passed with 64 percent of the vote, handing the governor a major victory on what had been until recently her signature issue.

Brewer had previously only dabbled in border issues but was now one of the major figures of American immigration politics. "Brewer's approval ratings have skyrocketed, catapulting her to the top of the polls in the gubernatorial race and launching what may be the biggest political comeback of the year in the U.S.," one conservative news outlet surmised.[69] Choosing the more popular side had aided her among the general electorate. Equally important, in the minds of her advisers, was the polarized nature of the national political environment that structured debate over the bill and that they saw as helping to solidify her position among right-wing Republicans who had just months earlier disparaged her. Coughlin recalled:

> There was a path where she could have potentially vetoed [SB 1070], if [Obama] had called her and said, "I'm coming out to Arizona. I'm gonna be there. I want to go down to the border with you. I want to understand this issue. I want you and me to work together to figure out what that means, to secure the border. 'Cause I believe what you're saying is that you don't want the law to be discriminatory towards people." . . . So my viewpoint was—and it was validated then by what happened with her popularity—what the president essentially did [instead] was make her an iconic hero in this highly partisan environment.

Notwithstanding whether cooperation between Obama and Brewer truly represented a viable possibility for either of them, there was no question that the contrast between Brewer and her supposed liberal and establishment critics had considerably aided her. As one erstwhile rival for the Republican gubernatorial nomination lamented later, "She's certainly captured the imagination of most of the conservative pundits that are listened to by many of your typical Republican voters. . . . Her name is daily mentioned on most of the shows, so she's getting astounding amounts of free advertising, and it's very, very difficult to compete with that in this atmosphere."[70] Bruce Merrill, a veteran Arizona political scientist and pollster, observed: "The more the liberal media rails against Arizona and against [Brewer], the more it helps her."[71]

The Obama administration's May announcement that it would redeploy the National Guard to the border met with a response from Brewer both expressing skepticism and taking credit for getting the federal government to act.[72] Brewer's meeting with Obama at the White House on June 3—which the two described as "cordial" despite an ongoing though largely one-sided war of words[73]—underlined the stature she had gained from signing SB 1070. In the shadow of an impending federal legal challenge against Arizona, the civility of the exchange did little to close a rift of a markedly partisan character. Kanefield recalled: "I went and met with President Obama and the governor to talk about 1070 after its passage but before the federal lawsuit. And [this] was the point the president was making, which was that 'we need to address this as a comprehensive national solution. We can't have a patchwork of state laws.' Those were his exact words. And the governor's point was, 'You're not doing anything.'"

In tandem with Brewer's star rising—and consistent with the quandary long faced by border-hawk opponents—the political aftermath of SB 1070 had hugely complicated matters for Terry Goddard, the state attorney general and leading Democratic candidate for governor.[74] He recalled:

> I personally thought [SB 1070] had severe constitutional problems, but it also was very bad policy. . . . We saw that it was a tidal wave of public opinion, and I thought the responsible commentary would always be seen as pro-immigrant and anti–law enforcement, which, of course, especially the second part, I wasn't and didn't want to be in that camp. . . . But people didn't ask any questions at that point. The hysteria or the rush to find a quick, easy, and understandable solution was so intense that nobody wanted to hear, for example, that 50 percent or more of the people in this country without documentation came across legally.

Having led nearly all polls against Brewer until late April, by June Goddard's position had flipped. Although having said he opposed SB 1070 as litigation brewed against the law, Goddard underlined that he intended to fulfill his constitutional role as attorney general and represent the state against legal challenges, also urging the federal Department of Justice not to file an additional lawsuit against it.[75] But Brewer maneuvered to strip Goddard of the authority to represent Arizona in court.[76] "She signed [SB 1070], and I said publicly I thought it was bad policy and bad idea," Goddard said later. "I didn't ever say it was unconstitutional because if I said that, then I was obligated to oppose it or not to do anything legally [to defend it], and I thought it was my job if I could find any way to support it to do so, which alienated both sides of the equation. The governor's people didn't want me anywhere near it, and my supporters thought, 'Well, he shouldn't be supporting it in any way.' But I thought I'd taken an oath on that point."

After confirmation that the federal Justice Department would file its suit,[77] Goddard stepped aside, despite maintaining that moves to strip him of his role as Arizona's attorney general in responding to this legal challenge were unconstitutional.[78] This maneuver marked the end of what had become for him a politically awkward episode but did not alleviate what he saw as the larger difficulty of positioning himself in regard to the bill. "Goddard would much rather be talking about Arizona's economic malaise and all of the cuts to public education, parks and health care during Gov. Jan Brewer's tenure, even if the attorney general has a much more motivated Hispanic base than he did before the governor signed SB 1070 into law," one analyst wrote.[79]

In advance of the primary elections to be held on August 24, Brewer cleared most of the Republican gubernatorial field, leaving only one minor challenger still campaigning against her. Other Republicans were campaigning on their support for SB 1070 in an election season they found overwhelmingly defined by this law. Crandall—facing a primary challenger recruited by right-wing activists outraged by Crandall's absence from the HB 2280 vote in 2009—had voted for SB 1070, and over the summer his primary opponent suspended his campaign to unseat Crandall. Even after Crandall's opponent had withdrawn, though, a number of right-wing activists continued to campaign for the challenger. "If I had said I want to execute anybody in the country illegally, it still would not have been good enough for that crowd," Crandall recalled. "You had to start using all of the platitudes. 'I'm for a secure border,' 'I'm for the rule of law.' . . .'Illegal means illegal,' or something like that. . . . They've done their polling, and, hey! these three things. . . . And if you try to talk about anything else in your campaign literature, it just falls flat."

As Crandall and his campaign consultants saw it, although as a relative moderate he had the loyalty of those who quietly favored a more moderate path on immigration, he needed to win over a certain number of more right-wing voters. In the political environment of 2010, running as a border hawk seemed to be the only way to do so. "And so there it is: 'I will secure the border,'" Crandall said. "No one even knows what that means, and no one even knows how to measure it!" Even after having suspended his campaign, the opponent up against Crandall in the Senate primary still won 40 percent of the vote. In such a climate, even Republicans who had voted for SB 1070 through gritted teeth made their support for it central to their campaigns. Pearce recalled of Republicans who had privately protested to him over SB 1070, "In their brochures, when they ran for office, I swear, you'd think that they wrote the bill."

Moving past the August primaries, even Democrats—to the extent they were campaigning in remotely competitive districts—felt the pressure to run as tough on border issues. "There were some long days knocking on doors because people were just—were really mad," said Eric Meyer, a Democrat who was running for reelection in his Republican-leaning House district. "That was the only election cycle, 2010, when I sent out a border flyer. You know, tough on the border. . . . It just wasn't me. It's far too caustic." The climate of intense concern about lawlessness emanating from the border seemed unable to be countered. As Meyer recalled, "I mean, you have the governor saying we've got beheaded people in the desert, and you could be next!" In an early September televised debate between the gubernatorial candidates, Goddard pressed Brewer repeatedly on much-criticized claims she had made on two occasions in June that authorities had found decapitated drug cartel victims in the Arizona desert.[80]

> TERRY GODDARD: What's hurting us economically are false statements made by Jan Brewer that Arizona has become so violent that we are a place of fear and we have beheadings in the desert. Those are false statements and cause people to think that Arizona is a dangerous place, and they don't come here and invest here because our governor has said such negative things about our state. And Jan, I call upon you to say there are no beheadings; that was a false statement and needs to be cleared up right now.
>
> JAN BREWER: You know, Terry, I will call you out. I think you ought to renounce your support and endorsement of the unions that are boycotting our state and trying to drive our economy into the ground— taking jobs away—
>
> TG: No way, no how. I've done everything I can to fight against it. They endorse me in spite of my views, not because of them.
>
> JB: Well, no, they endorse you because of their views, because you support what they're doing.
>
> TG: That's untrue, and we need to clarify that.[81]

The apparent difficulty of pinning down Brewer in this political environment, even about statements widely criticized as demonstrably false,[82] was underscored by how little she seemed hurt by an awkward and halting opening statement in that same debate, which media reported "as one of the most painful openings to a political debate in recent memory."[83] Unaffected in the polls, though, Brewer a few days later admitted she had misspoken on the decapitation matter, while making clear she would not be agreeing to further debates with Goddard: "I think it's pretty defined what he stands for and what I stand for," she said.[84]

Goddard found himself unable to gain much traction in public polls despite a substantive record on border-crime issues. Regarded as an aggressive state attorney general who used innovative means to combat drug cartels, particularly through intercepting their use of wire services to move money,[85] Goddard's work had culminated in a major settlement with the wire service Western Union that funded a border-state task force to combat money laundering.[86]

> INTERVIEWER: So there were obviously parts that you were working on as AG which were on, so to speak, the "right side of the issue" in terms of popular support. . . . I'm interested in your perceptions about why that wasn't enough to get you onside as being, you know, in the 2010 election, as being the authority on immigration stuff.
>
> TERRY GODDARD: Well, I mean, in fact, I was. And that didn't do any good. That didn't do any good. I think it ultimately boiled down to one line, and it was 1070.

Entering the final stretches of what just months before had looked like an eminently winnable contest for Goddard, the outcome appeared to be cast in the stone of a polarized immigration debate. "In that context, it didn't matter what else you'd done. If you weren't the person who brought forth 1070, you weren't truly protecting the border, you weren't truly fighting the immigration problem," Goddard recalled.

> When we did polling in September of 2010, we found that none of the push polls, where you ask, you know, different issues about Jan Brewer, whether they would change people's opinion of her . . . and none of them moved the needle more than two points. And I asked the pollster, "Well, OK—we just paid you to put this poll out. Which one of these issues . . . would move us closer to even or winning?" And her answer—she swallowed hard and said none of 'em would because the impact of Brewer's identification with 1070 was so strong that people basically, regardless of

what you said about her or in what other context you were trying to compare her, people looked only at that one thing, and that was "Jan Brewer, 1070." So [they would say], "Regardless of what you tell me about her, I think she's fine." In remarkably solid and across-the-board ways. So it wasn't about me. It wasn't about my record. It wasn't about anything else. The election was about 1070.

Brewer, who had begun the year in dire straits, won election to a full gubernatorial term by a 12 percent margin. In an election where Democrats were routed nationwide, the party in Arizona shed seats in the legislature, with Meyer one of the party's only vulnerable incumbents to hang on, and a number of relatively safer Democratic seats lost.

Border hawks awoke the morning after election day riding high. Brewer had been propelled forward by SB 1070 and personified the apparent mobilizing power of its brand of border-security politics. Democrats' losses in the legislature were so deep as to condemn them to "superminority" status: in the new legislature, they would hold only twenty of sixty seats in the House and nine of thirty in the Senate. The intraparty Republican battle on immigration seemed to have been settled decisively in the border hawks' favor. Soon after the election, Pearce—who had been leveraging his own increasing procedural power to advance his proposals—was designated the next president of the Arizona Senate.[87] It seemed that the nation's toughest measure on immigration would be only a first step.

DISCUSSION: CONTINGENCY AND CONFLICT IN SB 1070

SB 1070 had sweeping effects on Arizona politics—quickly amplifying the already pronounced ways in which the securitization of migration had worked as an exceptionally powerful tool of political mobilization. Indeed, these effects in Arizona were stark enough to evoke the type of transformation that securitization theorists have proposed security exacts upon political issues: the elevation beyond the "merely political" that cements elite authority, centers a state of exception, and reorders the broader the political scene. A policy that several years earlier had been broadly considered extreme and unacceptable was brought forward amid an alleged crisis and became law. Then, in the political heat that followed, those who had dared to voice objections were routed; the opposition washed away; a new political power structure, elevating the leaders supposedly protecting the state and its people, stood.

However, SB 1070's sweeping effects on the structure of political power in Arizona did not emerge from just one transformative juncture. Rather, this outcome was built from a years-long state of elevated issue salience and long-unfolding threat narratives, although even the political actors involved were surprised by the sheer level of political attention that the bill came to command. What produced such a moment, where border-security politics reached such great intensity, were two distinguishable though inherently linked political phenomena. For this moment to occur, the securitized subject matter was necessary but not sufficient: contingent political circumstances and longer veins in both Arizona and broader U.S. politics were also important. The confluence of these two factors enabled the securitization of policy to proceed more quickly and farther than before. On the one hand, this confluence resulted in an advancement of starkly securitized policy; on the other, it shot the issue to new heights in the media and the political agenda, giving immigration issues, which were adopting an increasingly hardened tone, an even greater air of dominance over Arizona politics.

INTRAPARTY REPUBLICAN DYNAMICS IN SB 1070

SB 1070 seemed to culminate trends outlined in the previous two chapters. Arizona's border hawks had continually managed to move powerful opposition, achieving escalating political victories that grew from policy makers' particular perceptions of the immigration issue's political workings, given its security content. With politicians across the board sharing broad impressions of these workings, between 2005 and 2008 an intense interparty security-politics competition took hold. After 2008, however, Republican intraparty competition—already escalating in the preceding years—became decisive to the direction of policy. The Republican office-holders making pivotal decisions in 2009 and 2010 were doing so in large part in reference to judgments they were making about internal Republican Party politics. Although always premised on the concept of incontestable general public support for greater security measures, political judgments about these intraparty dimensions differed in important ways from those in the preceding period.

Before 2009, hesitant Republicans had only rarely taken center stage against their party's border hawks, for two main reasons. First, with the Democrat Napolitano as governor, they often saw themselves as able to avoid the political difficulty of voting no on immigration bills with little cost to policy direction: to Napolitano's right, they expected that if a bill were unacceptable to them, it would be less acceptable to her, and she would veto it. Because hesitant Republicans had not previously seen themselves as the ultimate backstop against the border hawks, when one-party control arrived, decisive public opposition to the border hawks was not their default posture. This is an important factor in SB 1070 as a policy outcome that did not derive from larger political structures but rather found an opportunity through the contingencies of individuals' leadership and legislative styles.

Second and more structurally, non-border-hawk Republican policy makers saw themselves as more constrained than even Democrats regarding the range of action on immigration issues that they thought might politically succeed. Much of this difference emerged from their readings of a Republican Party primary electorate, which was, of course, quite irrelevant to Democrats. Right-wing activists had demonstrated a willingness to mobilize challenges against Republican immigration moderates, thus placing greater pressure on Republican officeholders to prove ideological purity on immigration issues than the general electorate did. The "pivot" ownership strategy (discussed in chapter 2), while occasionally attempted, was therefore even more difficult to execute: the required demonstration of credibility within the dominant problem conceptualization, upon which the pivot is performed, was particularly extreme, given the stridency of anti-immigration activists' demands. Lacking the agenda-setting prowess of Pearce, whose leadership on immigration made him a constant presence in the media, more moderate Republicans had to behave in an overwhelmingly reactive way in their efforts against the border hawks. These hesitant Republicans therefore resorted more to passive means: declining to act on bills in committee, convincing leadership to not bring bills to the floor, proposing safe-haven "counterbills," or, most notably in this chapter, absenting themselves from critical legislative votes.

A critical development for the success of SB 1070 was that these hesitant Republicans began to see such passive tools as no longer politically workable. Pearce's growing procedural power increasingly enabled him to outmaneuver opponents' attempts to bottle up his bills in committee. More crucially, though, Pearce and other policy makers on the far right leveraged the long-deepening intensity of right-wing activist engagement in Arizona Republican Party politics, eventually exposing forms of passive opposition that in the past may have offered their users plausible deniability. This was the lesson that the "Sanctuary Six" drew from their pillorying. Positioning on immigration has often been conceived of as taking place in a multidimensional space, where left–right position is significant, but so are factors such as ownership and issue salience.[88] The effect of Republican intraparty developments in Arizona was to remove these multidimensional aspects of competition as perceived political possibilities, aspects that had allowed for more potentially creative avenues of opposition, including trying to set the agenda with "countering" alternatives or passively deadlocking legislation.

Through right-wing hypervigilance and Pearce's clear agenda dominance, the process of positioning oneself on immigration became, in Republicans' eyes, effectively flattened, collapsed into a single dimension wherein one's left–right position on the border was the only factor that mattered. Crandall later described his reading of the one-dimensional political strategy in 2010: "So I'm trying to appeal to the Far Right. You've got that spectrum—you've got your number line. I know I've got all the votes here, toward the middle. . . . How do I carve out my little niche of the Far Right? And that's where you say, 'Okay, I need to use their own language to appeal to them.'" Of course, the difference between language and legislative behavior was by this point intensively policed by right-wing activists at Pearce's encouragement. With no other tools seemingly available, following along one's assertions in a scrupulously consistent way seemed the only viable choice.

NATIONAL POLITICS AND POLARIZATION IN THE ELECTIONS OF 2010

Those intraparty dynamics were shaped by an increasingly engaged right-wing grass roots. As 2010 progressed, however, the seemingly less engaged general-election audience became paramount. In appeals to this lower-information electorate, the apparent dimensionality of immigration positioning became even simpler: you were either for SB 1070 or against it. In Arizona immigration politics, this binary quality was a new development. Even amid the earlier consensus that immigration had to be treated as a security issue, politicians had not seen being politically "for" border security as an either–or proposition and had instead positioned themselves as supporting border security in ways that possessed considerable multidimensionality and texture. In 2010, this flexibility was no longer available to them: SB 1070 had become a litmus test for a border-security issue that had risen to peerless dominance on the Arizona political agenda, reshaping the distribution of power and proving a potent tool for those who captured its energy.

How did this change occur? Institutions had earlier seemed to play a key role in providing agenda-setting opportunities that anti–border hawks employed to create multidimensionality in the issue. By 2010, the governorship had transitioned from a politician who considered it important to counter Republican border hawks to one who was not primarily interested in border issues and was significantly preoccupied. The loss of that bully pulpit combined with an apparent paucity of other opportunities to rival Pearce's agenda-setting ability on immigration—especially within a Republican Party where policy makers saw relatively moderate positions as continuously losing credibility. With budget issues dominating at the state capitol, there was a noticeable lack of attention to even attempting such moves on immigration. In sum, by 2010 policy makers saw few alternative ways to plausibly represent themselves to the public as "tough on the border." SB 1070 was the only show in town; positioning oneself on immigration became exclusively a question about one's position on that bill.

Beyond policy makers' perceived inability to create viable alternative border-security positions, however, this state of affairs also grew from a nationalization of the issue that was seen to generate mighty headwinds that, as Goddard conveyed, suddenly placed immigration issues "way out of our grasp locally." Inasmuch as policy makers saw SB 1070 as entirely dominating the discourse on immigration in 2010 and immigration, in turn, as dominating Arizona state politics, they also understood these developments as accelerated by the immersion of Arizona's border-security politics within larger national dynamics and entrenched conflicts in U.S. politics. The rise of "negative partisanship"—wherein American voters are mobilized by a loathing of the party they oppose—has accompanied an increased partisan polarization mirroring each party's growing ideological homogeneity and the Republicans' especially pronounced movement rightward.[89] Although voter behavior has been slower to fall into this polarized pattern in U.S. state and local politics, this process has been progressing at those levels, too, and ossifying in the same way as at the national level.[90] Arizona political actors had been aware of this phenomenon, but the "nationalization" of SB 1070 in the days surrounding Brewer's signing of it was seen to activate the process suddenly, with far-reaching effects upon the issue's political development in the following months.

National media coverage of SB 1070—which also permeated Arizona—portrayed the bill within the context of familiar media tropes emphasizing existing lines of contention in U.S. politics.[91] In this manner, Brewer's aides saw Obama's interventions as assisting her in leveraging disputes over SB 1070 to her political benefit as a facet of broader partisan conflict.[92] Sparring with Obama became key to Brewer's primary strategy, making her a heroic figure to Republican primary voters, who were ultimately more motivated by Obama's purported villainy than by Brewer's earlier tax-hike apostasy. Meanwhile, staking out a viable "middle" position while these discourses swirled was seen as exceedingly difficult. The national attention given to SB 1070 not only solidified its position as the signal issue in Arizona politics in 2010 but also provided myriad opportunities for Brewer to seize upon her resulting close identification with it. Given that, as long believed, stronger enforcement measures were popular in Arizona, opponents of this legislation or of Brewer saw themselves with few options.

An overarching theme in this book has been how policy makers' choices to securitize immigration in Arizona were related to varied opportunistic calculuses that grew from Arizona political actors' particular circumstances. Brewer did not set out to further securitize immigration. Like many politicians before her, she did so principally to defend her political power and advance other signature policies. When further political benefits of securitization became evident, she leveraged border-security politics for all it was worth. Likewise, legislative Republicans who had never felt warm toward the border-hawk agenda found themselves defensively agreeing with hawks in April 2010 and offensively campaigning as hawks in November. In terms of policy objectives, Pearce and his allies reaped the benefits. Politically, the benefits were more broadly spread. The political appeal of choosing to securitize immigration seemed as strong as ever. However, these reasonings were heavily contingent: their appearance as the best political options available was based on how events were developing and how issues were playing out. Perhaps the foundation upon which the border-hawk victory was built was not as sturdy as it seemed.

***

In 2010, immigration and border politics in Arizona appeared to reach its full mobilizing power, transforming the political landscape. Security policies on immigration that had previously been regarded as extreme and unacceptable were embraced and enacted. Then, the political storm raging, those who hazarded to stand opposed were swept away. Underlying these dramatic events, however, were two key contingent developments. First, intraparty dynamics further intensified pressures on hesitant Republicans to obediently follow the border-hawk line. Then, after Jan Brewer's signature of the popular SB 1070, opponents of the border hawks, who already viewed themselves as facing a difficult predicament because of the issue's intensity, saw other possibly viable avenues vanish. Overwhelming media attention to the bill and the nationalization of conflict about it made Arizona's 2010 election into a binary question: whether a candidate supported or opposed the nation's toughest measure on unauthorized immigration. The huge scale of the issue seemed to make it impossible to reshape the election as about anything beyond this question.

The sweeping effects of SB 1070 and its aftermath on Arizona politics saw intraparty Republican disputes apparently settled in the populist radical Right's favor, Democrats further diminished, and the border hawks' formal power at an all-time high. Arizona's border hawks therefore were primed to enact even more of their broadening agenda. Yet although their victory had been momentous, its basis was more contingent than it might have appeared.

4

A LINE IN THE SAND

Arizona border hawks were riding high at the end of 2010. SB 1070 had won passage and gained broad public approval over vociferous opposition. The sweeping Republican electoral victories that followed were credited in large part to the border-hawk brand of politics. The legislators who had pressed hardest for the most aggressive actions on immigration had gained more formal power than ever before— led by Russell Pearce, the new president of the Arizona Senate. Yet 2011 proved to be a year when the border hawks faced unexpected challenges—a year that, in retrospect, participants in state politics say everything changed.

Entering 2011, the long crescendo of anti-immigration politics in Arizona seemed to have reached a consuming clamor. As the previous chapters showed, though, this dominant tone of danger and threat and the considerable power that leading champions of securitizing immigration had accrued through it did not mean that politics itself had transformed into something exceptional. The haggling of normal politics went on; the political tools to possibly turn a different direction remained, but they had not been used for reasons of political expediency. All of the events of the preceding years were contingent on political developments and in theory could have changed with the judgments of the human actors involved. Yet to those who would oppose this increasingly hard-line direction on immigration, this notional possibility would be cold comfort.

The direction of policy seemed crystal clear, and the political forces pushing that way were, from all indications, powerful. Certainly, no one who observed the events of 2010 in Arizona concluded that the political weight behind a security treatment of immigration was lessening. In principle, everything in politics is potentially fragile, subject to fate or fortune. But in Arizona at this time a whole generation of shrewd politicians had calculated, amid the grip of populist border-security politics, that there would be no victory in trying to force this trend to a halt. The SB 1070 episode seemed to confirm this reading of the situation. In the here and now of politics, how successfully can one battle such a strong tide?

In Arizona in 2005, a new border-security emergency quickly grew from shifting political moves and countermoves. Inversely, can such a powerful trend—its mobilizing power so strongly in evidence—suddenly disintegrate? Such a development would be surprising both to observers at the time and to those who study such topics. There is no single, main reading of how securitization processes end,[1] in part because even critical security scholarship tends to see the success of such processes largely as rooted in the power of securitizing political actors or security elites who entrench themselves through the securitization they enact, inculcating new social relations of insecurity and making the phenomenon difficult to challenge.[2] Amid such perspectives, although resistance by the subaltern who is affected by security practices has been studied, how securitization may be fully and successfully contested within arenas of "normal" politics has received less consideration.[3] The course of Arizona's immigration politics in 2011, therefore, opens a crucial window into what kinds of contestation may be effective against hard-line security politics—a matter of theoretical interest, indeed, but beyond that of pressing political importance. As the previous seven years of immigration politics in Arizona showed, the success of populist radical-right border hawks was difficult to beat back.[4] What sort of political mobilization could halt such a powerful trend?

This chapter argues that dramatic shifts can emerge from particular dynamics in the intensely politicized and contested nature of exclusionary securitizing developments. The heat of security politics does not simply translate into greater political support for securitizing authorities. It can also provoke a backlash politics and newly mobilize opponents. This chapter analyzes how, beyond instigating backlash among communities who face the brunt of securitized exclusion, these developments may in particular unsettle center-right forces by seeming to disturb the social conditions necessary for economic exchange and growth. In Arizona, this occurred in great part due to how visible social backlash, well positioned to attract media coverage, drew attention to the state's apparent transgressions according to widely shared concepts of rationality, thereby putting reputations and relationships of exchange at risk. Chapter 5 draws out this phenomenon in further theoretical detail, but this chapter shows how activist resistance interacted with center-right ambivalence toward securitizing logics to rapidly halt a long-advancing policy trend. In Arizona, these dynamics quickly threatened border hawks' heretofore amassing power.

Arizona's border hawks had both sown and reaped potent political dynamics—in particular apparently durable public support for mounting security action toward immigration as well as grassroots right-wing demands for movement on the issue—to convince fellow Republicans to go along with a hard line. Hispanic, liberal, and left-wing opposition within Arizona, though increasingly mobilized, had failed to make a major dent in SB 1070's general popularity. Opponents had also divided internally on whether to support boycotts, which had yielded more limited results than many within the opposition desired. However, business constituencies were growing more and more uneasy with even limited boycotts' potential implications for them amid the larger political response to border-hawk efforts. With Arizona Democrats weaker than at any time in recent memory, those factions within the Republican coalition that were never at ease with SB 1070 or its like faced a choice: they could continue to stay mostly quiet as border hawks pushed forward with their plans, or they could advocate more strongly for their own position—precisely at a moment when border hawks seemed to have amassed fearsome power. In turn, border hawks, aware of some Republicans' fatigue after SB 1070, faced a decision on how hard to push the next steps of their agenda. This brewing confrontation would come to a resolution in 2011. The aftermath would have lasting impacts on the direction of immigration politics in Arizona as well as on how we might understand the possibilities for contesting securitized border politics.

ANTI-IMMIGRATION CAPITAL

Republican domination of Arizona's November 2010 elections offered apparently decisive proof of the broad popularity of the anti-immigration politics of Republican border hawks, while establishing the state as fertile ground for the waxing Tea Party movement. Despite continuing legal challenges to Arizona's laws, politicians in other states were drawing inspiration from the passage of those laws. Pearce's well-established involvement in the American Legislative Exchange Council,[5] a conservative organization that diffuses "model bills" among U.S. state lawmakers, was helping to seed anti-immigration efforts elsewhere. By autumn 2010, measures modeled after SB 1070 were ready to be proposed in at least twenty other states.[6] Arizona was poised to be a national trendsetter.

The main proponents of border-hawk measures had risen to new heights within their own party, while the damage to Democrats—locked out of all major statewide offices and reduced to rumps in both chambers of the legislature—weakened opposition to an expanded right-wing agenda. Sen. Russell Pearce, the driving force behind SB 1070, was chosen by fellow Republicans in November 2010 to preside over an upper chamber where his party would control 70 percent of the seats. Pearce promised a "Tea Party Senate," talking up the importance of a number of newly salient conservative causes alongside the anti-immigration politics he had been laboring to advance for years.[7]

Amid the ascendance of new conservative causes in 2010 that had fueled Republican campaigns nationwide—for instance, opposition to Barack Obama's Affordable Care Act—in Arizona border-security politics retained a particular favored place within the right-wing agenda. SB 1070 had made Tea Party heroes of Pearce and Gov. Jan Brewer, and the bill had boosted many other Arizona Republicans in their campaigns. To border hawks, that autumn's vote of confidence indicated the tailwinds behind their agenda. Many Republicans arrived at the state capitol in January ready to legislate further on the border.

Steve Smith, for instance, had run as a Republican for a Senate seat in Pinal County—a place where old-style, rural Democratic Party politics had dominated since before statehood but that was undergoing a political shift as exurban development emanating from Phoenix ballooned its population. Running hard on a border-security platform, Smith, a first-time candidate, defeated a Latina Democratic incumbent from a family rooted in Pinal County politics for decades. Smith recounted: "Certainly my hallmark issue was border security, stopping illegal immigration, no social services for illegals, things like that. . . . That issue clearly resonated with our voters. And I was the first Republican senator elected in our district since statehood, so [in] about one hundred years. . . . I think at the time it was still a Democrat district [by voter registration], so it's not like you're just singing to the choir."

Victories such as Smith's appeared to demonstrate the success of border hawks in capturing the political mainstream, portending a continuing drumbeat of hawkish immigration legislation. All sides in the SB 1070 debate regarded that bill as having represented a major battle. But whereas many opponents of it believed it was overreaching, unconstitutional, and generally beyond the pale, border hawks as well as some of the Republicans who supported it more squeamishly saw it as a mere reinvigoration of existing laws against unauthorized immigration. In that view, although SB 1070 was a milestone political victory, what border hawks had achieved so far was only the beginning of a truly incisive policy agenda. Pearce pledged his attention to budget issues and offered to let other legislators take the lead on immigration, but as Senate president he promised to "help usher those bills if they're good public policy."[8]

Pearce had sporadically overcome fractures within the Republican Party to pass his legislation, most notably SB 1070, but these divisions had not yet disappeared. In 2010, although Republicans who in the past had in various ways opposed Pearce's efforts on immigration ran in their campaigns as tough on the border, this shift in political presentation did not entail a deepening enthusiasm for the merits of this kind of legislation. Republicans viewed as relative moderates had been progressively defeated in years of intraparty battles—for instance, former Rep. Bill Konopnicki, an open opponent of Pearce, losing a primary election for a Senate seat in 2010. However, many of the legislature's "closet moderates" on border issues who toed the line on SB 1070 lived to see another term. Rich Crandall, Adam Driggs, Nancy Barto, and John McComish—three members of the "Sanctuary Six" who had walked out on HB 2280 in 2009 and one Republican (McComish) who had voted no on it—were members of the incoming Senate supermajority, joining business-minded Republicans such as Michele Reagan, Steve Pierce, and Steve Yarbrough. The political dynamics behind the passage of SB 1070 had moved these lawmakers into lockstep with the populist Right within their party on that bill, so it seemed altogether logical that they might see similar benefits in supporting further hard-line measures.

Beyond the continued presence of sometime opponents, border hawks faced a couple of other brewing problems emerging from SB 1070's tempestuous aftermath. First was a sense among some Republicans that having two envelope-pushing state immigration laws in federal court was enough and that Arizona should step back from the issue to deal with budget matters and economic recovery. Although some more right-wing legislators such as Sen. Frank Antenori sympathized with this position, it tended to be voiced by the usual Republican immigration moderates.[9] More important, however, was the detrimental impact that some in the business community perceived SB 1070 to be having on Arizona's economy. The most sweeping calls for boycotts had not materialized, with Major League Baseball, for instance, ignoring the call to move its all-star game out of Phoenix in 2011.[10] Certainly, "the state's economy [hadn't] come to a screeching halt,"[11] but, anecdotally, some effects were noticeable in tourism and hospitality as some high-profile entertainment acts and conventions canceled plans in Arizona.[12] Tourism industry groups, the City of Phoenix, and progressive think tanks publicly quantified the estimated losses.[13] Regardless of the size of the impact, the backlash, boycott talk, and the negative tone of national media coverage of SB 1070 prompted concern among a business community that had generally said little about SB 1070 before it passed. Tourism industry lobbyists in particular stressed their position to lawmakers early in the 2011 legislative session.[14]

Overall, among Republican legislators, there was a lack of agreement about where things stood in terms of further border-hawk bills. Some were eager to seize the opportunity presented by their electoral victories to advance a broader immigration agenda. Smith recalled of the time when he entered the legislature in 2011:

> You have some people that are like, "Okay, finally now we can maybe get our house in order, so to speak, in terms of really addressing this problem" 'cause, again, 1070 was nothing other than a copy of federal law. And so it's not like it was this sweeping reform, right? It basically just

reiterated what federal law said you can do. . . . When I got to the legislature, it was like, "Now, let's kind of address this in all areas of society." That's when I said, alright, let's address it in our schools, which is one of the bills I ran. Let's address it in our hospitals.

At the same time, Russell Pearce's commitment to addressing the state budget and a measure of fatigue among some Republicans led some to believe that perhaps a "time-out" on immigration would ensue.[15] Although business-oriented Republicans, much like the border hawks, maintained that SB 1070 did not do what its opponents claimed it did, they nonetheless perceived it as having caused real problems. Crandall explained:

> People said, "Hey, the sky is gonna fall if you vote yes on this. . . . No Hispanics are going to come to Arizona because they'll just be pulled over, 'Show me your papers.'" And you read through it, and you say, "Wait—that's illegal if they do that." . . . It didn't matter. It was perception. A hundred percent of it was perception. . . . And then, sure enough, it all comes true. Boom. One after another. Cancelation, cancelation. Protest, boycotts. So then we come back together in January, the next session, and say, "Okay, let's don't do anything further."

Clearly, these two positions—one typified by Crandall, the other by Smith—were on a collision course. And if nothing else, SB 1070 had demonstrated the strengthening forces behind the hawkish side's tendency to prevail in such conflicts.

THE STOCKYARDS SEVEN

Pearce took the Senate gavel in January amid some uneasiness from the business community about the prospect of more immigration controversy but with a formidable reputation as "arguably the most powerful man in Arizona politics."[16] While often regarded as a bare-knuckle fighter, in leading his majority Pearce would also show a more accommodating side. "Ninety percent of the time, he and I were on the same page, and he was supportive," Crandall recalled of Pearce as Senate president. "He gave me [the chairmanship of the] Senate Education [Committee]. He supported big bills that I ran. . . . And so we had dialogue."

These conversations with relative moderates, according to Crandall, included the reservations they held about a number of immigration bills introduced early in the session as the next stage of the border-hawk agenda. SB 1308, sponsored by Pearce and Sen. Ron Gould, and SB 1309, sponsored by Pearce, Gould, and Smith, aimed to create a new category of "Arizona citizenship" and to restrict the issuance of birth certificates to the children of unauthorized immigrants. Advocates hoped these bills would spur litigation that would eventually prompt the U.S. Supreme Court to redefine the jus soli citizenship established by the Fourteenth Amendment by excluding children born to unauthorized immigrant parents. SB 1405, another Smith-sponsored bill, required hospitals to verify the lawful status of patients who could not present valid insurance information and to report those who could not prove they were present in the United States legally. SB 1407, sponsored by both Smith and Pearce and echoing some of the latter's previous proposals, sought to require public schools to report statistics on their numbers of unauthorized immigrant students. In February, Pearce also introduced SB 1611, another "omnibus" bill that would, among other measures, make it unlawful for unauthorized immigrants to drive a car in Arizona, require proof of legal status for the purposes of registering a vehicle, and exclude unauthorized immigrants from enrolling at any state higher-education institution. All of these measures caused concern for the Republican Caucus's relative immigration moderates. "We were very open: 'Hey, no, Russell, I can't go there. I can't go there,'" Crandall recalled, echoing a warning that Pearce had heard many times before.

On the other side of the aisle, Democrats possessed very little policy-making heft. But outside of the legislature, activist groups were devising their own ways to strike back against Pearce and, more broadly, against the right-wing border-policy push. The previous year's calls for boycotts had already caused some headaches for the Republicans. In January 2011, a small group of activists led by the labor organizer Randy Parraz began a campaign to recall Pearce from office using the recall provisions of the Arizona Constitution, which would force Pearce into a new election to defend his Senate seat. Hispanic community activists, particularly mobilized after SB 1070, were on high guard for further proposals from Pearce. These activists could now count on active backing from a broad array of organizations that may have supported them more quietly before but now coalesced in opposition to the border hawks as a matter of greater priority. In the early years of contention over immigration, "we were standing by ourselves! You had a handful of Latinos that were standing there," recalled Steve Gallardo, a Democratic legislative veteran who entered the Senate in 2011. Following the controversy over SB 1070, however, Gallardo stated, "you have an immigration march, you have labor involved, the Democratic Party, you have all these progressive groups. These groups were not with us [before]. They weren't. You didn't have the Sierra Club with us." While Arizona's left-leaning activist organizations occupied a clear minority position within the state's politics, they were closing ranks at a time when business groups within the Republican coalition were becoming more mobilized in urging a cooling-off on immigration issues.

As the legislative session of 2011 began, budget and economic bills indeed appeared to take precedence. Immigration measures still percolated through committees, but they met a less-than-enthusiastic reception. Pearce's position as Senate president meant that he could guide bills he favored to committees friendliest to their passage and control the flow of business to the floor, but the initial difficulties that his bills encountered soon raised eyebrows. By February, it was clear that "influential business groups," including the Arizona Chamber of Commerce and Industry, "[had] lined up against the immigration measures."[17] That month Pearce removed the two Fourteenth Amendment bills from the Senate Judiciary Committee—which, despite being chaired by his ally Gould, did not seem to have the votes to pass them—and moved them to the more amenable Appropriations Committee. In Senate Appropriations, Crandall was the sole Republican to vote against the bills. "We keep moving down this road, and the hotel industry is saying, 'Hey, we just barely convinced the world that we're not crazy,'" Crandall said in a media interview at the time. "What's the image we're trying to portray? Where does it stop?"[18] Border hawks brushed aside this argument. "We're not doing this because we enjoy doing these things," Gould said at the time. "We're doing it because it's essential to the survival of Arizona."[19] Pearce's omnibus bill, SB 1611, also squeaked through by a single vote in the Appropriations Committee.

Although the birthright citizenship bills had passed their initial test, Crandall told reporters that within the Senate as a whole he was not alone in his opposition. "There's numerous people who are 'no' now once you get it into the entire body."[20]

Crandall had strong reasons to believe this even though border hawks had often used the twin cudgels of popular support and grassroots vehemence to subdue Republican opposition. In a more social echo of the way moderate legislative Republicans had regularly met with each other in the past, at the start of the 2011 legislative session Crandall and like-minded Republican colleagues began meeting regularly in a private room at a long-established Phoenix steakhouse, the Stockyards Restaurant. "We called ourselves the 'Stockyards Seven,'" Crandall recalled: "Justice [Sandra Day] O'Connor, when she was a state senator . . . ,[21] her group would go and meet at the Stockyards. . . . We decided to resurrect that. People would come and mosey in, and we'd stay for two to three hours in the back room. They'd close the doors and let us have that whole back room to ourselves."

Although the group was not as numerically fixed as the epithet suggests—some members stopped attending over the course of these meetings, and others joined in later—meetings in early 2011 included several senators who bore border-related battle scars: Crandall, Driggs, and Barto (three of the Sanctuary Six) as well as McComish. Other members included business-oriented Republicans whose ideology resembled more traditional pre–Tea Party conservatism. These informal meetings allowed for like-minded colleagues to fraternize over the Senate scuttlebutt while building support for their own priorities. "We'd talk about [how] this or that bill's gonna be coming up—it was gossip," Crandall said.

Although the immigration-related bills circulating through the legislature in early 2011 did not seem to have a completely clear path forward, their lingering presence deepened the concern of business groups. On March 14, the Greater Phoenix Chamber of Commerce sent an open letter to Pearce signed by sixty-four business executives and asking him to ease off controversial immigration measures:

> We strongly believe it is unwise for the Legislature to pass any additional immigration legislation. . . . Arizona's lawmakers and citizens are right to be concerned about illegal immigration. But we must acknowledge that

when Arizona goes it alone on this issue, unintended consequences inevitably occur. . . . It is an undeniable fact that each of our companies and
our employees were impacted by the boycotts and the coincident negative image [after the passage of SB 1070]. Tourism, one of our state's largest industries and employment centers, also suffered. . . . Let us be clear:
*our dissension with legislative action on the state level does not translate
to our being "pro–illegal immigration."* . . . [W]e urge the Legislature to
redirect its energy by joining us in pressing the federal government for
meaningful immigration reform.[22]

Border hawks were unmoved. "I'm sorry, so we're gonna look at our economic footprint over what we're just supposed to be doing as a matter of
right and wrong, as a matter of law, as a matter of protecting our citizenry?" Smith later said in a typical formulation. "Hey, I'm a capitalist
like anybody else. However, I am not gonna put a company's economic
interest above safety and our country's safety interests." Against this position, Democrats were in league with business organizations, despite
some of the Democrats' allies on the left having instigated or supported
the boycotts. In addition to all the usual reasons Democrats opposed this
policy push, they found a complementing argument that further legislation on immigration would trigger more economic damage. "You want
another boycott of Arizona? You continue on and hurt Arizona's economy. Go ahead. Do these bills," Gallardo explained elected Democrats'
arguments on the matter. "It got the Chamber [of Commerce] involved
big time. I did not see them more involved than in the 2011 fight," he
recalled.

Major business lobbies by this point seemed clearly prepared to provide the kind of political cover that unenthusiastic Republicans had found
lacking in the SB 1070 debate. But those Republicans' willingness to vote
against such measures still had not been tested against the border hawks'
continued use of grassroots pressure and broad popularity to twist the
arms of the unwilling. After the new immigration bills' relatively rocky
committee approvals, many legislators were unsure about when and
whether Pearce would move them to the floor at all. "We weren't expect-
ing them," Crandall said. "We knew they were out there, but we thought
that Russell understood well enough that, hey, we were never going to be
a yes on those." With the possibility of confrontation brewing as Pearce

made moves to usher the bills along, the issue arose in the back room of the Stockyards.

> RICH CRANDALL: There's just so much hearsay that what are we going to do if these bills come up? . . . And we've been meeting for at least two or three months at the Stockyards. . . . So we had that, and we were prepared. We were prepared that when they came up, we were going to vote no.
>
> INTERVIEWER: All of you together.
>
> RC: All of us together. . . . Everybody had met with us, just saying, "Hey, guys, we need you to be our backstop to any more crazy stuff. We can't afford any more of this. . . ." We're starting to think a little more pragmatic: How about we focus on other issues besides immigration, once and for all? . . . And so we were prepared because we had been having those meetings.

On March 16, two days after the business executives delivered their open letter, Pearce held the gavel as Senate Republicans passed a number of contentiously negotiated budget-slashing bills. The day marked an applauded moment in Pearce's leadership as he led his caucus to a unified conclusion and advanced the session's centerpiece legislation. The next day he brought the five immigration bills to the Senate floor.

Pearce had in the past pushed bills to the floor even with fellow Republicans vowing their opposition—sometimes succeeding at calling their bluff (as with SB 1070) and at other times failing. His gambit on March 17 was therefore an audacious but not unprecedented bet that the forces that had consolidated Republicans behind his agenda in 2010 would again be what counted most in the end. "We had told Russell we were gonna be a no on it. He knew that. I think he thought that, 'oh, when you have to go to the Board of Truth, you're gonna be a yes on this. I'm sure you are,'" Crandall recalled. The decision to cause action on these bills on that day came as a surprise to those not directly involved in advancing them. With the Senate's nine Democrats solid in their opposition, the bills could tolerate only five Republican defections if they were to pass.

The initial hour and a half of discussion on the floor during the Committee of the Whole—during which senators heard amendments and moved the bills toward final votes—played out largely as a debate between the bills' Republican sponsors and the chamber's Democrats. Democrats offered blistering critiques, usually aimed at the political center. "If an individual comes into a hospital, hospitals are in the business of doing one thing, and that is to save and preserve life. That being the case, I just don't see how hospitals are going to now have to become ICE agents," Democratic senator Leah Landrum Taylor said regarding SB 1405. Commenting on one of the provisions of SB 1611, Pearce's omnibus bill, Democratic senator David Schapira said: "To say that our community colleges and universities are also going to have to be immigration agents, that they also are going to have to determine immigration status, and that now not only can they not offer in-state tuition—which is said and done—they can't even admit a student, again, I ask: What is the cost to our future as a state and as a country when we pass legislation that says we will no longer educate our students?" "What state makes it illegal to go to college?!," Gallardo asked more pointedly. Some sounded warnings about racism. "Personally, I feel that there is a lot of hate associated with these bills," Democratic senator Olivia Cajero Bedford commented. It was largely Gallardo who raised the specter of business opposition that loomed over the entire debate. "There's a reason why many members within the business community have come out and opposed so many of these bills," Gallardo said. "Do we want another round of national boycotts on the state of Arizona?"[23]

In response, repeating long-standing arguments, the Senate's Republican border hawks disputed that the bills represented anything radical or discriminatory, contending that they instead simply extended existing legal principles and aimed to address major issues for which the public was demanding answers. Regarding the Fourteenth Amendment bills, the border hawks were saying, as Smith put it, "All we really want to do with this is let's ask the Supreme Court, 'You tell us,' and let them make the decision for us." Pearce argued that birthright citizenship for the U.S.-born children of unauthorized residents was "nothing but amnesty through birth." Smith also defended his own proposal addressing hospitals, SB 1405, as straightforward and simple: "We are not turning our hospital admin people into ICE agents. . . . I just want them to make a phone call. No detaining, no arresting, no laborious reports. A simple phone call. It'd be no different if we saw someone breaking into a car outside." Border hawks were unmoved by talk of outside opposition. "That's the kind of black eye I'd like to have," Pearce said. "America's on our side, from coast to coast. . . . All [SB 1611] does is to codify what the voters have spoken on time and time again. Enough is enough."[24] Each bill moved forward to final consideration without roll-call votes.

The silence of the Stockyards group then ended. While the chamber was casting its ballots on the first measure—SB 1308, one of the Fourteenth Amendment bills—Sen. Steve Yarbrough rose to explain his vote against it:

> I am appropriately described as a hawk when it comes to the issue of illegal immigration. I believe I've voted for every measure intended to address illegal immigration during my time in the legislature. . . . So, is there any sufficiently compelling reason to vote no? Well, yes, there is clearly one: I do not believe these bills will accomplish their objective. I am persuaded that they will not result in getting the United States Supreme Court to address the fundamental question of whether the Fourteenth Amendment would allow birthright citizenship to not be extended to the U.S.-born children of illegal immigrants.[25]

"It's very difficult to tailor legislation to specifically get the Supreme Court to take certiorari for it. . . . [I]f someone has better language, they should have amended this bill," Sen. Andy Biggs, the majority leader, said in defense of the measure.[26] During the vote on SB 1309, which would create a separate legal category of Arizona citizenship, Sen. Adam Driggs rose to make a more categorical objection than had been voiced so far. Holding a signed copy of *The Making of America* by the right-wing Mormon writer W. Cleon Skousen, Driggs quoted Skousen on the citizenship clause of the Fourteenth Amendment:

> "The provision gives every human being born or naturalized in the United States the RIGHT"—and he puts "right" in all-caps—"to citizenship in both the United States and the state where the person resides. The only exceptions are children born to foreign diplomats, and children born to enemies during wartime occupation." The only exceptions—to a person I respect greatly, and I know other people in this chamber respect this man greatly also, because this book is on desks of members in this chamber.[27]

As no votes began to light up the Senate's electronic voting display, border hawks invoked the possible consequences of defying what they portrayed as public opinion. Gould said: "Apparently what you're saying here is that you're unwilling to attempt to remove an incentive for people to illegally immigrate into the United States. So when your constituents come up and ask you, 'Why don't you do something about this?,' you can reflect back on this bill and how this bill failed. So I'd be kind of interested to see how you're going to explain yourself to your constituent emails that'll start coming in momentarily."[28]

Both Senate citizenship bills failed by significant margins—SB 1308 on a 12–18 vote and SB 1309 on an 11–19 vote. Senators Barto, Crandall, Driggs, McComish, Yarbrough, John Nelson, and Michele Reagan all held the line against both of them, as did Republican dissenters Frank Antenori and Steve Pierce.

With the day not proceeding as border hawks had hoped, the Senate moved to consider Smith's bills—SB 1405, regarding hospitals, and SB 1407, regarding data gathering by public schools. Smith rose to defend the first of these measures:

> The State of Arizona spends between $700 and $800 million per year—per year—on free health care for illegals. We just passed a budget yesterday, and our budget shortfall was over $1 billion, as you know. . . . We wouldn't have made the cuts that we had to make yesterday—tough cuts, very tough cuts. You've got understand: Whose money do you want to cut and take? The agencies'? Education? Your tax dollars? Your children's tax dollars? Or, stop giving free things to do those who don't deserve it?[29]

Crandall replied with some incredulity. "The largest percentage of uncompensated care at any hospital is from emergency services," he said. "And I appreciate when Senator Smith was drafting this bill, he excluded that part. . . . You cannot stand up and say we could have avoided yesterday's cuts had this bill passed."[30] Barto offered a more ambivalent appraisal:

> It's a really difficult bill for me to vote on because I agree so much with my colleagues voting aye. . . . I would score very well if I voted aye on dealing with illegal immigration. I think it would have an impact. But I think it would have a more negative impact on our business community

and the citizenry, and the rights of Arizona and U.S. citizens. . . . How much regulation are we going to put on private business to address this problem? I think this is a good line to draw at this point in time.[31]

To many who were voting yes, however, fiscal impacts were clearly secondary. Sen. Sylvia Allen said:

I also agree with the senator. . . . who explains that the bill doesn't save us any money. It's a statement saying that we have problems in our state created by people who care less about honoring our laws, but want to come here and reap the benefits of our lifestyle that people before them paid the price to do! And it's wrong that we do not turn this back on them, and instead we're the ones who are wrong and we're the ones who are in trouble, and we're the ones who are called racists![32]

Closing debate on SB 1405 as it was failing, Pearce dismissed the claims that the issue was complex. "It's a very simple issue: enforce the law," he said. "I don't know why we make this such a difficult issue. As a nation we stand for something. Either we stand as a nation, or we'll fall as a nation divided. . . . Almost everybody here ran on the issue of fixing the broken border problem. Well, you have a chance to do it, folks. Either you believe it, or you don't. Your vote is what is gonna be recorded, and make that clear to your constituents."[33]

In the following debate on SB 1407, Smith spoke as the no votes mounted: "I know my constituents ask, 'How many kids are in our school system illegally?' and unfortunately my answer is, 'I don't know.' This would just be a way to collect data with no penalty to the school system for noncompliance. Guys, if we can't vote [yes] on this one, my goodness! . . . Don't you care about knowing the answer? I do. My constituents do." "It appears that we will have some work to do before the next election with our folks out in the world as we run some citizens' initiatives since we can't seem to get this stuff out of the legislature," Gould commented as voting on that measure finished.[34] SB 1405 failed on a 12–18 vote, and SB 1407 fell 14–16.[35]

Finally, the Senate considered Pearce's proposed omnibus bill SB 1611. Up to the point of the third-reading debate, Republicans had been identifying numerous flaws in the measures, while Democrats stayed silent. As debate on the bills reached their end, however, McComish mentioned the elephant in the room:

> Before our session, I believe everybody in this body would have agreed that the economy, and trying to drive our economy forward, was probably the most important thing that we could do. . . . I believe that [the immigration bills] could be, potentially—if we were to continue with them—a detriment to the growth of our economy. . . . I got a letter today from a group of business leaders, sixty owners and presidents, CEOs, of our very largest corporations in the state of Arizona. . . . I will take their advice before any other group I can think of in terms of what's going to drive our economy forward, and they say bills such as 1611 are not the answer. . . . The Arizona Business Coalition did a survey amongst our people, and while they said that illegal immigration was important, it was not listed anywhere near the top. . . . Members, like many of you, I supported Senate Bill 1070, and I still do. However, it seems obvious to me that it's time for us to take a time out on immigration, and I vote no.[36]

With McComish joined by the same six Republicans in opposition, the afternoon was amounting to a major defeat for Pearce and his allies. The dissenters were "way more than just two or three people," Crandall pointed out later, recalling how Pearce "rip[ped] us from the dais like there is no tomorrow . . . as he gives his vote explanation to close the board." "Folks, apparently there ought to be a law about honesty in brochures and honesty in campaigning," Pearce began his remonstration.

> I stand on the side of citizens, not a bunch of businessmen that write me a letter. . . . Beheadings in Chandler, contract killings in Casa Grande, twelve Phoenix police officers killed and maimed by illegal aliens. . . . Fifteen-year-old in Scottsdale raped, fifteen-year-old in Guadalupe kidnapped and raped. Officer Brian Terry, sent to confront armed bandidos with beanbags.[37] $2.7 billion to educate, medicate, and incarcerate. Apparently it's not a big deal. The voters have spoken loud and clear. . . . But you know what? It took me a while on 1070, too. I introduced it in '05, '06, '07, '08, '09, and 2010 before we had a governor that would sign

it. . . . Once they cross that border, it's your neighborhood, your education, your health care, your citizens that are impacted. It's you that pay
a price. And it's your responsibility, who take the oath of office, to defend
these laws and protect our citizens! You can't keep passing the buck to
somebody else! The only impediment to enforcing our laws is the lack of
political courage on the part of our elected and appointed officials. You
bear the burden and responsibility of the costs and the maimings and
the death! It's gotta stop, folks. I know you care as much as I care. You've
gotta use the tools that are available to you to fix this problem. You have
to. Your citizens deserve it. Your nation deserves it. You have an
obligation.[38]

With Pearce's bill failing on an 11–19 vote in the chamber he led,
observers quickly recognized the afternoon as a potential turning point.
"In an abrupt change of course, Arizona lawmakers rejected new anti-
immigration measures on Thursday, in what was widely seen as capitulation
to pressure from business executives," wrote the *New York Times*. "[But]
state politicians and other officials interviewed after the bills' defeat said
it was too soon to tell whether the turnabout represented a long-term
change."[39]

Still, it did seem as if the change had come about due to some major
shifts. The mobilization of business lobbies against threatening anti-
immigration politics that had seen accusations of racism prominently
leveled against Arizona—if not against policies that had a very direct
impact on businesses' operations—greatly reshaped hesitant Republicans'
perceptions of their possibilities. To business-friendly Republican
legislators with existing preferences for less state-level immigration legislation, this mobilization very strongly signaled that they would now find
previously lacking political support in opposing the border hawks, even
despite the popular appeal of restrictive policies and a febrile party grass
roots. These Republicans also sensed safety in numbers. "Even today,
that far-right, rabid group . . . want [border-hawk legislation] voted [in].
That's why it still came up" in 2011, Crandall explained later. "And to know
that you've got some people who have your back—I mean, the fact that
there were seven of us meeting every two weeks at the Stockyards—that
gave me the courage to say, 'Hey, I'm a 'no' on this.'"

THEY THAT SOW THE WIND

Whatever the defeats of March 17 seemed to portend at the time, they did not entail a complete halt in immigration-related legislation. Work progressed on a handful of lesser border-hawk priorities as well as on bills occupying the now long-standing consensus on state enforcement against human and drug smuggling. Early in the legislative session, Governor Brewer had signed a bill solidifying earlier efforts to remove the state attorney general from a lead position in defending SB 1070 in court, giving legislative leaders and the governor the lead instead (SB 1117). By March 17, the Senate had already passed a Gould-sponsored measure to prohibit state agencies from accepting consular cards as valid ID, by then a long-time border-hawk goal. That measure, SB 1465, eventually passed the House in April and was signed by Brewer. A provision to require proof of citizenship or qualified residency to receive public-housing benefits (SB 1222) had also already passed the Senate but was held in the House. HB 2191, sponsored by Rep. Jim Weiers, the former House Speaker, sought to retrospectively apply the prohibition on unauthorized immigrants receiving punitive damages in civil trials, which voters had passed in 2006 as Proposition 102, in order to help vacate an award made in a civil judgment against the border vigilante Roger Barnett in 2004.[40] Brewer signed that bill into law.

Indeed, if read based on the number of bills passed alone, the 2011 session could seem relatively productive in terms of border-security legislation. SB 1225, a bill that classified forgery as a felony if it were used to obtain a dwelling as a smuggling drop house, was also signed by Brewer in April; it was an unusual product of the Republican legislature in featuring a Democrat, Sen. Kyrsten Sinema, as one of its primary sponsors. SB 1046, which the legislature also passed and Brewer signed, required that the state discharge youths in custody if the federal government enforced a detainer for an immigration proceeding. HB 2102, sponsored by Rep. John Kavanagh, required photo ID proof of citizenship or lawful status to obtain any state ID, including a fingerprinting clearance card for the latter. It was also among the April border bills signed into law. Yet even while these immigration-related bills were being signed by Brewer in April, the U.S. Court of Appeals for the Ninth Circuit upheld a lower court's injunction against much of SB 1070 taking effect. This decision signaled the difficult legal terrain ahead for the law as appeals courts began siding with the Obama administration against Arizona.[41]

In addition to the previous legislation was one border-related measure sponsored by Sen. Steve Smith not brought to the Senate floor on March 17. SB 1406 allowed the governor to enter into an interstate compact to build the border fence that hawks argued the federal government refused to construct and created a trust fund to gather private donations for that purpose. The idea of building a border fence, at an estimated cost of $2.8 million per mile,[42] with donated funds seemed remote to many. Indeed, the trust fund eventually wound down after collecting only $220,000.[43] Smith, though, saw his proposal as, at the very least, a move in the right direction.

Despite the success of those bills, the desire to legislate on the border was clearly waning among Arizona policy makers as a whole at the same time that SB 1070–inspired efforts in other states foundered.[44] General fears about the economy had tamped down enthusiasm and narrowed border hawks' room for maneuver. "As much as [U.S. representative] Raúl Grijalva gets criticized for calling for the boycott of Arizona, it worked!," Gallardo recalled. As the legislative session closed, it seemed that a new configuration had emerged wherein legislating on immigration was hemmed in by a combination of Hispanic and (later) left-wing backlash and newly emphatic business objections triggered by activist boycott threats. Indeed, business lobbies sustained their mobilization beyond March 17, making a point to help those who had stood on their side, even if not exactly positioning themselves against Republican border hawks whose politics they saw as damaging. Crandall recalled: "They finally started, the chambers [of commerce], playing in political races, raising money for you. That was the biggest one. It was the fund-raising. They had a big fund-raiser for us. . . . And that was the first time they had really stepped up to say, 'No, we're gonna support the pragmatic Republicans.' . . . And so [opponents] started, instead of calling us the 'Sanctuary Six,' they started calling us the 'Country Club Republicans.'"

As the "Country Club Republicans" barb suggests, despite vocal opposition from Hispanic organizers, left-wing activist groups, and business elites, it was not evident that the border hawks had lost support among either the right-wing grass roots or the political center. It was unclear, therefore, that threats to resort to popular pressure and ballot initiatives—invoked directly on the Senate floor during the March 17 debates—had truly lost their menace.

In June, though, the newly active opposition succeeded in lodging enough voter signatures to recall Pearce from the Senate and force him to defend his seat in a new election, which would be run under rules distinct from those followed in regular elections. His allies considered the threat to be weak, and even most sympathizers viewed the effort as a longshot. "Pearce won his previous contests by wide margins, and his political allies dismiss the recall as little more than an annoyance for such a proven campaigner," a press report said at the time, quoting Kavanagh as characterizing the recall effort as "a gnat on the rump of an elephant."[45] Nevertheless, the leaders of the recall effort believed that Pearce was vulnerable given the form of a recall election, in which all candidates would compete on the same ballot, without partisan primaries beforehand. From the beginning, Parraz, the labor organizer orchestrating the recall petition drive, had envisioned that Democrats would refrain from nominating a candidate in Pearce's heavily Republican Mesa district and would instead gamble that a more moderate Republican would emerge to challenge him.[46]

This prospect became more and more possible as anti-Pearce activists gathered their signatures and events in the legislature played out. In an uncomfortable development for Republican unity, tension had magnified between the border hawks and business lobbies. But Pearce was also becoming a figure of controversy within the Mormon community, which is politically important in statewide Republican politics and particularly in Pearce's home city of Mesa. In 2011, the Church of Jesus Christ of Latter-day Saints worked with business groups to water down an SB 1070–inspired bill in Utah.[47] The church was also beginning to promote a more openly humanitarian position on immigration in Arizona, partially because church leaders believed that Pearce, a Mormon, was damaging the church's image among Hispanic Americans and people in Latin America,[48] a potential threat to Mormon evangelization. After SB 1070 was passed, Mormon leaders in Arizona and at the church's headquarters in Salt Lake City, Utah, had begun privately to urge a shift on the issue among Mormon policy makers. Crandall recalls a prelegislative session social meeting of Mormon politicians—including himself, Pearce, Biggs, Driggs, former House Speaker Kirk Adams, and others—convened by church leaders. Although a normal part of the annual calendar for Mormon politicians, the meeting in 2011 turned fractious:

> The conversation was to be around "Hey, guys, remember these are human beings, children of God," things like that. . . . And it's just heated and contested. . . . So fast forward about three or four months. All of us Mormons get a letter from Salt Lake, just saying, "Guys, remember, these are human beings you're talking about." You know, Russell and the whole conversation's around these "lesser" people and just trashing on them. . . . You've got five Hispanic congregations in Mesa that have lots of illegals that are Mormon. We don't ask, "What's your citizenship status?" when you get baptized. . . . So it was really heated, and the church just divided, to where the final straw for me was when a bunch of Hispanics went and protested against Russell Pearce at the [Mesa] Temple.

The divisions that had opened up within a number of normally conservative blocs—Republicans, business, the Mormon community—created an opportunity in the Pearce recall for a more moderate, business-oriented, Mormon Mesa Republican. The dreams of Pearce's opponents were fulfilled later that summer when a local businessman, Jerry Lewis, announced he would run in the November recall election. Lewis, as a media report said at the time, "fits to a T the profile that recall organizers have said they wanted. He's a Republican, active in the Church of Jesus Christ of Latter-day Saints, conservative, family-oriented (seven children) and a stalwart in grass-roots causes [such] as Boy Scouts and Little League."[49] Lewis's campaign sought to avoid a direct confrontation on immigration issues, arguing in more general terms for a change in priorities:

> For the last several years many of my neighbors and I have been concerned about the actions of some of our state political leaders. . . . [W]e haven't felt that the tone and priorities of our senator have accurately reflected who we are. . . . We can work with our wonderful city leaders to bring sustained economic growth to Mesa. We can work with our school administrators to improve the quality of our education and we can work with all people to solve problems without constantly bickering, name calling, and law suits.[50]

The *Economist* captured in a lengthy article the recall election's domination by questions of tone:

> It has become a bizarre contest. Like Mr Pearce, Mr Lewis is a Mormon
> and a conservative Republican. "This is a Mormon family feud," says
> Dave Richins, a Mesa councilman (and also Mormon and Republican,
> like most local leaders). What makes it odd is that "I don't disagree
> with Pearce on much," Mr Lewis insists. . . . Yes, he would have opposed
> SB1070, but for the parts of it that are excessive, not because it is wrong
> in principle. . . . So tone and style have become substance in this
> race. . . . Next to Mr Pearce's aggression, Mr Lewis embodies niceness
> and politeness. . . . Mr Lewis is "a way of getting Pearce's policies with-
> out the asshole," as one Mormon Republican says.[51]

As summer turned to autumn, Pearce's supporters began to take seriously the threat from Lewis. Pearce's backers, including Tea Party groups,
touted their candidate's immigration record and lambasted Lewis as a
pawn of left-wing activists. A third entrant into the race, Olivia Cortes,
was later revealed to be a sham candidate recruited by Pearce's supporters, meant to siphon the district's Hispanic voters away from Lewis.
Cortes eventually withdrew from the race, though too late for her name
to be removed from the ballot. This episode ended up being an embar-
rassment for Pearce, seeming to typify the aggressive style for which he
had been criticized.[52] Just a year after Republicans across Arizona rode to
victory on the back of his biggest legislative accomplishment, Pearce's
political future was in trouble. On November 8, the results of the recall
election confirmed this.

> Political experts will spend years analyzing how a political novice
> emerged from obscurity in west Mesa to knock off Arizona's most pow-
> erful lawmaker in Tuesday's unprecedented recall election. But analysts
> and people involved in the fierce campaign pointed Wednesday to an
> array of factors in Jerry Lewis' improbable upset victory over Senate Pres-
> ident Russell Pearce. Those factors include: The nature of the recall
> itself, which allowed Democrats and independents to vote in what
> amounted to an "open primary" election pitting two Republicans against
> each other. The influence of outside groups, some aligned with liberal
> causes, that allied with the conservative Lewis to knock off the even more

conservative Pearce. Political blunders by Pearce and, more spectacularly, by his supporters. Dissatisfaction with Pearce's tone, style and priorities. Unhappiness among Mormon voters over the image that Pearce, a Mormon, had cast on their religion. Lewis himself, described by backers as the "perfect" candidate to challenge a politician of his own religion and party.[53]

Notwithstanding what factor was most important in Pearce's losing his seat by a 12 percent margin—about 2,700 votes—the development made clear that the defeat of his five immigration bills in March had been more than a temporary setback for the populist anti-immigration movement he led. Pearce, though, appeared to have few regrets. "If being recalled is the price for keeping one's promises," he said on election night, "so be it."[54]

THE END OF AN ERA

The events of 2011 in Arizona have come to be seen as no passing blip but rather the moment a major shift became clear. Jonathan Paton, the Republican legislative sponsor of many smuggling-related bills, reflected later on what "marks the beginning and the end of where I think you can look at it as a distinct era in Arizona politics": "So, 2004 . . . that was the year that Prop 200 was on the ballot. There were things that happened before that, but that really, at least for me and I think for a lot of people, that sort of signaled the beginning of that [era]. It reached its climax with the Rob Krentz murder and Senate Bill 1070, and then I think right around the time that Russell Pearce had [five] immigration bills that all failed in the Senate, I think that's kind of when that era ended." Smith reflected ruefully on the stillbirth of the expanded border-security agenda he had hoped to bring to the fore in the Senate in the heady aftermath of the 2010 elections.

My first year, with Russell as president, there were five immigration bills introduced. Two or three of them were mine. And it was on the one fateful night where all five were put up at once, and they were, all five, defeated on the same night in the Senate.[55] And that's when the turn started happening, where people said, "Hey, we've had enough. Let's take a break. We've got 1070. Everybody's on fire about this. . . ." So, literally, when the ink was barely dry from 1070 passing the session before, the next session, some didn't want to see any more of that happen. And that's why there really hasn't been anything passed since.

What, precisely, had changed? Pearce's recall loss seemed to confirm a real shift had occurred, though the significance of his political demise to the movement's decline in Arizona remained, to those involved, somewhat hazy. From one perspective, the loss of Pearce—who had done more than any other individual to doom the previous elite consensus that the State of Arizona had no policy-making role on the border—was a significant pragmatic blow to the border-hawk movement. As Kavanagh recalled, "There wasn't any kind of a formal anti-illegal-immigration caucus. It was very informal. . . . I would say 80 percent of the movement was Russell Pearce. Almost all of them were his bills that he pushed through very effectively. And the rest of us either supported his bills, or we ran a few of our own bills, as I did."

The loss of Pearce the legislative ringleader also entailed the loss of Pearce the perennial media presence. "He was the one that every reporter would go to, and they usually didn't have to because he'd usually be in front of a microphone somewhere," recalled Jeff Flake, a Mormon Republican with moderate inclinations on immigration who was elected to the U.S. Senate in 2012. "Not having him at the tip of newscasts, criticizing or organizing events and press conferences—it just makes for a different environment."[56] At the same time, some former legislators, including Kavanagh and Smith, see Pearce's removal as an isolated incident that reflected little on the legitimacy of the movement.

JOHN KAVANAGH: The Pearce recall wasn't a backlash against illegal-immigration legislation. I think it was a backlash against Russell Pearce's style—you know, a good friend of mine, still a good friend of mine, but he was pretty outspoken in many ways. And they basically turned their sights on him, and they looked for every little thing, things which were innocent that could be twisted. I mean, it became a real character assassination campaign against him. And then they found a successful candidate who was willing—in his own community—who was willing to run against him. And that was the end of it all. And the other big thing was that it was done as a recall. Had it been a regular election, then it would have been a Republican primary, and only Republicans would have voted, and he would not have been voted out of office. . . .

INTERVIEWER: Yeah. But there wasn't any concern that the general kind of mood was—

JK: Not at all. I'm not concerned about it today. I think my district is still solidly anti–illegal immigration.

Indeed, recall elections did not emerge as a successful general tactic against other border hawks—though this may be because the issue began to decline on Arizona's agenda. Political defeats in Arizona due to alleged immigration extremism, even after 2011, have been only sporadic. With a phalanx of likeminded lawmakers in office at the time, why did no one else pick up Pearce's border-hawk banner? In part, Pearce's removal from office in November occurred amid a string of legal developments that eviscerated much of SB 1070. This trend culminated in the U.S. Supreme Court's decision in *Arizona v. United States* (567 U.S. 387), handed down on June 25, 2012, which permanently ruled out that the law would ever be implemented fully as intended and held that federal law preempted the creation of a state offense for not carrying immigration documents and that stops for not carrying such documentation could not be prolonged.[57] Pearce himself reflected on his removal from office and the decline of the border-hawk movement in Arizona:

INTERVIEWER: 1070 happened, but after that things seemed to have dropped off. What's behind that?

RUSSELL PEARCE: Well, I blame the courts and the Obama administration in general. And our Congress and others. Talk is cheap. They continue to talk about it and do nothing. The courts continue to make unconstitutional rulings. . . . So people throw up their hands and say, "You can't win! You can't win!" And it is hard. It is hard. You think, where do you go from here? . . .

I: Do you think that what happened with your recall dissuaded people from doing this kind of thing?

RP: I think it did, but they didn't understand the recall, the fact that it's a jungle election, there's no primary. They refused to recruit a

Democrat. They recruited a liberal Republican with no record. They did all kinds of games, and they paid people to go around and get people illegally registered.[58] We know that. So anyway, a lot of shenanigans took place, but it cost me the election. And I think it had an impact on folks. The governor got elected because of 1070, and I got recalled because of 1070—it makes you kind of wonder about it, you know? . . . But you know what? I respect the will of the people, right or wrong. What happened happened, and it doesn't change what I believe, and it won't change my efforts.

However, Pearce's failure to recapture a Senate seat in a Republican primary in 2012 against the entrepreneur Bob Worsley suggests that his political difficulties extended beyond the particular conditions of a recall election.[59]

The new political dynamic limiting state action on border- and immigration-related issues has held in the time since then, even following the ascendancy of Donald Trump at a national level. Relative moderates among legislative Republicans consistently denied border-hawk revivals in the subsequent years—including attempts by Smith in 2016 to revive measures similar to the failed bills of 2011.[60] Indeed, for Democrats and generally for those who oppose the right wing in Arizona, the post–SB 1070 episode seemed to reveal an effective formula for defeating right-wing legislation on contentious social controversies primed for national media coverage. Democrats and opposition groups used the experience in 2014 to secure Brewer's veto of SB 1062, a measure that aimed to shield business owners who refused to provide services related to same-sex marriages, which had previously passed the legislature with Republican support.[61] Chad Campbell, a Democrat in the state House during the time of both bills, 1070 and 1062, commented:

If we knew what we know now, I think in the days following the passage of 1070, you would have seen the business community come out against it, you would have seen a better-organized and larger-scale protest. You would have seen a much more concerted effort from not just the Latino community but [also from] a diverse group of people, communities coming together opposing it. That's what happened with [SB] 1062. And you would have gotten that veto, I think. I really do believe that. I think we learned from that . . . [to] use the media and the national exposure to our advantage in certain situations to kill that legislation.

The lack of legislative traction for immigration measures after 2011 has not equated to the utter disappearance of the border from Arizona politics. When in 2012 the U.S. Department of Homeland Security, under Napolitano, rescinded many of Arizona's 287(g) local-enforcement agreements following the Supreme Court's decision in *Arizona v. United States*, Brewer retorted, "The Obama administration has fought the people of Arizona at every turn—downplaying the threat that a porous border poses to our citizens, filing suit in order to block our State from protecting itself, unilaterally granting immunity to tens of thousands of illegal aliens living in our midst, and now this."[62] After the Obama administration announced in June 2012 the Deferred Action for Childhood Arrivals (DACA) policy, granting a form of contingent leave to some people brought to the United States unauthorized as children, Brewer signed an executive order interpreting Arizona law as prohibiting those affected by DACA from being issued state driver's licenses, thus positioning Arizona as much more hard-line than other states.[63] Indeed, Brewer maintained a combative stance on the border, if more often in tone than in policy. Despite the reassertion of business concerns in Arizona with respect to border issues, Chuck Coughlin, a consultant and close confidant of Brewer, later characterized the possibility of leading politics more openly back toward a trade-oriented view of the Arizona-Mexico border as entailing political risks that seemed too steep to the governor:

> I don't think she was willing to risk that political capital. . . . I mean, think about the fights that she went through, the political fights that she went through on the budget, on Medicaid restoration,[64] and still remains a hugely popular Republican figure. I think she worried. I think she worried, despite polling numbers, which I continued to show her, that her popularity amongst Republicans would suffer as a result of that. I could assure her that it would be tough, tough to go look at your friends in the eye and say, "We're wrong about this; we need to go here." But she'd done that on multiple occasions. . . . Somebody's who's shown that kind of political courage I can't ask to do any more.

Indeed, in internal Arizona Republican Party politics the border and unauthorized immigration have continued to be prominent issues. Amid a "crisis" of unauthorized Central American minors arriving at the

U.S.-Mexico frontier in 2014, border issues became the major issue in the Republican gubernatorial primary. Candidates rushed to the right.[65] "[In] the governor's race [in 2014] . . . it was still polled as the number-one issue, border security," Smith pointed out. However, as Dennis Burke, Napolitano's former gubernatorial chief of staff, reflected in an interview in early 2015, Doug Ducey, the Republican governor elected in that contest, "literally ran TV ads about how he was gonna secure the border, and then he gets into office, and he gives his [first] State of the State speech [in 2015] and barely mentioned it."

While Arizona Republican leaders turned more ambivalent on this kind of immigration politics, the aftermath of these episodes had solidified and energized a young activist base that was mobilizing against these border policies through notable groups such as Puente and Living United for Change in Arizona (LUCHA). The most visible advocate of hard-line immigration enforcement who was still in office—Maricopa County Sheriff Joe Arpaio—faced increasingly fervent and well-organized opposition.[66] His "sweeps" yielded mounting legal problems that inhibited his pursuit of this approach; for instance, a federal court in 2012 accused him of contempt for allegedly purposefully ignoring its orders from a civil rights lawsuit.[67] Organized opposition to Arpaio led by Hispanic activists and exhaustion with his approach in some more moderate Republican quarters led to the defeat of the sheriff who was at one time the state's most popular politician by an 11.2 percent margin in his bid for a seventh term in 2016, even as Donald Trump narrowly carried Maricopa County—and with it Arizona—in the presidential election.[68]

After 2016, in the face of this new political configuration, statewide Republican officials showed limited inclination to revive the border-hawk style embraced by Pearce, Arpaio, and Brewer. Although hesitant to criticize aggressive federal action on immigration during the Trump administration and willing to use the issue against Democrats,[69] Ducey, a former business executive, did not make immigration a primary issue in his governorship. In 2019, he quietly dropped efforts to maintain Brewer's ban on DACA recipients' obtaining driver's licenses.[70] Nevertheless, potential ruptures to this settlement arose under Ducey's watch. In November 2019, Tucson voters overwhelmingly defeated Proposition 205, which sought to declare Tucson a "sanctuary city" and (against remaining elements of SB 1070) to greatly limit the city's cooperation with federal immigration agencies.[71] Following this vote, some Republicans again sensed possible profit from more concerted anti-immigration politics. When the Arizona Legislature reconvened in 2020, Ducey quickly backed moves to ask voters to enshrine SB 1070's ban on sanctuary cities in the state constitution (HCR 2036, SCR 1007). Advocates of these measures were taken aback by a vociferous opposition in the form of organized protests and contested legislative hearings that brought international pressure to bear on Arizona.[72] A familiar combination of "mounting pressure from the business community and outrage from immigrant rights groups" moved Ducey to drop the effort within weeks,[73] bringing to a close a controversy widely blamed on the governor's miscalculation. Nonetheless, as asylum seekers from Central America again increased in numbers in 2021, Ducey returned to the tactics of criticizing the federal government and sending 250 Arizona National Guard troops to the border, moves that Democrats decried as stunts.[74] With the arrival of Joe Biden in the White House, Ducey increasingly rallied Republican governors with criticisms of Democratic border and immigration policy—though without a strong accompanying policy program in the Arizona Legislature.[75] Thus, the relative quiescence of Arizona's immigration politics—although seemingly long-lasting—still must be taken with a grain of salt.

For years, the apparently unassailable popularity of immigration restriction and border-security measures as well as the expectation that populist border hawks would kindle and exploit this popularity guided policy on immigration in Arizona in a single, securitized direction. Although a new elite consensus cooler on such an approach has developed, the extent to which basic public attitudes toward the issue of unauthorized immigration really changed can be questioned. "I would just again highlight that it is not the people that have said we've had enough of this," Smith said in 2015. "It's all politics."

DISCUSSION: A NEW SETTLEMENT

In 2010, immigration dominated the Arizona political agenda completely—SB 1070 in particular—delivering momentous victories to those

who had positioned themselves as border hawks. By the end of 2011, however, the issue was tremendously diminished, if not gone entirely from the
agenda, despite the designs of the issue's powerful champions—the most
prominent of whom suffered a sudden end to his political career. As an
unsurpassed tool for political mobilization and power seeking, the passage of SB 1070 seemed to constitute an apotheotic moment in Arizona
politics for the securitization of the border and unauthorized migration.
Quickly, however, the political heavens began realigning to push the border hawks back down to earth. What from the outside had seemed like a
powerful new consensus about the border and immigration had been built
on shifting sands. A new, rapidly emerging political configuration on
immigration mined previous contention on the issue to offer fresh
opposition.

In two ways, the border hawks might be understood as victims of their
own success. The first is visible in the contrast between the period of interparty security-politics competition and the period of one-party Republican control, when intraparty dynamics paved the way to SB 1070. As a
result of the interlocking political logics adopted by the diverse array
of actors who had occupied veto points over the issue, the period of
interparty competition featured a creeping securitization of immigration. It also effectively meant broader inclusion in making these policies:
periods of open contestation with Democrats had generally produced
outcomes in which either the border hawks were subverted completely
(sometimes with the help of opponents within the Republican Party), or
their goals were significantly tempered. These results kept border politics
in a pattern, where even groups that disliked the resulting compromises
were hesitant to undermine their pivoting allies in office. During this
time, Democrats, Hispanic organizations, left-wing groups, and business
muddled on, and Republican border hawks continued to press their
agenda forward against these foils. The greatest political losers at this
time were Republicans targeted as soft on the border.

However, after the transition to a period of one-party control, the
border hawks, with SB 1070, succeeded politically on largely their own
terms. But this outcome triggered a backlash among those groups that
had previously accepted (however coolly) past compromises. Some
among these groups saw SB 1070 as racist and beyond the pale; others
may not have agreed with this view but saw the resulting brouhaha as

unacceptable. First among these newly mobilized opponents were Hispanic activists, left-wing groups, and Democrats, followed later by business lobbies and the Church of Jesus Christ of Latter-day Saints. The breaking open of the issue agitated greater potential opposition and forced the mobilization of the border hawks' foes within the dominant Republican Party,[76] who, with Democrats diminished, now had to act more firmly regarding their preferences.

Second, although the "nationalization" of SB 1070 had helped Arizona Republicans (especially Jan Brewer) to sweeping victories in 2010, it also ironically helped to undo Arizona's border-hawk movement not long after that. If submerging SB 1070 into intense and highly visible national politics seemed to leave border hawks' opponents with few workable political strategies in the short run, it was this critical national gaze, scrutinizing Arizona for racism, that in the slightly longer run unnerved key members of the Republican coalition, including business interests and some Mormon voters. The intense activist response to SB 1070 fed coverage by national political media, which moved the business community to mobilize based on its previously loosely held preference for more relaxed immigration policy and, in turn, strengthened the spines of business's officeholding allies. Business-oriented Republican immigration moderates had previously stood down lest they be isolated. Now they were encouraged by a mobilized business lobby to adopt their originally more moderate stance on the issue.

This specific type of opposition to securitization—its logics and values—seems to be a particular species not accounted for in accounts of either desecuritization or resistance to security practices.[77] Those accounts usually imply a fuller rejection of security logics than what took place in Arizona: although the border hawks' opponents, including Hispanic and left-wing activists, halted the trend that the border hawks championed by eliciting a veto from the Center Right, actually rescinding SB 1070 has been a bridge too far. How can we understand this form of opposition, and what, exactly, made it so effective in Arizona? These questions are explored at length in the following chapters as part of assessing the possible implications of what happened in Arizona for border-security politics farther afield.

The border hawk Steve Smith reflected that the fall of Arizona's populist border-hawk movement and the securitization trend it championed was "all politics." The end of the movement did not emerge from any apparent, sudden shift in public opinion. Nor, indeed, had Arizona's immigration politics at any point tracked objective, empirical measurement of the border's security "problems." What had changed, yet again, was the unfolding political game.

As this chapter charts, contextual developments prompted key policy makers—especially business-minded Republicans—to develop new understandings of their political landscape, which encouraged actions against further securitization that had been unthinkable just a year earlier. Because of the activation of business interests in the aftermath of the SB 1070 controversy, it made more sense to many Republicans to stand with business against border hawks than to continue to securitize immigration, as they had done earlier in order to retain their political seats. The ability of somewhat hazy economic arguments to swiftly trump a securitized way of dealing with the border that had just reached its apparent apogee is, on face, a surprising development—both in view of the powerful political dynamics that seemed to have driven the security approach forward and in view of past securitization theory. Examined empirically, though, the coherent political rationalities underlying this development come into sharper view. SB 1070 had seemed poised to usher in a new political era. And it did—but the opposite of a future that had appeared most likely.

After all, the rise of securitization on the tide of populist border-security politics in Arizona had equally been "all politics" in just the same sorts of ways. With the arc of this book's narrative now fully in view—revealing the contingent politics that built the securitization of immigration in Arizona and then later doomed this trend—what can we surmise, overall, about the larger meanings this story might reveal about the politics of security? What did the qualities of security do to politics in this case, and what allowed these effects to be at least in part undone?

5

THE POLITICAL GAME OF SECURITY
ON THE ARIZONA BORDER

Party Competition, Populism, and Countersecuritization

Why does security so often come to dominate the policy treatment of immigration—even when the immigration issue is complex, the ways to possibly address it are diverse, and potential public support appears to exist for a variety of other approaches? This book has explored this basic puzzle in examining the politics of immigration in Arizona, especially as its securitized policies toward immigration from 2004 to 2011 appeared disconnected from any objective changes in border-security "problems" and its swings in policy direction belied the stability predicted by structural accounts of immigration policy. Of course, beyond Arizona, a pattern of securitizing immigration is also recognizable in immigration politics across much of the post–Cold War West.[1] This chapter takes the conceptual implications of the events in Arizona described in the previous chapters and situates these implications within larger theoretical discussions in security studies and political science about the politics of immigration and security. The goal is to help sharpen our theories about how security—particularly in regard to immigration—operates in our politics and changes the political game.

Distilling the theoretical implications of events in Arizona, this chapter articulates several distinct arguments about the politics of security that emerge from this study. The first two pertain to the growth and dominance of security understandings of migration that result in securitized policies. First, the chapter elaborates how the logics of populism and security interact with significant empirical effect on the strategies of governing elites—which helps to explain why, amid substantial contestation about immigration, policy debates so quickly collapse around a shared "common sense" that articulates security meanings with a populist twist that governing elites see as a sharp political challenge. The chapter also helps to address uncertainties in the populism and migration policy literatures regarding why governing elites so often respond with strategies that "mainstream" populist positions previously regarded as extreme. It argues that considering the specific social meanings of security and the ways that it shapes concepts of political responsibility operating in competitive politics is key to explaining why governing elites "mainstream" rather than resist populist-right positions on this issue. Second, drawing a parallel with ideational concepts of populism, the chapter argues that security can be understood as introducing Hobbesian concepts into the political game, while the game itself remains "normal" rather than being elevated to an exceptional state. This view allows us new insight into the concepts of responsibility that shape security politics in distinctive ways.

Viewing the case from the other end—the end of the intense period of border-security politics in Arizona—this chapter analyzes and specifies the countersecurity logic that eventually prevailed within Arizona's Center Right, bringing the state's long-lasting securitizing trend to a close. Against previous theorizations of what may end securitization processes, this countersecuritization drew from cosmopolitan orientations rooted in liberal concerns about security harming civil society. These concerns concretely manifested in alarm that Arizona was seen as transgressing universalized standards of reasonability, which imperiled the pursuit of exchange and growth. A securitization effort that had been legitimized in particularist terms—specifically regarding the dangers and anxieties experienced by a narrow community—became delegitimized in cosmopolitan ones.

These arguments spelled out in this chapter have broader implications for our understandings of "security politics." At the start, this book suggested that the key processes by which immigration becomes "securitized" differ from the ones most typically theorized. In the latter readings, security—by implying the urgent need for something or someone to survive—shifts an issue from being about choice and competition among different social visions to being about the necessity of a single, overwhelming objective and the authority needed to pursue it.[2] Examining concrete cases makes clear that it is untenable to maintain the sharp distinction that has underlain much analysis of the securitization of issues—between "normal" politics and "exceptional" security.[3] However, it has not always been clear just how, if this is the case, we ought to understand the distinct qualities that security seems to bring into politics—including the new acceptance of what was previously regarded as extreme. To this end, this book has presented an alternative lens with which to view and apprehend this aspect of securitization. "Normal" politics continues— politicians continue to pursue the same sorts of political goals—but security very much still matters because it affects the ways that it seems to make political sense for policy makers to deal with an issue. Security changes the political game.

The story of Arizona's immigration politics makes clear the intense political haggling that drove forward a years-long securitization trend, which underlines the importance of scholarship that has focused increasingly on how an issue can "be about security and at the same time remain within the regular sphere of politics"—that is, "conceptualization[s] where security and normal politics are combined."[4] Such scholarly calls have been made previously, but this book has answered them in a new way by detailing how this combination works in politicians' interpretations— that is, at the level of actually practiced politics in a major case of the securitization of migration. The focus is not on how old security issues of intelligence and defense have become "repoliticized"[5] but on how a new security issue emerged in a U.S.-Mexico border state and how in the entire arc of its trajectory this security issue was political through and through.

The preceding chapters detail these episodes of jockeying for power, deal making, arm-twisting, turnabout, one-upmanship, disputation, and backstabbing among purported friends. So far, so normal—as far as politicians go. However, the previous chapters also show how Arizona's immigration politics took shapes that, if not abnormal enough to constitute a different kind of political life, are clearly distinctive. These attributes have from the beginning driven interest in the securitization concept: the rapid disruption of previously established policy settlements, the muting of dissension over whether a policy issue is indeed one of security, and the new acceptance of measures that would have previously been considered too extreme to be countenanced. If it is not empirically tenable to hold that these effects are the consequence of security's exception from the normal—if, indeed, an issue can be debated as about security without an automatic escalation to exceptionalist or even clearly "extraordinary" politics[6]—then what exactly does security do to politics that produces these effects?

Others have proposed some useful ideas but have not entirely put to rest the question. Migration-politics scholars, more predisposed to seeing ordinary politics at play in such processes, have interpreted such securitization approaches taking hold across the political spectrum as a "contagion" emanating from the Far Right.[7] Yet the wide variety of possible ways for governing elites to deal with radical-right populist challengers raises the question of just why this contagion spreads.[8] "Mainstreaming" of these radical views is a multiactor and multidirectional process,[9] so what drives such familiar patterns? The sudden collapse of Arizona's securitization trend in 2011 underlines the extent to which the border-security crescendo was built not upon political transformations brought forth by an extraordinary character found within security[10] but upon contingent political circumstances. The unexpectedness of this rapid reversal raises further questions. The force of securitization seems strong. What is powerful enough to fell it? When reversals of such securitization processes have often proven tricky to grasp,[11] further insight into the ways they can unfold could be significant.

It is clear that competitive politics are at play throughout the many episodes of this book's narrative, so this chapter attempts to synthesize what these many episodes amount to. If there is an elusive "politics of security," this effort works to identify the particular characteristics of the reshaped political game that comes into being when security takes hold—the changes that security can introduce to political competition, shifting calculations and moving political life toward recognizable and often troubling effects. This chapter draws a line from these questions to the clear populist bent of those who often push for the hardest line against immigration and to the kinds of political mobilizations that may effectively counteract the securitization juggernaut.

The purpose of this examination is not to proclaim new laws of "security politics," applicable generally to all cases of securitization or even just to all securitizations of migration. Single-case studies cannot do this.[12] Indeed, if there is one overarching observation to draw from Arizona's twists and turns, it is that particular contexts are essential to the unfolding of security politics. These developments depend both on a locale's larger social structures, such as its particular racial politics or institutions of direct democracy, as well as on its local happenstance—the killing of a rancher or a meeting at a steakhouse. The operation of security does not reduce to a single transversal script acted out the same everywhere.[13]

Even so, although security takes hold differently across varying contexts, it stands to reason that some kind of consistent meaning is attached to it that is essential to understanding both its significance in social life and how it can be said to "work" politically.[14] This chapter's examination grows from those studies that have sought to identify, among varying cases, the core ideational claims of securitization[15] and employs such explorations to ask how the presence of security in issue contestation can affect the choices of policy makers. This chapter offers some propositions for how security "works" within and upon competitive immigration politics and affects the calculations and judgments of political actors in this politics. Because this question has not been extensively explored in earlier security studies, this in-depth single-case study is well suited to offering such initial theoretical propositions.[16]

This chapter therefore presents some broad initial theoretical propositions in two veins. The first examines how securitization emerged and consolidated in Arizona: pushed forward by securitization logics, connected to populist meanings that opened an avenue to question elite security judgments, and deepened by a particular resulting image of political responsibility that cast a wide shadow of political accountability across immigration politics. Second, this chapter identifies the particular form of countersecurity logic that emerged with political success in 2011 and how activist criticism of the racism of securitization, though not accepted wholesale by other political actors, interfaced with a larger cosmopolitan countersecurity rationality focused on universalism and reason. This discussion sketches security politics from its other, equally important face: how through shifting political rationalities securitization might end.

SECURITIZING IMMIGRATION:
POPULISM, RESPONSIBILITY, AND THE
COMMON SENSE OF SECURITY

The preceding chapters sketched how across time the securitization of immigration in Arizona emerged from changing political calculations. This process was a product of policy makers' changing political rationalities.[17] To grasp why these approaches were the ones that made the most sense to the actors who chose them, it is worth considering, in broad terms drawn from literature on the party politics of immigration, three classical ideal-type modes of navigating political issues.[18] The first—perhaps the likeliest to spring to mind when imagining "typical" politics—is to hold to one's preferred position in an issue debate and try to win it. The second is to try to suppress the issue's salience, shifting debate to different terrain. It is the third—to change one's position in the direction of one's competitor's—that resonates with the "contagion" hypothesis in migration-politics literature and the literature about the "mainstreaming" of far-right views and that seems most evoked by the types of consensus envisioned as typical of securitized politics.

The idea of security as possessing a constrained kind of politics, with timid opposition, is most contrasted against the first ideal type of navigating political issues: open competition. This type of opposition, sometimes in tandem with efforts to downplay the issue, was indeed what Arizona policy makers who opposed the securitization of immigration initially tried to do when the issue began to gain attention. Following the success of Proposition 200 in 2004, though, opposing politicians quickly came to believe that this strategy was not working; Proposition 200's passage occasioned the "alarmed discovery" that treating immigration as a threat possessed manifest mobilizing power. As chapter 2 detailed, these politicians sought an alternative that "resonated."

Policy makers began to see a downplaying strategy as futile for a few major reasons. One was the extent to which fearfulness or anxiety seemed to pervade public debate about immigration. In the eyes of elites, this pervasion of fear gave popular conceptions about the existence of a problem a fixed quality. Policy makers began to believe that, as an opening principle, the issue had to be at least addressed sympathetically. As Kyrsten Sinema, at the time serving as a Democrat in the Arizona Legislature, argued, "What you have to say is, 'I see that you're worried, it makes sense that you're worried, of course you're worried, that's normal and valid to be worried, and here are some ideas that could work better than the proposal that you've been offered.' . . . Don't criticize it 'cause it's valid and real. Be kind about it because it's real. And then try to offer a better solution." Sinema's emphasis on a "solution" implies that this approach was not merely a matter of sympathetic rhetoric. A second aspect of the situation in Arizona that policy makers began to accept as a basic fact was the perceived public demand for policy makers to act on the immigration issue. As Tim Nelson, general legal counsel in the Governor's Office, recalled, "When there's a real sentiment, you've gotta be responsive to the sentiment in some fashion. . . . [A] 'veto, veto, veto, no, no, no' approach would be perceived as not responsive to the sentiment."

Immigration thus transformed from the pet concern of a small number of elected border hawks into an issue regarding which all sides were trying to develop an active strategy. Nevertheless, it might have been conceivable for a new stance both to sympathize with public worry and to promise action without relying overwhelmingly on security interpretations of the problem—especially given that everyone seemed to accept that irregular migration dynamics were driven by economic forces. Or even while admitting there was some kind of problem, a response might have still contested its essence, preserving as an option something more like the open-contestation ideal type of politics. Instead, the alternative stance that did develop traded heavily on security concepts within a narrowed field of debate. What exactly was going on here?

Such strategies followed from several aspects of security issues that, although not necessarily unique to them, provide some explanation for the distinct politics of securitization. Importantly, though, security logics did not work alone to force these shifts. Essential to security's advancement as a problem conception was the populist articulation of security concern by the political actors pushing hardest on the issue, enabled by the consonance of many core claims of populism and securitization. Both security and populism shaped the approaches that Arizona's nonpopulist governing elites took in response. Indeed, advocating security is made simpler for populist radical-right border hawks by the essential shared logics between security and populism. Accordingly, security is also a key part of explanations for how right-wing anti-immigrant politicians so successfully reorient "mainstream" politics. This synergy had decisive impacts on Arizona's political game.

SECURITIZATION AND POPULISM: SHARED LOGICS, SHARED POLITICS

The previous chapters make clear the overwhelming sense of difficulty that Arizona's non-border-hawk policy makers felt in trying to convincingly articulate the superiority of an alternative, nonsecurity path when pitted against border-hawk populism in a competitive situation. Border hawks' intuitive arguments seemed to resonate within the media ecosystem, with the public's anxieties, and against the seeming aloofness of a downplaying response, which came across as denialist. The populist outsiders' ability to put governing elites on their back feet is both a key aspect of the Arizona case and a major puzzle for a securitization concept that has tended to read security as axiomatically strengthening the hand of elite insiders by engendering deference to authority amid threat. Security logics are supposed to empower "top leaders," and these leaders are supposed to be able to use their authority and political capital to quash challenges to them over defining security.[19] In Arizona, though, these governing elites were defensive and eventually had to decide that they needed to live with the reality of a security framing that had been foisted upon them by an initially marginal legislative faction. Why?

A key part of the answer lies in the interrelationship between the logics of security and populism, particularly as these logics are articulated by far-right radical populists. Indeed, populism and securitization share core ideational components that can bind together into a shared "common sense." This single logic was illustrated earlier in examining Russell Pearce's border-security arguments in chapter 1. In Arizona, these populist and security logics complemented each other in ways that shifted political calculations and drove forward the securitization trend. In short, populism articulates security meanings in a manner that corrodes elites' authority to define security in context.[20]

As chapter 1 discusses, it is analytically productive to employ similar "ideational" approaches to identify the presence of populist and security logics in political processes that yield securitized policies. Earlier chapters identified how Arizona's radical-right populists mapped a moral dichotomy of lawbreaking and law keeping onto the key populist distinction between the elite and the people—defining "the people" as in line with the moral quality of the law and against a criminality that is self-evidently dangerous to society, unacceptable, and also racialized. Nonetheless, it remains somewhat unclear just why this portrayal came to compel the political positioning of a wide number of actors who might normally oppose it. Delving further into the case, however, demonstrates that the security logic underlying exclusionary securitization and the logic mobilized by radical-right populists share three essential elements.

Indeed, as has often been said about security politics, "populist politics is not ordinary, routine politics."[21] If securitization can invoke a "politics of the extraordinary" that contends fundamentally over the content and ends of a community,[22] populism clearly contests similar turf. However, the logic of populism articulates with a crucial twist certain ideas reflected in classical articulations of security: it introduces an inextricable antielitism that casts elites as part of the problem rather than as the only authorities competent to enact the solution.[23] This casting foils any association between security and the automatic empowerment of elites, and it introduces a potentially sharp political predicament for governing elites. In this reversal may lie an answer to the question of why—in Arizona and elsewhere—radical-right populists often seem so successful at catalyzing a security treatment of immigration and "mainstreaming" their preferred policies even when the distribution of political power initially seems stacked against them.

What are these commonalities between populism and securitization? First, populism and security share pretensions of broad reach. Radical-right populism in particular shares a homogenizing holism that the securitization literature has associated with the political theory of Thomas Hobbes and Carl Schmitt.[24] Security's logic of the sovereign embodying the whole community against enemies parallels the general will key to populism's logic. As in the logic of security, in the "logic of populism . . . the empty place of power is closed by a substantive image of the people as a homogeneous unity."[25] Both populist politics and security politics, therefore, purport to represent the whole (genuine) community and to mobilize this attitude in exclusionary ways against the community's alleged enemies. In the case of the populist radical Right, this attitude is mobilized against both what is considered a corrupt internal elite and this elite's clients, "typically, asylum-seekers, immigrants, minorities who have been granted special treatment, welfare recipients and so on."[26]

Second, both security and populism fixate on the fear that autonomy, as linked to a general will, is being compromised. Of course, this fixation reflects the centrality of sovereignty in both logics. For the populist radical Right, popular sovereignty and national sovereignty are basically equated—especially against elites who are considered to degrade the nation.[27] In parallel, as the security agenda widens and entities beyond the state become "referent objects" to secure, autonomy stands out as a critical object that needs to be secured. Security's logic says, "If we do not tackle this problem, everything else will be irrelevant (because we will not be here *or will not be free to deal with it in our own way*)."[28] Immigration emerges as a bugbear because the purported threat that it will deluge the community strikes upon "political autonomy in the double sense of independent identity and functional integrity rather than the physical survival of a political unit."[29] The notion that voting or claims making by "illegal" immigrants voting erodes the autonomy of the community through an undeserved participation in the body politic melds into images of violence, invasion, and the community being overrun.

Third, despite the fact that both populism and security seem to summon highly charged politics, both also present themselves as self-evident and thereby apolitical. Security's logic is that contentious politics must be suppressed in the face of a threat to survival. Populism's logic dictates that the community's autonomy and general will must be rescued as a paramount goal that is similarly obvious. This presentation of security and populism strikes at a shared "common sense" between the two logics, articulated by Arizona border hawks such as Pearce. "It is common for populist leaders to employ a language of common sense, a political message that is intended to be non-ideological[,] . . . conveying the sense that they are speaking for, and to the ordinary people."[30] In truth, populists attempt to construct "common sense" according to specific political images.[31] Radical right-wing populists work particularly from a Hobbesian mythology,[32] which holds as self-evident the need to sanction authority to defeat threats or to enact "security" practices analogous to safety in everyday life. Border walls and the simplistic incantation to "enforce the law" exemplify this populist border-hawk brand of common sense.

From these similarities, it is easy to see how Arizona's populist border hawks mobilized security claims naturally, even credibly. Such security arguments are wholly consistent with the populist worldview. This creates an asymmetrical contest. When it comes to the need to securitize immigration, populist border hawks' exhortations contain no logical endpoint. If nonpopulist elites indulge in these arguments, however, they must continually defend the boundaries of the security treatment of an issue. Boundaries raise questions. Why declare an emergency but not punish employers? Why allow jails to investigate the immigration status of inmates but not require police to do the same of people they stop? For nonpopulist elites, to treat immigration as security when it has not been treated that way before requires justification; to populist border hawks, in contrast, this treatment is self-evident. Media dynamics favoring simplistic problem conceptions magnify this asymmetry.[33]

But what truly changes much larger political strategies—by making border hawks' arguments not just difficult to counter but also impossible for governing elites to ignore—is how border hawks' articulation of this border-security problem ties this common sense to the core of populist antielitism. This specific populist addition to the dynamic is not present in a logic of security alone. It creates vastly different political implications for "top leaders" who have normally been assumed to consolidate power through securitization processes. What they faced instead in Arizona was a populist security logic that sought to supplant or at least to constrain governing elites: according to this logic, elites are not the only solution to a security problem, as securitization accounts normally have presented; rather, they are a key part of the problem. In this sense, while security and populism complement each other and overlap in ways that facilitate a certain dynamic between them, each concept introduces distinct and important elements. Populism can be articulated in terms of any number of issues; in any of these issues, elite corruption is outrageous, but this outrage does not inherently map onto the urgency of ensuring some form of survival for some important entity. Rather, the latter is the particular quality that security logics bring, which makes it difficult for governing elites to ignore this challenge when that option may otherwise be a viable political strategy. Both elements therefore are essential to the emerging political quandary that governing elites face.

Consider how the populist border hawk Steve Smith reflected on his proposal to build a border wall versus mainstream elites' conceptualizations of border issues:

> The security things are commonsensical. You would hope that your nation is secured. Why do you have a fence around your backyard? Why do you have a lock on your door? . . . [Y]ou would hope that the simple, most fundamental tenet of any government is to protect your people. Of course! Yeah, duh, you've got to put a fence up. You've got to put a lock on your door. You've got to put a gate up. And so that is so . . . self-evident to people that it's "Yeah, you mean it isn't being done that way?" . . . Whereas now you talk about amnesty, it's like, "Whoa, we're gonna do what, for who, and why?" It's this so much more confounding argument.

Here, populism and security connect through—while adding something to—a distinct account of "common sense." In populist fashion, Smith points to the obviousness of the possible solution (a fence) refused by mainstream elites. This obviousness complements the "common sense" of security, the need to survive or defend oneself—in Hobbesian terms, the "most fundamental tenet" of government. Immigration is a threat, and common sense offers obvious ways to guard against it. Appealing to a "common" logic downplays the claim's contentiousness, presenting the populist border-hawk idea as obvious, even banal. Simultaneously, this "common sense" creates a vector by which governing elites' security judgments can be impeached: they stand accused of dismissing obvious solutions to an urgent problem. This dismissal is branded as outrageous and, by all appearances, corrupt.

Although opposed to these border-hawk logics in principle, governing nonpopulist policy makers in Arizona also began to believe that their positions were coming across in this negative way. The border hawks' apparent advantage had two parts. First, their messages about enforcing the law or the logic of barriers came across as intuitive, soundbite-ready "common sense." As the border-hawk politician Randy Graf said about gaining petition signatures to place Proposition 200 on the ballot, "When you told folks in its simplest form that this bill is going to require proof of citizenship for people to register to vote and an ID card when you go to the polls to vote and proof of citizenship or legal residency when they register for welfare, they couldn't sign it fast enough. Just common sense. Simple measures."[34]

Second, both refuting those points and offering alternatives entailed arguments that were significantly nuanced—thus straining the limitations of the media and the public as well as feeding border hawks' antielitist arguments. It was easy within these perceived limitations for border hawks to make an initial, resonant statement about a dire security problem; it was more complex to rebut this statement successfully. These dynamics, of course, corroded the inbuilt authority that governing elites have long been seen to possess in defining what is and is not a security issue.[35] This corrosion introduced major complications for mainstream politicians as they internalized a sense that, especially once the media had given attention to a dramatized irregular immigration issue, simpler appeals were primed to fare better in the competition for media and public attention.[36] How does one respond to the pervasive argument (or tautology) that "illegal means illegal"? Terry Goddard, the Democratic state attorney general who lost the gubernatorial election in the border-hawk annus mirabilis of 2010, offered a typical and telling account: "One of the things that was going on was master messaging. I mean, I still remember with great pain [Russell] Pearce's repeated question: 'What part of illegal don't you understand?' . . . I ask you: What's more compelling? A six-part fundamental immigration reform answer that says we're eventually going to provide a path to citizenship for 11 million people who broke the law when they came in this country or 'What part of illegal don't you understand'?"

In Arizona, media-friendly populist border-hawk arguments were thus seen as powerfully positioned to shape general public opinion against even vigorous contestation. This situation pinpoints how although public discourses about immigration are important in shaping the way elites navigate their positioning on these issues, so are readings of alternative possibilities permitted by existing political structures—readings that grow in part from political actors' broader understandings of media dynamics and elites' own assessment of their potential control over issue trajectories. Here, possibilities seemed very constrained: against the populist twist in security's logic, Arizona's governing elites saw themselves caught in a trap. Once this constrained position is accepted as part of the political game, it is clear how an apparent consensus emerges that the border problem is, in fact, a security problem: if one needs to adopt a sympathetic and active policy stance, the only viable versions are ones premised on a security characterization of the problem. In this way, the interaction of populist and securitization logics is a key causal mechanism driving the securitizing political positions taken by a wide array of policy makers.

This dynamic did not mean a staid consensus: the political game still evolved in competitive directions. Opponents of the border hawks attempted to distinguish themselves politically on the issue, which was the only visible way to neutralize it as a political threat to them. The effort that nonpopulist governing elites engaged in was, overall, relatively nuanced. It never accepted populist radical-right arguments wholesale but was pitched to voters on many of the same terms that the border hawks used. This approach sought partially to "capture" or "own" the immigration issue because elites accepted the public's fearfulness and anxiety as something that could not be argued against effectively.[37] This strategy was designed to work through a double act of agreeing while also disagreeing, thereby distinguishing elites' own position(s).

The search for an active, enforcement-oriented approach in Arizona meant in part emphasizing security measures that nonhawkish officials would find genuinely acceptable, thus minimizing true "movement" on the issue by not simply adopting border-hawk stances. The result was a security-oriented approach that emphasized using typical law enforcement measures to combat what opponents of the border hawks felt were legitimate problems, such as smuggling and "border crime." These measures were often intended to communicate simple symbolism. For instance, the focus on creating a state and local law enforcement role against human smuggling and trafficking contrasted with the populist border-hawk vision of widespread state and local enforcement of immigration law, yet both relied on similar symbolic resonance. In taking this approach, border hawks' opponents co-opted the intuitiveness of enforcement logics, remained acceptable to allies who viewed the security push with suspicion, and put a new spin on the issue to distinguish their appeal to the electorate while they attempted to steer debate away from the border hawks' most preferred ground.

These more moderate factions argued for the prudence of their own proposals against alleged extremism while also clearly seeking to steal some of the hard-liners' rhetorical thunder. They saw it as possible to oppose many parts of the border-hawk agenda from a position of relative political safety—supporting some measures while nixing others portrayed as going too far. Elites who make such moves have sometimes been portrayed as engaging in a thin populism,[38] but understanding populism ideationally—as necessarily containing some core ideas—clearly distinguishes such moves as something else. These political rationalities lack the Manicheanism at the core of populism as well as populist border hawks' radical drive. The response was about tactically managing a political problem—showing solicitude for public concern while maintaining a sense of the policy's complexity, accepting public opinion but not a general will. This response from more moderate factions is described more accurately as "demotic":[39] focusing on a closeness to ordinary people and their fears, as, for instance, Sinema expressed. Demoticism characterizes but does not alone make populism, and, indeed, nonpopulist elites can make demotic moves on a variety of issues. (In this way, it continues to make sense to distinguish between nonpopulist and populist political actors even after the latter's immigration positions have been "mainstreamed.") But the need to show closeness to a sense of widely held public fear shifts contestation about the border-security issue: the fault line in the debate moves away from the question of whether the security emphasis on the problem is misplaced and instead toward questions of prudence and focus.

Indeed, demotic moves became a way to play political offense as much as to stall populist opponents. These moves sought to recapture "control" of immigration issues from the border hawks by centering discussion on a different, more moderate position. Rather than tightly controlling securitization, however, this strategy created political opportunities for further securitization of the issue beyond what moderates desired—as underscored in particular during the debate over introducing state-level employer sanctions (explored in chapter 2). Even though Democrats were unenthusiastic about employer sanctions as policy, they initially championed the issue in 2005. Aiming to cleave border-hawk Republicans and the party's business constituency, Democrats also sought to demonstrate their willingness to act on the issue in a way that contrasted with actions taken by their partisan opponents. In 2007, however, border hawks called this bluff by using the broad popularity of sanctions proposals, the threat of a more draconian employer-sanctions ballot measure, and compromises with nervous business-aligned Republicans to win passage of a state-level employer-sanctions bill despite the fact that few political elites (including many Republicans) actually wanted one. The border hawks' aggressive strategy made a substantial number of policy makers feel as if they had been painted into a corner, which they viewed as limiting their politically viable options when it came to opposing the policy. Amid this ownership maneuver, the constant need to win credibility in line with the dominant problem conception—which, as mentioned, is an asymmetrical challenge that mainstream elites face but populist border hawks do not—allows securitization to creep forward even after moderates have successfully "captured" the issue.

In contrast to the Democrats, hesitant Republicans, rather than seeking to distinguish their own position, increasingly followed a strategy of visibly falling in line behind the border-hawk vanguard. Republican officials who opposed the border hawks were often conservatives aligned with business. They occupied different political situations than Democrats, especially in having to deal with a party grass roots that was enthusiastic about hard-line policy, more interested in ideological purity than in party unity, and especially mobilized by populist-right invocations. Some Republicans who were cool on the securitization of migration did for a time similarly attempt co-optation or resonance theft, sometimes by introducing "counterbills" to those championed by the border hawks— measures dealing with similar issues but in ways that Republican "closet moderates" found more acceptable. However, elected Republicans who opposed the border-security push increasingly saw more open forms of opposition as politically unworkable, and so they limited themselves to tactics that were passive or behind the scenes. Eventually, though, they began to see even those tactics as politically risky, especially after the "Sanctuary Six" episode of 2009. The political possibilities now severely constricted in their eyes, hesitant Republicans stood down—a necessary condition for the passage of the centerpiece border-hawk law, SB 1070.

The overarching impression emerging here is not of the dominance of a logic of security necessity but rather of interlocking logics of political expediency, given the understood structure of the immigration issue's politics. In contrast to readings of the logic of security as exceptional, though, it is important to point out that security is not unique in this kind of effect on political contestation. Although the developments outlined in the previous paragraphs seem to resonate with the issue trajectory that the securitization concept imagines, this kind of lopsidedness in contestation due to similar perceived limitations also occurs with respect to other issues. For instance, in fiscal policy the logic of balancing the budget and the logic of reducing public debt have similar properties because the logic of fiscal laxity is much more difficult to articulate successfully than the logic of fiscal tightening.[40] Similar things might be said about arguments concerning welfare dependency or crime and punishment.[41]

At the same time, even this collapse of political messages around intuitive logics under populist pressure seems not to capture the entire reason behind securitization in Arizona—especially the aspect of enduring, intense activity surrounding immigration issues. Indeed, even if one feels so boxed in that one has to alter one's position on an issue, there are many possible ways to go about it. One might accept defeat and attempt to move on by agreeing to a settlement, or one might change positions while also trying to change the topic in the hope political debate will move on. Especially amid divided government, one might also deadlock policy passive-aggressively, speaking in the same rhetorical tones and co-opting some measures put before you while at the same time initiating little and waiting for the moment to pass. Aggressively adopting a partially co-opted version of your opponent's problem conception, while clearly striving to "own" the issue, is merely one option. The analysis in the next section helps to identify why many Arizona political elites saw it as the only workable one.

RESPONSIBILITY MADE ACCOUNTABILITY: HOBBES'S REFLECTION IN THE POLITICAL GAME

Even given the sharp challenge of populist border-hawk pressure, why did so many of Arizona's political elites continually run toward the immigration issue, piling on attention and initiatives over the course of years, rather than try to seek to close the book on it or to run away from it? Here, again, the particular importance of security logics—and not just of populism—comes to the fore because they introduce key meanings that shape the political contest in consequential ways: the particular concept of political responsibility amid urgency and threat that emanate from the security problem conception had a key effect on shaping strategic political decisions.

The resort by Arizona governing elites to an ownership "capture" strategy for border security—rather than to another possible strategy that is less active—reflects the perception that a "security" issue is not one that can be stepped away from with political ease. Indeed, in competitive politics responsibility implies accountability. If securitization is at base a process where an issue becomes treated as one of security from among other possible conceptualizations, then it is important to grasp the implication of problem definitions for specifically political concepts of responsibility. The dimensions of responsibility that are implied by competing notions of a problem's nature are what give these debates their political essence: it is why they are not just philosophical exercises to convince an audience of the most justified label for a problem.[42] We can already see from events in Arizona how this process is laden with the politics of accountability for addressing a security problem. It is clear that different positions on the nature of the issue hold, implicitly or explicitly, that different people ought to do something about the problem. "In this sense—of responsibility—the structure of public problems has a political dimension to it."[43] Political responsibility is different from the facts of causation, instead turning on who is charged with solving or alleviating the problem and thereby subject to political "reward or punishment."[44] Here, again, the logic of security brings into political competition distinctive meanings that shape how political actors believe it makes political sense to address securitization.

Indeed, as Juha Vuori has written, "security brings with it deontic powers"—that is, ones related to duty and obligation—"of usually major significance."[45] And as Andrew Neal has underlined, in dealing with more traditional national-security issues, political actors often understand that the ability to "play politics" with these issues is constrained by the need to (be seen to) act responsibly. Such duties exist in deep relation to accountability in the political sense in that these actors' political futures depend on appearing to be faithful to these duties.[46] However, acting based on accountability in a democracy is inescapably and deeply interpretive. Voters' instructions to policy makers are muddled, which means that acting according to notions of responsibility is a matter of policy makers' interpretations—how they understand and anticipate the expectations being placed upon them.

This fundamental context helps us to grasp the significance of responsibility and accountability concepts in this case of securitization. In a way, the question of why Arizona's nonhawkish policy makers began to feel it was necessary to deal with immigration in the hawkish way they did—the birth of the whole phenomenon—is, at the very first instance, a question of responsibility. These policy makers had to accept that what had always been described as a "federal responsibility" was now seen to be the responsibility of state-level political actors, too. To officials at the subnational level, having a central government to blame for immigration problems while holding no real responsibility for them might seem a politically optimal arrangement. So why did they begin to accept responsibility?

In the beginning, this idea of responsibility for state-level actors to deal with immigration emerged from the border hawks' right-wing ideological commitments. These concepts lean hard on a realist philosophical concept of security as the first responsibility of government. This raised the question of whether the federal government's failure to perform this responsibility—which was loudly accepted as a fact by all sides of the debate in Arizona—implied that any government authority, therefore, possessed a duty to step into the void. At first, few political figures in Arizona had an interest in pursuing more aggressive immigration policy as a matter of duty: it seemed a fraught venture to step into the "black hole" of attempting, with limited tools, to govern irregular migration, a potentially insoluble problem.[47] It was only after the issue burst onto the agenda that whether and how to do so became relevant questions.

For some policy makers, a rise in the immigration issue's salience activated a sense of responsibility to devote attention to it. Some legislators felt a duty to respond to what seemed to be both a major political issue in their constituencies and a real problem. Others felt the need, amid the issue's salience, to safeguard the interests of a given community in a climate of policy change. Those with more liberal sensibilities felt a need to address real problems while suppressing scapegoating and overheated politics. Some policy makers believed that acting "responsibly" would bring political success; others believed it would not affect their personal political fortunes; and still others believed that to act on the issue in the most responsible way, in an ethical sense, would risk political danger. If policy makers, then, sought to "take responsibility" according to their own individual conceptions of it, then this would have meant a continued basic clash of ideas: political debate would have proceeded as a competition among clearly distinct problem conceptions and notions of responsibility.

Although there is a tradition in securitization studies of analyzing the ethics of securitizing,[48] to those inscribing security in Arizona responsibility was not primarily about ethics but about politics. The sense of "political responsibility" that loomed over Arizona immigration politics seemed to enforce a consensus on what "taking responsibility" meant politically—a homogenization of and apparent constraint on the possibilities for contestation that is a hallmark of securitized politics. This is the idea of a shared accountability with broad characteristics that differing policy actors analytically agree upon. Political responsibility is less drawn from one's own beliefs than imposed in ways that emerge from the prevalent conceptualization of a given problem.[49]

For a time—even after the acknowledgment that there was a problem at the border and that it was (at least partially) one of security—a significant portion of Arizona's political elite continued to assert that fixing the problem was the responsibility of someone else (federal officials). Any success that this strategy initially met was short-lived, however. Although this claim never went away, gradually it fell clearly into the background as the debate shifted to what the state would do and as devising action became the most important facet of political strategy. Where security went, responsibility surely followed.

In most political issues, the argument that one has no real control over something that has always been someone else's problem is usually effective in avoiding taking responsibility for it—even where, as in security, discussion tends to center upon intuitive logics. Take again, for instance, government debt: it may be common for politicians at any level to rail against it, but even if the problem is allegedly huge, for it to spill the banks of settled responsibility—for a state governor, for instance, to accept imposed responsibility to reduce the ignored federal deficit—would be unusual. Security seems different, however. It introduces a distinct possibility of responsibility diffusing throughout the political system and casting a shadow of accountability that is unusually long. This diffusion contradicts the image that the securitization of an issue focuses responsibility for it, presumably on governing executives. The possibility for insecurity to manifest anywhere and the basic concept of security as a responsibility of "government" generally imply that any government official has potential responsibility in that area. Although this quality is distinctive, the extent to which it is unique to security (at least in its traditional conceptions) is again questionable: such a concept of responsibility also appears possibly reflected in, for instance, the political logics of humanitarian assistance or safeguarding human rights or protecting children's welfare.[50]

Arizona policy makers saw it as difficult to convince voters that the distinctions between federal and state responsibility for immigration and border policy were very meaningful. The difficulty of complicated messages again came into play here. Policy makers often commented in interviews that voters' understanding of federalism was thin. Mike Haener, a gubernatorial aide, recounted the likely progression of such a conversation: "'Why can't you fix the immigration problem? You're the governor.' 'Well, it's federal.' 'Who cares? You're the governor. They're coming across our border—you fix it.' 'But it's not really our border, it's the U.S. border.' You can't explain that!" Yet despite policy makers' impression that across all policy areas there is general lack of the public's understanding of the division of powers in U.S. federalism, most political controversies still tend to be contained in settled bounds of responsibility. Arizona policy makers believed voters were "frustrated" and "wanted something done" about the border, but this is also the case for many other issues that do not break loose in the same way the border issue did in Arizona.

In Arizona, a strong concern emerged among policy makers that, notwithstanding the existing settlement, it looked as if they were dodging responsibility for border security. Amid the populist border-hawk attack, they eventually decided not to challenge this assignment of responsibility but instead to embrace it partly, often with considerable reluctance. The mantle of responsibility was very hard to shake off. Goddard concisely explained the dilemma: "It's awfully hard to say as an Arizona state official, 'This is a federal problem, and the federal response has been totally inadequate.' . . . You start defending an administration that's done a terrible job on the immigration side. They [the public] ask you, 'What's your solution?' 'Well, we should work with the immigration authorities to fix it.' That's inherently incredible."

As Goddard recounts, that approach basically "play[ed] into Russell [Pearce]'s hands." This assigned responsibility was politically very difficult to dodge through any type of more passive action. Any attempt to validate voter frustration about the problem—a move to which, as discussed earlier, there seemed to be no politically workable alternative— only ended up strengthening the border hawks' basic implication that the broken border had become a state responsibility, at least in part. It is only a short distance from this development to the possibility of being held accountable for inaction on the problem. The security nature of the problem diffused the sense of political responsibility for it, while, as Goddard's reflections imply, the taking of responsibility further entrenched and validated security as the main problem conception.

At the point that state-level responsibility to address the problem has been accepted, the possible frontiers of restrictive immigration policy quickly expand. Amid the new responsibility for the state government to use its levers of power to confront the border-security problem, the boundaries containing securitized policy are already weakened. The possible sites for addressing immigration anxiety become as diffused and abundant as the crevices of state government activity in the United States. As a result, security understandings are adopted by new levels of government and become a force in new facets of policy—what perhaps we mean most basically by "securitization." At this point—where the problem conception cannot be rejected because rejection does not seem politically workable and the responsibility implicit in the problem conception cannot be dodged without the strong prospect of accountability—the logic of taking control of the issue rather than running away from it politically asserts itself. "Ownership" becomes doubly appealing with the impossibility of disownership if one cannot avoid being pinned down over the issue. With myriad new areas of policy opened to securitization, hesitant actors seek to seize this imposed responsibility in order to recenter the conversation on what they consider a more palatable position, but this position already sits on emphatically securitized terrain.

Yet the question remains: What is behind the success of this call for such a total response to this particular problem, beyond the bounds of how responsibility has traditionally been assigned, when calls for a similar total response on other issues seem likely to fail? Why do responsibility and accountability require for this particular issue not just a response but rather an active and sustained one with an all-hands-on-deck logic, where on other issues a press conference might do? The answer to these questions is key to understanding how political actors in Arizona saw the problem logic implied by security—one that heavily conditioned "pitching in" as responsible and politically viable and "stepping out" as politically risky, nigh lethal. This political problem perception links the Machiavellian phenomenon of security politics, where political survival is the kind of survival most clearly at stake,[51] to indelible Hobbesian undertones in the meanings that security logics bring to an issue and that summon anxiety about survival in a more fundamental way.

Indeed, the undercurrent of anxiety that Arizona policy makers viewed as pervading the politics of immigration and the border seemed to invoke a broad sense of responsibility to address an uncontrolled security problem—a sense of the prioritization of security as a response to fear and the potential of threat. That a vein of fear underlay Arizona's immigration politics was a basic observation among policy makers. The logic of addressing this unease implicitly proposed the mobilization of extra measures, outside of the previously ordinary, to attempt to confront it: the premise went that such measures at least were a start in addressing the problem. Of course, the State of Arizona, not traditionally involved in border security, had few ordinary measures to address it anyway; thus, nearly any response would nudge security practices beyond where they formerly had been in the state. Although not the same as the classical, exceptionalist imperative of suspending the normal to address the problem, this problem conception at least implied the necessity of thinking and acting outside the box. The scale of anxiety on the issue was complemented by the reading that voters had little sense of why it had not been solved. This frustration was seen as politically potent enough to move voters to discard abstract disputation about federal responsibility in favor of their own version of proper accountability. Politicians followed along.

To note a Hobbesian undertone in this dominant problem conception and its implications for accountability does not suggest that politics was transformed at a fundamental level into something Hobbesian. We can see Hobbes's reflection in the political game without therefore assuming that the political game has changed under pressure into something exceptional. We can see how debates can be *about* security in the sense of revolving around certain meanings associated with security,[52] can lead to certain clearly recognizable security practices,[53] and can adopt certain recognizable political patterns but not inherently entail exceptionalist treatment or summon an extraordinary politics. Though political debate prominently features the content of security logics in political discourse, the invocation of such logics—even when politically successful at enacting security practices—does not suspend the normal haggling of politics. What it does change, however, are the ways in which it makes sense to haggle.

Indeed, the presence of pluralistic competition throughout this case shows how politics, even if unusual, was still be "normal" in the objects of its game. The securitized policy direction instead resulted from formal consent provided to this policy path by policy makers acting on their understandings of the political responsibility and accountability that unfurled from the problem. These reasons seemed compelling. But the eventual defeat of the border hawks in 2011 demonstrates that however strong these political logics may have appeared, under the right conditions they could be neutralized. Border hawks never ceased to mobilize their conceptions of the border-security problem. Pearce's speech from the dais of the Arizona Senate after five of his favored enforcement bills were defeated on March 17, 2011, is well remembered: "Once they cross that border, it's your neighborhood, your education, your health care, your citizens that are impacted. It's you that pay a price. And it's your responsibility, who take the oath of office, to defend these laws and protect our citizens! You can't keep passing the buck to somebody else! The only impediment to enforcing our laws is the lack of political courage on the part of our elected and appointed officials. You bear the burden and responsibility of the costs and the maimings and the death!"[54]

But this incendiary call to take up responsibility became the last gasp of Pearce's border-hawk movement. It points to the dimension of political responsibility not as an unshakably firm structure for political action in the security realm but rather as something embedded in shared understandings of competitive politics—what politicians perceive constituencies to demand of them in a situation. By 2011, it seemed possible to resist this call amid the charge that the border hawks were legislating with disregard for the consequences, in particular those for Arizona's economy.

As uneasy constituencies began to signal their willingness to stand openly against the securitized direction of state-level immigration policy, their usual elite allies saw a receding of the prospect of being held responsible for thwarting this approach. Having before moved even dedicated foes into action, Pearce's exhortation fell on deaf ears in new political conditions. The juggernaut of securitization ground to a halt.

COUNTERING SECURITIZATION: COSMOPOLITANISM, RATIONALITY, AND ECONOMY

The securitization of migration and the border in Arizona grew from seemingly compelling—though ultimately contingent—political logics. These political logics' contingent nature emerges clearly in the sudden loss of their former pull. A complete accounting of "security politics" in the Arizona case means understanding the countervailing political forces that so dramatically relocated political accountability and halted the securitization trend. The most pivotal force behind the decline of securitized border politics in Arizona was a form of countersecurity contestation based on broad cosmopolitan ideals and concerns, which were stirred amid the tempest of post–SB 1070 politics.

In the aftermath of the national political firestorm provoked by the bill, with opposing Hispanic activists mobilized and media coverage of the state's purported racism pervasive, Arizona's business lobbies became much more assertive. Calling for a "time-out" on the issue, they finally provided political cover to natural allies in the Republican Party who had been targets of border-hawk arm-twisting. Business-aligned Republicans were the pivotal bloc in the Senate's defeat of the border hawks' major policy proposals in March 2011. Left-wing opponents successfully recalled Pearce from the Senate that summer, and forces within the business community and the Church of Jesus Christ of Latter-day Saints supported Pearce's more moderate Republican opponent that November. Pearce's defeat helped make clear that the era of Arizona's populist border-security politics had truly ended. In light of the long and steadily building policy trend that these developments followed, two closely related questions arise:

What motivated this form of opposition, and why did it arise when it did and not earlier?

This type of opposition is difficult to pinpoint in existing literatures on both security politics and migration politics. Within securitization theory, which has viewed securitization as a strong tool for political mobilization, it is a surprise that such a quick political reversal of an apparently successful securitization process could occur at all. Even moving into the newer theoretical ground opened for conceptualizing "security politics," this mode of opposition is difficult to characterize. Most scholarly attention on opposing security has been devoted to some idea of "desecuritization," which could hold the promise of reversing whatever effects security brings to politics, but discussing such a process empirically is difficult because there are competing definitions of it.[55] In its original formulation, desecuritization means a return to "normal" politics,[56] but if security politics in this instance remained thoroughly normal (that is, not "exceptional" or "extraordinary"), then the concept clearly does not fit. A more transformative notion of desecuritization might refer to reformulating social relations conditioned by security practices toward something more radically democratic,[57] but that reformulation is also not really in evidence in Arizona. The eventually successful opposition to securitization there did not seek to accomplish a move away from any deeper social relations of security: the pivotal business Republicans did not seek even to repeal securitized policies such as SB 1070; rather, they merely wanted a halt to securitization as a political trend.

In this sense, the opposition resembles not so much any form of desecuritization as it does a thinner "countersecuritization,"[58] providing some kind of countering force if not a theoretically opposite one. This type of countersecuritization that happened in Arizona does not fit easily within established readings of resistance to security, either. Resistance is analytically bound up with subalternity or some kind of subordinate political position: in this way, security is "contested among top dogs, and resisted by underdogs."[59] Resistance to security has been gainfully theorized, but the enduring image of securitization's domineering implications over political life has limited the conceptualization of how security may be a matter of open elite political contest. It seems accurate, though, to see resistance and contestation as "two interacting poles."[60] Indeed, it is impossible to imagine what happened on the floor of the Arizona

Legislature in 2011 without acknowledging previous resistance and backlash from grassroots activists who highlighted the extent to which SB 1070 targeted Hispanics in Arizona by summoning longer narratives of Hispanic immigrants' threat to white America.[61] This raises the question of how precisely these dual forms of opposition—from Hispanic activists and the business-aligned Center Right—interact.

Beyond security scholarship, the successful countersecuritization in Arizona does not sit easily within the immigration politics literature, either. Political economy views on immigration-policy processes make it a central prediction that business lobbies will succeed in opposing immigration restriction and impart a stability and incrementalism upon policy. The benefits of immigration are concentrated upon businesses, which have incentives to lobby against immigration restrictiveness and are also easy to organize. In contrast, the costs of immigration are spread diffusely among a general public that is difficult to organize into an influential political force.[62] These facts explain an "expansionary bias" of liberal-democratic immigration policy making,[63] where the general public's desires for greater restriction are systematically unmet.

It is clear in Arizona that business lobbies engaged—eventually—in elite politics to push back successfully against the restrictive, securitized demands that politicians saw emanating from public opinion. Their role, however, was quite different from the one predicted by a political economy model, wherein businesses lobby against restriction in order to ensure their supply of workers. In Arizona, there is a puzzling disparity between the efforts of business amid the debate over employer-sanctions proposals and in the aftermath of SB 1070. On the one hand, HB 2779, the employer-sanctions bill, seemed to pose a direct threat to businesses' supply of labor, with potentially great costs for businesses that ran afoul of the law. Business was clearly cool to this idea, but policy makers recall business lobbying on this measure as wishy-washy. After HB 2779 passed, business mounted no effort to push back against border hawks or the larger securitization trend. On the other hand, SB 1070 posed no direct threat to businesses' operations or labor supply. The border-hawk proposals of 2011 were also poised to have direct effects much smaller than those of HB 2779, yet these pieces of legislation spurred a major business mobilization, which quickly effected a political shift. Why?

A more interpretivist view in understanding "interests"—as understood and constructed but not objectively deduced from conditions[64]—helps in this analysis. To begin, it is useful to examine the effort in 2007 to protect what were seen as "business interests" against the border-hawk push for an employer-sanctions bill. Anti-border-hawk policy makers in both parties were frustrated that business lobbies did not engage more directly in this debate. While business seemed concerned about the prospect of a draconian ballot initiative—a threat that moved center-right legislators to negotiate with border hawks—it still never settled on a strategy that was clear to its legislative allies. Nonetheless, these allies continued trying to safeguard what they regarded as private-sector interests during their negotiations, even under what they felt as significant political strain. That effort was a relative success. Business groups privately expressed a preference that the governor veto HB 2779 but that they could live with the result.

In this case, pro-business legislators did not act on behalf of business primarily as a response to lobbying. Rather, in many quarters of Arizona politics—and especially in much of the Republican Party—creating "pro-business" policy resembled a more philosophically rooted programmatic idea.[65] On a salient issue with clear stakes such as employer sanctions, it was not necessary for business to coherently lobby to get what it would regard as a tolerable result because crucial policy-making roles were occupied by committed advocates of similarly conceptualized business interests. If low-regulation "pro-business" policy making serves as a prominent programmatic idea, then the representation of some broadly shared concept of "business interests" is assured on issues where it is clear to participants that businesses have a stake, even if there is a simultaneous concern about security.

This absence of business lobbying contrasts with the effort by businesses to campaign against the further securitization of immigration in 2011. Pro-business Republicans had not thought of SB 1070 as having especially much to do with business and were satisfied that it did not actually do the troubling racist things its opponents claimed. Business lobbies themselves did not decisively intervene on the bill, despite some concerns. At first glance, the five major immigration bills on the agenda in 2011 were similar.[66] The threats that those bills were eventually thought to pose were of a completely different sort than the threats of HB 2779 and emerged from the shadow of the uncomfortable context of how SB 1070 had opened a Pandora's box of incendiary conflict.

Other contrasts between these two episodes are illuminating. In the employer-sanctions episode of 2007, amid concern about the possible consequences of a popular ballot measure, elite politics was a realm of safety for business interests: in elite policy-making settings, business easily monitored developments on familiar terrain, and the environment already played host to a programmatic idea sympathetic to business. In such a realm—notwithstanding political winds or even a powerful push for securitization—outcomes are seen as controllable. But the events after SB 1070 played out in a very different arena. The problem was not the policy outcome per se but the resulting political tempest. The battle was in the national media and wider cultural currents. The event was both too big and too nebulous for its outcomes to be easily controlled. Here, the possible damage was not to businesses' operations or to their particular brands but indirectly to Arizona's reputation in the emotive context of a backlash against exclusionary security practices, which were harshly criticized for asserting racist hierarchies.[67] In a context where negative repercussions are difficult to rein in through narrow interventions, the only political action apparently able to meet the challenge is to counter the securitization trend as a whole. This is what business ended up advocating in Arizona. Sympathetic lawmakers quickly grasped this expanded business interest after observing the political fallout and hearing business's case directly. Non-border-hawk policy makers acted upon this preference when business took actions to help them feel politically safer in doing so than they had before this point.

In a political economy view, taking such a position against reputational harm might be a narrow matter of self-interest—a dollars-and-cents insurance move against the risk of bottom-line damage. It is certainly correct to see this position as a matter of self-interest, but it is also essential to pinpoint the concept of self-interest at work and how it relates in particular to the logic that it was mobilized to oppose—that of securitization unbridled. Questions of security, so intertwined with the very notion of sovereign power, axiomatically evoke the anxiety that the state, in its power, hazards the harming of individuals or society. This anxiety is, of course, at the heart of the liberal tradition. The liberal response to limit the state has long been closely associated with the political advocacy of business and industry. This view of security is ambivalent toward security: those who hold this view might variously be wary of security practices as overbearing and unjust, while also understanding security as essential to civil society. The idea of security being modulated due to economic considerations that coexist alongside security logics is strange if security is supposed to be characterized by necessity and the suffocation of choice. Yet this modulation nevertheless seems strongly present in empirical instances of "security politics."[68] Neal identifies in such instances a clash between contrasting visions of security: between the traditional realist-descended Hobbesian "logic of security" that has provided the dominant account of security in security studies and an alternative liberal concept akin to a security logic genealogized by Michel Foucault.[69]

Foucault's analysis of security has been seen as a loose end in his work,[70] but his charting of how security understandings in modernity have evolved appears increasingly relevant in a world where security is contested more and more in competitive political arenas. In his lectures on the topic, Foucault works to separate security from his famous concept of discipline. In this account, amid the advent of liberal philosophy that conceptually separates the state (and politics) from other social domains such as the economy, security derives its moral justification from accepting the organic variability of these distinct domains: in a crucial way, security "lets things happen."[71] Raisons d'état, the state's own reasons, are no longer the paramount moral criterion. Instead, the functioning of these other domains, in particular the market, comes to be regarded as what "tell[s] the truth" about the quality of state policy.[72] Rather than seeing a constant need to ward off threat to ensure survival at all costs, security in this concept means accepting some risk and that security practices must be tuned so as not to smother other social domains.[73]

A similar concept of security seemed to be operating among the business-aligned Republicans who became the most pivotal opponents of Arizona's border hawks. Their already-tepid support for securitization ended as discussions of possible damage to the market arose in response to the prominence of critics who denounced Arizona's immigration laws as racist. Pearce's calls for responsibility, argued from a premise of necessity, were rebutted successfully with the contention that other economic and social developments were revealing border-hawk politics to be *irresponsible.* As these opponents took pains to express, however, their newfound opposition was not to "security" per se (they emphasized they did not support "illegal immigration") but to the negative relation of this particular securitization to the economic domain.

This opposition was premised not upon a clear interest in how the proposed or enacted policies would concretely affect businesses' affairs. Rather, it drew from a broader sense of the market telling the truth about policy—or, as Foucault labels it, the market's "veridiction." Countersecuritization in Arizona emerged, then, not from a quantified or strictly grounded sense of self-interest but from an anticipatory reading of a nebulous market and how that market would respond to the insistence that businesses avoid tainting themselves by association with Arizona's racist immigration laws. Impressions of market response—as translated by business leaders—functioned as a critical indicator to center-right policy makers of both the needed direction of policy and how the politics of the issue were likely to unfold. Indeed, in 2011 the common refrain was not that the boycotts had caused much damage to businesses individually; there seemed to be limited evidence of this. Rather, the possibility of future damage to Arizona at a more holistic level was feared. (This seems to accord with the feeling of many activists, reflected in media coverage, that the anti–SB 1070 boycotts had been wan.) This contrast between the concrete and the ethereal mirrors an earlier observation. For businesses, proposed regulations that have direct impacts on their operations are easily influenced by the programmatic ideas of businesses' policy-maker allies or, failing that, by lobbying. These regulations can be dealt with narrowly. Larger, atmospheric developments, however, seen to possibly damage the overarching abstract "market," are altogether more difficult to control. They require broader interventions, such as a complete countersecuritization. The concern in this case was not just that society could be damaged by state actions, which is a classic concern in political economy, but that damage could result from the exclusionary politics of the state and its citizens apart from the material effect of state intervention as a matter of economic policy.

In this sense, the countersecuritization that ultimately succeeded in the Arizona case was cosmopolitan—which contextualizes the self-interest at play within particular constructions of interest, outlooks on society, and understandings of security. The perceived potential damage to Arizona's economy or to the market was seen as happening because the border-hawk politics of the state was branding Arizona in the eyes of *others*: Arizona was being cast as insular, racist, and "crazy." The paramount concern to the countersecuritizers was what future possibilities this development threatened. It is essential to note that this concern did not belong only to business or to the economic sphere. It resonated clearly within the Church of Jesus Christ of Latter-day Saints, which saw its evangelism threatened by Arizona's border-security politics. Entities in society that rely on visions of a future of some greater universalism, beyond the borders of the polit-ical community—whether to pursue profit, gain enlightenment, or sow salvation—mobilized together. They might be seen as wanting to secure something, too—to possess their own "referent object"[74]—but not one of the cherished underpinnings of things as they are (such as the state, soci-ety, or the environment) that are normally associated with the conserva-tive, realist "logic of security." Rather, what these elements in society sought to secure was the possibility of some yet unrealized future of greater universalism.

Securitization, as mobilized by the border hawks, threatened such a possibility with the encroachment of a Hobbesian worldview that strengthens boundaries—literally or figuratively—around the political community, thus effecting exclusion.[75] To Arizona's eventual counterse-curitizers, this exclusionary politics was never ideal, but it became intol-erable when this exclusion reached a point where it appeared to trans-gress the sensibilities of others beyond Arizona by underlining long-standing narratives of racist hierarchies in ways that no longer escaped prominent notice. Discord resulted. When what it means to be "modern" is universalized, the disinterested "other" serves the role of clarifying what it means to be rational.[76] Amid this universalized sense of rationality, actors—whether governments or businesses—derive much of their legitimacy from being similar to others. Locally, "too much uniqueness . . . violates the principles of rational actorhood," which disin-terested others serve to clarify[77]—a risk that "going it alone on immigra-tion" in Arizona began to invite too recklessly.

Of course, this situation mirrors the classic dichotomy between the particular and the universal, which possesses a distinctive link to secu-rity. The traditional, Hobbesian view of security is particularist par excel-lence, revolving entirely around the survival of a defined and bounded group. The notion of security as a politics of the extraordinary similarly revolves around the notion that clarifying the meaning of the political community mobilizes the community in uncommon ways. An alternative security logic, rooted in liberal thinking, counters this understanding with universalist appeals to transversal or objective ideas of reasonable action. Populism mirrors the classic Hobbesian security logic, rejecting elite subscription to cosmopolitan values as a betrayal of the community.[78] Indeed, a political fault line in Arizona deepened in 2011 over whether outside objections to SB 1070 were relevant or not. If security practices "remain socially binding so long as they respond to commonly accepted values,"[79] the two sides of this debate drew from distinct, competing wells of purported legitimacy: one particular and realist, the other universal and rationalist. These models of legitimacy summoned two imagined roles of the police and of state coercion generally. One role was to "secure and guarantee the daily routines of general order . . . that makes the governance of the territory possible"[80]—an idea connected to community policing and to an image of security that "lets things happen" by providing conditions for the possible liberal flourishing of society. The other role, supporting SB 1070 and measures like it, drew on the simultaneous image of enforcing the law as symbolizing "the prevailing cultural characteristics of particular political communities."[81] In Arizona, in conflict with prevailing notions of liberal, universalized reason, the latter position stood for the defense of a particular kind of society—an autonomous, upstanding, and law-abiding (white) citizenry—against the arrival of criminal Hispanic hordes that border hawks labeled as an "illegal invasion."

Those center-right figures in Arizona advocating for countersecuritization fretted about what others outside the state—Mexican businesses, national activist groups, Barack Obama, even late-night comedians—thought and said about SB 1070 and Arizona. Border hawks pointedly did not. They discounted these figures as interlopers without Arizonans' best interests at heart. To cosmopolitan elements attuned to outsider "others," though, hearing heated assertions that Arizona had transgressed shared values stripped legitimacy from the state's securitization efforts. At stake was Arizona's broad acceptability. The Sturm und Drang of Arizona's parochial security politics imperiled this acceptability regardless of whether these charges against the state, at the level of policy effect, were actually true. This border-security situation reprised historical experiences of Arizona as a pariah—in its allegedly "uncivilized" prestatehood days and during the Martin Luther King Jr. holiday controversy of the 1980s and 1990s. Those experiences helped these particular countersecurity accounts of interests and legitimacy to resonate politically.

How did this form of opposition—a cosmopolitan countersecuritization awakened by the contentiousness of activist claims—yet again change the political game? How did it so successfully work in Arizona politically, given the compelling security-politics logics that had preceded it? As this opposition's cosmopolitan nature implies, it arises when the behavior of the political community has drawn a judgment, voiced by others, that it has transgressed shared standards of acceptability or reasonableness. The border-hawk policy drive, with its underlying assertion of exclusion and its racial undertones, had long been a source of unease.[82] But in the context of a securitization trend that is difficult to oppose politically, tolerating unease is less costly than trying to cure it if a crucial delegitimizing influence—the negative judgment of disinterested "others"—is absent. A key step in countersecuritization is for conflicts to break into the open and thus to gain a wider audience beyond the community's borders.

In Arizona, this break happened only thanks to activists who responded to SB 1070 in ways that helped win and sustain broad attention to the issue, precipitating a backlash that portrayed the issue in an emotionally polarized way that captured national media attention.[83] Before 2009, the potential of "resistance" was, in effect, held in check by the existing political configuration and by the particular security-politics strategies adopted by the resisters' most natural elite allies. These allies worked to undercut or temper border-hawk initiatives even while more broadly accepting the security "problem." Border-hawk proposals thus saw success largely in the form of negotiated compromises. These compromises, in the eyes of many would-be opponents, were designed to be able to be lived with and thus allowed many politicians to pursue other priorities while de facto limiting the fuel for the fire of those who would resist these policies. Border hawks were frustrated in achieving their larger goals, but securitization still crept forward in policy as the border-hawk movement was nourished politically by a mixed diet of success and frustration. Only when the border hawks later resoundingly won a political battle on largely their own terms did long-simmering unease finally reach a boil and new resources for dele-gitimation become available.

How exactly did the countersecuritizers fashion this newly available political material into a winning strategy that prevailed politically? The previous section noted their success at reformulating responsibility when it came to border and immigration policy, rebutting the border hawks' Hobbesian responsibility logic with the contention that the market, as reflecting universalized reason, was proving that group unwise. The extent to which the countersecuritizers actually convinced the public more broadly of this is questionable. Indeed, no one in this saga ever seemed to crack the apparent complexity of public opinion on immigration in Ari-zona. Rather, the countersecuritizers' victory was narrower. At the very least, this intervention appears to have used the skepticism of rational "others" to cast a shadow of doubt over the reasonableness of continuing down the securitized policy path. Most broadly, this delegitimizing move succeeded at relocating political accountability when it came to border and immigration policy making. Business and Mormon constituencies rich in Republican political capital backed an effort to reshape account-ability for Republican would-be allies who advocated the countersecuri-tization position. In the aftermath of the SB 1070 tempest, this cosmopolitan countersecuritization argument was victorious, at least on its own nar-row terms. The delegitimation it pursued was plausible enough to work for the political purpose of counterbalancing the political threats posed by the border-hawk movement.

Such a "countersecuritization" move can be seen as a subset of a broader type of case—again, situating security within the run of other political topics. As discussed earlier, this cosmopolitan position is not against secu-rity per se as it draws from a liberal tradition with an ambivalent stance toward the classical security concept. The most basic question was not whether Arizona politics was too security focused but rather whether this focus meant the state's politics was extremist and racist. It is telling that forces that had opposed SB 1070 drew heavily from that episode to defeat the "religious liberty" law in 2014 that they saw as exclusionary toward LGBT people but that had little apparent relation to security, at least as classically understood.[84] Likewise, opposition in 2016 to a "religious lib-erty" law passed in Mississippi and to a North Carolina law restricting what public bathrooms transgender people can use triggered a familiar political sequence: activist backlash, national media focus, boycott announcements, performance and conference cancellations, and business opposition.[85] The pattern repeated when Arizona Republicans again broached a state constitutional ban on "sanctuary cities" in 2020, from which they quickly backed off.[86] Cosmopolitan opposition arises only out of some broader sense of right conduct. In twenty-first-century America, despite (or concurrently with) the rise of far-right politics and white nationalism, exclusion may be such a third rail—a value perceived as opposite to the progressive and modern. Securitization is only one of many forces seen to exclude, which can spark a common set of cosmopolitan concerns about moral failure, reputational damage, harm to economic exchange, and the appearance of being "crazy" or rogue. This opposition is less about security per se than about exclusion and extremism—as well as, inherently, about the mirror-image cosmopolitan values of universalism and reasonableness. The cosmopolitan countersecuritization that took place in Arizona might, therefore, be seen as a particular application of a larger mode of opposition against forms of politics judged too exclusionary and extreme to tolerate, an opposition awakened by the costly stigmatization this politics augurs. Security is one of many possible types of exclusionary approach that might be opposed by the same interests with the same tactics and for the same reasons.

The success or even the existence of this form of contestation against securitization is contextual. Those who were ideologically primed to espouse this countersecuritization position happened to occupy a pivot point in Arizona politics. The position was permitted by the fact that business has long occupied a central place in Arizona's political culture. Arizona's business-aligned conservatives in 2011 held the keys to the failure of border-hawk bills due to the ideological composition of the Arizona Senate—just as they long had, including in previous years when they had declined to turn those keys. The fact that the ideology behind this countersecuritization often holds a prominent place within the Center Right suggests that it could be important in many political contexts. In another political configuration, however, this opposition might not have an opportunity to emerge, or it might find itself entangled in debates lasting much longer than the year that the assertion of this countersecuritization logic took in Arizona. And as happened for many years in Arizona, policy progressions can long unfold, undergirded by recognizable images of racial or social hierarchy, yet not trigger the backlash necessary to set this kind of cosmopolitan countersecuritization in motion. The reassertion of business interests over populist, security-driven, and restrictive immigration policy is by no means assured. What this means for arenas beyond Arizona is explored in the final chapter.

This chapter has synthesized the particular interactions of security and populism logics as well as the notions of responsibility emanating from security meanings that fueled the securitization of migration in Arizona. It has specified the particular cosmopolitan countersecuritization logic that was eventually activated by the intensity of securitized politics and was mobilized to bring a powerful securitization trend to a close. The securitization process in Arizona seemed to possess remarkable political momentum, rooted in securitization's sheer mobilizing power. But viewed in terms of the political rationalities of the people involved in making policy decisions, the hold of security over immigration policy looks quite different. Security logics were aided by populist logics in consolidating this hold; the interaction of these logics was a key mechanism in reshaping the political game for nonpopulist governing elites due to how it articulated securitarian meaning in an antielitist way that corroded governing elites' credibility. The politics of security can indeed resemble the politics of other issues where, amid competition, politicians resort to crowding around intuitive arguments that seem primed for messaging success. However, the progress of securitization seems powered by a particular security-related concept of responsibility that renders stepping out of the issue politically unworkable and pushes the political strategies of would-be opponents of securitization further toward "ownership" efforts that risk entrenching the securitization phenomenon itself. The political game surrounding securitization looks difficult to play, indeed, if one does not especially desire securitized policy outcomes.

But the swift defeat of Arizona's border hawks in 2011 suggests that what seems politically workable when it comes to security, even against such apparently compelling logics, changes with context. The mobilization of new forces of opposition can inspire yet more possibilities, drawing from new, competing wells of legitimacy, changing the game yet again. The defeat of Arizona's border hawks might be considered a mere example of business reasserting its power following an anomalous period of populist immigration policy making, but this interpretation is too simple. What halted the securitization trend in Arizona was the interaction of activist resistance and elite contestation. These developments mobilized a broader form of opposition rooted in cosmopolitan concepts against what the border hawks' opponents saw as the stigmatization of Arizona as racist and extreme—a costly transgression of more broadly held values and sources of legitimation.

While the securitization of immigration and the border in Arizona seemed to follow from powerful political dynamics, the fact that this trend was ultimately arrested suggests that contestation over security issues always remains possible. In this sense, understanding securitization as emerging from actors' political rationalities is key to grasping the success of securitization as momentary—as merely contingent rather than transformational. The two categories of theoretical insight drawn from this case help to establish what we mean by "security politics"—a form of politics that is different or distinctive in some of its patterns and forms and yet still resolutely "normal," a political game that is in essential ways like any other.

6

APPRAISING ARIZONA

Possibilities for Immigration Politics

his book began with the idea that the rise and decline of Arizona's border-security politics have something important to say
about broader developments in the world: the growing treatment
of immigration as a security issue and the mainstreaming of hard-line
positions on immigration that would have previously been regarded as
extreme. As much as Arizona was painted as an extremist outlier in the
aftermath of SB 1070[1]—a portrayal, indeed, key to the state's eventual
change of course—it has become clearer in recent years that what happened there fits within larger trends. In the years since the events described
here, Arizona has frequently been painted as at the center of wider U.S.
political controversies, its immigration politics foreshadowing Donald
Trump's.[2]

This book has sketched a full portrait of how the political game surrounding these issues evolved in Arizona, with a volatility that belies
structural accounts that predict much more stability in immigration politics. It has worked to pinpoint just why, for years, the presence of populist and security logics in immigration politics together so effectively
pushed competing politicians in one overarching policy direction. It has
also identified how rival concepts emerged with enough political force to
successfully counter a seemingly relentless securitizing trend—cementing
a new settlement on immigration in state government in Arizona and, as
elections in 2018 and 2020 would suggest, a new political configuration

in the state. In this configuration, not only is there greater partisan parity than before, but also for Republicans the immigration issue has not seemed to serve the same mobilizing and vote-winning roles that it once did. This book's narrative has also underlined the importance of political institutions, social context, contingent developments, and combinations of characters—indeed, place—in how events unfolded. So, in the end, just what can Arizona teach us about the possibilities for border-security politics elsewhere in the world?

This chapter looks to specify the relevance of this book's theoretical insights when it comes to the immigration politics of both the Center Right and the Center Left. In Arizona, the Center Left played an important role in the period of border-security politics' rise. How to counter challenges on immigration has been a major issue for center-left parties following a political period that across countries has overall been trying for them.[3] As this book has argued, inculcating security meanings within immigration politics allows the populist radical Right an especially plausible route not just to co-opt the rest of the political Right but also to make claims to the political Center—both of which challenge traditional center-left governing parties. This chapter argues that although the Center Left does not, across all contexts, enjoy clear answers on how to approach immigration, the Arizona case illustrates limits to the issue-ownership maneuvers that may work in the short run to secure power but in the long run favor the Center Left's opponents' positioning and feed into continuing political dilemmas for it. Recent difficulties that the Center Left has faced in many countries may not inherently come down to immigration, but it is nonetheless clear that when center-left governing elites securitize immigration, this securitization primes the issue for further radicalization when power changes. The Arizona case underlines how the Center Left's willingness to compromise its preferred positions on immigration in order to retain power—because the issue sat outside its main policy vision—was key to the issue's securitizing drift and the "mainstreaming" of more radical positions. The movement of immigration issues—in particular the interests of settled communities with immigrant backgrounds—further into the core issues of center-left coalitions stands to change political calculations, as has happened in Arizona. This shift opens up new political pathways for how the issue can be treated, as has also occurred in the state.

On the other side of the political spectrum, this chapter picks up on the Arizona Center Right's sudden reassertion of a relatively moderate immigration position—following years of deepening acceptance of the populist radical Right's push on this issue—to ask whether center-right forces today maintain the capacity for such a turn. The Arizona case shows that in some situations the Center Right may be a crucial faction in stopping hard-line immigration policy trajectories: it was the pro-business, relative Center Right that in Arizona ultimately held the balance between a continued securitization of immigration and a halt to that trend. Yet the prospect of reaping political benefits from accommodating the Far Right is a perennial consideration; Republicans in the United States seem to have become the "party of Trump," and Europe's traditional conservative governing parties tilt continually rightward on immigration.[4] To what extent does the Arizona case present an important caveat? This chapter identifies this center-right countersecuritization position as situational rather than deeply principled: it is activated only by the impression that the social environment has become intolerably tense—perhaps due to "brown backlash" but especially to the feeling, occasioned by dramatized resistance that captures media attention, that important outsiders are forming negative judgments about the political community's insularity and exclusionary tendencies. Voters long associated with the Center Right but alienated by exclusionary right-wing immigration politics can also shift in ways that alter the political landscape more broadly. Indeed, Russell Pearce's election losses have echoed in the Arizona Democratic Party's rising fortunes in previously Republican-voting predominantly white suburbs in the Trump era, a key element of an unfolding reconfiguration of Arizona state politics. In combination, the political processes surrounding the securitization of migration, although often exhibiting notable patterns, are also indeterminate and complex—with the possibility to lead to unexpected places and novel political settlements.

The final chapter of a scholarly book is normally where the author cautions readers about the limits of the research. This whole chapter should, indeed, be read as a caution about the ability to generalize from this one case to others. Single cases, examined in depth, can tell us much—indeed, perhaps more than most presume.[5] Yet the findings from studying them must be put to the test elsewhere before larger conclusions can be drawn from them.[6] Beyond extrapolating to different places, time also changes

situations. At the start of the events in this narrative, few had heard of
Barack Obama, and fixtures of today's politics, such as Twitter, did not
exist. By the end of this period in 2011, the Syrian boy Alan Kurdi, whose
drowning in the Mediterranean Sea shamed Europe, had not yet even
been born. Neither had a populist radical-right outfit as much discussed
in recent years as Alternative für Deutschland.

Indeed, perhaps our political world has changed in some fundamental
ways since the events of this book took place—or, alternately, too many
preexisting social processes have deepened or advanced for Arizona's
populist border-security politics to say much about today's world. U.S.
partisan polarization, the radicalization of the Right, the popularity of
anti-immigration politics among those identifying as Republicans, and
partisan realignment have grown apace since 2011—processes the Trump
presidency both grew from and deepened. Events in Europe since 2011—
in particular in the Mediterranean in 2015—have entrenched a securitized
European border governance,[7] while the coronavirus pandemic has
hindered the movement of people. In Australia, the state of exception in
closing borders due to COVID was profound but also followed years of
draconian offshore detention policies toward those who arrive by boat.[8]
European populist radical-right parties in the 2010s continued on the
gradual upward trajectory they have enjoyed since the late 1990s.[9]
The League in Italy and the Freedom Party in Austria have leveraged
coalition dynamics to gain power over immigration policy in government, at least for a time. Trump himself, despite the ambiguity of his
future ambitions at present, has fully centered radical-right politics
within America's big-tent right party, the Republicans. Meanwhile, some
in Central Europe's more authoritarian Right, such as Hungary's Viktor
Orbán, have sought to consolidate their power by campaigning against
immigration in hyperbolic terms.[10] Although Arizona is a particular
case, it can also be read within these much larger trends. And, indeed,
the waning power of this politics in Arizona may have similarly fore-
shadowed the dip in Trump's fortunes.

Even in drawing from the strengths of this research to try to identify
its broader implications, it is worth specifying one limitation or particu-
larity of this book at this point. To try to understand why securitizing
immigration made sense to Arizona's politicians—to better understand
the political game that emerged around these issues—this book has taken

an actor-centered and interpretive approach.[11] It has sought to understand how political elites took stock of their situation to devise solutions to dilemmas they faced when past ways of doing things no longer appeared to be viable.[12] Clearly, however, what happened was not all about elites. Activists and voters played an essential role in events and in the development of a new political settlement in Arizona[13]—just as one might hopefully assume they would in a democracy. The political game very often extrapolated from the properties that policy makers perceived in an anxious electorate. At the same time, concerted mobilization by Arizonans had decisive effects. Arizona's eventual turnabout in 2011 was inconceivable without dedicated protest led by Hispanic activists in the aftermath of SB 1070, which catalyzed media coverage, negative outsider impressions of the state, and business concern. As Roxanne Lynn Doty has demonstrated, security analyses can miss a lot by failing to notice how security problems are constructed and contested beyond the official arena.[14] Although this book has not focused on activists in Arizona, other scholarship has.[15] Inasmuch as these resistances and mobilizations seek—partially or eventually—to counter a hard-line trend in policy, this book can reflect on what combination of events and circumstances can lead to desired outcomes.

One thing that emerges clearly from the Arizona case is that elite decision dynamics on immigration policy have something less than a straightforward relationship to public opinion. Major shifts in policy approach can emerge even without a sense that the public has changed its view on key aspects of immigration. Indeed, public polling in Arizona throughout the period discussed showed consistent support for both security approaches to immigration and nonsecurity measures, such as new channels for legal migration and broad regularization programs.[16] What seem to have a closer relationship to policy changes are coalition dynamics and particular mobilizations. Indeed, one might surmise this from how the Trump administration executed hard-line immigration policies even while Americans' attitudes toward immigration continued to gradually warm,[17] as has occurred in many western European countries.[18] Arizona is especially important, however, in showing that the inverse can also hold: mobilizations and coalition dynamics can halt exclusionary securitizing trends in migration policy, not just advance them, again without perceptible short-term shifts in public perceptions of the issue and even just after immigration issues reach peak salience—at least under certain conditions.

Nonetheless, it is clear that no reliable silver bullet exists in relation to these kinds of politics or across contexts.[19] Although this chapter delves further into the dynamics that halted Arizona's securitization trend, specifies the Center Right's critical role, and discusses what seemed to work to move it into opposition, the evolution of our political world since 2011 suggests that this effort at extrapolation—tricky to pull off under any circumstances—is even more complicated than before. Nevertheless, the chapter concludes by surveying what within the shifts in Arizona's politics has seemed to last. The state's change from reliable Republican redoubt to a competitive "purple state" in the aftermath of intense immigration politics may be instructive—even if the state has particular demographics that may facilitate such a trend.[20] Perhaps the tumult of Arizona's experience may show how these politics can change in a somewhat more positive direction.

THE CENTER LEFT AND THE CHALLENGE OF BORDER-SECURITY POLITICS

Border-security politics have proven a formidable—and frequently commented upon—challenge in this century for the traditional governing center-left parties of Western democracies. Democrats in the United States may be said to be perennially in disarray, but the European Center Left has suffered a decline in popularity so deep it has been called a crisis.[21] This party family faces some similar issues on both sides of the Atlantic. Changes in economic and societal structures have destabilized the support base of parties that had counted as a key constituency the industrial working class. Rising right-wing populism, growing from complex social disillusionments,[22] has increased the salience of immigration issues, which exacerbate conflicting ideological pulls within these parties' preexisting support bases:[23] more culturally progressive and liberal elements may clash with working-class elements frequently portrayed as more socially conservative, whose general favoring of state intervention may extend to immigration policy in particular. A debate has emerged here: while activists increasingly challenge center-left parties over their immigration stances, analysts who see such challenges as cleaving "white working-class" support from center-left parties have questioned whether these parties should make efforts to avoid associations with activists who increasingly organize against punitive, racialized policies, including with respect to immigration.[24]

It is clear from the Arizona case and others that the Center Left, when in power, has often inscribed securitization in immigration policy—as Labour governments did in Britain and the Socialists did in France. What are the viable alternatives? The larger troubles of the Center Left in Arizona seem largely to have ensued after the Democrats' departure from power following the elections of 2008, and immigration is but one issue that has seemed to beset this party family. Yet although immigration may not be at the core of the Western Center Left's ills, the issue, in introducing frequently hyped tensions for preexisting party coalitions, has not seemed to help the situation. But whereas Arizona Democrats' immigration issue-ownership maneuvers, appealing to some measure of conservative "law and order" cultural views as a political strategy, seemed successful at capturing the middle as long as the Democrats held power, elsewhere since 2009 this kind of effort seems to have a more mixed track record—as the woes of British Labour and the Italian Democrats would suggest.

Pressures for center-left parties to avoid "mainstreaming" securitizing approaches to immigration championed by the populist Right come at a delicate time of noticeable transformation in their base of support and in the aftermath of substantial challenges from the left, both within and outside traditional party structures. The basic fact is that immigration has never been a core campaign issue for the traditional governing parties of the Western Center Left. Economic justice or the more recent Third Way objective of growth with greater social equality[25] has typically been social-democratic parties' raison d'être; U.S. Democrats arrived at a similar place via a different ideological path. To this vision, immigration has most often been secondary, however much the scapegoating of immigrants runs afoul of progressive political commitments. Much as in Arizona, immigration's rise on the global agenda is liable to be seen as a wrinkle in best-laid plans, threatening to disrupt the pursuit of "higher" priorities. Confronted with the sharp populist security challenge this book describes, ownership or capture seems a more appealing approach than tactics that fully stake one's power in taking an oppositionally contesting stand on a second-rate issue. Using power on what matters is important, but first one must gain and keep that power.[26]

In Arizona, the Center Left adopted securitizing approaches that often compromised on immigration precisely because it was not an area where most Democrats in Arizona's policy-making system sought to make changes to pursue their preferred social vision, which made immigration an issue acceptable to compromise on. Indeed, throughout this narrative, Arizona Democrats maintained a sense that there was little they could do about immigration within the federal system. Importantly, Democrats enacted some securitized policies they agreed with—such as antismuggling laws—while at other times they held their noses, such as on employer sanctions, and in other cases they rejected particular proposals as racist and extremist. In any case, they were making decisions on an issue that did not, on the whole-party level, fit into their key motivations or agenda. As a former Democratic governor's chief of staff said about immigration, "It's not an issue that we wanted to drive the debate. It was not, from our perspective, the most important issue. It wasn't a policy priority of ours. But it was what was most interesting to voters." Of course, as chapter 5 explained, voter interest was seen as dominated by a populist "common sense" of security.

The question of whether center-left parties should be seen either to align with or alternately to eschew ascendent movements against punitive racialized policies has become its own major topic. Indeed, the politics surrounding this question has been shifting. Increased activism about and social discussion of systemic racism—and shifts in the social attitudes of more liberal whites toward the claims of racial minority groups[27]—may fundamentally disrupt perceptions of what securitizing policies are politically opportune.[28] Compromising in a securitized direction is a clear option for center-left figures in the central circles of power if immigration stands outside the core issues of concern: making policy toward immigration constitutes a matter of managing a political problem, not an opportunity to assert important principles or to hold the line on a social vision.

Limiting concessionary stances by the Center Left is therefore difficult unless immigration moves farther into its core agenda as a rights issue with racial justice implications and certain lines that cannot be crossed. As chapters 1 and 2 explained, part of the Arizona Center Left's approach to positioning itself on immigration was highlighting support for policies gesturing to enforcement with which center-left politicians were already mostly comfortable. This approach minimized true movement on the issue in terms of the Center Left's policy stances but accommodated a securitization trend it would probably not otherwise have embraced. In Arizona, accommodating positions included supporting measures such as antismuggling laws, checking the immigration status of inmates, and including immigration status as an aggravating factor in criminal sentencing. In this sense, limiting the Center Left's enthusiasm for securitizing migration is partly about drawing lines internally about which ideas go too far—especially inasmuch as they entrench larger discourses of minorities as threats. Drawing lines, though, is not necessarily the same as embracing the demands of movements that advance racial justice claims.

Getting these lines drawn within parties may entail truly difficult work for activists: party figures may resist, given data on less-educated white voters' hesitance to embrace a politics more skeptical of law-enforcement and security logics and the argument that this politics does constitute part of a political platform that helps to win majority support. However, looking at the longer trajectory of what happened in Arizona—understanding these issues as subject not to static public opinion but to dynamic political processes—tells a somewhat different story: Arizona immigration politics and to some extent national immigration politics as well have evolved since the end of the period described in this book's narrative. For one, pro-immigrant activists' work may have grown easier in the aftermath of the Trump presidency. The Trump administration introduced a number of extreme and draconian policies on immigration, from the thinly veiled "Muslim ban" to family separation.[29] Indeed, in his border wall Trump found at last one border-security measure the U.S. public broadly opposed—a feat Arizona's border hawks did not clearly achieve.[30] Trump's policies were largely novel and extreme enough to most voters that Democrats could oppose them vocally without moving their positions on immigration or border security. Trump's divisive qualities made this tactic much easier: where in 2006 it made sense to many congressional Democrats to support the Secure Fence Act after comprehensive immigration reform foundered, they felt no such compunction on a wall advocated by a champion of much less subtextual racist appeals.[31] And this is not just a result of conservatives moving out of the Democratic Party: individual policy makers have embraced new positions.

At the same time, activists in the United States seem to be playing their own autonomous part in drawing lines within Democratic Party politics, reorienting prevailing Democratic attitudes toward immigration as the party increasingly draws support from those less likely to see immigration as a threat. In Arizona, the coming-of-age of a Hispanic political generation in the shadow of SB 1070 and Sheriff Joe Arpaio's "crime-suppression" sweeps has had an important impact on these shifts.[32] The previous expectation had been that Hispanic activists and wider political constituencies would accept a less-bad option that kept a lid on the brewing immigration issue, embraced broadly supported policies justifiable as substantive public-safety measures (for instance, combating smuggling), and at least gestured toward more humane immigration approaches against the palpable threat of an ascendant populist radical Right. As the previous chapter argued, Arizona Democrats' partial success in tempering the populist radical-right immigration agenda kept their coalition in an uneasy stasis. The process seemed to work at keeping the worst-case scenarios at bay, averting disaster or true disruption. In the end, a stronger counterpunch to this trend was triggered only when the issue broke open into more direct confrontation and contestation, especially over racism's presence in immigration politics, inviting a wider political backlash beyond elite machinating.

To earlier governing Democrats, the ascendancy of immigration issues risked disruption to their core agenda. For younger, frequently Hispanic activists mobilized by the insecurity sown by figures such as Pearce and Arpaio, justice toward immigrants and opposition to racism in law enforcement represented an essential part of their social vision. Where "white backlash" occurred in Arizona, a "brown backlash" followed that seems to have had at least equally important long-run effects. Both within Arizona and outside it, "Dreamer" activism by people brought unauthorized to the United States as children has been successful at establishing within the Democratic Party increasingly firm support for regularization measures and at making hard-line positions on immigration enforcement less viable for Democratic elites.[33] Democrats held a strong line against Trump's wall, but other immigration-enforcement issues remain divisive—as the left-wing exhortation to "abolish ICE" demonstrates and as intraparty dismay over early Biden administration border policies shows.[34] Research focused specifically on elites' relationship to activists may help to pinpoint how such campaigns can succeed.

The counterargument, of course, is that by forcing center-left officials to heed them, activists are forcing center-left parties into political peril. Assessing whether this is correct is not as straightforward as it may seem. Governing center-left parties in Europe have often lost despite making the kinds of immigration compromises ripe to upset activists—even in an environment where the consequences of this upset may be less politically risky because pro-immigrant activism in the less-diverse Europe is generally weaker than in historic settler countries such as the United States.[35] The recent electoral performances of such European center-left parties have not offered shining evidence that putting aside pro-immigrant constituencies in an attempt to woo the center pays off with any reliability. Conservative parties are structurally seen to "own" social control issues,[36] so any salience immigration control has may simply favor these conservative parties in ways very difficult to effectively combat. However, this does not mean that the inverse is necessarily true—that a less hard-line stance on immigration would fare better. Larger discursive situations form a key part of the dilemma. As the previous chapter detailed, Democrats in Arizona felt by 2005 that public fearfulness about immigration had to be accepted, that their stance had to be based on this feeling, and that they needed to embody action. It is difficult to poke holes in their argument, in part because this research is designed to understand the logics that were at play rather than to hold them to some objective test. Indeed, it may be that in some places and times the Center Left faces such a robust environment of fear, whether precipitated mainly by events or by the media, that it is left with little other short-term, tactical choice than to accommodate harder-line stances on immigration. Further detailed process-tracing research about other cases of center-left responses to populist border-security challenges is needed to yield more systematic answers.

In Arizona, Democrats actually succeeded at keeping power through ownership-and-capture maneuvers toward a securitized immigration issue. They tumbled from power in Arizona only due to other political circumstances—the shakeout from the presidential election of 2008, which the Democratic candidate won. As a result, it is impossible to tell whether Arizona Democrats would have eventually been caught out misreading the public, would have worn out allies' patience, or would have finally exhausted the Republicans to the point where the issue faded away (though the patterns analyzed in this book suggest that the last possibility is unlikely). It is clearer that when Republicans came to power in Arizona for contingent reasons, the immigration issue was ripe for exploitation. This suggests that even if the Center Left loses power for reasons that have little fundamentally to do with immigration—one valid reading of its recent plight across Western democracies—its previous actions on that particular issue can set the stage for continued movement in securitized directions by normalizing securitized treatment in public discourses that then have further feedback effects on party positioning and resulting policy.[37] Activists and citizens, however, need not think solely in terms of the short-run need to keep power or of advocating for ideas that are already popular. Nor must they confine themselves to the limits of the tactical rear-guard actions of those in power who, in principle, should be sympathetic to their claims. They can instead work with a view toward the longer run in devising political strategies and social campaigning to shape social discourses and attitudes.

In the United States today, these issues increasingly seem able to mobilize a growing, motivated constituency of voters either alienated by aggressive anti-immigrant efforts or genuinely more sympathetic to immigrants. This mobilization already seems to be making new kinds of center-left positioning more tangibly viable than before. Indeed, U.S. public attitudes overall seem to be becoming more pro-immigrant thanks to more assertive claims making and demographic change. Nonetheless, as this chapter has argued, this phenomenon has no direct relationship to policy direction. In fact, whatever association there is seems likely to weaken as the two major U.S. parties continue to polarize, sort ideologically, and see immigration issues in increasingly opposite ways. Perhaps any action on immigration is poised to be met by reaction—though the Arizona case shows that the populist radical Right will often proceed with the same hard-line agenda regardless of whether the stances its adversaries choose are accommodating or resolute.

Even more concretely, the evolving coalition that rejects these sorts of hard-line positions to immigration—either as racist or, more mildly, as divisive—is appearing to realign Arizona's politics. A progression of white backlash, brown backlash, business-oriented response, and voter reaction is having clear effects. Democrats have risen from the lows of 2010 to their greatest levels of electoral support in decades. They won a U.S. Senate election in 2018 for the first time in thirty years with Kyrsten Sinema, whose approach to immigration the preceding pages describe. In 2018, Democrats also won two other major statewide offices and more seats in the state House of Representatives than they had since 1964. And, of course, in 2020 Arizona voters not only elected a second Democrat, Mark Kelly, to the U.S. Senate but by 10,457 votes delivered the state's electoral votes to Joe Biden in the nation's presidential race, the smallest raw margin of any state in the election—supporting a Democrat for president for only the second time since 1948. In the post–SB 1070, post-2016 environment, a more vocal and insistent pro-immigrant activist corps has increasingly mobilized Hispanic voters, melding with growing white suburban disillusionment with immigration hard-liners. This trend has continued producing changes beyond Joe Arpaio's momentous defeat in his bid for a seventh term as Maricopa County sheriff in 2016.[38] Events in 2010 were an important moment, but even more significant may be the less expected political process that followed. Perhaps such developments are not as tangible for other places, but perhaps Arizona can serve as an example.

THE CENTER RIGHT AND THE DECLINE OF ARIZONA'S BORDER POLITICS

Perhaps even more telling implications emerge from Arizona regarding opposition to hard-line immigration policy by the Center Right—a faction that has often seemed to be either bowled over by or cynically exploiting the anti-immigration politics that it has helped to mainstream.[39] Indeed, the Center Right's role has often been underanalyzed, given the considerable power it retains over immigration politics across Western democracies.[40] For relatively moderate conservatives, accommodating more far-right forces is perennially enticing because those forces often hold the promise of mobilizing particularly fervent support. How this relationship unfolds can have major implications for whether societies develop in democratic and inclusive fashions.[41] Tension between factions that differ on immigration has become typical for parties on the right.[42] The inevitable danger for the relatively moderate Right is that it, rather than the radical Right, will end up being co-opted and that accommodating stances toward radical upstarts will provide the latter an opportunity to usurp the moderates.[43] Indeed, in Arizona this risk was made especially palpable because of how openly populist border hawks were willing to attack fellow Republicans. Republicans disinclined to the border-hawk agenda did not hold a firm line against it, providing the key condition for the acceleration of the securitization trend—and, concretely, for SB 1070—after 2008, when their Democratic foes had lost power in Arizona.

Yet Arizona also clearly provides a case of the relative Center Right turning against the populist radical Right even after it looked as if the former had been disciplined into full obedience on immigration. In 2011, Arizona's business-oriented Republicans turned into key allies for countering further hard-line, security-oriented policy on immigration and the border. Does this mean that those advocating for a different approach to immigration should hesitate to give up on the Center Right? How should it be approached?

The previous chapters have tried to decode the pattern of the Center Right's behavior in Arizona—at first resisting at least some of the securitization trend, then caving under pressure, then reasserting its original view when its co-optation seemed complete. This constant change created a level of turbulence in immigration policy that belies structural accounts that predict much greater stability.[44] In discerning just what makes for center-right opposition to hard-line policy, it is important to note that the Center Right's particular moments of defiance were not simple matters of principle, brought forward when policies went beyond what it could tolerate. Indeed, in a way, the issue was not at base about policy at all. The fact that these Republicans were not ideologically committed border hawks was important but only because it raised the possibility of their opposition. Clearly, this latent disagreement was not itself sufficient to produce a public fracture. Rather, the key to understanding these center-right figures' calculations is to see how situational those calculations were. A sense of philosophical disagreement did not provide the ultimate say in whether these figures were compelled to object. Instead of anything so categorical, the key was how this policy direction seemed likely to play out against broader standards of tolerance and reasonableness held by others outside of the state and especially how this contrast might affect the market.

Business-aligned Republicans in the Arizona Legislature routinely felt bullied by populist border hawks and the latter's grassroots supporters, yet they also proved adept at swallowing their objections when they perceived political benefit in doing so. Tensions on immigration between the Center Right and the populist radical Right most often have not been explored as an intraparty matter because relevant cases have mostly been in western Europe, where electoral systems typically favor the formation of separate populist radical-right parties.[45] For the Center Right, dealing with radical-right populists in the same party and competing against a separate party are naturally different things. In systems with primary elections, these factions may compete for primary votes. They do not, however, compete within the general electorate, which may strengthen the incentives to band together—especially for business-oriented conservatives if they tap into far-right passion as a route to power for the party as a whole.

Traditional governing conservative parties may be tugged to the right on immigration in competing against populist radical-right parties in systems that feature both types of parties.[46] When big-tent conservative parties contain an assertive populist radical-right faction, the shift to the right might occur more quickly as the logics of making peace between factions and presenting a united front prevail. This might be especially so when party leadership is institutionally weak, as in the United States, and thus ineffective at tamping down far-right attacks against party moderates.[47] Arizona saw the Republicans' relative immigration moderates repeatedly seek to keep peace within the party despite disagreements. Border hawks, led by Pearce, also compromised on occasion to win more moderate Republicans' acquiescence to their proposals, despite attacking them publicly for their differences. Intraparty politics continually tilted rightward, especially on immigration, driving forward this dynamic.

Tension on immigration emerges naturally not just within center-left parties but also within principal right parties as culturally conservative or ethnonationalist elements clash with market liberals and key business constituencies.[48] Business is the presumed winner in this battle: classic political economy accounts of immigration policy see business as an organized pro-immigration interest that can easily trump scattered anti-immigration forces to drive expansionary policy.[49] What happened in Arizona, however, suggests a much more complex positioning by business. Business did not always stand fully in opposition to border hawks' hard-line efforts. On the measures most relevant to business, such as employer sanctions, it in fact sought narrow interventions that would protect its direct interests rather than aim to quash a larger hard-line policy direction. When businesses did finally intervene in 2011 to turn back the securitization trend, this intervention was not driven by the narrow self-interest (in aiming to secure a pool of labor) that, according to political-economy accounts, motivates them. What was much more important were larger, atmospheric conditions—the dust kicked up by the political brouhaha that followed SB 1070. It was this development— national and international attention painting Arizona as racist and extreme and thus promising reputational damage—that truly exacerbated latent tension on immigration among Republicans.

The Arizona case suggests that it cannot simply be presumed that business and business-aligned center-right policy makers will naturally assert less strict immigration positions or that these positions will prevail in a big-tent right party such as the Republican Party. This caveat offers a correction to more structural accounts and advises a need to understand in a more granular way business logics in the immigration politics of the twenty-first century. In the Trump period, business constituencies often abided extreme immigration policies amid deregulation and tax cuts, seeming only to visibly—perhaps temporarily—break with the Trumpist element of the Republican Party after the storming of the U.S. Capitol on January 6, 2021.[50] Because businesses' interests can be narrowly protected within immigration regimes that are broadly restrictive or hard-line, business opposition is not enough for opponents of these policies to rely on. Beyond this, however, the Arizona case suggests that the Center Right retains—even silently—a classical liberal sensibility in which it is sensitive to being seen as broadly reasonable and to protecting future possibility and growth from the threat of exclusion, isolation, and tumult.

Although that sort of business objection may sound philosophical— rooted, as the previous chapter explained, in a classic liberal reformulation of how security policy is justified—it is in reality much more situational. Events in Arizona suggest that if policies seem to be going over smoothly enough, then the Center Right will tolerate quite a few developments about which it may feel uneasy, but the level of this toleration can change with context. In assessing the likelihood of backlash or disruption, center-right figures will look to the larger political, social, and economic environment. They will be content to follow the populist right-wing path, allaying factional tension, as long as things overall look fine. The real problems for Arizona's Center Right arrived with a growing sense of upheaval—the feeling that others were judging the state negatively and, most importantly, that larger doubts about Arizona were starting to affect the market, which provides a truer verdict than anything else on the merits of policy. What stirred all these sensations was not a sense of principled disagreement but the fact that activist resisters inside and outside Arizona were raising a ruckus.

Activists in Arizona called for protests and boycotts, which unnerved business even as though the boycotts' impact was mixed. Activist efforts were certainly aided by the media fixation on the state—suggesting that easily dramatized, emotive, media-friendly narratives are another key part of fomenting this variety of center-right squeamishness. Business-aligned legislators in Arizona were particularly concerned that outsiders were, as a result of the media attention, seeing the state as racist, rogue, or "crazy." In their view, these problems were not a property of the policies that SB 1070 inherently contained—indeed, these policy makers were convinced that the bill was not as problematic as alleged—but rather a quality of the larger social reaction to the law. Activist protest was thereby able to move a cohort very ideologically different than itself into action, not by finding areas of agreement in a consensus-building effort but by making the other cohort uncomfortable. This negative feeling prompted center-right policy makers—with business support—to halt the securitization trend in Arizona in 2011. Scholarship examining this activism therefore can offer key insights into how these goals were achieved. By reaching a broad audience and prompting critical commentary, the protests worked—not in the short run necessarily, but much more clearly in the medium and long run.

What happened in Arizona therefore might serve as a sort of guide to the kinds of political developments that unnerve crucial business communities and their center-right allies when it comes to immigration politics—the kinds of events that turn these two groups from enablers of racist enforcement policies into a factor in inhibiting them. However, the lack of a consistently decisive principle in motivating this turn and, instead, the reliance on contingent events and the development of a certain kind of atmosphere or mood to trigger the turn suggest that precipitating it can be difficult under any circumstance. Matt McDonald discusses similar cosmopolitan countersecurity arguments that activists have aimed at Australia's extreme offshore-detention policies for asylum seekers and how those arguments have not yet seemed to work.[51] In Arizona, historical experiences, in particular the Martin Luther King Jr. holiday controversy from 1986 to 1992, may have softened a certain segment of Arizona Republicans to these kinds of accusations. Or for such an atmosphere to develop, a polity may need to be saturated by a larger media environment that portrays the locale in question more harshly, driving home negative outside perceptions. This seems likelier for U.S. states, which are immersed in a national media environment, than for countries that possess distinct media ecosystems, notwithstanding the international news media. In any case, the conditions for precipitating this kind of center-right opposition seem tricky to capture.

There are, furthermore, reasons to think that this kind of opposition might have become even harder to mobilize today. The Trump presidency seemed to represent a rightward shift in world politics that has not quickly abated with his defeat. As far as domestic politics goes, in comparison to Arizona's border hawks Trump was the leader of the national Republican Party rather than just the orchestrator of an assertive anti-immigration faction vying for power in a single state. This greater status naturally hugely alters calculations among Republicans about when it may be wise to abandon accommodation of far-right elements who champion anti-immigration views—both because of the strong support Trump summons among the party base and because the whole party's reputation, at least in the short run, is strongly bound to his. Republicans, even those whose earlier comments suggested they would disagree with Trump, have been very cautious to criticize him,[52] even following his attempts to seize power after losing the 2020 election. Of course, underlying these recent calculations are some more basic developments that have occurred in American politics since 2011. They include many of the very same dynamics that strengthened the border hawks' hand in Arizona for so long. Partisan polarization has advanced at an elite level as the U.S. Right has become disproportionately radicalized.[53] Anti-immigration positions have become more popular among Republican voters (or anti-immigration voters have increasingly moved into the Republican camp).[54] As has been evident at a national level since at least the Tea Party movement, populist criticism of Republican officials is ripe to sting, especially when voters underestimate just how loyally partisan their representatives are.[55] For any interested Republican officeholder, finding viable middle ground on immigration issues has thus become even harder.

Activating the kind of center-right opposition that happened in Arizona depends on the sense that a political community is being seen by others as transgressing some kind of important shared norms about reasonableness or inclusion. In this regard, the effect of Trump's presence upon world politics—amplifying hype about a "populist wave"[56]—is important. Even if suspect as an analytical matter, simply the perception that the liberal consensus emergent with the post–Cold War condition is starting to crack puts in question to what extent this cosmopolitan countersecurity logic still holds traction. In a world where a right-wing populist can win the White House, Britain votes to leave the European Union, and right-wing authoritarians hold power in countries as diverse as Russia, India, and Brazil, it becomes more difficult to argue that policies breaching universal rationalist values are embarrassingly out of step. Whereas Arizona's anti-border-hawk activists were able to point to outside condemnation to ground a sense that the border hawks had pushed things beyond the pale, what has become "mainstreamed" in the meantime may create a permissive environment for more radical right-wing or authoritarian politics.

The possibility for a countersecuritization moment in larger-scale politics—whether in the United States or western Europe—therefore seems more remote precisely because of the apparent scale of global political changes. At the same time, dispute roils on: instead of the development of a restrictive consensus, a battle for more humane values, including regarding immigrants, is very much being waged. After all, Trump managed to make his signature immigration-enforcement policy the one that Americans generally seem to oppose: the wall.

In the end, whether the Center Right represents a crucial constituency at all in halting a hard-line trend on immigration—as happened in Arizona—depends on the contextual distribution of power. Sometimes the Center Right occupies the crucial pivot point, but not always. In Arizona, it seemed to be the only force in a realistic position to stop the border hawks; this is perhaps one reason why it finally stepped up to the plate to do so, whereas in previous years it could have counted on Democrats to fight that battle. Where there is fierce and more even partisan competition, as on the U.S. national stage, perhaps this intraparty fracturing is less likely to happen, however.[57] The fact that sweeping Republican victories at the polls vanquished Republicans' electoral foes so much that it set the stage for a factional battle that finally killed Arizona's securitization trend illustrates the topsy-turvyness, the unpredictability, of politics. In a political realm with such inherent unpredictability, even as the number of moderate Republicans dwindles and American politics ossifies, it would be rash to be certain we will never be surprised. And on a broader scale, the Center Right will always contain the seeds of dispute with the more radical Right on immigration—if only they can be brought to germinate.

ARIZONA, 2022

Amid the seemingly enduring patterns we see in border-security politics across many locales, this book has underlined how this politics is still one that we shape together toward a wide spectrum of possible outcomes. Even when racialized accounts portraying immigration as a threat have demonstrated strong mobilizing power and yielded securitized, exclusionary ways of governing migration, this is not the end of the story. By tracing the narrative of immigration politics in Arizona, this book has illustrated that we cannot fully understand this kind of politics through individual, seemingly exceptional moments or by boiling it down to how these issues appear to play in focus groups or public polls. Rather, this kind of security politics plays out in a long and complex process, including moves, countermoves, and interacting strategies that produce certain outcomes but over time may lead to other, very different ones. Even though it can appear sometimes that securitized politics follows a single dominant script, politics is always a field of active dispute, twists, and turns: unexpected possibilities can emerge.

In the end, then, we turn to what such a process has left in place in Arizona at the time of writing this book—twelve years on from the passage of SB 1070 and eleven years after the state reached the end of an era of especially intense border-security politics. Today's Arizona is not politically placid; it remains center stage for major controversies in U.S. politics.[58] It is a divided place—politically very closely divided indeed.[59] But that close division in itself marks a major change. Democrats took both of Arizona's seats in the U.S. Senate between 2018 and 2020, and Joe Biden carried Arizona by the narrowest raw-vote margin of any state. Republicans held both chambers of the state legislature, but only by a single seat in each. Much of this new partisan parity grows from sustained mobilizations by younger Hispanic Arizonans: activists and organizers who combated the likes of Pearce and Arpaio from the outside—leading protests, lobbying efforts, community immigration law clinics, and voter registration drives in the heat of earlier border-security politics—in many cases now hold office.[60] They and the countermobilization they led are often credited for finally making manifest a long-prophesied purpling of the state.[61]

Although the decreasing dominance of the Republican Party has not yielded a larger moderating trend within the party, it is also clear that the functions of the immigration issue for Republicans have shifted. In the aftermath of Trump's defeat, Arizona Republicans have maintained and even deepened their Trumpist positioning, including through a widely condemned "audit" into the presidential election results that was called by state senate Republicans.[62] As the state party has lurched to the right, there is no question that many Republican officeholders remain supportive of hard-line immigration policy. However, the immigration issue is not functioning in the way it used to within the Arizona Republican Party's efforts to mobilize its supporters or win general election votes. Gone are Russell Pearce, who led a concerted legislative attempt to treat immigrants as a threat, and Joe Arpaio, who made a point of menacing Hispanic communities. Both have failed in political comeback attempts, and neither has any close imitator on the Arizona political scene of the early 2020s. Although the current Republican governor, Doug Ducey, has taken the initiative to orchestrate Republicans in criticizing the Democratic presidential administration on its handling of the border, he has been forced to quickly retreat from other efforts to leverage state-level immigration action for partisan gain.[63] Republicans seeking to replace Ducey as governor seem otherwise occupied, with the Trump-endorsed candidate echoing expected far-right immigration positions but campaigning more prominently on different right-wing grievances surrounding COVID-19 and the 2020 election.[64]

Furthermore, Arizona voters in 2022 have the opportunity to undo a ban that Pearce led (with the passage of Proposition 300 in 2006) on unauthorized residents of Arizona accessing in-state university tuition rates, which would allow Dreamers more equal access to higher education—a reversal made possible by a legislative referral (SCR 1044) supported in roll-call votes by seven Republican legislators.[65] This would have been unthinkable a decade earlier. Where institutions of direct democracy had been leveraged by radical-right populists to drive more exclusionary measures through the ballot box and reconfigure elite strategies in more hard-line directions, perhaps those actions may now be, at least in small part, reversed.

This new political configuration grows from the history and dynamics of the state's earlier immigration struggles and cannot be separated from them. At the same time, these new dynamics may open some spaces for Arizonans to move beyond old debates. Democrats overall are more reluctant than before to take security-heavy or punitive approaches toward immigration. Where Democrats had earlier abandoned calling Pearce's policies racist, feeling that this message was falling flat, today openly discussing racial justice is much more common. The new generation of Hispanic officeholders, who often cut their teeth in struggles against Pearce and Arpaio, "want to move past opposing those who have opposed them, and to be defined by the positive changes they make"; in this sense, the SB 1070 era can be understood as the start of a wider and enduring mobilization.[66]

And such activists may increasingly find at least some measure of common ground with the kinds of white suburban voters who decided to boot Pearce from office in 2011, having tired of his style, priorities, and divisiveness. Arizona's suburbanites—among them a sizeable number of chamber-of-commerce-style, white, professional-class voters—were another key constituency in Democrats' gains in 2018 and 2020.[67] The particular demographics of Arizona—with relatively few rural white voters and a large (sub)urbanized population—may particularly favor the emergence of this kind of political configuration.[68] Nonetheless, even as Arizona's future remains unsettled, its political landscape at the beginning of this decade is markedly different than its landscape at the beginning of the previous decade, in ways that not so long ago would have been difficult to predict.

The goal of this book has been to illuminate the story of Arizona to clarify the political processes that surround the securitization of migration—a trend that has swept across not just the Sonoran Desert but also the Mediterranean Sea and many other places besides. This book has analyzed how securitization may deepen because of how security meanings shape competitive politics around immigration—how these developments can be driven by dynamics of party competition, attempts to capture issue ownership, one-upmanship, and the distinct political logics that decision makers adopt for how purported security issues are politically best dealt with. It can seem very difficult indeed to shift these dynamics given how entrenched securitizing approaches to immigration have become. Yet this book has equally shown how the heat of security politics and resistance to racialized, exclusionary security policies can power new countersecurity logics, create unlikely political allies, and perhaps in the end bring about new and unexpected political configurations. Security politics is fluid, just like the rest of our social lives: it always preserves the chance for new possibilities to take hold. How our governments treat people on the move has increasingly become subject to the political games that surround security, but the rules of these games ultimately are up to us as citizens.

APPENDIX

METHODOLOGY

PROCESS-TRACING APPROACH

This book employs an "explaining-outcome" process-tracing approach that aims to reconstruct a sufficient explanation of a puzzling case outcome—or, in this instance, differing puzzling outcomes across time.[1] Although all process-tracing research aims to identify the "causal mechanisms" that operate between contextual circumstances and particular process outcomes, case-oriented process-tracing research employs a broad sense of the concept, as Derek Beach and Rasmus Brun Pedersen observe,[2] because the research is trying to explain a particular case through as many mechanisms as may be required for a sufficient explanation rather than focusing parsimoniously on a single generalizable mechanism. Mechanisms in general go beyond the establishment of correlations to "tell us how things happen: how actors relate, how individuals come to believe what they do or what they draw from past experiences, how policies and institutions endure or change, how outcomes that are inefficient become hard to reverse, and so on."[3] In this light, processes are conceptualized as "frequently occurring combinations or sequences of mechanisms."[4]

Chapter 1 establishes three main puzzling outcomes of the Arizona case to be explained through the construction of a process narrative:[5] first, the escalating securitization of immigration and the border, which did not in any sense track the metrics usually employed to measure border-security problems; second, the overwhelming security-oriented policy response in Arizona state government between 2004 and 2010, puzzling given substantial support in public polls for a number of other kinds of responses to the immigration issue; and third, the longer policy trajectory from a relaxed disposition toward unauthorized immigration to an intense securitization trend and then to a rapid halt to that trend, a sequence that belies expected securitization trajectories as well as structural explanations of immigration-policy stability. In all of those respects, coming to an explanation of the case depends on identifying mechanisms that operate between the larger contextual conditions and particular outcomes in terms of policy and resulting political configurations.

Explaining-outcome process-tracing studies often rely upon inductive research strategies to build sufficient explanations of their case outcomes; after all, this kind of case explanation is needed only if there is a lack of existing generalizable propositions that apply to the case. In particular, the project for this book was spurred by a need to investigate the interactions of security meanings with competitive political strategies—an area undertheorized such that there is no straightforward preexisting explanation for the Arizona case's development. Although it has been proposed that Copenhagen School–style securitizing moves constitute a causal mechanism,[6] in post-Copenhagen sociological securitization studies there has been much less attention to a more appropriate reading of securitization as a *process* (leading to security practices) that is composed of particular mechanisms.[7] In this sense, the goal of this book's analysis is to inductively develop new propositions of the mechanisms that allow for a sufficient explanation of events within the securitization (and, later, countersecuritization) process in Arizona.[8] The ability of process-tracing methods to introduce the researcher to explanations that might not have been evident[9] is particularly significant for these inductive purposes.

Indeed, although this kind of process-tracing research is "case oriented"—focused on developing a sufficient explanation of the case rather than propositions intended to be fully generalizable—case-oriented process-tracing analyses will nonetheless "often have theoretical ambitions that reach beyond the single case."[10] Single-case studies can in fact be particularly well suited for theory building regarding relationships that have not been extensively explored.[11] The richness of "within-case" data that deal with a range of actors, moments in time, and observations gives the researcher the opportunity to grapple with complexity and ambiguities in ways that are not just empirically precise but also potentially theoretically productive.[12] Single-case studies can provide valuable theoretical propositions, even if not sufficient grounds for generalizations, in process-tracing studies as in qualitative research more generally.[13]

One of the challenges of process-tracing research is to identify mechanisms that serve a causal function and are not just congruent to the sequence being examined.[14] This may be less urgent in what Beach and Pedersen call case-oriented (rather than theory-oriented) process tracing because of expectations that particular case explanations will encompass contextual factors. However, this consideration is nonetheless significant for research that has any aims to generate theoretical propositions with possibly greater relevance. Part of the answer to how such robustness is achieved within this research design lies in the single-case study's extensive, detailed, within-case data, which underscore how a single-case study comprises, in reality, many hundreds of observed episodes:[15] this research traces the success or failure of hundreds of policy proposals and in the process of identifying larger, more generalized patterns among them engages in a focused discussion of the mechanisms yielding these patterns. Although many aspects of context remain crucial in the explanations offered in case-oriented process-tracing research, the discussion sections near the ends of the chapters in this book serve to focus on and analytically distinguish the key apparent mechanisms in explaining the case outcomes.

INTERPRETATION AND SITUATED AGENCY

Process tracing offers a clear approach for grasping participants' intersubjective understandings in decision-making processes that are characterized by ambiguity, by the emergence of new interpretive dispositions toward issues, and by dilemmas that emerge when existing ways of doing things no longer appear viable.[16] Process tracing can often take on a somewhat positivist character in testing the validity of hypotheses about given decision processes,[17] creating misperceptions about it that have left it a relatively seldom-used method within a securitization studies literature that often favors more critical and post-positivist analysis.[18] Indeed, these misperceptions are partly why, as chapter 1 argues, there is a lack of research into why policy decision makers choose securitizing approaches to immigration. Interpretive forms of process tracing, however, employ qualitative data to identify mechanisms of interest within the shifting interpretive dispositions of policy actors as a way of explaining how certain policy approaches become favored and others are ruled out.[19] This interpretive methodology accords with a Weberian view of subjective rationality, where actions are rational in that actors consciously relate action to meaning.[20] Indeed, if the central research question of this book is why policy actors in Arizona chose securitizing approaches to immigration among other available interpretations, then interpretive process tracing is a self-evidently valuable approach to recovering the mechanisms underlying the deliberative process that produced the outcomes to be explained. Drawing mainly on contemporaneous documents and elite interviews,[21] process tracing can reveal these reasonings in ways that discourse analysis cannot because policy makers' motives "may be excluded from the official discourse."[22]

A key strength of process-tracing research is that it allows a perspective that illuminates the significance of both context and agency in the processes examined.[23] Actors, of course, draw social meanings from their preexisting context but also can resist social regularities, attempt to create new ones, and generally innovate in response to dilemmas.[24] Here, the concept of "situated agency" becomes central to how interpretation explains action with respect to a Weberian concept of subjective rationality: "We can accept that people always set out against the background of a social discourse or tradition and still think of them as agents who can act and reason in novel ways to modify this background."[25] With this notion of situated agency, this research takes a fundamentally actor-centered approach to interpretation and favors "agent-oriented theory."[26] Such a perspective can take "the subjective understandings of leaders as funnels for other . . . factors" that shape decisions,[27] offering a way to understand what conditions represented compelling forces in the actors' views and thus shaped their beliefs and interpretive dispositions. Importantly, the use of historical-based understanding is distinguished from hermeneutical approaches;[28] if one accepts the constructivist premise that meanings can be sufficiently shared to constitute social facts,[29] then this research approach can serve the goal of inductive theory generation.

Although all process-tracing research relies on the careful sequencing of events that compose the process in question,[30] a method that works to construct narratives is in particular well equipped to preserve the sense that interpretive beliefs and understandings are connected to each other and to larger shared social understandings. This method is very distinct from "approaches that introduce meanings or beliefs as 'ideational variables' alongside other variables. . . . Narratives explain shared facts by postulating significant relationships, connections or similarities between them."[31] A clear consonance is evident between this form of political science narrative and interpretivist approaches to identifying causal mechanisms in that events in narratives are "revealed as possessing a structure, and order of meaning, that they do not possess as a mere sequence."[32]

IDENTIFICATION OF RELEVANT POLICIES (WITHIN-CASE EVENTS)

Because process tracing still always relies upon sequencing, this study identified relevant policy proposals in Arizona (within-case events) around which policy makers' interpretations would be examined with the goal toward identifying the political rationalities underlying this securitization process. Policy proposals were identified through several main sources. Secondary literature easily identified those Arizona policies from this period that had gained substantial academic attention already. However, only rarely did the literature provide sequencing information about policies that had not already come to generally prominent attention.[33] More significant resources in this regard were (1) the online archives of the Arizona State Legislature, which provided a complete record of proposed bills in the state legislature as well as summaries, committee records, and voting records, and (2) news media accounts, accessed largely through the Nexis database (discussed later). Further official sources such as the *Arizona Administrative Register* allowed for the sequencing of relevant administrative decisions. Interviews with policy actors also allowed for the sequencing of less visible policy changes, such as funding decisions and policies regarding enforcement that did not require specific pronouncement.

In total, this book identifies 118 proposed or enacted policies in the main period of study between 2003 and 2011. This number allows for a broad tracing of the larger policy environment in Arizona; many of these proposals (in particular bills in the legislature that did not advance) did not yield extensive coverage in the media or otherwise. This large survey of sequenced events provided for a broader understanding of the policy-making climate and ensured that the process account was not wrongfully skewed toward events that had already dominated the secondary literature. Beyond sequencing, the survey also informed interviews and other further research.

Like most process-tracing research, this project employed multiple methods of empirical investigation: both interviews with policy actors relevant to the decisions under discussion (as discussed in a later section) and, preceding that, document analysis.

DOCUMENT COLLECTION AND ANALYSIS

An initial period of data gathering focused on the collection and analysis of relevant documents, preceding a planned period of interview fieldwork that would provide the essential data about interpretations by policy actors in the case.

It is a common position that the limits of interviews as a method mean "they cannot be relied upon as the sole methodology."[34] Documents therefore occupy a secure methodological place alongside elite interviews in this sort of case-study design.[35] Document gathering and analysis aimed to serve several analytical functions. First, they aided in sequencing, described earlier. Second, they informed planned interviews, either by aiding in interview sampling or in developing appropriate questions for particular interviewees. The "decisional" method of sampling for elite interviews (as discussed in the next section)[36] relies on identifying before interview fieldwork some of the individual policy elites involved in making a decision. Documents frequently provided this information. In addition, referring to documents is a crucial part of an interviewer's preparation of appropriate questions,[37] and documents can also be used during the interview itself to prompt the interviewee,[38] a tactic occasionally employed in this research.

Third, documents were gathered to provide primary data in their own right, which they can do even about interpretive matters such as political elites' beliefs.[39] Especially regarding political controversies, contemporaneous journalism and government documents contain information about policy makers' beliefs about problems and politics as well as their rationalities for action. The political elites interviewed would often refer to political positions or problem conceptions that had been contemporaneously documented; documents therefore provided important context for interviews that could go on only for a limited duration. The process of reaching an interpretive analysis of political decisions relied on both forms of data. In general, policy makers were aware of how their decisions had been documented and interpreted at the time, which often formed the background of how they discussed their choices in interviews. Documents therefore provided context for depth in interpretive analysis—though they were necessarily read as empirical evidence with the understanding that they were not produced in reference to the research question[40] and were shaped by their contemporaneous purposes and their likely intended audiences.[41]

Fourth, perhaps the most discussed use of documents in relation to interview data involves the process of "triangulation." Drawing upon "different forms of evidence around the same event"[42] serves the interest of accuracy in empirical studies examining qualitative data, even in studies that take an interpretivist approach because interviews usually present at least some interpretive complexities.[43] "Triangulation" can refer either to using different methods to bring new data into the interpretive mix or, more traditionally, to making sure that each data source aligns factually with the other sources.[44] Both types of triangulation were necessary approaches at different points in this research. For instance, given the time that had passed since the events some interviewees were discussing, it was important to compare their accounts and recalled sequences against the contemporaneous documentary record. Documents helped to sequence events and ground interviews in order to illuminate how different interview accounts of the same events fit together. Triangulation also did not exclusively mean falsification: policy-maker recollections that sometimes seemed unlikely were bolstered by the documentary record.

In sum, this project consulted hundreds of contemporaneous press and government documents, more than six hundred of which were coded (see the later section on coding). Press accounts came from a very large number of local and national media sources available through the Nexis database. However, especially large numbers of media documents came from the *Arizona Capitol Times*, an "insider" political publication; the *Arizona Republic*, a mass-market newspaper; and the Associated Press Phoenix political desk. As mentioned earlier, the online archives of the Arizona Legislature were a significant source of documents, providing in particular the minutes of hearings, summaries of draft bills prepared by legislative staff, legislative voting records, and governors' veto letters and signing statements. Archives held by the Arizona Secretary of State's Office provided access to other important documents such as the texts of executive orders.

SAMPLING AND INTERVIEWING POLICY ACTORS

The method most central to process tracing is "conducting elite interviews to establish the decisions and actions that lay behind an event or series of events."[45] A semistructured interview format allowed for a focus on some dedicated topics and policies and for the interviewee to teach the interviewer about aspects of the research problem,[46] which is critical to inductively grasping the actors' own categories that guided action.[47]

In process-tracing research, nonprobability methods are the only relevant way to sample interviewees;[48] this project identified interviewees both from documents and through snowball sampling. It followed the "decisional" or decision-based model of nonprobability sampling,[49] which sought to interview policy elites who were specifically relevant to certain policy decisions. The identity of many such individuals, in particular elected officials, is evident from public records. Snowball sampling was used in addition to gain a sense of which provisionally identified participants were indeed most relevant to the particular decisions and sometimes to identify new possible interviewees. In cases where many decision makers are already known, it is easier to identify different starting points for various rolling "snowballs" and to ensure that these starting points differ in respects significant to the research. This study carefully pursued a number of different "starting points" for sampling in order to interview relevant people of varying parties, institutional positions, and ideological factions. Because of the decisional basis of sampling, interviewee demographics were skewed toward those typical of state elected offices— that is, white, male, older. Access to interviewees benefited from the generally more open environment of U.S. state government.[50]

Twenty-seven semistructured elite interviews were conducted: twenty-six in person in Arizona in fieldwork from November 2014 to February 2015 and one over the phone in June 2015. Each of the interviewees had been either an elected official or an adviser to the governor during the period under study. All of these discussions were audiorecorded with the interviewees' permission and later fully transcribed. Interviews tended to last around an hour but ranged from twenty minutes to one hour and forty-five minutes. Somewhat unusually for political interview research, interviews were not conducted with promises of anonymity because of the public profile of the interviewees and their identifiability due to their involvement in well-known episodes.

The full list of interviewees is presented in table A.1.

CODING AND NARRATIVE CONSTRUCTION

Documents were coded using NVivo before interviews were conducted; following the conclusion of data gathering, interview data were also thematically coded using NVivo. Coding employed themes identified from both the initial document analysis and new information gathered in interviews. The codes related to both specific policies (e.g., "employer sanctions," "local enforcement," "SB 1070") and institutions (e.g., "legislature," "police," "federal government") as well as to larger themes in securitization and general political analysis (e.g., "exceptionalism," "party politics"). To facilitate sequencing and the construction of the case narrative, event- and year-based codes were created to order events. Passages of the interviews were coded according to the content or themes of particular parts of the interview.

Following data collection, events were laid out in sequential maps to better identify policy-making patterns and to aid in the eventual construction of narratives. This process included extensive mapping of voting records and tracing policies to previously proposed (or defeated) versions

TABLE A.1 List of Interviewees

Interviewee	Relevant Office	Party (2003–2011)	Interview Date	Interview Location
Bill Brotherton	State representative, 1998–2003; state senator, 2003–2007	D	January 28, 2015	Phoenix
Dennis Burke	Governor's chief of staff for policy, 2003–2007; chief of staff, 2007–2009	D	January 13, 2015	Phoenix
Jennifer J. Burns	State representative, 2003–2009	R	November 24, 2014	Marana
Chad Campbell	State representative, 2007–2015	D	December 2, 2014	Phoenix
Chuck Coughlin	Consultant; adviser to governor, 2009–2015	R	December 18, 2014	Phoenix
Rich Crandall	State representative, 2007–2011; state senator, 2011–2013	R	December 10, 2014	Mesa
Tony Estrada	Santa Cruz County sheriff, 1993–2021	D	February 10, 2015	Nogales
Steve Gallardo	State representative, 2003–2009; state senator, 2011–2015	D	January 28, 2015	Phoenix
Terry Goddard	State attorney general, 2003–2011; candidate for governor, 2010	D	June 24, 2015	by phone
Mike Haener	Deputy chief of staff for legislative affairs to the governor, 2003–2009	D	January 23, 2015	Phoenix
Pete Hershberger	State representative, 2001–2009	R	November 24, 2014	Tucson
Russ Jones	State representative, 2005–2007, 2009–2013	R	February 6, 2015	Yuma
Joseph Kanefield	State election director, 2004–2009; general counsel to governor, 2009–2011	R (de facto)	November 6, 2014	Phoenix

Name	Party	Experience	Date	City
John Kavanagh	R	State representative, 2007–2015	January 6, 2015	Phoenix
Jeanine L'Ecuyer	D	Press secretary to governor, 2004–2005; communications director, 2005–2009	November 11, 2014	Phoenix
Phil Lopes	D	State representative, 2003–2011	January 16, 2015	Tucson
Juan Mendez	D	State representative, 2013–2017	December 11, 2014	Phoenix
Eric Meyer	D	State representative, 2009–2017	December 4, 2014	Phoenix
Tim Nelson	D	General counsel to the governor, 2003–2008	November 17, 2014	Phoenix
Tom O'Halleran	R	State representative, 2001–2007; state senator, 2007–2009	January 27, 2015	Village of Oak Creek
Jonathan Paton	R	State representative, 2005–2009; state senator, 2009–2010	February 2, 2015	Scottsdale
Russell Pearce	R	State representative, 2001–2009; state senator, 2009–2011; Arizona Senate president, 2011	February 11, 2015	Phoenix
Martín Quezada	D	Analyst/policy adviser, Arizona House of Representatives, 2002–2005; state representative, 2012–2015	December 8, 2014	Phoenix
Ed Rheinheimer	R	Cochise County attorney, 2005–2015	January 19, 2015	Oro Valley
Kyrsten Sinema	D	State representative, 2005–2011; state senator, 2011–2012	December 5, 2014	Phoenix
Steve Smith	R	State senator, 2011–2013; state representative, 2013–2015	December 22, 2014	Phoenix
Jim Walsh	D	Pinal County attorney, 2007–2013	January 26, 2015	Oracle

in order to track events across time. Events were therefore mapped and sequenced in order to thematically identify relevant patterns. These maps provided structure for the collation of qualitative interview and documentary data related to specific episodes, which were then reduced to the most illustrative or explanatory material involving those events.

In this way, narrative construction proceeded by relying on codes that linked policy-maker interview data and documents to particular episodes, policies, and years. This construction was often cross-coded with the themes identified, which were then used to draft analytical sections. In the drafting of the case narrative, policy-makers' retrospective accounts were synthesized and triangulated against each other and the documentary record in order to build as accurate a sequence and narrative as possible with the data.[51] The division of the narrative into separate thematically focused chapters followed only after larger maps of events had been completed and noteworthy patterns and mechanisms identified. This process helped to construct the "theoretically explicit narrative" that constitutes the case study.[52]

ACKNOWLEDGMENTS

This book has been a long time in coming. I recall sitting at my desk as a summer intern in Phoenix in 2004, reading over some newspaper articles and press releases, and starting to think that this immigration issue looked to become bedeviling. That was half a lifetime ago. One gathers a lot of debts in such a span. The immigration politics that has unfolded during this time has not always been edifying, but I have been fortunate to be able to spend the time I have tracing it and trying to understand it. Whatever I have produced from this effort is, of course, not mine alone.

First among those to thank are the people who literally made the research—the people in Arizona whom I interviewed. They gave generously of their time and recollections and allowed this book to be. A number of them also helped to connect me with other respondents and enriched the research in that way, too. I extend my thanks to them all.

Second, many people gave me guidance and encouragement as a researcher. Christina Boswell and Andrew W. Neal are chief among them, always offering kind and thoughtful support for me and for this work. There are others as well whom I came to know at the University of Edinburgh, and the university itself provided me with crucial financing for this project. It was there, amid the company of excellent researchers, that I learned (I hope) how to be a scholar. I am grateful.

Third, there are those who helped to make this research into this book. In the process, I benefited from the advice of Richard Freeman and Hugh Bochel. Ian O'Grady gave me valuable feedback. Stephen Wesley at Columbia University Press has been an excellent editor for a first book, someone who has ably shepherded it—and me—through an unfamiliar process. I appreciate this.

Last, there are those who have supported me as a person through this undertaking. They include, certainly, the many people—too many to name here—who still make Arizona home for me. There are also the scholars whom I was fortunate to have as friends in the years when I was doing this work: again, too many to name all of them, but Taylor Spears, Alexander R. Hensby, and Sara Casella Colombeau stand out. And, of course, my loved ones have helped me in multifarious ways: my parents, Christine Coffey and Terrence Slaven; and my wife, Kirsten Craig, who has been my constant supporter. My thanks to them and my love.

NOTES

INTRODUCTION: ARIZONA AND THE RISE OF POPULIST BORDER-SECURITY POLITICS

1. Russell Pearce, quoted in Ted Robbins, "The Man Behind Arizona's Toughest Immigrant Laws," *Morning Edition*, National Public Radio, May 1, 2008.

2. Josh Barro, "Before Donald Trump, There Was Jan Brewer," *Upshot* (*New York Times* blog), February 10, 2016, https://www.nytimes.com/2016/02/11/upshot/before-donald -trump-there-was-jan-brewer.html.

3. Gary P. Freeman, Randall Hansen, and David L. Leal, *Immigration and Public Opinion in Liberal Democracies* (London: Routledge, 2013); David Johann and Kathrin Thomas, "Need for Support or Economic Competition? Implicit Associations with Immigrants During the 2015 Migrant Crisis," *Research and Politics* 5, no. 2 (2018): 1–8; Scott Blinder, "Imagined Immigration: The Impact of Different Meanings of 'Immigrants' in Public Opinion and Policy Debates in Britain," *Political Studies* 63, no. 1 (2015): 80–100.

4. Jens Hainmueller and Daniel J. Hopkins, "The Hidden American Immigration Consensus: A Conjoint Analysis of Attitudes Toward Immigrants," *American Journal of Political Science* 59, no. 3 (2015): 529–48; Francine Segovia and Renatta Defever, "The Polls—Trends: American Public Opinion on Immigrants and Immigration Policy," *Public Opinion Quarterly* 74, no. 2 (2010): 375–94.

5. See, for instance, Nick Vaughan-Williams, *Vernacular Border Security: Citizens' Narratives of Europe's "Migration Crisis"* (Oxford: Oxford University Press, 2021).

6. Amada Armenta, "Who Polices Immigration?," in *Protect, Serve, and Deport: The Rise of Policing as Immigration Enforcement* (Berkeley: University of California Press, 2017), 15–35.

7.   "The assumption is that security practices result from securitization. No security practices without securitization" (Thierry Balzacq, "Legitimacy and the 'Logic' of Security," in *Contesting Security: Strategies and Logics*, ed. Thierry Balzacq [Abingdon, U.K.: Routledge, 2015], 2). That is, securitization is whatever process leads to security practices—notwithstanding how much this may resemble previous theoretical models.

8.   Philippe Bourbeau, "Moving Forward Together: Logics of the Securitisation Process," *Millennium* 43, no. 1 (2014): 187.

9.   See Paul James Pope and Terence M. Garrett, "America's Homo Sacer: Examining U.S. Deportation Hearings and the Criminalization of Illegal Immigration," *Administration and Society* 45, no. 2 (2013): 179–82; Nik Theodore, "Policing Borders: Unauthorized Immigration and the Pernicious Politics of Attrition," in *The Police and Society: Touchstone Readings*, 4th ed., ed. Victor E. Kappeler and Brian P. Schaefer (Long Grove, IL: Waveland Press, 2019), 515; Gabriel J. Chin, Carissa Byrne Hessick, and Marc L. Miller, "Arizona Senate Bill 1070: Politics Through Immigration Law," in *Arizona Firestorm: Global Immigration Realities, National Media, and Provincial Politics*, ed. Otto Santa Ana and Celeste González de Bustamante (New York: Rowman and Littlefield, 2012), 77; and Clariza Ruiz De Castilla, "Citizenship Constructions: Rhetoric, Immigration, and Arizona's SB 1070," PhD diss., University of Texas at Austin, 2013, 4.

10. Doris Marie Provine and Gabriella Sanchez, "Suspecting Immigrants: Exploring Links Between Racialised Anxieties and Expanded Police Powers in Arizona," *Policing and Society* 21, no. 4 (2011): 468–79.

11. Clara Eroukhmanoff, "'It's Not a Muslim Ban!' Indirect Speech Acts and the Securitisation of Islam in the United States Post-9/11," *Global Discourse* 8, no. 1 (2018): 5–25.

12. Patrick Kingsley, "Migration to Europe Is Down Sharply. So Is It Still a 'Crisis'?," *New York Times*, June 27, 2018, https://www.nytimes.com/interactive/2018/06/27/world/europe/europe-migrant-crisis-change.html.

13. Adam Isacson, Maureen Meyer, and Ashley Davis, "Border Security and Migration: A Report from Arizona," Washington Office on Latin America, December 5, 2013, https://www.wola.org/analysis/border-security-and-migration-a-report-from-arizona/; Ruth Ellen Wasem, "US Immigration Policy: Chart Book of Key Trends," Congressional Research Service, March 7, 2013, 12, http://digitalcommons.ilr.cornell.edu/key_workplace/1032/.

14. Dennis Wagner and Ronald J. Hansen, "Poll: Worker Verification Even More Popular," *Arizona Republic*, July 25, 2010; Pew Research Center for the People and the Press, Pew Hispanic Center, "America's Immigration Quandary: No Consensus on Immigration Problem or Proposed Fixes," March 30, 2006, http://www.people-press.org/2006/03/30/americas-immigration-quandary/.

15. Hilary Cunningham, "Transnational Politics at the Edges of Sovereignty: Social Movements, Crossings, and the State at the US-Mexico Border," *Global Networks* 1, no. 4 (2001): 369–87.

16. Terry Greene Sterling and Jude Joffe-Block, *Driving While Brown: Sheriff Joe Arpaio Versus the Latino Resistance* (Oakland: University of California Press, 2021); Emine

Fidan Elcioglu, *Divided by the Wall: Progressive and Conservative Immigration Politics at the U.S.-Mexico Border* (Oakland: University of California Press, 2020); René Galindo, "Repartitioning the National Community: Political Visibility and Voice for Undocumented Immigrants in the Spring 2006 Immigration Rights Marches," *Aztlan* 35, no. 2 (2010): 37–64; Michael Scherer, "Why the Latino Vote in Arizona Could Be Decisive in 2012," *Time*, February 22, 2012, http://swampland.time.com/2012/02/22/why-the-latino-vote-in-arizona-could-be-decisive-in-2012/.

17. For instance, see Gary P. Freeman, "Modes of Immigration Politics in Liberal Democratic States," *International Migration Review* 29, no. 4 (1995): 881–902.

18. Andrew W. Neal, "'Events, Dear Boy, Events': Terrorism and Security from the Perspective of Politics," *Critical Studies on Terrorism* 5, no. 1 (2012): 107–20; see also Patrick A. Mello and Dirk Peters, "Parliaments in Security Policy: Involvement, Politicisation, and Influence," *British Journal of Politics and International Relations* 20, no. 1 (2018): 4.

19. Jonas Hagmann, Hendrik Hegemann, and Andrew W. Neal, "The Politicisation of Security: Controversy, Mobilisation, Arena Shifting. Introduction by the Guest Editors," *European Review of International Studies* 5, no. 3 (2018): 4.

20. Martha Finnemore and Kathryn Sikkink, "Taking Stock: The Constructivist Research Program in International Relations and Comparative Politics," *Annual Review of Political Science* 4, no. 1 (2001): 391–416; Joseph R. Gusfield, *The Culture of Public Problems: Drinking-Driving and the Symbolic Order* (Chicago: University of Chicago Press, 1981).

21. Barry Buzan, Ole Wæver, and Jaap de Wilde, *Security: A New Framework for Analysis* (Boulder, CO: Lynne Rienner, 1998); Ole Wæver, "Securitization and Desecuritization," in *On Security*, ed. Ronnie D. Lipschutz (New York: Columbia University Press, 1995), 46–86.

22. Buzan, Wæver, and de Wilde, *Security*, 5.

23. Carsten Bagge Laustsen and Ole Wæver, "In Defence of Religion: Sacred Referent Objects for Securitization," *Millennium* 29, no. 3 (2000): 709; Hagmann, Hegemann, and Neal, "The Politicisation of Security"; Adam Côté, "Agents Without Agency: Assessing the Role of the Audience in Securitization Theory," *Security Dialogue* 47, no. 6 (2016): 553.

24. See, for instance, Matt McDonald, "Securitization and the Construction of Security," *European Journal of International Relations* 14, no. 4 (2008): 563–87; Felix Ciută, "Security and the Problem of Context: A Hermeneutical Critique of Securitisation Theory," *Review of International Studies* 35, no. 2 (2009): 301–26; Alison Howell, "The Global Politics of Medicine: Beyond Global Health, Against Securitisation Theory," *Review of International Studies* 40, no. 5 (2014): 961–87; and Jef Huysmans, "Revisiting Copenhagen: Or, On the Creative Development of a Security Studies Agenda in Europe," *European Journal of International Relations* 4, no. 4 (1998): 479–505.

25. Neal, "'Events, Dear Boy, Events,'" 107.

26. Michael C. Williams, "Words, Images, Enemies: Securitization and International Politics," *International Studies Quarterly* 47, no. 4 (2003): 511–31.

27. Buzan, Wæver, and de Wilde, *Security*, 23–24.

28. Fiona de Londras, "Politicisation, Law, and Rights in the Transnational Counter-Terrorism Space: Indications from the Regulation of Foreign Terrorist Fighters," *European Review of International Studies* 5, no. 3 (2018): 116.

29. Michael C. Williams, "Securitization as Political Theory: The Politics of the Extraordinary," *International Relations* 29, no. 1 (2015): 115, https://doi.org/10.1177/0047117814526606c.

30. Fred Vultee, "Securitization as a Theory of Media Effects: The Contest Over the Framing of Political Violence," PhD diss., University of Missouri at Columbia, 2007.

31. See Thierry Balzacq, "The Three Faces of Securitization: Political Agency, Audience, and Context," *European Journal of International Relations* 11, no. 2 (2005): 171–201; Thierry Balzacq, "A Theory of Securitization," in *Securitization Theory: How Security Problems Emerge and Dissolve*, ed. Thierry Balzacq (Abingdon, U.K.: Routledge, 2011), 1–30; Jef Huysmans, *The Politics of Insecurity: Fear, Migration, and Asylum in the EU* (Abingdon, U.K.: Routledge, 2006); Roxanne Lynn Doty, "States of Exception on the Mexico-US Border: Security, 'Decisions,' and Civilian Border Patrols," *International Political Sociology* 1, no. 2 (2007): 113–37; Mark B. Salter, "Securitization and Desecuritization: A Dramaturgical Analysis of the Canadian Air Transport Security Authority," *Journal of International Relations and Development* 11, no. 4 (2008): 321–49; and Holger Stritzel, *Security in Translation: Securitization Theory and the Localization of Threat* (Basingstoke, U.K.: Palgrave Macmillan, 2014).

32. Georgios Karyotis, "Securitization of Migration in Greece: Process, Motives, and Implications," *International Political Sociology* 6, no. 4 (2012): 390–408.

33. Karyotis, "Securitization of Migration in Greece," 393.

34. Rita Floyd, "Extraordinary or Ordinary Emergency Measures: What, and Who, Defines the 'Success' of Securitization?," *Cambridge Review of International Affairs* 29, no. 2 (2016): 677–94; Didier Bigo, "Security and Immigration: Toward a Critique of the Governmentality of Unease," *Alternatives* 27, special issue (2002): 63–92; Jef Huysmans, *Security Unbound: Enacting Democratic Limits* (Abingdon, U.K.: Routledge, 2014).

35. Roxanne Lynn Doty, *The Law Into Their Own Hands: Immigration and the Politics of Exceptionalism* (Tucson: University of Arizona Press, 2009); Scott D. Watson, "'Framing' the Copenhagen School: Integrating the Literature on Threat Construction," *Millennium* 40, no. 2 (2012): 279–301; Myriam Dunn Cavelty, *Cyber-security and Threat Politics: US Efforts to Secure the Information Age* (Abingdon, U.K.: Routledge, 2008); Holger Stritzel, "Security, the Translation," *Security Dialogue* 42, nos. 4–5 (2011): 343–55.

36. Paul Roe, "Actor, Audience(s), and Emergency Measures: Securitization and the UK's Decision to Invade Iraq," *Security Dialogue* 39, no. 6 (2008): 615–35; Fred Vultee, "Securitization as a Media Frame: What Happens When the Media 'Speak Security,'" in *Securitization Theory*, ed. Balzacq, 77–93; Lee Jarvis and Tim Legrand, "'I Am Somewhat Puzzled': Questions, Audiences, and Securitization in the Proscription of Terrorist Organizations," *Security Dialogue* 48, no. 2 (2017): 149–67.

37. Nils Brunsson, *The Organization of Hypocrisy: Talk, Decisions, and Actions in Organizations* (New York: Wiley, 1989).

38. Philippe Bourbeau, *The Securitization of Migration: A Study of Movement and Order* (Abingdon, U.K.: Routledge, 2011), 43.

39. Christina Boswell, "Evasion, Reinterpretation, and Decoupling: European Commission Responses to the 'External Dimension' of Immigration and Asylum," *West European Politics* 31, no. 3 (2008): 491–512.

40. Buzan, Wæver, and de Wilde, *Security*, 176.

41. See Valerie M. Hudson, "Foreign Policy Analysis: Actor-Specific Theory and the Ground of International Relations," *Foreign Policy Analysis* 1, no. 1 (2005): 1–30; and Juliet Kaarbo, "A Foreign Policy Analysis Perspective on the Domestic Politics Turn in IR Theory," *International Studies Review* 17, no. 2 (2015): 189–216.

42. Karyotis, "Securitization of Migration in Greece."

43. Deborah Stone, *Policy Paradox: The Art of Political Decision Making*, 2nd ed. (New York: Norton, 1997); Neal, "'Events, Dear Boy, Events.'"

44. Wæver, "Securitization and Desecuritization."

45. Williams, "Securitization as Political Theory"; Thierry Balzacq, "Securitization Theory: Past, Present, and Future," *Polity* 51, no. 2 (2019): 343.

46. Mike Slaven, "Populism and Securitization: The Corrosion of Elite Security Authority in a US-Mexico Border State," *Journal of Global Security Studies* 6, no. 4 (2021): 7 (online only; articles individually paginated).

47. See, for instance, Jef Huysmans, "Migrants as a Security Problem: The Dangers of 'Securitizing' Societal Issues," in *Migration and European Integration: The Dynamics of Inclusion and Exclusion*, ed. Robert Miles and Dietrich Thranhardt (London: Pinter, 1995), 53–72; Huysmans, *The Politics of Insecurity*; Christina Boswell, "Migration Control in Europe After 9/11: Explaining the Absence of Securitization," *Journal of Common Market Studies* 45, no. 3 (2007): 589–610; Andrew W. Neal, "Securitization and Risk at the EU Border: The Origins of FRONTEX," *Journal of Common Market Studies* 47, no. 2 (2009): 333–56; Claudia Aradau and Jef Huysmans, "Mobilising (Global) Democracy: A Political Reading of Mobility Between Universal Rights and the Mob," *Millennium* 37, no. 3 (2009): 583–604; and Bourbeau, *The Securitization of Migration*.

48. Jef Huysmans, "Security! What Do You Mean? From Concept to Thick Signifier," *European Journal of International Relations* 4, no. 2 (1998): 226–55; Huysmans, *The Politics of Insecurity*, 1–13.

49. Buzan, Wæver, and de Wilde, *Security*, 23–29.

50. Kyrsten Sinema, "No Surprises: The Evolution of Anti-immigration Legislation in Arizona," in *Punishing Immigrants: Policy, Politics, and Injustice*, ed. Charis E. Kubrin, Marjorie S. Katz, and Ramiro Martinez Jr. (New York: New York University Press, 2012), 62–90.

51. These concerns are most prominent in critical security scholarship but are quite widespread. See Claudia Aradau, "Security and the Democratic Scene: Desecuritization and Emancipation," *Journal of International Relations and Development* 7, no. 4 (2004): 388–413; Ian Loader and Neil Walker, *Civilizing Security* (Cambridge: Cambridge University Press, 2007); Ole Wæver, "Politics, Security, Theory," *Security Dialogue* 42, nos. 4–5 (2011): 465–80; Huysmans, *Security Unbound*; and Philippe Bourbeau and Juha A.

Vuori, "Security, Resilience, and Desecuritization: Multidirectional Moves and Dynamics," *Critical Studies on Security* 3, no. 3 (2015): 1–16.

52. See, for instance, Andrew W. Neal, "Normalization and Legislative Exceptionalism: Counterterrorist Lawmaking and the Changing Times of Security Emergencies," *International Political Sociology* 6, no. 3 (2012): 260–76; Kathryn Marie Fisher, *Security, Identity, and British Counterterrorism Policy* (New York: Springer, 2016); Paul Roe, "Is Securitization a 'Negative' Concept? Revisiting the Normative Debate Over Normal Versus Extraordinary Politics," *Security Dialogue* 43, no. 3 (2012): 249–66; Floyd, "Extraordinary or Ordinary Emergency Measures"; and Michael Lister, "Explaining Counter Terrorism in the UK: Normal Politics, Securitised Politics, or Performativity of the Neo-liberal State?," *Critical Studies on Terrorism* 12, no. 3 (2019): 416–39.

53. See, for instance, Mello and Peters, "Parliaments in Security Policy"; Hendrik Hegemann, "Toward 'Normal' Politics? Security, Parliaments, and the Politicisation of Intelligence Oversight in the German Bundestag," *British Journal of Politics and International Relations* 20, no. 1 (2018): 175–90; and Andrew W. Neal, *Security as Politics* (Edinburgh: Edinburgh University Press, 2019).

54. Myriam Dunn Cavelty and Matthias Leese, "Politicising Security at the Boundaries: Privacy in Surveillance and Cybersecurity," *European Review of International Studies* 5, no. 3 (2018): 53.

55. Neal, *Security as Politics*, 115–60.

56. Neal, *Security as Politics*; Hegemann, "Toward 'Normal' Politics?"; Mello and Peters, "Parliaments in Security Policy."

57. Mike Slaven, "The Promise of 'Politicisation' in Security Studies," *European Review of International Studies* 7, no. 1 (2020): 110–15.

58. João Carvalho, "The Front National's Influence on Immigration During President François Hollande's Term," in *Do They Make a Difference? The Policy Influence of Radical Right Populist Parties in Western Europe*, ed. Benjamin Biard, Laurent Bernhard, and Hans-Georg Betz (Colchester, U.K.: ECPR Press, 2019), 37–56; Leila Hadj Abdou and Didier Ruedin, "The Austrian People's Party: An Anti-immigrant Right Party?," *Journal of Ethnic and Migration Studies*, early online, 2021, https://www.tandfonline .com/doi/full/10.1080/1369183X.2020.1853904.

59. Neal, *Security as Politics*.

60. Stone, *Policy Paradox*, 2. This observation about the necessity to possess power to pursue all political ends is echoed in international relations theorizing as canonical as that of Hans J. Morgenthau; see Morgenthau, *Politics Among Nations: The Struggle for Power and Peace*, 7th ed. (New York: McGraw-Hill Education, 2005), 29.

61. Dunn Cavelty, *Cyber-security and Threat Politics*; Sarah Léonard and Christian Kaunert, "Reconceptualizing the Audience in Securitization Theory," in *Securitization Theory*, ed. Balzacq, 57–76; Vultee, "Securitization as a Media Frame."

62. Cas Mudde, "Three Decades of Populist Radical Right Parties in Western Europe: So What?," *European Journal of Political Research* 52, no. 1 (2013): 1–19; Tim Bale,

"Supplying the Insatiable Demand: Europe's Populist Radical Right," *Government and Opposition* 47, no. 2 (2012): 256–74.

63. Cas Mudde, "The Populist Zeitgeist," *Government and Opposition* 39, no. 4 (2004): 541–63; Ben Stanley, "The Thin Ideology of Populism," *Journal of Political Ideologies* 13, no. 1 (2008): 95–110.

64. Pippa Norris, *Radical Right: Voters and Parties in the Electoral Market* (Cambridge: Cambridge University Press, 2005); Aurelien Mondon and Aaron Winter, *Reactionary Democracy: How Racism and the Populist Far Right Became Mainstream* (London: Verso, 2020); Cas Mudde, *The Far Right Today* (Cambridge: Polity Press, 2019).

65. Mudde, *The Far Right Today*, 130.

66. Norris, *Radical Right*, 264.

67. Robert Harmel and Lars Svåsand, "The Influence of New Parties on Old Parties' Platforms: The Cases of the Progress Parties and Conservative Parties of Denmark and Norway," *Party Politics* 3, no. 3 (1997): 315–40; Joost van Spanje, "Contagious Parties: Anti-immigration Parties and Their Impact on Other Parties' Immigration Stances in Contemporary Western Europe," *Party Politics* 16, no. 5 (2010): 563–86.

68. Tim Bale, Christoffer Green-Pedersen, Andréa Krouwel, Kurt Richard Luther, and Nick Sitter, "If You Can't Beat Them, Join Them? Explaining Social Democratic Responses to the Challenge from the Populist Radical Right in Western Europe," *Political Studies* 58, no. 3 (2010): 410–26.

69. Bonnie M. Meguid, "Competition Between Unequals: The Role of Mainstream Party Strategy in Niche Party Success," *American Political Science Review* 99, no. 3 (2005): 347–59.

70. Meguid, "Competition Between Unequals"; Bale et al., "If You Can't Beat Them, Join Them?"

71. Elaborations of number-line models have been prominent in some political science approaches to immigration-issue positioning. See, for instance, Jane Green, "When Voters and Parties Agree: Valence Issues and Party Competition," *Political Studies* 55, no. 3 (2007): 629–55; and Jane Green and Sara B. Hobolt, "Owning the Issue Agenda: Party Strategies and Vote Choices in British Elections," *Electoral Studies* 27, no. 3 (2008): 460–76.

72. See, for instance, Balzacq, "Legitimacy and the 'Logic' of Security"; Thierry Balzacq, "The 'Essence' of Securitization: Theory, Ideal Type, and a Sociological Science of Security," *International Relations* 29, no. 1 (2015): 103–13; and Bourbeau, "Moving Forward Together."

73. Mudde, "The Populist Zeitgeist"; Bale, "Supplying the Insatiable Demand"; Jan-Werner Müller, *What Is Populism?*, digital ed. (Philadelphia: University of Pennsylvania Press, 2016).

74. Pontus Odmalm and Eve Hepburn, "Mainstream Parties, the Populist Radical Right, and the (Alleged) Lack of a Restrictive and Assimilationist Alternative," in *The European Mainstream and the Populist Radical Right*, ed. Pontus Odmalm and Eve Hepburn (London: Routledge, 2017), 1–27.

75. Thorsten Wojczewski, "'Enemies of the People': Populism and the Politics of (In) Security," *European Journal of International Security* 5, no. 1 (2020): 5–24; Bohdana Kurylo, "The Discourse and Aesthetics of Populism as Securitisation Style," *International Relations*, early online, 2020, https://journals.sagepub.com/doi/full/10.1177/004711 7820973071.

76. See, for instance, Xavier Guillaume, "Resistance and the International: The Challenge of the Everyday," *International Political Sociology* 5, no. 4 (2011): 459–62; Florent Blanc, "Poking Holes and Spreading Cracks in the Wall: Resistance to National Security Policies Under Bush," in *Contesting Security*, ed. Balzacq, 63–83; and Gary T. Marx, "Security and Surveillance Contests: Resistance and Counter-Resistance," in *Contesting Security*, ed. Balzacq, 15–28.

77. Wæver, "Securitization and Desecuritization"; Doty, "States of Exception on the Mexico-US Border."

78. Elisabeth Ivarsflaten, "What Unites Right-Wing Populists in Western Europe? Reexamining Grievance Mobilization Models in Seven Successful Cases," *Comparative Political Studies* 41, no. 1 (2008): 3–23; Daniel Oesch, "Explaining Workers' Support for Right-Wing Populist Parties in Western Europe: Evidence from Austria, Belgium, France, Norway, and Switzerland," *International Political Science Review* 29, no. 3 (2008): 349–73; Geertje Lucassen and Marcel Lubbers, "Who Fears What? Explaining Far-Right-Wing Preference in Europe by Distinguishing Perceived Cultural and Economic Ethnic Threats," *Comparative Political Studies* 45, no. 5 (2012): 547–74.

79. Doty, *The Law Into Their Own Hands*, 10–11.

80. Wæver, "Securitization and Desecuritization," 57.

81. Slaven, "Populism and Securitization."

82. Kerem Nisancioglu, "Racial Sovereignty," *European Journal of International Relations* 26, no. 1 (2020): 39–63; Catarina Kinnvall, "Ontological Insecurities and Postcolonial Imaginaries: The Emotional Appeal of Populism," *Humanity and Society* 42, no. 4 (2018): 523–43.

83. Lucy Mayblin and Joe Turner, *Migration Studies and Colonialism* (Cambridge: Polity, 2021), 49; Maggie Ibrahim, "The Securitization of Migration: A Racial Discourse," *International Migration* 43, no. 5 (2005): 163–87.

84. Leo R. Chavez, *The Latino Threat: Constructing Immigrants, Citizens, and the Nation*, 2nd ed. (Stanford, CA: Stanford University Press, 2013); Reece Jones, *White Borders: The History of Race and Immigration in the United States from Chinese Exclusion to the Border Wall* (Boston: Beacon, 2021).

85. Huysmans, *The Politics of Insecurity*; Jonas Hagmann and Myriam Dunn Cavelty, "National Risk Registers: Security Scientism and the Propagation of Permanent Insecurity," *Security Dialogue* 43, no. 1 (2012): 79–96; Giacomo Orsini, "Securitization as a Source of Insecurity: A Ground-Level Look at the Functioning of Europe's External Border in Lampedusa," *Studies in Ethnicity and Nationalism* 16, no. 1 (2016): 135–47.

86. Eric Van Rythoven, "The Securitization Dilemma," *Journal of Global Security Studies* 5, no. 3 (2020): 478–93.

87. See Wæver, "Securitization and Desecuritization"; Thierry Balzacq, Sara Depauw, and Sarah Léonard, "The Political Limits of Desecuritization: Security, Arms Trade, and the EU's Economic Targets," in *Contesting Security*, ed. Balzacq, 104–21; and Jef Huysmans, "The Question of the Limit: Desecuritisation and the Aesthetics of Horror in Political Realism," *Millennium* 27, no. 3 (1998): 569–89.

88. Eric Van Rythoven, "A Feeling of Unease: Distance, Emotion, and Securitizing Indigenous Protest in Canada," *International Political Sociology* 15, no. 2 (2021): 251–71.

89. Juha A. Vuori, "Contesting and Resisting Security in Post-Mao China," in *Contesting Security*, ed. Balzacq, 29–43.

90. Huysmans, "The Question of the Limit."

91. Bourbeau and Vuori, "Security, Resilience, and Desecuritization"; Olaf Corry, "Securitisation and 'Riskification': Second-Order Security and the Politics of Climate Change," *Millennium* 40, no. 2 (2012): 235–58.

92. Leila Hadj Abdou, Tim Bale, and Andrew Peter Geddes, "Centre-Right Parties and Immigration in an Era of Politicisation," *Journal of Ethnic and Migration Studies*, early online, 2021, https://www.tandfonline.com/doi/full/10.1080/1369183X.2020.1853901.

93. Perry Bacon Jr., "What Is Really Behind Trump's Controversial Immigration Policies?," *FiveThirtyEight* (blog), June 19, 2018, https://fivethirtyeight.com/features/what-is-really-behind-trumps-controversial-immigration-policies/; Marisa Abrajano and Zoltan L. Hajnal, *White Backlash: Immigration, Race, and American Politics* (Princeton, NJ: Princeton University Press, 2015), 63–87.

94. Derek Beach and Rasmus Brun Pedersen, *Process-Tracing Methods: Foundations and Guidelines* (Ann Arbor: University of Michigan Press, 2013), 18–21; see the appendix for greater detail on process tracing. Also see Jeffrey T. Checkel, "Process Tracing," in *Qualitative Methods in International Relations: A Pluralist Guide*, ed. Audie Klotz and Deepa Prakash (New York: Palgrave Macmillan, 2008), 114–27. For use of process tracing in a study of securitization of migration, see Corey Robinson, "Tracing and Explaining Securitization: Social Mechanisms, Process Tracing, and the Securitization of Irregular Migration," *Security Dialogue* 48, no. 6 (2017): 505–23.

95. On "theoretically explicit narratives," see Tulia G. Falleti, "Process Tracing of Extensive and Intensive Processes," *New Political Economy* 21, no. 5 (2016): 455–62. Tulia G. Falleti and Julia F. Lynch also offer a clarifying definition of the "causal mechanisms" central to process-tracing analysis: "Mechanisms describe the relationships or the actions among the units of analysis or in the cases of study. Mechanisms tell us how things happen: how actors relate, how individuals come to believe what they do or what they draw from past experiences, how policies and institutions endure or change, how outcomes that are inefficient become hard to reverse, and so on" ("Context and Causal Mechanisms in Political Analysis," *Comparative Political Studies* 42, no. 9 [2009]: 1147).

96. Robinson, "Tracing and Explaining Securitization."

97. John Gerring, "What Is a Case Study and What Is It Good For?," *American Political Science Review* 98, no. 2 (2004): 341–54; Kathleen M. Eisenhardt and Melissa E.

Graebner, "Theory Building from Cases: Opportunities and Challenges," *Academy of Management Journal* 50, no. 1 (2007): 25–32.

98. See Martin Rein and Donald A. Schön, "Problem Setting in Policy Research," in *Using Social Research in Public Policy Making*, ed. Carol H. Weiss (Lexington, MA: Lexington Books, 1977), 235–54; and Bryan D. Jones and Frank R. Baumgartner, *The Politics of Attention: How Government Prioritizes Problems* (Chicago: University of Chicago Press, 2005).

99. Colin Hay, "Ideas and the Construction of Interests," in *Ideas and Politics in Social Science Research*, ed. Daniel Béland and Robert Henry Cox (Oxford: Oxford University Press, 2010), 65–81; Vivien A. Schmidt, "Speaking of Change: Why Discourse Is Key to the Dynamics of Policy Transformation," *Critical Policy Studies* 5, no. 2 (2011): 106–26.

100. Gabriel A. Almond and Stephen J. Genco, "Clouds, Clocks, and the Study of Politics," *World Politics* 29, no. 4 (1977): 489–522.

101. Mark Bevir and R. A. W. Rhodes, *Governance Stories* (London: Routledge, 2006), 4.

102. Marc Geddes, "The Explanatory Potential of 'Dilemmas': Bridging Practices and Power to Understand Political Change in Interpretive Political Science," *Political Studies Review* 17, no. 3 (2019): 239–54.

103. Kaarbo, "A Foreign Policy Analysis Perspective."

104. Bevir and Rhodes, *Governance Stories*, 26.

105. Mikkel Vedby Rasmussen, *The Risk Society at War: Terror, Technology, and Strategy in the Twenty-First Century* (Cambridge: Cambridge University Press, 2006), 5.

106. Bent Flyvbjerg, "Rationality and Power," in *Readings in Planning Theory*, ed. Scott Campbell and Susan S. Fainstein (Oxford: Blackwell, 2003), 318–29; Giandomenico Majone, *Evidence, Argument, and Persuasion in the Policy Process* (New Haven, CN: Yale University Press, 1989).

107. David Knoke, "Networks of Elite Structure and Decision Making," *Sociological Methods and Research* 22, no. 1 (1993): 23–45.

108. Oisín Tansey, "Process Tracing and Elite Interviewing: A Case for Non-probability Sampling," *PS: Political Science and Politics* 40, no. 4 (2007): 765–72.

109. Glenn Beamer, "Elite Interviews and State Politics Research," *State Politics and Policy Quarterly* 2, no. 1 (2002): 86–96.

110. All interviews occurred between November 2014 and June 2015. See the appendix.

111. Alexander L. George and Andrew Bennett, *Case Studies and Theory Development in the Social Sciences* (Cambridge, MA: MIT Press, 2005), 6; Darren G. Lilleker, "Interviewing the Political Elite: Navigating a Potential Minefield," *Politics* 23, no. 3 (2003): 207–14.

112. Philip H. J. Davies, "Spies as Informants: Triangulation and the Interpretation of Elite Interview Data in the Study of the Intelligence and Security Services," *Politics* 21, no. 1 (2001): 73–80.

113. Kimberly Rapanut, "How Did SB 1070 Affect You?," *Cronkite News* (blog), March 31, 2020, https://cronkitenews.azpbs.org/2020/03/31/sb-1070-reader-callout/; Daniel Gonzalez, "SB 1070 Galvanized Many Latino Activists to Run for Office," *Arizona Republic*, February 18, 2020.

1. A BORDER EMERGENCY IS BORN

1. Mike Slaven, "Populism and Securitization: The Corrosion of Elite Security Authority in a US-Mexico Border State," *Journal of Global Security Studies* 6, no. 4 (2021): 7 (online only; articles individually paginated); Bohdana Kurylo, "The Discourse and Aesthetics of Populism as Securitisation Style," *International Relations*, early online, 2020, https://journals.sagepub.com/doi/full/10.1177/0047117820973071; Thorsten Wojczewski, "'Enemies of the People': Populism and the Politics of (In)Security," *European Journal of International Security* 5, no. 1 (2020): 5–24.

2. Katy Brown, Aurelien Mondon, and Aaron Winter, "The Far Right, the Mainstream, and Mainstreaming: Towards a Heuristic Framework," *Journal of Political Ideologies*, early online, 2021, https://doi.org/10.1080/13569317.2021.1949829; Aurelien Mondon and Aaron Winter, *Reactionary Democracy: How Racism and the Populist Far Right Became Mainstream* (London: Verso, 2020).

3. Mike Slaven and Christina Boswell, "Why Symbolise Control? Irregular Migration to the UK and Symbolic Policy-Making in the 1960s," *Journal of Ethnic and Migration Studies* 45, no. 9 (2019): 1479.

4. Didier Bigo, "Security and Immigration: Toward a Critique of the Governmentality of Unease," *Alternatives* 27, special issue (2002): 69.

5. Fiona de Londras, "Politicisation, Law, and Rights in the Transnational Counter-Terrorism Space: Indications from the Regulation of Foreign Terrorist Fighters," *European Review of International Studies* 5, no. 3 (2018): 116.

6. Fred Vultee, "Securitization: A New Approach to the Framing of the 'War on Terror,'" *Journalism Practice* 4, no. 1 (2010): 33–47.

7. Hendrik Hegemann, "Toward 'Normal' Politics? Security, Parliaments, and the Politicisation of Intelligence Oversight in the German Bundestag," *British Journal of Politics and International Relations* 20, no. 1 (2018): 175–90.

8. Gregor Aisch and Robert Gebeloff, "Mapping Migration in the United States," *New York Times*, August 15, 2014, http://www.nytimes.com/2014/08/16/upshot/mapping-migration-in-the-united-states-since-1900.html.

9. David R. Berman, *Arizona Politics and Government: The Quest for Autonomy, Democracy, and Development* (Lincoln: University of Nebraska Press, 1997), 1–2.

10. Anita Huizar-Hernández, *Forging Arizona: A History of the Peralta Land Grant and Racial Identity in the West* (New Brunswick, NJ: Rutgers University Press, 2019), 11.

11. Mary Kirk Laidlaw, "Why Arizona? The S.B. 1070 and the History of Immigration in the Southwestern Border States," master's thesis, Georgetown University, 2012, 14.

12. William D. Carrigan and Clive Webb, "The Rise and Fall of Mob Violence Against Mexicans in Arizona, 1859–1915," in *Lynching Beyond Dixie: American Mob Violence Outside the South*, ed. Michael J. Pfeifer (Champaign: University of Illinois Press, 2013), 110–31.

13. Celeste González de Bustamante, "Arizona and the Making of a State of Exclusion, 1912–2012," in *Arizona Firestorm: Global Immigration Realities, National Media, and Provincial Politics*, ed. Otto Santa Ana and Celeste González de Bustamante (New York: Rowman and Littlefield, 2012), 19–37; Katherine Benton-Cohen, "Immigration and

Border Politics in Arizona, Then and Now," in *Back to the Border: A Historical Comparison of U.S. Border Politics*, ed. Katherine Benton-Cohen and Geraldo Cadava (Washington, DC: Immigration Policy Center, 2010), 7; Paul Frymer, "'A Rush and a Push and the Land Is Ours': Territorial Expansion, Land Policy, and U.S. State Formation," *Perspectives on Politics* 12, no. 1 (2014): 134.

14.   Christine Marin and Luis F. B. Plascencia, "Mexicano Miners, Dual Wage, and the Pursuit of Wage Equality in Miami, Arizona," in *Mexican Workers and the Making of Arizona*, ed. Luis F. B. Plascencia and Gloria H. Cuádraz (Tucson: University of Arizona Press, 2018), 223–26.

15.   Benton-Cohen, "Immigration and Border Politics in Arizona," 8.

16.   Jeanne M. Powers, "Forgotten History: Mexican American School Segregation in Arizona from 1900–1951," *Equity and Excellence in Education* 41, no. 4 (2008): 467–81.

17.   F. Chris Garcia, Christine Marie Sierra, and Maier Murdock, "The Politics of Women and Ethnic Minorities," in *Politics and Public Policy in the Contemporary American West*, ed. Clive S. Thomas (Albuquerque: University of New Mexico Press, 1991), 198. On the deportation efforts, see Francisco E. Balderrama and Raymond Rodriguez, *Decade of Betrayal: Mexican Repatriation in the 1930s* (Albuquerque: University of New Mexico Press, 2006); and Juan Ramon Garcia, *Operation Wetback: The Mass Deportation of Mexican Undocumented Workers in 1954* (Westport, CN: Greenwood Press, 1980).

18.   Alex P. Oberle and Daniel D. Arreola, "Resurgent Mexican Phoenix," *Geographical Review* 98, no. 2 (2008): 171–96.

19.   Leo R. Chavez, *The Latino Threat: Constructing Immigrants, Citizens, and the Nation*, 2nd ed. (Stanford, CA: Stanford University Press, 2013), 3.

20.   Mark Berman, "Arizona's Experience with Controversial Laws and Boycotts," *Washington Post*, February 26, 2014, http://www.washingtonpost.com/news/post-nation/wp/2014/02/26/arizonas-experience-with-controversial-laws-and-boycotts/.

21.   C. Wesley Buerkle, Michael E. Mayer, and Clark D. Olson, "Our Hero the Buffoon: Contradictory and Concurrent Burkean Framing of Arizona Governor Evan Mecham," *Western Journal of Communication* 67, no. 2 (2003): 187–206.

22.   Michelle Ye Hee Lee, "Recalling Arizona's Struggle for MLK Holiday," *Arizona Republic*, January 15, 2012.

23.   See Evan Serpick, "Public Enemy Look Back at 20 Years of 'By the Time I Get to Arizona,'" *Spin*, November 10, 2011.

24.   Carrigan and Webb, "The Rise and Fall of Mob Violence against Mexicans in Arizona."

25.   Berman, *Arizona Politics and Government*, 166.

26.   Gordon Morris Bakken, "The Arizona Constitutional Convention of 1910," *Arizona State Law Journal* 1978, no. 1 (1978): 1–30.

27.   Micaela Anne Larkin, "Labor's Desert: Mexican Workers, Unions, and Entrepreneurial Conservatism in Arizona, 1917–1972," PhD diss., University of Notre Dame, 2008.

28.   Jack L. August, "Water, Politics, and the Arizona Dream: Carl Hayden and the Modern Origins of the Central Arizona Project, 1922–1963," *Journal of Arizona History* 40, no. 4 (1999): 391–414.

29. Ronald J. Hrebenar and Clive S. Thomas, eds., *Interest Group Politics in the American West* (Salt Lake City: University of Utah Press, 1987).

30. Judith Gans, "The Economic Impact of Immigrants in Arizona," in *Arizona Firestorm*, ed. Santa Ana and González de Bustamante, 47–70.

31. Berman, *Arizona Politics and Government*, 62–63.

32. Garcia, Sierra, and Murdock, "The Politics of Women and Ethnic Minorities," 217.

33. Susan Gonzalez Baker, "The 'Amnesty' Aftermath: Current Policy Issues Stemming from the Legalization Programs of the 1986 Immigration Reform and Control Act," *International Migration Review* 31, no. 1 (1997): 5–27.

34. Patrisia Macías-Rojas, "Immigration and the War on Crime: Law and Order Politics and the Illegal Immigration Reform and Immigrant Responsibility Act of 1996," *Journal on Migration and Human Security* 6, no. 1 (2018): 1–25; Austin T. Fragomen, "The Illegal Immigration Reform and Immigrant Responsibility Act of 1996: An Overview," *International Migration Review* 31, no. 2 (1997): 438–60.

35. A citizens' initiative is an institution of direct democracy that allows citizens to place proposed legislation directly on the ballot after meeting a substantial signature threshold. An initiative becomes law with a majority of the popular vote, thus bypassing governing elites.

36. James Crawford, *Language Loyalties: A Source Book on the Official English Controversy* (Chicago: University of Chicago Press, 1992), 218–23.

37. Wayne E. Wright, "The Political Spectacle of Arizona's Proposition 203," *Educational Policy* 19, no. 5 (2005): 662–700.

38. Tony Payan, *The Three U.S.-Mexico Border Wars: Drugs, Immigration, and Homeland Security* (Westport, CN: Praeger Security International, 2006), 67.

39. Berman, *Arizona Politics and Government*, 173.

40. Anthony York, "R.I.P. Prop. 187," *Salon*, July 30, 1999; David S. Broder, "A Wedge That Keeps Splitting," *Washington Post*, April 21, 1999.

41. Peter Andreas, "Politics on Edge: Managing the US-Mexico Border," *Current History* 105, no. 688 (February 2006): 64.

42. Payan, *The Three U.S.-Mexico Border Wars*, 68.

43. Reece Jones, *Border Walls: Security and the War on Terror in the United States, India, and Israel* (London: Zed Books, 2012), 31; Ted Hesson, "Why Arizona Is Ground Zero for Immigration Policy," Fusion, October 9, 2013, http://fusion.net/justice/story/reasons-arizona-ground-immigration-policy-15288.

44. Roxanne Lynn Doty, "Bare Life: Border-Crossing Deaths and Spaces of Moral Alibi," *Environment and Planning D: Society and Space* 29, no. 4 (2011): 599–612; Vicki Squire, *Post/Humanitarian Border Politics Between Mexico and the US: People, Places, Things* (Basingstoke, U.K.: Palgrave Macmillan, 2015).

45. Peter Andreas, *Border Games: Policing the U.S.-Mexico Divide* (Ithaca, NY: Cornell University Press, 2000), 6–7.

46. Megan Boehnke, "Arizona Immigration Law Revives Memories of 1997 Chandler Roundup," *Arizona Republic*, April 28, 2010.

47. Adam Isacson, Maureen Meyer, and Ashley Davis, "Border Security and Migration: A Report from Arizona," Washington Office on Latin America, December 5, 2013, https://www.wola.org/analysis/border-security-and-migration-a-report-from-arizona/.

48. Jones, *Border Walls*, 32.

49. Jones, *Border Walls*, 39–45.

50. David J. Bier, "The 9/11 Legacy for Immigration," *Independent Review* 26, no. 2 (2021): 205–24.

51. All quotations from policy makers come from interviews conducted for this book unless cited otherwise; ellipses indicate omissions rather than pauses. See the table in the appendix for a list of the interviews conducted.

52. Roxanne Lynn Doty, *The Law Into Their Own Hands: Immigration and the Politics of Exceptionalism* (Tucson: University of Arizona Press, 2009), 64–82.

53. All seats in both chambers of the Arizona Legislature are up for election every two years. Both chambers use the same districts, with one senator and two House members elected per district. Elected executive officers—the governor, attorney general, secretary of state, and others—serve four-year terms.

54. Josh Goodman, "Goodbye Moderate Governors, Hello Partisans," *Governing*, October 2010, http://www.governing.com/topics/politics/goodbye-moderate-governors-hello-partisans.html.

55. Kyrsten Sinema, "No Surprises: The Evolution of Anti-immigration Legislation in Arizona," in *Punishing Immigrants: Policy, Politics, and Injustice*, ed. Charis E. Kubrin, Marjorie S. Katz, and Ramiro Martinez Jr. (New York: New York University Press, 2012), 64.

56. Le Templar, "Napolitano Vetoes Voter Identification Bill," *East Valley Tribune*, June 27, 2003, http://www.eastvalleytribune.com/news/article_ae2f6fb6-bba3-568e-bf0c-7be060 89fa42.html.

57. Governor Janet Napolitano to Secretary of State Jan Brewer, re: HB 2345, June 26, 2003; all of Governor Napolitano's veto letters and signing statements are archived by the Arizona State Legislature and are available on the legislature's website as "Governor's Letters," https://www.azleg.gov/governors-letters/.

58. For consistency, the label *border hawks* is used throughout to describe Pearce's group of legislators and other aligned public officials.

59. See Cas Mudde, "The Populist Zeitgeist," *Government and Opposition* 39, no. 4 (2004): 541–63; and Slaven, "Populism and Securitization."

60. Darin David Barney and David Laycock, "Right-Populists and Plebiscitary Politics in Canada," *Party Politics* 5, no. 3 (1999): 317–39.

61. Gijs Schumacher and Kees van Kersbergen, "Do Mainstream Parties Adapt to the Welfare Chauvinism of Populist Parties?," *Party Politics* 22, no. 3 (2016): 300–312; Ann-Cathrine Jungar and Anders Ravik Jupskås, "Populist Radical Right Parties in the Nordic Region: A New and Distinct Party Family?," *Scandinavian Political Studies* 37, no. 3 (2014): 226; Cas Mudde, "Three Decades of Populist Radical Right Parties in Western Europe: So What?," *European Journal of Political Research* 52, no. 1 (2013): 9.

62. Slaven, "Populism and Securitization."

63. The Arizona State Legislature meets every year in a regular session that begins in January and adjourns at a varying date (always by July) and in occasional special sessions.

64. Hil Anderson, "Analysis: Ariz. Prop Localizes Immigration," United Press International, October 26, 2004.

65. Max Blumenthal, "Backlash on the Border," *Salon*, October 18, 2004; Carrie Kahn, "State of US Immigration Reform in 2004," *Weekend All Things Considered*, National Public Radio, January 1, 2005.

66. Of the fifty-six Republicans then in the Arizona Legislature, twenty-one were listed in a press release as planned participants in a pro–Proposition 200 rally in September 2004. Although many of the twenty-one were considered to be in the right-wing faction of the caucus, the number also included some members more often identified as traditional conservatives.

67. Beth DeFalco, "New PAC Formed to Fight Immigration Initiative," Associated Press State and Local Wire, September 9, 2004.

68. Ananda Shorey, "Activists in Arizona Pushing Immigration Measure Aimed at Preventing Fraud," Associated Press, October 5, 2004.

69. Antonio Gonzalez, "Proposition 200," *Tavis Smiley*, National Public Radio, September 21, 2004.

70. Jacques Billeaud, "Arizona Lawmakers Vote to Impose New Restrictions on Immigrants," Associated Press State and Local Wire, May 12, 2005.

71. Proposition 200 left unresolved which forms of identification were valid for voting. In Arizona, elections rules are drafted by the secretary of state, the highest official in charge of elections and also first in the line of succession to the governorship, and have the force of law upon the approval of the attorney general and governor.

72. Paul Davenport, "Napolitano Vetoes Bill to Implement Prop 200 Voting ID Mandate," Associated Press State and Local Wire, April 1, 2005; Anabelle Garay, "Attorney General Delays Implementing Voting Provision of New Law," Associated Press State and Local Wire, February 10, 2005.

73. Jim Small, "28 Bills Cover Illegal Border Crossers," *Arizona Capitol Times*, June 10, 2005.

74. Jacques Billeaud, "Two Local Agencies in Arizona Form Smuggling Squads as New Law Is Set to Take Effect," Associated Press, July 29, 2005.

75. In Arizona, a referendum, in contrast to a citizens' initiative, is a law that both houses of the legislature can vote to refer to voters for approval, bypassing the governor.

76. Steve Gallardo, quoted in Jacques Billeaud, "State Lawmakers Take Crack at Immigration Problems," Associated Press State and Local Wire, January 17, 2005.

77. Kyrsten Sinema, quoted in Small, "28 Bills Cover Illegal Border Crossers."

78. Ben Miranda, a House Democrat from a majority Hispanic district, died in 2013, before I did the research for this book.

79. Bill Hess, "During Hearing on Immigration Bill, Local Officials Push for Resources; Residents Share Their Viewpoints," *Sierra Vista Herald*, March 5, 2005.

80. Small, "28 Bills Cover Illegal Border Crossers."

81. Governor Janet Napolitano to Senate President Ken Bennett, re: SB 1306, May 20, 2005.

82. Governor Janet Napolitano to House Speaker Jim Weiers, re: HB 2709, May 2, 2005.

83. Governor Janet Napolitano to House Speaker Jim Weiers, re: HB 2030, May 20, 2005.

84. Phil Lopes, quoted in Small, "28 Bills Cover Illegal Border Crossers."

85. Amanda Lee Myers, "Lawmakers Say Prosecutor Misinterpreting Immigration Law," Associated Press State and Local Wire, March 24, 2006.

86. Chavez, *The Latino Threat*, 135–56; Doty, *The Law Into Their Own Hands*, 73.

87. As expected, the federal government never paid these state incarceration costs, despite Arizona's notional entitlement to reimbursement under the federal State Criminal Alien Assistance Program.

88. Jacques Billeaud, "Local Police Examine Their Role in Combating Illegal Immigration," Associated Press State and Local Wire, July 12, 2005; Janet Napolitano, "Executive Order 2005-13: Summit on Immigration Enforcement Strategies," June 3, 2005, *Arizona Administrative Register* 11, no. 25 (2005): 2328–329.

89. Janet Napolitano, "Executive Order 2005-30," October 20, 2005, *Arizona Administrative Register* 11, no. 44 (2005): 4320–321.

90. Jacques Billeaud, "Governor Orders State Contractors to Ensure Hirings Are Legal," Associated Press State and Local Wire, November 1, 2005.

91. US Immigration and Customs Enforcement, "Memorandum of Agreement," September 20, 2005.

92. "287(g) agreement" is the normal term for such agreements, after the section of the federal Immigration and Nationality Act that authorizes them.

93. Janet Napolitano, "Declaration of Emergency: Arizona-Mexico International Border Security Emergency," August 15, 2005, Wayback Machine, http://web.archive.org/web /20060625024629/http://azgovernor.gov/dms/upload/DE~081605~AZMEXBorder Security.pdf.

94. Barry Massey, "N.M., Ariz. Governors Ignite Debate, Score Politically with Border Declarations," Associated Press, August 30, 2005; Phil Riske, "Arizona Governor Steps Up Border Battle," *Arizona Capitol Times*, August 19, 2005.

95. Jacques Billeaud, "Immigration to Occupy a Part of Arizona's Political Debate in Future," Associated Press State and Local Wire, May 16, 2005; see also Christina Boswell and Elisabeth Badenhoop, "'What Isn't in the Files, Isn't in the World': Understanding State Ignorance of Irregular Migration in Germany and the United Kingdom," *Governance* 34, no. 2 (2021): 335–52.

96. Barry Buzan, Ole Wæver, and Jaap de Wilde, *Security: A New Framework for Analysis* (Boulder, CO: Lynne Rienner, 1998), 29.

97. Bigo, "Security and Immigration," 69.

98. See, for instance, Doty, *The Law Into Their Own Hands*, 68; Buzan, Wæver, and de Wilde, *Security*, 21; and Jonathan White, "Emergency Europe," *Political Studies* 63, no. 2 (2015): 300–318.

99. See, for instance, Claudia Aradau, "The Perverse Politics of Four-Letter Words: Risk and Pity in the Securitisation of Human Trafficking," *Millennium* 33, no. 2 (2004): 251–77; and Nicole J. Jackson, "International Organizations, Security Dichotomies, and the Trafficking of Persons and Narcotics in Post-Soviet Central Asia: A Critique of the Securitization Framework," *Security Dialogue* 37, no. 3 (2006): 299–317.

100. See, for instance, Nikos Papastergiadis, "The Invasion Complex in Australian Political Culture," *Thesis Eleven* 78, no. 1 (2004): 8–27; and Hein de Haas, "The Myth of Invasion: The Inconvenient Realities of African Migration to Europe," *Third World Quarterly* 29, no. 7 (2008): 1306.

101. Philippe Bourbeau, "Moving Forward Together: Logics of the Securitisation Process," *Millennium* 43, no. 1 (2014): 187.

102. Jonas Hagmann, Hendrick Hegemann, and Andrew W. Neal, "The Politicisation of Security: Controversy, Mobilisation, Arena Shifting. Introduction by the Guest Editors," *European Review of International Studies* 5, no. 3 (2018): 3–29.

103. Slaven, "Populism and Securitization," 7.

104. Philippe Bourbeau, *The Securitization of Migration: A Study of Movement and Order* (Abingdon, U.K.: Routledge, 2011), 42.

105. Andrew W. Neal, *Security as Politics* (Edinburgh: Edinburgh University Press, 2019), 42.

106. See, for instance, Holger Stritzel, "Security, the Translation," *Security Dialogue* 42, nos. 4–5 (2011): 343–55; and Thierry Balzacq, "Legitimacy and the 'Logic' of Security," in *Contesting Security: Strategies and Logics*, ed. Thierry Balzacq (Abingdon, U.K.: Routledge, 2015), 1–9.

107. Neal, *Security as Politics*; Felix Ciută, "Security and the Problem of Context: A Hermeneutical Critique of Securitisation Theory," *Review of International Studies* 35, no. 2 (2009): 301–26.

108. Mike Slaven, "The Promise of 'Politicisation' in Security Studies," *European Review of International Studies* 7, no. 1 (2020): 110–15.

109. Mudde, "The Populist Zeitgeist," 543.

110. Cas Mudde, "Populism: An Ideational Approach," in *The Oxford Handbook of Populism*, ed. Cristóbal Rovira Kaltwasser, Paul A. Taggert, Paulina Ochoa Espejo, and Pierre Ostiguy (Oxford: Oxford University Press, 2017), 29–34.

111. Ben Stanley, "The Thin Ideology of Populism," *Journal of Political Ideologies* 13, no. 1 (2008): 95–110.

112. Mudde, "Populism," 31.

113. Mudde, "Populism," 38.

114. On "Manichean moralism," see Michael Tonry, "Explanations of American Punishment Policies: A National History," *Punishment and Society* 11, no. 3 (2009): 377–94.

115. Jungar and Jupskås, "Populist Radical Right Parties in the Nordic Region"; Schumacher and van Kersbergen, "Do Mainstream Parties Adapt to the Welfare Chauvinism of Populist Parties?"; Matthijs Rooduijn, "Vox Populismus: A Populist Radical Right Attitude Among the Public?," *Nations and Nationalism* 20, no. 1 (2014): 80–92.

116. Dorothy E. Roberts, "Race, Vagueness, and the Social Meaning of Order-Maintenance Policing," *Journal of Criminal Law and Criminology* 89, no. 3 (1999): 775–836; Michelle Alexander, *The New Jim Crow: Mass Incarceration in the Age of Colorblindness* (New York: New Press, 2010).

117. Doris Marie Provine and Gabriella Sanchez, "Suspecting Immigrants: Exploring Links Between Racialised Anxieties and Expanded Police Powers in Arizona," *Policing and Society* 21, no. 4 (2011): 468–79.

118. Ernesto Laclau, *Politics and Ideology in Marxist Theory: Capitalism, Fascism, Populism* (London: New Left Books, 1977); Ernesto Laclau, *On Populist Reason* (London: Verso, 2005).

119. Kirk A. Hawkins and Cristóbal Rovira Kaltwasser, "The Ideational Approach to Populism," *Latin American Research Review* 52, no. 4 (2017): 516.

120. Thierry Balzacq, "Enquiries Into Methods: A New Framework for Securitization Analysis," in *Securitization Theory: How Security Problems Emerge and Dissolve*, ed. Thierry Balzacq (London: Routledge, 2011), 31–53.

121. Balzacq, "Legitimacy and the 'Logic' of Security," 2; Bourbeau, "Moving Forward Together," 187.

122. Balzacq, "Legitimacy and the 'Logic' of Security." The main alternative perspective would be the hermeneutical view. See Ciuță, "Security and the Problem of Context."

123. See, for instance, Thierry Balzacq, "The 'Essence' of Securitization: Theory, Ideal Type, and a Sociological Science of Security," *International Relations* 29, no. 1 (2015): 103–13; and Balzacq, "Legitimacy and the 'Logic' of Security"; and Bourbeau, "Moving Forward Together."

124. Buzan, Wæver, and de Wilde, *Security*, 33.

125. Bigo, "Security and Immigration"; Balzacq, "Legitimacy and the 'Logic' of Security," 2.

126. On causal mechanisms, see Tulia G. Falleti and Julia F. Lynch, "Context and Causal Mechanisms in Political Analysis," *Comparative Political Studies* 42, no. 9 (2009): 1143–166.

127. Bryan D. Jones and Frank R. Baumgartner, *The Politics of Attention: How Government Prioritizes Problems* (Chicago: University of Chicago Press, 2005), 56.

128. Ruud Koopmans and Paul Statham, "Migration and Ethnic Relations as a Field of Political Contention: An Opportunity Structure Approach," in *Challenging Immigration and Ethnic Relations Politics: Comparative European Perspectives*, ed. Ruud Koopmans and Paul Statham (Oxford: Oxford University Press, 2000), 13–56.

129. Tim Bale, Christoffer Green-Pedersen, Andréa Krouwel, Kurt Richard Luther, and Nick Sitter, "If You Can't Beat Them, Join Them? Explaining Social Democratic Responses to the Challenge from the Populist Radical Right in Western Europe," *Political Studies* 58, no. 3 (2010): 410–26; Bonnie M. Meguid, "Competition Between Unequals: The Role of Mainstream Party Strategy in Niche Party Success," *American Political Science Review* 99, no. 3 (2005): 347–59.

130. Pippa Norris, *Radical Right: Voters and Parties in the Electoral Market* (Cambridge: Cambridge University Press, 2005); Joost van Spanje, "Contagious Parties: Anti-immigration Parties and Their Impact on Other Parties' Immigration Stances in Contemporary Western Europe," *Party Politics* 16, no. 5 (2010): 563–86; Aristotle Kallis, "Far-Right 'Contagion' or a Failing 'Mainstream'? How Dangerous Ideas Cross Borders and Blur Boundaries," *Democracy and Security* 9, no. 3 (2013): 221–46.

131. For this "puzzling" concept, see Hugh Heclo, *Modern Social Politics in Britain and Sweden* (New Haven, CN: Yale University Press, 1974).

132. See Bourbeau, *The Securitization of Migration*, 42; and Stefano Guzzini, "Securitization as a Causal Mechanism," *Security Dialogue* 42, nos. 4–5 (2011): 335–36.

133. This is a typical populist response to elite assertions that issues are complicated. See Margaret Canovan, "Trust the People! Populism and the Two Faces of Democracy," *Political Studies* 47, no. 1 (1999): 6.

134. Jacques Billeaud, "Poll: Prop. 200 Won Support from Blue-Collar Workers," Associated Press State and Local Wire, November 3, 2004.

135. Ole Wæver, "Securitization and Desecuritization," in *On Security*, ed. Ronnie D. Lipschutz (New York: Columbia University Press, 1995), 46–86; Claudia Aradau, "Security and the Democratic Scene: Desecuritization and Emancipation," *Journal of International Relations and Development* 7, no. 4 (2004): 388–413; Jef Huysmans, *Security Unbound: Enacting Democratic Limits* (Abingdon, U.K.: Routledge, 2014); Ian Loader and Neil Walker, *Civilizing Security* (Cambridge: Cambridge University Press, 2007).

136. Lee Jarvis and Tim Legrand, "'I Am Somewhat Puzzled': Questions, Audiences, and Securitization in the Proscription of Terrorist Organizations," *Security Dialogue* 48, no. 2 (2017): 149–67.

137. Neal, *Security as Politics*, 125–38. See also Jarvis and Legrand, "'I Am Somewhat Puzzled.'"

2. SECURING VICTORY

1. On ownership, see David B. Holian, "He's Stealing My Issues! Clinton's Crime Rhetoric and the Dynamics of Issue Ownership," *Political Behavior* 26, no. 2 (2004): 95–124.

2. This kind of more abstract discussion of threat construction is most often manifest in discourse analysis. For a discussion, see Andrew W. Neal, "'Events, Dear Boy, Events': Terrorism and Security from the Perspective of Politics," *Critical Studies on Terrorism* 5, no. 1 (2012): 107–20.

3. Georgios Karyotis, "Securitization of Migration in Greece: Process, Motives, and Implications," *International Political Sociology* 6, no. 4 (2012): 390–408.

4. On legitimacy, see Didier Bigo, "Security and Immigration: Toward a Critique of the Governmentality of Unease," *Alternatives* 27, special issue (2002): 63–92; on power, see Deborah Stone, *Policy Paradox: The Art of Political Decision Making*, 2nd ed. (New York: Norton, 1997).

5. Andrew W. Neal, *Security as Politics* (Edinburgh: Edinburgh University Press, 2019), 43.

6. "Europe's Populists Are Waltzing Into the Mainstream," *Economist*, February 3, 2018, https://www.economist.com/briefing/2018/02/03/europes-populists-are-waltzing -into-the-mainstream; Cas Mudde, *The Far Right Today* (Cambridge: Polity Press, 2019); see also Aurelien Mondon and Aaron Winter, *Reactionary Democracy: How Racism and the Populist Far Right Became Mainstream* (London: Verso, 2020).

7. See Mondon and Winter, *Reactionary Democracy*; and Cas Mudde, "Three Decades of Populist Radical Right Parties in Western Europe: So What?," *European Journal of Political Research* 52, no. 1 (2013): 1–19.

8. Janet Napolitano, quoted in John Pomfret, "At Front Line of Immigration Debate," *Washington Post*, June 25, 2006, http://www.washingtonpost.com/wp-dyn/content /article/2006/06/24/AR2006062400785.html.

9. Napolitano's policy of making all-day kindergarten available to all Arizona children was promoted as one of her signature accomplishments.

10. Amanda Ripley and Karen Tumulty, "America's Five Best Governors," *Time*, November 21, 2005.

11. Erica Werner, "Western Governors Call for Guest Worker Plan, Immigration Reform," Associated Press, February 28, 2006.

12. Pomfret, "At Front Line of Immigration Debate."

13. Survey USA, "Arizona Governor Approval Tracking Poll," 2006, http://www.surveyusa .com/client/PollTrack.aspx?g=d1c42d6f-c0c6-4784-b108-6fbd136adf03.

14. Christian Palmer, "Possible Use of Radar, Cameras to Thwart Illegal Immigration Advances," *Arizona Capitol Times*, February 17, 2006.

15. Governor Janet Napolitano, "State of the State Address," Phoenix, January 9, 2006.

16. "2006 State of the State," *Horizon*, KAET Channel 8, Phoenix, January 9, 2006, https:// azpbs.org/horizon/2006/01/state-of-the-state-reaction/.

17. Larry Rohter, "National Guard Is Used in a Test to Curb Drug Flow from Mexico," *New York Times*, August 22, 1988, http://www.nytimes.com/1988/08/22/world/national -guard-is-used-in-a-test-to-curb-drug-flow-from-mexico.html.

18. Napolitano, "State of the State Address," January 9, 2006.

19. Arizona State Legislative Staff, "HB 2701: National Guard Mobilization; Border; Appropriation. As Transmitted to the Governor," fact sheet, Arizona State Legislature, 2006; all documents from the Arizona State Legislature are available in the legislature's online archives at https://www.azleg.gov/.

20. Arizona State Legislature, Committee on Federal Mandates and Property Rights, "Minutes of Meeting, Committee on Federal Mandates and Property Rights," February 6, 2006, http://www.azleg.gov/legtext/47leg/2r/comm_min/house/0206%20fmpr.doc.htm.

21. Janet Napolitano, "Executive Order 2006-6: Authorizing Increased National Guard Assistance at the Border," March 8, 2006, *Arizona Administrative Register* 12, no. 11 (2006): 842–43.

22. Governor Janet Napolitano to House Speaker Jim Weiers, re: HB 2701, March 9, 2006; all of Governor Napolitano's veto letters and signing statements are archived online by the Arizona State Legislature as "Governor's Letters" at https://www.azleg.gov /governors-letters/.

23. John Allen, quoted in Jacques Billeaud, "Ariz. Gov. Orders More Troops to the Border," Associated Press, March 8, 2006.

24. Janet Napolitano, quoted in Billeaud, "Ariz. Gov. Orders More Troops to the Border."

25. Janet Napolitano, campaign commercial, 2006, https://www.youtube.com/watch ?v=8yipIomcWU8.

26. Governor Janet Napolitano to Senate President Ken Bennett, re: SB 1157, April 17, 2006.

27. Arizona State Legislative Staff, "HB 2837: Shared Revenues; Sanctuary Policy; Limitation," fact sheet, Arizona State Legislature, 2006.

28. Randal C. Archibold, "In Cost and Vitriol, Race in Arizona Draws Notice," *New York Times*, September 11, 2006, http://www.nytimes.com/2006/09/11/us/politics/11arizona .html.

29. Leo R. Chavez, *The Latino Threat: Constructing Immigrants, Citizens, and the Nation*, 2nd ed. (Stanford, CA: Stanford University Press, 2013), 157–80.

30. The largest such march, on April 10, 2006, drew an estimated 100,000 to 300,000 participants (Wilson Center, "Immigrant Rights Marches, Spring 2006," 2006, https://www .wilsoncenter.org/sites/default/files/media/documents/publication/Data.pdf). See also Matt A. Barreto, Sylvia Monzano, Ricardo Ramírez, and Kathy Rim, "Mobilization, Participation, and Solidaridad: Latino Participation in the 2006 Immigration Protest Rallies," *Urban Affairs Review* 44, no. 5 (2009): 736–64; and Heather Silber Mohamed, "Can Protests Make Latinos 'American'? Identity, Immigration Politics, and the 2006 Marches," *American Politics Research* 41, no. 2 (2013): 298–327.

31. Yvonne Wingett and Daniel Gonzalez, "Immigrants Protested in Valley, Cities Across U.S.," *Arizona Republic*, March 28, 2006; Sheryl Gay Stolberg, "After Immigration Protests, Goal Remains Elusive," *New York Times*, May 3, 2006, http://www.nytimes .com/2006/05/03/us/03assess.html.

32. Terry Greene Sterling and Jude Joffe-Block, *Driving While Brown: Sheriff Joe Arpaio Versus the Latino Resistance* (Oakland: University of California Press, 2021), 66.

33. Alia Beard Rau, "Limit on Illegal-Immigrant Lawsuits Faces Test of Constitutionality," *Arizona Republic*, May 30, 2011.

34. Jacques Billeaud, "Legislature Puts 2 Immigration Proposals on Ballot; 3 Others Fail," Associated Press State and Local Wire, June 22, 2006.

35. Jacques Billeaud, "Immigration Proposals Clear Senate with Punishments for Businesses," Associated Press State and Local Wire, May 9, 2005; Jacques Billeaud, "Lawmakers Stifle Proposed Punishments for Employers of Immigrants," Associated Press State and Local Wire, April 19, 2005.

36. Amanda Aguirre, quoted in Phil Riske, "Leader: Arizona Democrats Want Business Involved in Immigration Reform," *Arizona Capitol Times*, June 3, 2005.

37. See Margaret Canovan, "Taking Politics to the People: Populism as the Ideology of Democracy," in *Democracies and the Populist Challenge*, ed. Yves Mény and Yves Surel (Basingstoke, U.K.: Palgrave Macmillan, 2002), 32.

38. Greg Patterson, "Queen's Gambit Accepted," *Espresso Pundit* (blog), October 26, 2007, http://www.espressopundit.com/2007/10/queens-gambit-a.html.

39. Napolitano, "State of the State Address," January 9, 2006.

40. Brandy Petrone, "Strike Everything Amendment to H.B. 2577, Relating to Employment; Licensing; Immigration Policy," bill summary, Arizona State Legislature, April 18, 2006.

41. Paul Davenport, "Napolitano Cool Toward GOP Immigration Bill for State," Associated Press State and Local Wire, May 18, 2006.

42. Governor Janet Napolitano to House Speaker Jim Weiers, re: HB 2577, June 6, 2006.

43. Phil Riske, "Interview with Democrat Governor Napolitano," *Arizona Capitol Times*, July 28, 2006.

44. Rebecca Gambler, "Border Patrol: Goals and Measures Not Yet in Place to Inform Border Security Status and Resource Needs," U.S. Government Accountability Office, February 26, 2013, http://www.gao.gov/products/gao-13-330t.

45. Jim Small, "Dead Bill in Ariz. Barring Acceptance of Mexican ID Card Springs to Life," *Arizona Capitol Times*, April 13, 2007.

46. Governor Janet Napolitano to Senate President Timothy S. Bee, re: SB 1236, May 8, 2007.

47. Jim Small, "Illegal Immigration Heats Up in House with Competing Bills," *Arizona Capitol Times*, February 16, 2007.

48. Bill Konopnicki, quoted in Ted Prezelski, "Konopnicki's Speech," *Rum, Romanism, and Rebellion* (blog), February 21, 2007, Wayback Machine, https://web.archive.org/web/20070301101133/http://www.rumromanismrebellion.net/2007/02/21/konopnickis-speech/.

49. The Arizona Legislature's ability to modify a law passed by voters is very constrained. It requires a three-quarters vote in each chamber and must pass the legal test that the modification can only further the intent of the voters.

50. Robert Pear and Carl Hulse, "Immigration Bill Fails to Survive Senate Vote," *New York Times*, June 28, 2007, http://www.nytimes.com/2007/06/28/washington/28cnd-immig.html?mtrref=www.google.co.uk&gwh=8FA29BE0D2C16681F88AC233565899D6&gwt=pay.

51. Governor Janet Napolitano to House Speaker Jim Weiers, re: HB 2779, July 2, 2007.

52. Russell Pearce, interviewed in the segment "Employer Sanctions," *Arizona Horizon*, KAET Channel 8, Phoenix, July 9, 2007, transcript, https://azpbs.org/horizon/2007/07/one-on-one-20/.

53. Patterson, "Queen's Gambit Accepted."

54. Leith van Onselen, "How Phoenix Housing Boomed and Busted," *New Geography* (blog), November 6, 2011, http://www.newgeography.com/content/002517-how-phoenix-housing-boomed-and-busted.

55. Catherine Reagor, Matt Dempsey, and Ryan Konig, "Phoenix-Area Real Estate Collapse Echoed Troubles," *Arizona Republic*, October 9, 2011.

56. Chris Lukinbeal and Laura Sharp, "Performing America's Toughest Sheriff: Media as Practice in Joe Arpaio's Old West," *GeoJournal* 80, no. 6 (2015): 881.

57. See Jize Jiang, "The Politics of Punishment and Protection: A Comparative Historical Analysis of American Immigration Control, 1990–2017," *Law and Policy* 42, no. 2 (2020): 125–61. For more on "penal populism" in general, see John Pratt, *Penal Populism* (New York: Routledge, 2007).

58. Terry Greene Sterling, "The Handcuffing of Sheriff Joe," *National Journal*, August 2, 2014, https://www.nationaljournal.com/s/72886/handcuffing-sheriff-joe.

59. William Finnegan, "Sheriff Joe," *New Yorker*, July 13, 2009, http://www.newyorker.com/magazine/2009/07/20/sheriff-joe.

60. Ashley Bates, "The Napolitano Files: The Opportunistic Immigration Record of the New UC President," *East Bay Express*, January 22, 2014, http://www.eastbayexpress.com/oakland/the-napolitano-files/Content?oid=3816442.

61. John Dougherty, "In the Crosshairs," *Phoenix New Times*, June 24, 2004, https://www.phoenixnewtimes.com/news/in-the-crosshairs-6431626.

62. See Melissa Hickman Barlow, "Race and the Problem of Crime in 'Time' and 'Newsweek' Cover Stories, 1946 to 1995," *Social Justice* 25, no. 2 (1998): 149–83; and Marc Mauer, *Race to Incarcerate* (New York: New Press, 1999).

63. E. J. Montini, "How Thomas, Arpaio Changed Migrant Debate," *Arizona Republic*, July 8, 2008.

64. Greene Sterling and Joffe-Block, *Driving While Brown*, 51–63.

65. Paul Giblin, "Reasonable Doubt: Arpaio's View on Who to Go After Has Changed," *East Valley Tribune*, July 9, 2008, http://www.eastvalleytribune.com/arizona/immigration/article_d94db972-9cc9-5953-a2bf-c743ae837a39.html.

66. Lisa Magaña, "Arizona's Immigration Policies and SB 1070," in *Latino Politics and Arizona's Immigration Law SB 1070*, ed. Lisa Magaña and Erik Lee (New York: Springer, 2013), 19–26.

67. Paul Giblin, "Deputies Arrest 13 in Migrant Patrols: 9 Taken Into Custody Are Suspected of Being Illegals," *East Valley Tribune*, March 22, 2008.

68. Joe Arpaio, quoted in Giblin, "Deputies Arrest 13."

69. Finnegan, "Sheriff Joe."

70. Ryan Gabrielson and Paul Giblin, "Reasonable Doubt: Sweeps Break the Rules," *East Valley Tribune*, July 11, 2008, http://www.eastvalleytribune.com/news/image_a3fc6e58-4a66-5bba-8927-6f7a45f5d247.html.

71. J. J. Hensley and Senta Scarborough, "Arpaio, Gascón a Study in Contrasts," *Arizona Republic*, June 29, 2008; Ray Stern, "Mesa Police Chief George Gascón Stares Down Sheriff Joe Arpaio," *Phoenix New Times*, July 10, 2008, http://www.phoenixnewtimes.com/news/mesa-police-chief-george-gascn-stares-down-sheriff-joe-arpaio-6426648.

72. Judith A. Greene, "Local Democracy on ICE: The Arizona Laboratory," in *Outside Justice: Immigration and the Criminalizing Impact of Changing Policy and Practice*, ed. David C. Brotherton, Daniel L. Stageman, and Shirley P. Leyro (New York: Springer, 2013), 40.

73. Governor Janet Napolitano, "State of the State Address," Phoenix, January 14, 2008.

74. No relation to Tim Nelson, the general counsel to the governor from 2003 to 2008.

75. Jacques Billeaud, "Group Urges Governor to Veto Immigration Bill," Associated Press, April 23, 2008.

76. Jim Small and Christian Palmer, "Arizona Governor Napolitano Acquiesces to Dems' Plea for Veto," *Arizona Capitol Times*, May 2, 2008.

77. Governor Janet Napolitano to House Speaker Jim Weiers, re: HB 2807, April 28, 2008.

78. John Nelson, quoted in Small and Palmer, "Arizona Governor Napolitano Acquiesces to Dems' Plea for Veto."

79. Christian Palmer, "Illegal Immigration Ballot Proposal Touted After Arizona Governor Vetoes Similar Bill," *Arizona Capitol Times*, May 9, 2008.

80. Ronald J. Hansen, "Bills Seek Temporary Foreign-Worker Program," *Arizona Republic*, February 8, 2008.

81. Ronald J. Hansen and Betty Beard, "Ariz. Seeks to Reshape Immigrant Farm Labor," *Arizona Republic*, February 7, 2008.

82. Marsha Arzberger, quoted in Faye Bowers, "Arizona Considers a Guest Worker Program of Its Own," *Christian Science Monitor*, March 31, 2008, http://www.csmonitor .com/USA/Politics/2008/0331/p02s02-uspo.html.

83. Luige del Puerto, "New Legislation Makes Major Changes to Arizona's Proposed Guest-Worker Program," *Arizona Capitol Times*, April 10, 2008.

84. Luige del Puerto, "Arizona State Senator Attempts to Stall Guest-Worker Program: The Gould Amendments," *Arizona Capitol Times*, May 9, 2008.

85. Ron Gould and Russell Pearce, quoted in Luige del Puerto, "An Amendment Purgatory in Arizona Legislature," *Arizona Capitol Times*, May 9, 2008.

86. Luige del Puerto, "Lawmakers Split on Arizona Guest-Worker Program," *Arizona Capitol Times*, January 18, 2008.

87. Luige del Puerto, "Arizona's Guest-Worker Bill Moves to Back Burner," *Arizona Capitol Times*, May 16, 2008.

88. Phil Gordon, "Cesar Chavez Day Speech," Phoenix, March 28, 2008, video, https://www .youtube.com/watch?v=PTnCqEwUpwA.

89. Mayor Phil Gordon to U.S. Attorney General Michael B. Mukasey, re: Request for Civil Rights Investigation of the Maricopa County Sheriff, April 4, 2008, https://www.aclu .org/other/letter-mayor-attorney-general-requesting-civil-rights-investigation -maricopa-county-sheriff.

90. Casey Newton and J. J. Hensley, "Gordon Blasts Arpaio Over Migrant Sweeps," *Arizona Republic*, March 29, 2008.

91. Paul Giblin and Ryan Gabrielson, "Reasonable Doubt: Sweeping Powers," *East Valley Tribune*, July 13, 2008, http://www.pulitzer.org/winners/ryan-gabrielson-and-paul -giblin.

92. Gordon, "Cesar Chavez Day Speech."

93. Janet Napolitano, "Executive Order 2008-22: State Felony and Fugitive Detail," May 12, 2008, *Arizona Administrative Register* 14, no. 22 (2008): 2157.

94. Joe Arpaio, quoted in Lindsey Collom, "Arpaio Cut Out of State Funding," *Arizona Republic*, May 14, 2008.

95. Mike Nizza, "Immigration Enforcement Funds Slashed in Arizona," *The Lede* (*New York Times* news blog), May 14, 2008, http://thelede.blogs.nytimes.com/2008/05/14 /immigration-enforcement-funds-slashed-in-arizona/.

96. Yvonne Wingett, "$1.6 Mil OK'ed for Arpaio's Illegal-Immigrant Program," *Arizona Republic*, May 21, 2009.

97. Matthew Benson, "Napolitano Endorses Obama for President," *Arizona Republic*, January 12, 2008.

98. Jennifer Ludden, "Immigration Issue Doesn't Divide McCain, Obama," *Morning Edition*, National Public Radio, June 10, 2008.

99. Dana Goldstein, "Janet Napolitano and the New Third Way," *American Prospect*, July 1, 2008, http://prospect.org/article/janet-napolitano-and-new-third-way; Spencer S. Hsu,

"Homeland Security Pick Napolitano Praised by Left and Right Alike," *Washington Post*, November 21, 2008, http://www.washingtonpost.com/wp-dyn/content/article/2008/11/20/AR2008112001567.html.

100. Paul Davenport, "Arizona Primes for a New Governor and Different Path," Associated Press Online, January 21, 2009.

101. Jean-Thomas Arrighi de Casanova, "Making Immigration in a Multinational Context: Border Struggles and Nation-Building in Contemporary Scotland and Catalonia," in *The Politics of Immigration in Multi-level States: Governance and Political Parties*, ed. Eve Hepburn and Ricard Zapata-Barrero (Basingstoke, U.K.: Palgrave Macmillan, 2014), 108–29.

102. Mike Slaven, "Populism and Securitization: The Corrosion of Elite Security Authority in a US-Mexico Border State," *Journal of Global Security Studies* 6, no. 4 (2021): 14 (online only; articles individually paginated).

103. Henrik Bech Seeberg, "How Stable Is Political Parties' Issue Ownership? A Cross-Time, Cross-National Analysis," *Political Studies* 65, no. 2 (2017): 475–92.

104. Jane Green and Sara B. Hobolt, "Owning the Issue Agenda: Party Strategies and Vote Choices in British Elections," *Electoral Studies* 27, no. 3 (2008): 460–76.

105. Pontus Odmalm and Betsy Super, "Getting the Balance Right? Party Competition on Immigration and Conflicting Ideological 'Pulls,' " *Scandinavian Political Studies* 37, no. 3 (2014): 301–22.

106. Holian, "He's Stealing My Issues!"

107. Holian, "He's Stealing My Issues!," 101.

108. Stone, *Policy Paradox*, 2.

109. Ole Wæver, "Securitization and Desecuritization," in *On Security*, ed. Ronnie D. Lipschutz (New York: Columbia University Press, 1995), 46–86.

3. THE TOUGHEST MEASURE

1. Michael C. Williams, "Securitization as Political Theory: The Politics of the Extraordinary," *International Relations* 29, no. 1 (2015): 115; Thierry Balzacq, "Securitization Theory: Past, Present, and Future," *Polity* 51, no. 2 (2019): 331–48.

2. For discussion of the unsettling nature of this kind of shift to societies' liberal identities, see Michael C. Williams, "Securitization and the Liberalism of Fear," *Security Dialogue* 42, nos. 4–5 (2011): 453–63.

3. Andrew W. Neal, *Security as Politics* (Edinburgh: Edinburgh University Press, 2019).

4. Jens Rydgren, "Is Extreme Right-Wing Populism Contagious? Explaining the Emergence of a New Party Family," *European Journal of Political Research* 44, no. 3 (2005): 413–37; Tim Bale, "Supplying the Insatiable Demand: Europe's Populist Radical Right," *Government and Opposition* 47, no. 2 (2012): 256–74; Cas Mudde, "Three Decades of Populist Radical Right Parties in Western Europe: So What?," *European Journal of Political Research* 52, no. 1 (2013): 1–19.

5.   Cas Mudde, *The Far Right Today* (Cambridge: Polity Press, 2019), 130.

6.   Daniel Ziblatt, *Conservative Parties and the Birth of Democracy* (Cambridge: Cambridge University Press, 2017).

7.   David Smith, "How Trump Captured the Republican Party," *Guardian*, June 10, 2018, https://www.theguardian.com/us-news/2018/jun/09/donald-trump-republican-party; S. V. Date, "Two Years In, the Republican Party Faces an Uncertain Future in Trump's Image," *Huffington Post*, January 20, 2019, https://www.huffingtonpost.com/entry/trump-gop-face_us_5c425823e4b0a8dbe171600b.

8.   Mike Sunnucks, "Arizona Budget Deficit Labeled Country's Worst," *Phoenix Business Journal*, February 28, 2008, http://www.bizjournals.com/phoenix/stories/2008/02/25/daily29.html.

9.   Governor Jan Brewer, "Inaugural Address," Phoenix, January 21, 2009.

10. Matthew Benson, "Brewer Promises to Downsize, Cut Spending," *Arizona Republic*, January 22, 2009.

11. Mary Jo Pitzl and Matthew Benson, "House GOP Ousts Jim Weiers as Leader," *Arizona Republic*, November 7, 2008.

12. Under the Arizona Constitution, tax increases require legislative supermajorities. Brewer's strategy therefore rested on the legislature's referring the measure to voters, which it could do with simple majority votes.

13. Randal C. Archibold, "Mexican Drug Cartel Violence Spills Over, Alarming U.S.," *New York Times*, March 22, 2009, http://www.nytimes.com/2009/03/23/us/23border.html; Reece Jones, *Border Walls: Security and the War on Terror in the United States, India, and Israel* (London: Zed Books, 2012), 32.

14. "Kidnapping Capital of the U.S.A.," *Nightline*, ABC News, February 12, 2009, http://abcnews.go.com/Blotter/story?id=6848672&page=1; Ciara O'Rourke, "McCain Says Phoenix Is the Second Kidnapping Capital in the World," Politifact Texas, June 28, 2010, http://www.politifact.com/texas/statements/2010/jun/28/john-mccain/mccain-says-phoenix-second-kidnapping-capital-worl/; Dave Biscobing and Mark LaMet, "Truth Behind Phoenix Kidnapping Statistics," ABC15 Arizona, July 25, 2013, Wayback Machine, https://web.archive.org/web/20141024191300/http://www.abc15.com/news/local-news/investigations/truth-behind-phoenix-kidnapping-statistics.

15. Phil Gordon, testimony, U.S. Senate Committee on Homeland Security and Governmental Affairs, *Southern Border Violence: State and Local Perspectives*, 111th Cong., 1st sess., April 20, 2009, https://www.hsgac.senate.gov/imo/media/doc/042009Gordon.pdf.

16. Russell Pearce, "Let's Put an End to Illegal-Migrant Catch and Release," *Arizona Republic*, June 25, 2009.

17. Howard Fischer, "Cities, Towns Cannot Block Enforcement of Immigration Laws," Capitol Media Services, April 15, 2009; Russell Pearce, "I Never Did Give Them Hell. I Just Told Them the Truth, and They Thought It Was Hell," July 14, 2009, available within the court filing at https://www.aclu.org/sites/default/files/field_document/715-6_exhibit_e_-_pochoda_declaration_1.pdf.

18. Janice Almond, "Strike Everything Amendment to H.B. 2280; Relating to Illegal Aliens; Trespassing; Enforcement," bill summary, Arizona State Senate, June 24, 2009; all documents from the Arizona State Legislature are available in the legislature's online archives at www.azleg.gov.

19. Luige del Puerto, "Clergy Ejected from Committee—Dems in Arizona Follow," *Arizona Capitol Times*, June 24, 2009.

20. Jacques Billeaud, "Arizona House Rejects Immigration Enforcement Bill," Associated Press, July 1, 2009.

21. See Christopher S. Parker and Matt A. Barreto, *Change They Can't Believe In: The Tea Party and Reactionary Politics in America* (Princeton, NJ: Princeton University Press, 2014), 153–89.

22. Jeremy Duda, "Sen. Pearce Pushed, Prodded, and Pandered to Pass His 'Legacy Bill,'" *Arizona Capitol Times*, April 23, 2010.

23. Chewie Shofir, "Crandall, Driggs, Quelland, Mason, & Konopnicki Tried to Have It Both Ways on Immigration," Sonoran Alliance, July 13, 2009, https://sonoranalliance .com/crandall-driggs-quelland-mason-konopnicki-tried-to-have-it-both-ways-on -immigration/. See also "Your Legislators Hard at Work, Taking a Dive—We Name Names," *Seeing Red AZ* (blog), July 1, 2009, https://seeingredaz.wordpress.com/2009 /07/01/your-legislators-hard-at-work-taking-a-dive-we-name-names/.

24. Sample talking point quoted in a court filing, *Valle del Sol et al. v. Michael B. Whiting et al., US District Court*, District of Arizona, CV-10-01061-PHX-SRB, https://www.aclu .org/files/assets/715-6_exhibit_e_-_pochoda_declaration_1.pdf.

25. Duda, "Sen. Pearce Pushed, Prodded, and Pandered to Pass His 'Legacy Bill.'"

26. Jim Small, "Arizona State Senator Russell Pearce: Stemming Illegal Immigration Is Arizona's Top Priority," *Arizona Capitol Times*, October 21, 2009.

27. Russell Pearce, quoted in Jim Small, "Arizona Senator Russell Pearce Sets Out to Eliminate 'Sanctuary' Policies, Create New Fines for Business," *Arizona Capitol Times*, October 12, 2009.

28. Matthew Benson, "Brewer Says State Still Needs More Revenue," *Arizona Republic*, December 1, 2009.

29. Luige del Puerto, "2010 Predictions: Political Races, Payday Loans, Racinos, Taxes, Immigration on Tap," *Arizona Capitol Times*, December 28, 2009.

30. "Toplines—2010 Arizona GOP Primary for Governor's Race—January 20, 2010," Rasmussen Reports, January 20, 2010, http://www.rasmussenreports.com/public_content /politics/elections/election_2010/election_2010_governor_elections/arizona/questions /toplines_2010_arizona_gop_primary_for_governor_s_race_january_20_2010.

31. Governor Jan Brewer, "2010 State of the State Address," Phoenix, January 10, 2010.

32. Mary Jo Pitzl, "Arizona Budget Passes; Cuts Total $1.1 Billion," *Arizona Republic*, March 12, 2010.

33. A mirroring bill was introduced in the House as HB 2632.

34. See Luis F. B. Plascencia, "Attrition Through Enforcement and the Elimination of a 'Dangerous Class,'" in *Latino Politics and Arizona's Immigration Law SB 1070*, ed. Lisa

Magaña and Erik Lee (New York: Springer, 2013), 93–127; and Alex Balch, "Twenty-First Century: Attrition by Enforcement," in *Immigration and the State: Fear, Greed, and Hospitality*, ed. Alex Balch (London: Palgrave Macmillan, 2016), 151–73.

35. Duda, "Sen. Pearce Pushed, Prodded, and Pandered to Pass His 'Legacy Bill.'"

36. SB 1070 ended up containing a similar provision, but one where legal standing was no longer defined as broadly as it had been. It was now limited to Arizona residents rather than applying to any American and stipulated that losing litigants would have to pay court fees.

37. Shar Porier, "Slain Rancher Was Beloved; Described as Good Samaritan," *San Pedro Valley News-Sun*, March 31, 2010.

38. Judson Berger, "Rancher's Murder Exposes Deadly Gaps in Border Policing, Tancredo Says," FoxNews.com, March 30, 2010, http://www.foxnews.com/politics/2010/03/30 /border-killing-exposes-deadly-gaps-immigration-policy-tancredo-says.html.

39. Dennis Wagner, "Slain Arizona Rancher Mourned by Friends, Neighbors: Death Is Blamed on Failure by U.S. to Secure the Border," *Arizona Republic*, April 1, 2010.

40. Randal C. Archibold, "Immigrants Are Focus of New Curbs," *New York Times*, March 24, 2010; Luige del Puerto, "Arizona Senate OKs Bill to Prohibit 'Sanctuary Cities,'" *Arizona Capitol Times*, February 15, 2010.

41. Evan Wyloge, "'Trespass' Removed from Arizona Immigration Bill," *Arizona Capitol Times*, March 30, 2010.

42. Arizona House of Representatives, Committee on Military Affairs and Public Safety, "Minutes of Meeting, Committee on Military Affairs and Public Safety," March 31, 2010, https://www.azleg.gov/legtext/49leg/2R/comm_min/House/033110%20MAPS.pdf.

43. Arizona House of Representatives, Committee on Military Affairs and Public Safety, "Minutes of Meeting," March 31, 2010.

44. Mary Jo Pitzl and Daniel Gonzalez, "Tough Immigration Bill OK'ed by Arizona House," *Arizona Republic*, April 14, 2010; Ewen MacAskill, "Arizona Goes It Alone with Strict Immigration Bill: Harshest Rules in US Target Workers Without Papers. It Will Lead to Harassment of Latinos, Opponents Say," *Guardian*, April 15, 2010; Nicholas Riccardi, "Arizona Passes Strict Illegal Immigration Act," *Los Angeles Times*, April 13, 2010.

45. Evan Wyloge, "Sen. Pearce's Controversial Immigration Enforcement Bill in Arizona Morphs Again," *Arizona Capitol Times*, April 14, 2010.

46. Pearce here is seemingly referring in part to Kris Kobach, an anti-immigration legal activist who helped to draft SB 1070 and was later elected the Kansas secretary of state.

47. Arizona State Legislature, *April 13, 2010—House Third Reading #1*, video, 2010, https:// www.azleg.gov/videoplayer/?eventID=2010041233&startStreamAt=1027.

48. Arizona State Legislature, *April 13, 2010—House Third Reading #1*.

49. Arizona State Legislature, *April 13, 2010—House Third Reading #1*.

50. Arizona State Legislature, *April 13, 2010—House Third Reading #1*.

51. Meyer was not present in the House on the day of the final vote on SB 1070.

52. Robert Leger, "Q&A with Outgoing Sen. Carolyn Allen," *Arizona Republic*, May 16, 2010.

53. Ewen MacAskill, "Arizona Goes It Alone with Tough Immigration Laws," *Guardian*, April 14, 2010, https://www.theguardian.com/world/2010/apr/14/arizona-tough-immigration-laws.

54. Martin Kady, "Grijalva: Boycott My Home State," *On Congress* (*Politico* blog), April 20, 2010, http://www.politico.com/blogs/on-congress/2010/04/grijalva-boycott-my-home-state-026514.

55. Jan Brewer, quoted in Stephen Lemons, "Jan Brewer Stomps Out of Chicanos por la Causa to the Chants of 'Veto the Bill,'" *Feathered Bastard* (*Phoenix New Times* blog), April 22, 2010, http://www.phoenixnewtimes.com/blogs/jan-brewer-stomps-out-of-chicanos-por-la-causa-to-the-chants-of-veto-the-bill-6501856.

56. Randal C. Archibold, "An Unexpected Governor Takes an Unwavering Course," *New York Times*, April 25, 2010.

57. Jan Brewer, "Statement by Governor Jan Brewer," press conference, Phoenix, April 23, 2010.

58. Jan Brewer, "Executive Order 2010-09: Establishing Law Enforcement Training for Immigration Laws," April 23, 2010, *Arizona Administrative Register* 16, no. 21 (2010): 856–57.

59. Brewer, "Statement by Governor Jan Brewer," emphasis in the original official text version.

60. Jonathan J. Cooper, "Ariz. Immigration Law Target of Protest," Associated Press, April 26, 2010, http://www.nbcnews.com/id/36768649/ns/us_news-life/t/ariz-immigration-law-target-protest/.

61. Brewer, "Statement by Governor Jan Brewer."

62. Barack Obama, "Remarks by the President at Naturalization Ceremony for Active-Duty Service Members," Washington, DC, April 23, 2010, https://obamawhitehouse.archives.gov/the-press-office/remarks-president-naturalization-ceremony-active-duty-service-members.

63. Manuel Chavez and Jennifer Hoewe, "National Perspectives on State Turmoil: Characteristics of Elite U.S. Newspaper Coverage of Arizona SB 1070," in *Arizona Firestorm: Global Immigration Realities, National Media, and Provincial Politics*, ed. Otto Santa Ana and Celeste González de Bustamante (New York: Rowman and Littlefield, 2012), 189–202.

64. Erin Kelly, "Ariz. Immigration Bill Has National Impact," Gannett News Service, April 23, 2010.

65. Casey Newton and Ginger Rough, "Arizona Governor Signs Bill Revising New Immigration Law," *Arizona Republic*, May 1, 2010.

66. Barack Obama, "Remarks by the President at Ottumwa, Iowa, Town Hall," Ottuma, Iowa, April 27, 2010, https://obamawhitehouse.archives.gov/realitycheck/the-press-office/remarks-president-ottumwa-iowa-town-hall.

67. Alia Beard Rau, "Poll: 52% in Arizona Back Immigration Law," *Arizona Republic*, May 4, 2010; Jeffrey M. Jones, "More Americans Favor Than Oppose Arizona Immigration Law," Polling Report, Gallup, April 29, 2010, http://www.gallup.com/poll/127598/Americans-Favor-Oppose-Arizona-Immigration-Law.aspx; "The Backlash Begins," *Economist*, May 6, 2010, http://www.economist.com/node/16060133; Pew Research Center, "Broad

Approval for New Arizona Immigration Law," Polling Report, May 12, 2010, http://www
.people-press.org/2010/05/12/broad-approval-for-new-arizona-immigration-law/.

68. Anna Ochoa O'Leary, Andrea J. Romero, Nolan L. Cabrero, and Michelle Rascón, "Assault on Ethnic Studies," in *Arizona Firestorm*, ed. Santa Ana and González de Bustamante, 97–120.

69. Katie Cobb, "Immigration Law Breathes Life Into Brewer's Re-election Campaign," *FoxNews*, June 12, 2010, http://www.foxnews.com/politics/2010/06/10/immigration-law -breathes-life-brewers-election-campaign.html.

70. John Munger, quoted in Cobb, "Immigration Law Breathes Life Into Brewer's Re-election Campaign."

71. Bruce Merrill, quoted in Cobb, "Immigration Law Breathes Life Into Brewer's Re-election Campaign."

72. Andrew Malcolm, "In Her Own Words: Arizona Gov. Jan Brewer on Obama's National Guard Border Troop Decision," *LA Times Blogs—Top of the Ticket*, May 26, 2010, http:// latimesblogs.latimes.com/washington/2010/05/jan-brewer-on-obama-national-guard -decision.html.

73. Devin Dwyer and Sunlen Miller, "Obama, Arizona Gov. Jan Brewer Hold 'Cordial' Meeting on Immigration," *ABC News*, June 3, 2010, http://abcnews.go.com/Politics /Media/president-obama-arizona-governor-jan-brewer-talk-immigration/story ?id=10807615; Stephanie Condon, "Arizona Gov. Jan Brewer: Obama Isn't Doing His Job," *CBS News*, May 21, 2010, http://www.cbsnews.com/news/arizona-gov-jan-brewer -obama-isnt-doing-his-job/.

74. Josh Goodman, "AZ-Governor: Terry Goddard's Immigration Balancing Act," *Governing: Politics* (blog), June 2, 2010, Wayback Machine, https://web.archive.org/web /20100605075157/http://www.governing.com/blogs/politics/Terry-Goddard-Immigration .html.

75. Casey Newton, "Goddard Tells Justice Dept. He Will Defend Ariz. Immigration Law," *Arizona Republic*, May 29, 2010.

76. Andrew Malcolm, "Arizona Gov. Jan Brewer Abruptly Suspends State's Attorney General from Illegal Immigrant Law Defense," *LA Times Blogs—Top of the Ticket*, May 28, 2010, http://latimesblogs.latimes.com/washington/2010/05/jan-brewer-arizona-illegal -immigrant-law.html.

77. Randal C. Archibold and Mark Landler, "Justice Dept. Will Fight Arizona on Immigration," *New York Times*, June 18, 2010, http://www.nytimes.com/2010/06/19/us/politics /19arizona.html.

78. Attorney General Terry Goddard to Governor Jan Brewer, June 18, 2010. http://media .phoenixnewtimes.com/4951069.0.pdf.

79. Goodman, "AZ-Governor."

80. Dana Milbank, "Headless Bodies and Other Immigration Tall Tales in Arizona," *Washington Post*, July 11, 2010, http://www.washingtonpost.com/wp-dyn/content/article /2010/07/09/AR2010070902342.html.

81. "Clean Elections Debate: Candidates for Governor," *Arizona Horizon*, KAET Channel 8, Phoenix, September 1, 2010, https://www.c-span.org/video/?295287-1/arizona-governor -debate.

82. Robert Farley, "Gov. Jan Brewer Talks of Beheadings in the Arizona Desert," Politifact, September 8, 2010, http://www.politifact.com/truth-o-meter/statements/2010/sep/08/jan-brewer/gov-jan-brewer-talks-beheadings-th-arizona-desert/.

83. Paul Davenport, "Arizona Governor Stumbles During Debate," Associated Press, September 2, 2010.

84. Brad Knickerbocker, "Jan Brewer Corrects the Record on Headless Bodies in the Desert," *Christian Science Monitor*, September 4, 2010, http://www.csmonitor.com/USA/Politics/The-Vote/2010/0904/Jan-Brewer-corrects-the-record-on-headless-bodies-in-the-desert; Jan Brewer quoted in Howard Fischer, "Brewer: No More Debates—Period," Capitol Media Services, September 3, 2010, http://tucson.com/news/local/govt-and-politics/elections/brewer-no-more-debates---period/article_cfb8fb2a-20a9-59d0-9276-ffaf4067b082.html.

85. "A Conversation with Terry Goddard, Attorney General of Arizona," *Washington Post*, April 5, 2009, http://www.washingtonpost.com/wp-dyn/content/article/2009/04/03/AR2009040301909.html?sid=ST2010020503071.

86. Sean Holstege, "Western Union $94M Settlement Broadens States' Investigative Powers," *Arizona Republic*, February 12, 2010.

87. Mark Duggan, "Russell Pearce Elevated to Arizona Senate President," Arizona Public Media, November 4, 2010, https://www.azpm.org/p/top-news/2010/11/3/2019-russell-pearce-elevated-to-arizona-senate-president/.

88. Jane Green, "When Voters and Parties Agree: Valence Issues and Party Competition," *Political Studies* 55, no. 3 (2007): 629–55; Jane Green and Sara B. Hobolt, "Owning the Issue Agenda: Party Strategies and Vote Choices in British Elections," *Electoral Studies* 27, no. 3 (2008): 460–76; Pontus Odmalm, "Party Competition and Positions on Immigration: Strategic Advantages and Spatial Locations," *Comparative European Politics* 10, no. 1 (2012): 1–22; Pontus Odmalm and Tim Bale, "Immigration Into the Mainstream: Conflicting Ideological Streams, Strategic Reasoning, and Party Competition," *Acta Politica* 50, no. 4 (2015): 365–78.

89. Alan I. Abramowitz and Steven Webster, "The Rise of Negative Partisanship and the Nationalization of U.S. Elections in the 21st Century," *Electoral Studies* 41 (2016): 12–22; George C. Edwards III, *On Deaf Ears: The Limits of the Bully Pulpit* (New Haven, CN: Yale University Press, 2003).

90. Abramowitz and Webster, "The Rise of Negative Partisanship."

91. Chavez and Hoewe, "National Perspectives on State Turmoil."

92. For the polarizing role that the presidential bully pulpit can play, see Edwards, *On Deaf Ears*.

4. A LINE IN THE SAND

1. Thierry Balzacq, Sara Depauw, and Sarah Léonard, "The Political Limits of Desecuritization: Security, Arms Trade, and the EU's Economic Targets," in *Contesting Security: Strategies and Logics*, ed. Thierry Balzacq (Abingdon, U.K.: Routledge, 2015), 104–21.

2.   Andrew W. Neal, " 'Events, Dear Boy, Events': Terrorism and Security from the Per-
     spective of Politics," *Critical Studies on Terrorism* 5, no. 1 (2012): 107; Columba Peoples,
     "The Securitization of Outer Space: Challenges for Arms Control," *Contemporary
     Security Policy* 32, no. 1 (2011): 82; Thierry Balzacq, Sarah Léonard, and Jan Ruzicka,
     " 'Securitization' Revisited: Theory and Cases," *International Relations* 30, no. 4 (2016):
     530; Jan Huysmans, *The Politics of Insecurity: Fear, Migration, and Asylum in the EU*
     (Abingdon, U.K.: Routledge, 2006); Didier Bigo, "Security and Immigration: Toward a
     Critique of the Governmentality of Unease," *Alternatives* 27, special issue (2002): 63–92.

3.   Juha A. Vuori, "Contesting and Resisting Security in Post-Mao China," in *Contesting
     Security*, ed. Balzacq, 29–43.

4.   Cas Mudde, "Three Decades of Populist Radical Right Parties in Western Europe: So
     What?," *European Journal of Political Research* 52, no. 1 (2013): 1–19.

5.   Alexander Hertel-Fernandez, *State Capture: How Conservative Activists, Big Businesses,
     and Wealthy Donors Reshaped the American States—and the Nation* (Oxford: Oxford
     University Press, 2019), 52–55.

6.   Garin Groff, "SB 1070: A Year Later Few States Still Feel Arizona Immigration Law's
     Allure," *East Valley Tribune*, April 19, 2011.

7.   Howard Fischer, "Pearce Plans to Run Chamber as Tea Party Senate," *East Valley Tri-
     bune*, November 3, 2010, http://www.eastvalleytribune.com/arizona/article_5f7425e4
     -e79f-11df-babb-001cc4c002e0.html.

8.   Russell Pearce, quoted in Paul Davenport, "Time-Out for Ariz. on Illegal Immigration
     in 2011?," Associated Press State and Local Wire, October 9, 2010.

9.   Davenport, "Time-Out for Ariz. on Illegal Immigration in 2011?"

10. George Vecsey, "All-Star Game 2011: Protests, Yes, but No Boycott," *New York Times*,
     July 10, 2011, http://www.nytimes.com/2011/07/11/sports/all-star-game-2011-protests-yes
     -but-no-boycott.html.

11. Bob Christie, "Arizona Boycott Cost State $140 Million Over Immigration Law, Study
     Finds," Associated Press, November 18, 2010.

12. Marc Lacey, "Immigration Advocates Are Split Over Arizona Boycott," *New York Times*,
     September 14, 2011, http://www.nytimes.com/2011/09/15/us/immigration-advocates-are
     -split-over-arizona-boycott.html.

13. Marshall Fitz and Angela Kelley, "Stop the Conference: The Economic and Fiscal Con-
     sequences of Conference Cancellations due to Arizona's S.B. 1070," Center for Ameri-
     can Progress, Washington, DC, November 2010.

14. Evan Wyloge, "Arizona Hospitality Industry Fears More Immigration Backlash in
     2011," *Arizona Capitol Times*, March 7, 2011.

15. Davenport, "Time-Out for Ariz. on Illegal Immigration in 2011?"

16. J. Weston Phippen, "Russell Pearce's Immigration Law Led to Boycotts of Arizona and
     Ended His Career. He's Not Sorry," *National Journal*, December 17, 2014, http://www
     .nationaljournal.com/next-america/population-2043/russell-pearces-immigration
     -law-led-boycotts-arizona-ended-his-career-hes-not-sorry.

17. Luige del Puerto, "Arizona's Immigration Hardliners Seemed to Have True Believers,
     but Some Republicans Are Straying from the Flock," *Arizona Capitol Times*, Febru-
     ary 25, 2011.

18. Rich Crandall, quoted in Wyloge, "Arizona Hospitality Industry Fears More Immigration Backlash in 2011."

19. Ron Gould, quoted in Wyloge, "Arizona Hospitality Industry Fears More Immigration Backlash in 2011."

20. Rich Crandall, quoted in del Puerto, "Arizona's Immigration Hardliners."

21. Sandra Day O'Connor served in the Arizona Legislature as a Republican from 1969 to 1975, including as Senate majority leader. Her reputation as a pragmatic consensus builder surely reflected upon these legislators' self-image.

22. Drew Brown et al. (Greater Phoenix Chamber of Commerce) to Senator Russell Pearce, re: CEOs on Immigration, March 14, 2011, emphasis in the original, https://graphics8 .nytimes.com/packages/pdf/us/20110316-CEOS-IMMIGRATION-ARIZONA.pdf.

23. Arizona State Legislature, *March 17, 2011—Senate Floor Session Part 1—Committee of the Whole #1*, video, https://www.azleg.gov/videoplayer/?eventID=2011031183&startSt reamAt=1774.

24. Arizona State Legislature, *March 17, 2011—Senate Floor Session Part 1—Committee of the Whole #1*.

25. Arizona State Legislature, *March 17, 2011—Senate Floor Session Part 2—Third Reading #1*, video, https://www.azleg.gov/videoplayer/?eventID=2011031170&startStreamAt=2077.

26. Arizona State Legislature, *March 17, 2011—Senate Floor Session Part 2—Third Reading #1*.

27. Arizona State Legislature, *March 17, 2011—Senate Floor Session Part 2—Third Reading #1*.

28. Arizona State Legislature, *March 17, 2011—Senate Floor Session Part 2—Third Reading #1*.

29. Arizona State Legislature, *March 17, 2011—Senate Floor Session Part 2—Third Reading #1*.

30. Arizona State Legislature, *March 17, 2011—Senate Floor Session Part 2—Third Reading #1*.

31. Arizona State Legislature, *March 17, 2011—Senate Floor Session Part 2—Third Reading #1*.

32. Arizona State Legislature, *March 17, 2011—Senate Floor Session Part 2—Third Reading #1*.

33. Arizona State Legislature, *March 17, 2011—Senate Floor Session Part 2—Third Reading #1*.

34. Arizona State Legislature, *March 17, 2011—Senate Floor Session Part 2—Third Reading #1*.

35. Barto and Yarbrough moved to the "yes" column on this bill.

36. Arizona State Legislature, *March 17, 2011—Senate Floor Session Part 2—Third Reading #1*.

37. Brian Terry was a U.S. Border Patrol agent killed on duty in Arizona in December 2010, whose murder became a pervasive news story and a national conservative cause célèbre.

38. Arizona State Legislature, *March 17, 2011—Senate Floor Session Part 2—Third Reading #1*.

39. Richard A. Oppel Jr., "Arizona, Bowing to Business, Softens Stand on Immigration," *New York Times*, March 18, 2011, http://www.nytimes.com/2011/03/19/us/19immigration .html.

40. Howard Fischer, "House Advances Measure to Deny Illegal Immigrants Punitive Damages," Capitol Media Services, February 16, 2011, http://www.eastvalleytribune.com /arizona/immigration/article_60db7d6a-3a3d-11e0-9b04-001cc4c03286.html.

41. Jerry Markon, "Court Upholds Block on Parts of Arizona Immigration Law," *Washington Post*, April 11, 2011, https://www.washingtonpost.com/politics/appeals_court _upholds_justice_challenge_on_ariz_law/2011/04/11/AFbyUKLD_story.html.

42. Bob Christie, "Effort to Build Arizona Border Fence Appears Dead," Associated Press, November 6, 2013.

43. Alia Beard Rau, "Cochise County Sheriff to Get Donations Meant for Border Wall," *Arizona Republic*, November 9, 2015.

44. Groff, "SB 1070"; A. Elena Lacayo, "One Year Later: A Look at SB 1070 and Copycat Legislation," National Council of La Raza, April 19, 2011, https://www.unidosus.org/wp-content/uploads/2021/07/A_look_at_SB_1070.pdf.

45. Marc Lacey, "Russell Pearce, Conservative Champion, Faces Recall in Arizona," *New York Times*, June 18, 2011, http://www.nytimes.com/2011/06/19/us/19recall.html.

46. Amy McMullen, "Inside the Russell Pearce Recall," *Salon*, November 12, 2011, http://www.salon.com/2011/11/12/russell_pearce_open2011/.

47. Lee Hockstader, "The 'Utah Way' Toward Immigration Reform," *Washington Post*, March 10, 2011.

48. David Montero, "Arizona Law: Buyer's Remorse?," *Salt Lake Tribune*, May 5, 2011.

49. Gary Nelson, "Mesa Republican Seeks to Unseat Russell Pearce," *Arizona Republic*, July 27, 2011.

50. Jerry Lewis, quoted in Stephen Lemons, "Russell Pearce Challenger Jerry Lewis Takes on the Critics, Swears Off All Freebies," *Feathered Bastard* (*Phoenix New Times* blog), September 23, 2011, http://www.phoenixnewtimes.com/blogs/russell-pearce-challenger-jerry-lewis-takes-on-the-critics-swears-off-all-freebies-6499423.

51. "Bully Meets Nice Guy," *Economist*, November 5, 2011, http://www.economist.com/node/21536608.

52. Alia Beard Rau, "Olivia Cortes Withdraws from Pearce Recall Race," *Arizona Republic*, October 7, 2011; Howard Fischer, "State Election Officials Launch Investigation Into Cortes Signs," *East Valley Tribune*, September 30, 2011, http://www.eastvalleytribune.com/arizona/article_7d3c8468-ebc2-11e0-a350-001cc4c03286.html.

53. Gary Nelson, "Dethroned: Host of Factors Helped Oust Russell Pearce," *Arizona Republic*, November 10, 2011.

54. Art Thomason, Jim Walsh, and John D'Anna, "Russell Pearce on Verge of Historic Loss in Recall," *Arizona Republic*, November 8, 2011.

55. This actually happened in the afternoon, though perhaps the misremembering of this fact reflects the mood of defeat.

56. Jeff Flake, quoted in David Weigel, "Fortress Arizona? How the Border State's Anti-immigration Movement Packed Up and Called It Quits," *Slate Magazine*, May 2, 2013.

57. Hiroshi Motomura, *Immigration Outside the Law* (Oxford: Oxford University Press, 2014), 60.

58. It is unclear what, if any, evidence exists for the claim that people were illegally registered to vote.

59. Gary Nelson, "Worsley Beats Russell Pearce in Mesa Senate Race," *Arizona Republic*, August 29, 2012.

60. Ben Giles and Gary Grado, "Senators Foil Revival of 3 Tough Immigration Bills," *Arizona Capitol Times*, February 26, 2016.

61. Alia Beard Rau, Yvonne Wingett Sanchez, and Mary Jo Pitzl, "Arizona Gov. Jan Brewer Vetoes Senate Bill 1062," *Arizona Republic*, February 26, 2014.

62. Jan Brewer, quoted in Linda Valdez, "Arizona Politicians Weigh in on 287(g)," *Insiders* (*Arizona Republic* blog), June 25, 2012, no longer available online.

63. Eyder Peralta, "Arizona Gov. Issues Executive Order Limiting New Immigration Policy," National Public Radio, August 15, 2012, http://www.npr.org/sections/thetwo-way /2012/08/15/158897138/arizona-gov-issues-executive-order-limits-new-immigration -policy.

64. In 2014, with Democratic legislative members' help, Brewer subverted Republican leadership in the Arizona Legislature by securing passage of a budget that expanded Medicaid enrollment in Arizona—legislation that was controversial among Republicans because it utilized Medicaid-expansion provisions of Obama's Affordable Care Act of 2010. See Kyle Cheney and Jason Millman, "Brewer Wins Medicaid Expansion," *Politico*, June 13, 2014, http://www.politico.com/story/2013/06/arizona-medicaid-expansion -jan-brewer-092723.

65. Bob Christie, "Immigration Leads Arizona's Governor's Race Issues," Associated Press, July 30, 2014, http://www.washingtontimes.com/news/2014/jul/30/immigration-leads -arizona-governors-race-issues/?page=all.

66. This opposition to Sheriff Arpaio is extensively explored in Terry Greene Sterling and Jude Joffe-Block, *Driving While Brown: Sheriff Joe Arpaio Versus the Latino Resistance* (Oakland: University of California Press, 2021).

67. Megan Cassidy, "Sheriff Joe Arpaio in Contempt of Federal Court, Judge Rules," *Arizona Republic*, May 16, 2016.

68. Fernanda Santos, "Sheriff Joe Arpaio Loses Bid for 7th Term in Arizona," *New York Times*, November 9, 2016, https://www.nytimes.com/2016/11/09/us/joe-arpaio-arizona -sheriff.html.

69. Anita Snow, "GOP Ads Target Arizona Democrat on Immigration," Associated Press, September 20, 2018, https://apnews.com/d6bf8582eb8d4d41bcd6edb6d7a7fbe5.

70. Howard Fischer, "Ducey Abandons Suit to Stop Deferred Action Recipients from Getting Driver's Licenses," *Arizona Capitol Times*, January 24, 2019, https://azcapitoltimes .com/news/2019/01/23/ducey-abandons-suit-to-stop-dreamers-from-getting-drivers -licenses/.

71. Jacey Fortin and Emily S. Rueb, "Tucson Rejects Sanctuary Status as Places Across U.S. Vote on Their Futures," *New York Times*, November 6, 2019, https://www.nytimes.com /2019/11/06/us/arizona-tucson-sanctuary-city.html.

72. Maria Polletta, "Sanctuary Cities Ban: Why Gov. Ducey Backed Off Plan for State Constitution," *Arizona Republic*, February 22, 2020.

73. Bob Christie, "Arizona Governor Pulls Immigration Plan Amid Business Revolt," Associated Press, February 21, 2020, https://abcnews.go.com/Politics/wireStory/arizona -governor-pulls-immigration-plan-amid-business-revolt-69131856.

74. Maria Polletta and Rafael Carranza, "Ducey Asks Homeland Security for Money to Dispatch National Guard to Border," *Arizona Republic*, March 26, 2021.

75. Mark Brodie, "Ducey, 25 Other GOP Governors Call for Meeting About Border with Biden," *Fronteras*, KJZZ, Phoenix, September 22, 2021, https://fronterasdesk.org/content /1718857/ducey-25-other-gop-governors-call-meeting-about-border-biden.

76. Indeed, the idea that one-party domination can encourage the destabilization of party coalitions is borne out in other studies of state and local politics in the United States. See Peter Bucchianeri, "Party Competition and Coalitional Stability: Evidence from American Local Government," *American Political Science Review* 114, no. 4 (2020): 1055–70.

77. Balzacq, Depauw, and Léonard, "The Political Limits of Desecuritization"; Gary T. Marx, "Security and Surveillance Contests: Resistance and Counter-Resistance," in *Contesting Security*, ed. Balzacq, 15–28; Vuori, "Contesting and Resisting Security in Post-Mao China"; Jef Huysmans, "The Question of the Limit: Desecuritisation and the Aesthetics of Horror in Political Realism," *Millennium* 27, no. 3 (1998): 569–89.

5. THE POLITICAL GAME OF SECURITY ON THE ARIZONA BORDER: PARTY COMPETITION, POPULISM, AND COUNTERSECURITIZATION

1. Jef Huysmans, "The European Union and the Securitization of Migration," *Journal of Common Market Studies* 38, no. 5 (2000): 751–77.

2. Ole Wæver, "Securitization and Desecuritization," in *On Security*, ed. Ronnie D. Lipschutz (New York: Columbia University Press, 1995), 46–86; Barry Buzan, Ole Wæver, and Jaap de Wilde, *Security: A New Framework for Analysis* (Boulder, CO: Lynne Rienner, 1998); Michael C. Williams, "Words, Images, Enemies: Securitization and International Politics," *International Studies Quarterly* 47, no. 4 (2003): 511–31.

3. Roxanne Lynn Doty, "States of Exception on the Mexico-US Border: Security, 'Decisions,' and Civilian Border Patrols," *International Political Sociology* 1, no. 2 (2007): 113–37; Andrew W. Neal, "Normalization and Legislative Exceptionalism: Counterterrorist Lawmaking and the Changing Times of Security Emergencies," *International Political Sociology* 6, no. 3 (2012): 260–76.

4. Myriam Dunn Cavelty and Matthias Leese, "Politicising Security at the Boundaries: Privacy in Surveillance and Cybersecurity," *European Review of International Studies* 5, no. 3 (2018): 53; Thierry Balzacq and Stefano Guzzini, "Introduction: 'What Kind of Theory—If Any—Is Securitization?,'" *International Relations* 29, no. 1 (2015): 100.

5. Andrew W. Neal, *Security as Politics* (Edinburgh: Edinburgh University Press, 2019).

6. Michael C. Williams, "Securitization as Political Theory: The Politics of the Extraordinary," *International Relations* 29, no. 1 (2015): 114–20.

7. Pippa Norris, *Radical Right: Voters and Parties in the Electoral Market* (Cambridge: Cambridge University Press, 2005); Joost van Spanje, "Contagious Parties: Anti-immigration Parties and Their Impact on Other Parties' Immigration Stances in Contemporary Western Europe," *Party Politics* 16, no. 5 (2010): 563–86; Aristotle Kallis, "Far-Right 'Contagion' or a Failing 'Mainstream'? How Dangerous Ideas Cross Borders and Blur Boundaries," *Democracy and Security* 9, no. 3 (2013): 221–46.

8. Tim Bale, Christoffer Green-Pedersen, Andréa Krouwel, Kurt Richard Luther, and Nick Sitter, "If You Can't Beat Them, Join Them? Explaining Social Democratic Responses

to the Challenge from the Populist Radical Right in Western Europe," *Political Studies* 58, no. 3 (2010): 410–26; Bonnie M. Meguid, "Competition Between Unequals: The Role of Mainstream Party Strategy in Niche Party Success," *American Political Science Review* 99, no. 3 (2005): 347–59.

9.   Katy Brown, Aurelien Mondon, and Aaron Winter, "The Far Right, the Mainstream, and Mainstreaming: Towards a Heuristic Framework," *Journal of Political Ideologies*, early online, 2021, https://doi.org/10.1080/13569317.2021.1949829.

10. Neal, *Security as Politics*, 17.

11. Thierry Balzacq, Sara Depauw, and Sarah Léonard, "The Political Limits of Desecuritization: Security, Arms Trade, and the EU's Economic Targets," in *Contesting Security: Strategies and Logics*, ed. Thierry Balzacq (Abingdon, U.K.: Routledge, 2015), 104–21.

12. John Gerring, "What Is a Case Study and What Is It Good For?," *American Political Science Review* 98, no. 2 (2004): 341–54.

13. Felix Ciută, "Security and the Problem of Context: A Hermeneutical Critique of Securitisation Theory," *Review of International Studies* 35, no. 2 (2009): 301–26; Neal, *Security as Politics*, 42–83.

14. See Thierry Balzacq, "Legitimacy and the 'Logic' of Security," in *Contesting Security*, ed. Balzacq, 1–9; Thierry Balzacq, "The 'Essence' of Securitization: Theory, Ideal Type, and a Sociological Science of Security," *International Relations* 29, no. 1 (2015): 103–13; and Holger Stritzel, *Security in Translation: Securitization Theory and the Localization of Threat* (Basingstoke, U.K.: Palgrave Macmillan, 2014).

15. Balzacq, "Legitimacy and the 'Logic' of Security"; Balzacq, "The 'Essence' of Securitization."

16. Bent Flyvbjerg, "Five Misunderstandings About Case-Study Research," *Qualitative Inquiry* 12, no. 2 (2006): 219–45; Gerring, "What Is a Case Study and What Is It Good For?"

17. Here I mean the Weberian sense of subjective rationality (rather than an objective sense of "rational choice"), where behavior is understood as rational inasmuch that within the actor's view the behavior is oriented toward certain meanings. See Rogers Brubaker, *The Limits of Rationality: An Essay on the Social and Moral Thought of Max Weber* (London: Allen and Unwin, 1984).

18. Bale et al., "If You Can't Beat Them, Join Them?," 412–14.

19. Wæver, "Securitization and Desecuritization," 54.

20. Mike Slaven, "Populism and Securitization: The Corrosion of Elite Security Authority in a US-Mexico Border State," *Journal of Global Security Studies* 6, no. 4 (2021): 1–18 (online only; articles individually paginated).

21. Margaret Canovan, "Trust the People! Populism and the Two Faces of Democracy," *Political Studies* 47, no. 1 (1999): 6.

22. Thierry Balzacq, "Securitization Theory: Past, Present, and Future," *Polity* 51, no. 2 (2019): 343; Williams, "Securitization as Political Theory."

23. Bohdana Kurylo, "The Discourse and Aesthetics of Populism as Securitisation Style," *International Relations*, early online, 2020, https://journals.sagepub.com/doi/full/10

.1177/0047117820973071; Thorsten Wojczewski, "'Enemies of the People': Populism and the Politics of (In)Security," *European Journal of International Security* 5, no. 1 (2020): 5–24.

24. Williams, "Words, Images, Enemies."

25. Koen Abts and Stefan Rummens, "Populism Versus Democracy," *Political Studies* 55, no. 2 (2007): 406.

26. Margaret Canovan, "Taking Politics to the People: Populism as the Ideology of Democracy," in *Democracies and the Populist Challenge*, ed. Yves Mény and Yves Surel (Basingstoke, U.K.: Palgrave Macmillan, 2002), 32.

27. Angelos Chryssogelos, "State Transformation and Populism: From the Internationalized to the Neo-sovereign State?," *Politics* 40, no. 1 (2020): 22–37; Hans-Georg Betz and Carol Johnson, "Against the Current—Stemming the Tide: The Nostalgic Ideology of the Contemporary Radical Populist Right," *Journal of Political Ideologies* 9, no. 3 (2004): 322.

28. Buzan, Wæver, and de Wilde, *Security*, 24, my emphasis.

29. Jeff Huysmans, *The Politics of Insecurity: Fear, Migration, and Asylum in the EU* (Abingdon, U.K.: Routledge, 2006), 61.

30. Andrej Zaslove, "The Dark Side of European Politics: Unmasking the Radical Right," *Journal of European Integration* 26, no. 1 (2004): 323.

31. Steve Patten, "Preston Manning's Populism: Constructing the Common Sense of the Common People," *Studies in Political Economy* 50, no. 1 (1996): 95–132.

32. Johan Tralau, "Introduction: Thomas Hobbes, Carl Schmitt, and Three Conceptions of Politics," in *Thomas Hobbes and Carl Schmitt: The Politics of Order and Myth*, ed. Johan Tralau (Abingdon, U.K.: Routledge, 2011), 3–16.

33. Stephen Hilgartner and Charles L. Bosk, "The Rise and Fall of Social Problems: A Public Arenas Model," *American Journal of Sociology* 94, no. 1 (1988): 53–78.

34. Randy Graf, quoted in "Proposition 200 in Arizona," *Marketplace*, National Public Radio, October 13, 2004.

35. See Wæver, "Securitization and Desecuritization."

36. For a broader model of issue competition, see Hilgartner and Bosk, "The Rise and Fall of Social Problems."

37. See David B. Holian, "He's Stealing My Issues! Clinton's Crime Rhetoric and the Dynamics of Issue Ownership," *Political Behavior* 26, no. 2 (2004): 95–124.

38. Jan Jagers and Stefaan Walgrave, "Populism as Political Communication Style: An Empirical Study of Political Parties' Discourse in Belgium," *European Journal of Political Research* 46, no. 3 (2007): 319–45.

39. Luke March, "Left and Right Populism Compared: The British Case," *British Journal of Politics and International Relations* 19, no. 2 (2017): 282–303.

40. Sidney Plotkin and William E. Scheuerman, *Private Interest, Public Spending: Balanced-Budget Conservatism and the Fiscal Crisis* (London: Black Rose Books, 1994).

41. See David O. Sears, "The Role of Affect in Symbolic Politics," in *Citizens and Politics: Perspectives from Political Psychology*, ed. James H. Kuklinski (Cambridge: Cambridge University Press, 2001), 14–40.

42. Joseph R. Gusfield, *The Culture of Public Problems: Drinking–Driving and the Symbolic Order* (Chicago: University of Chicago Press, 1981); contrast this discussion of the nature of problem definition with the dominant speech-act concept in securitization literatures discussed in Georgios Karyotis, "Securitization of Migration in Greece: Process, Motives, and Implications," *International Political Sociology* 6, no. 4 (2012): 391.

43. Gusfield, *The Culture of Public Problems*, 13.

44. Gusfield, *The Culture of Public Problems*, 14.

45. Juha A. Vuori, "Contesting and Resisting Security in Post-Mao China," in *Contesting Security*, ed. Balzacq, 41.

46. Neal, *Security as Politics*, 134–39.

47. "Black hole" from Jacques Billeaud, "Immigration to Occupy a Part of Arizona's Political Debate in Future," Associated Press State and Local Wire, May 16, 2005.

48. See, for instance, Buzan, Wæver, and de Wilde, *Security*, 34; Claudia Aradau, "Security and the Democratic Scene: Desecuritization and Emancipation," *Journal of International Relations and Development* 7, no. 4 (2004): 388–413; and Rita Floyd, "Just and Unjust Desecuritization," in *Contesting Security*, ed. Balzacq, 122–37.

49. Gusfield, *The Culture of Public Problems*.

50. Nina Perkowski, "Frontex and the Convergence of Humanitarianism, Human Rights, and Security," *Security Dialogue* 49, no. 6 (2018): 457–75; Joanne Warner, *The Emotional Politics of Social Work and Child Protection* (Bristol, UK: Policy Press, 2015).

51. Andrew W. Neal, "'Events, Dear Boy, Events': Terrorism and Security from the Perspective of Politics," *Critical Studies on Terrorism* 5, no. 1 (2012): 107–20.

52. Dunn Cavelty and Leese, "Politicising Security at the Boundaries," 53.

53. Balzacq, "Legitimacy and the 'Logic' of Security," 2; Philippe Bourbeau, "Moving Forward Together: Logics of the Securitisation Process," *Millennium* 43, no. 1 (2014): 187.

54. Arizona State Legislature, *March 17, 2011—Senate Floor Session Part 2—Third Reading #1*, video, https://www.azleg.gov/videoplayer/?eventID=2011031170&startStreamAt=2077.

55. Balzacq, Depauw, and Léonard, "The Political Limits of Desecuritization."

56. Wæver, "Securitization and Desecuritization."

57. Jef Huysmans, "Migrants as a Security Problem: The Dangers of 'Securitizing' Societal Issues," in *Migration and European Integration: The Dynamics of Inclusion and Exclusion*, ed. Robert Miles and Dietrich Thranhardt (London: Pinter, 1995), 53–72; Jef Huysmans, "The Question of the Limit: Desecuritisation and the Aesthetics of Horror in Political Realism," *Millennium* 27, no. 3 (1998): 569–89.

58. Aradau, "Security and the Democratic Scene," 399; Ian Paterson and Georgios Karyotis, "'We Are, by Nature, a Tolerant People': Securitisation and Counter-Securitisation in UK Migration Politics," *International Relations*, early online, 2020, https://journals.sagepub.com/doi/full/10.1177/0047117820967049.

59. Vuori, "Contesting and Resisting Security in Post-Mao China," 31.

60. Thierry Balzacq, "Part I, Resistance: Editor's Introduction," in *Contesting Security*, ed. Balzacq, 12.

61. Leo R. Chavez, *The Latino Threat: Constructing Immigrants, Citizens, and the Nation*, 2nd ed. (Stanford, CA: Stanford University Press, 2013).

62. Gary P. Freeman, "Modes of Immigration Politics in Liberal Democratic States," *International Migration Review* 29, no. 4 (1995): 881–902; Gary P. Freeman, "National Models, Policy Types, and the Politics of Immigration in Liberal Democracies," *West European Politics* 29, no. 2 (2006): 227–47.

63. Freeman, "Modes of Immigration Politics in Liberal Democratic States," 882.

64. See Colin Hay, "Ideas and the Construction of Interests," in *Ideas and Politics in Social Science Research*, ed. Daniel Béland and Robert Henry Cox (Oxford: Oxford University Press, 2010), 65–81.

65. See Vivien A. Schmidt, "Speaking of Change: Why Discourse Is Key to the Dynamics of Policy Transformation," *Critical Policy Studies* 5, no. 2 (2011): 106–26.

66. The possible exception is the bill regarding hospital reporting, but hospital companies never became primary players in this debate.

67. See Eric Van Rythoven, "On Backlash: Emotion and the Politicisation of Security," *European Review of International Studies* 5, no. 3 (2019): 139–59.

68. Neal, *Security as Politics*, 236–68.

69. Neal, *Security as Politics*, 236–68; Michael Foucault, *Security, Territory, Population: Lectures at the Collège de France, 1977–78*, ed. Michel Senellart, trans. Graham Burchell (Basingstoke, U.K.: Palgrave Macmillan, 2009).

70. Didier Bigo, "Security: A Field Left Fallow," in *Foucault on Politics, Security, and War*, ed. Michael Dillon and Andrew W. Neal (Basingstoke, U.K.: Palgrave Macmillan, 2008), 93–114.

71. Foucault, *Security, Territory, Population*, 45.

72. Michel Foucault, *The Birth of Biopolitics: Lectures at the Collège de France, 1978–79*, ed. Michel Senellart, trans. Graham Burchell (Basingstoke, U.K.: Palgrave Macmillan, 2008), 32.

73. Bigo, "Security," 110–14.

74. For a discussion of liberals' referent objects to secure, see Michael C. Williams, "Securitization and the Liberalism of Fear," *Security Dialogue* 42, nos. 4–5 (2011): 453–63.

75. Claudia Aradau, "Security as Universality? The Roma Contesting Security in Europe," in *Contesting Security*, ed. Balzacq, 92.

76. John W. Meyer, "Globalization Sources and Effects on National States and Societies," *International Sociology* 15, no. 2 (2000): 233–48; John W. Meyer, "World Society, Institutional Theories, and the Actor," *Annual Review of Sociology* 36, no. 1 (2010): 1–20.

77. Meyer, "Globalization Sources and Effects on National States and Societies," 245.

78. Chryssogelos, "State Transformation and Populism."

79. Balzacq, "Legitimacy and the 'Logic' of Security," 3.

80. Ian Loader and Neil Walker, "Policing as a Public Good: Reconstituting the Connections Between Policing and the State," *Theoretical Criminology* 5, no. 1 (2001): 15.

81. Loader and Walker, "Policing as a Public Good," 20; Neil Walker, "Defining Core Police Tasks: The Neglect of the Symbolic Dimension?," *Policing and Society* 6, no. 1 (1996): 53–71.

82. See Eric Van Rythoven, "A Feeling of Unease: Distance, Emotion, and Securitizing Indigenous Protest in Canada," *International Political Sociology* 15, no. 2 (2021): 251–71.

83. See Van Rythoven, "On Backlash."

84. Alia Beard Rau, Yvonne Wingett Sanchez, and Mary Jo Pitzl, "Arizona Gov. Jan Brewer Vetoes Senate Bill 1062," *Arizona Republic*, February 26, 2014.

85. Niraj Chokshi, "'Not a Louisiana Value': Governor Adds Protection Against LGBT Job Discrimination," *Washington Post*, April 13, 2016, https://www.washingtonpost.com /news/post-nation/wp/2016/04/13/not-a-louisiana-value-governor-adds-protection -against-lgbt-job-discrimination/?wpmm=1&wpisrc=nl_daily202.

86. Maria Polletta, "Sanctuary Cities Ban: Why Gov. Ducey Backed Off Plan for State Constitution," *Arizona Republic*, February 22, 2020.

6. APPRAISING ARIZONA: POSSIBILITIES FOR IMMIGRATION POLITICS

1. Manuel Chavez and Jennifer Hoewe, "National Perspectives on State Turmoil: Characteristics of Elite U.S. Newspaper Coverage of Arizona SB 1070," in *Arizona Firestorm: Global Immigration Realities, National Media, and Provincial Politics*, ed. Otto Santa Ana and Celeste González de Bustamante (New York: Rowman and Littlefield, 2012), 189–202.

2. Lauren Gambino and Maanvi Singh, "The Arizona County That Could Decide the Future of Trump—and America," *Guardian*, October 27, 2020, https://www.theguardian .com/us-news/2020/oct/26/maricopa-county-phoenix-donald-trump-2020.

3. Tim Bale, Christoffer Green-Pedersen, Andréa Krouwel, Kurt Richard Luther, and Nick Sitter, "If You Can't Beat Them, Join Them? Explaining Social Democratic Responses to the Challenge from the Populist Radical Right in Western Europe," *Political Studies* 58, no. 3 (2010): 410–26.

4. David Smith, "How Trump Captured the Republican Party," *Guardian*, June 10, 2018, https://www.theguardian.com/us-news/2018/jun/09/donald-trump-republican-party; Markus Wagner and Thomas M. Meyer, "The Radical Right as Niche Parties? The Ideological Landscape of Party Systems in Western Europe, 1980–2014," *Political Studies* 65, no. 1 (2017): 84–107.

5. Bent Flyvbjerg, "Five Misunderstandings about Case-Study Research," *Qualitative Inquiry* 12, no. 2 (2006): 219–45.

6. John Gerring, "What Is a Case Study and What Is It Good For?," *American Political Science Review* 98, no. 2 (2004): 341–54.

7. Andrew Geddes and Leila Hadj-Abdou, "Changing the Path? EU Migration Governance After the 'Arab Spring,'" *Mediterranean Politics* 23, no. 1 (2018): 142–60; Nina Perkowski and Vicki Squire, "The Anti-policy of European Anti-smuggling as a Site of Contestation in the Mediterranean Migration 'Crisis,'" *Journal of Ethnic and Migration Studies* 45, no. 12 (2019): 2167–84.

8. Adrian Little and Nick Vaughan-Williams, "Stopping Boats, Saving Lives, Securing Subjects: Humanitarian Borders in Europe and Australia," *European Journal of International Relations* 23, no. 3 (2017): 533–56; Mark Isaacs, "Australia's Draconian Refugee

Policy Comes Home to Roost," *Foreign Policy* (blog), November 21, 2018, https://foreignpolicy.com/2018/11/21/australias-draconian-refugee-policy-comes-home-to-roost-nauru-manus-island-offshore-detention-scott-morrison-asylum-seekers/.

9. Tjitske Akkerman, Sarah L. de Lange, and Matthijs Rooduijn, "Inclusion and Mainstreaming? Radical Right-Wing Populist Parties in the New Millennium," in *Radical Right-Wing Populist Parties in Western Europe: Into the Mainstream?*, ed. Tjitske Akkerman, Sarah L. de Lange, and Matthijs Rooduijn (Abingdon, U.K.: Routledge, 2016), 2.

10. Ákos Bocskor, "Anti-immigration Discourses in Hungary During the 'Crisis' Year: The Orbán Government's 'National Consultation' Campaign of 2015," *Sociology* 52, no. 3 (2018): 551–68.

11. See Mark Bevir and R. A. W. Rhodes, "Interpretive Theory," in *Theory and Methods in Political Science*, 2nd ed., ed. David Marsh and Gerry Stoker (Basingstoke, U.K.: Palgrave Macmillan, 2002), 131–52.

12. Marc Geddes, "The Explanatory Potential of 'Dilemmas': Bridging Practices and Power to Understand Political Change in Interpretive Political Science," *Political Studies Review* 17, no. 3 (2019): 239–54.

13. Terry Greene Sterling and Jude Joffe-Block, *Driving While Brown: Sheriff Joe Arpaio Versus the Latino Resistance* (Oakland: University of California Press, 2021).

14. Roxanne Lynn Doty, "States of Exception on the Mexico-US Border: Security, 'Decisions,' and Civilian Border Patrols," *International Political Sociology* 1, no. 2 (2007): 113–37.

15. See Greene Sterling and Joffe-Block, *Driving While Brown*; Matt A. Barreto, Sylvia Monzano, Ricardo Ramírez, and Kathy Rim, "Mobilization, Participation, and Solidaridad: Latino Participation in the 2006 Immigration Protest Rallies," *Urban Affairs Review* 44, no. 5 (2009): 736–64; René Galindo, "Repartitioning the National Community: Political Visibility and Voice for Undocumented Immigrants in the Spring 2006 Immigration Rights Marches," *Aztlan* 35, no. 2 (2010): 37–64; Heather Silber Mohamed, "Can Protests Make Latinos 'American'? Identity, Immigration Politics, and the 2006 Marches," *American Politics Research* 41, no. 2 (2013): 298–327; Lisa Magaña and Erik Lee, eds., *Latino Politics and Arizona's Immigration Law SB 1070* (New York: Springer, 2013); and Denise Ann Fuller, "Creating Resistance on the Border: Coalitions and Counternarratives to S.B. 1070," PhD diss., Ohio State University, 2017.

16. Dennis Wagner and Ronald J. Hansen, "Poll: Worker Verification Even More Popular," *Arizona Republic*, July 25, 2010; Pew Research Center for the People and the Press, Pew Hispanic Center, "America's Immigration Quandary: No Consensus on Immigration Problem or Proposed Fixes," March 30, 2006, http://www.people-press.org/2006/03/30/americas-immigration-quandary/.

17. Carroll Doherty, Jocelyn Kiley, and Bridget Johnson, "Shifting Public Views on Legal Immigration to the U.S.," Pew Research Center, June 2018, https://www.pewresearch.org/politics/2018/06/28/shifting-public-views-on-legal-immigration-into-the-u-s/.

18. Eurobarometer data show overall a slight warming in attitudes across the European Union toward non-EU immigrants since 2015, especially in western Europe, and European Social Survey data show a warming of attitudes on a number of scales over time.

Generally, however, since this date European policy has grown more hard-line. See Timothy J. Hatton, "Refugees and Asylum Seekers, the Crisis in Europe, and the Future of Policy," *Economic Policy* 32, no. 91 (2017): 46; and "Europeans, on the Whole, Are Becoming More Positive About Foreigners," *Economist*, July 21, 2018, https://www.economist.com/europe/2018/07/21/europeans-on-the-whole-are-becoming-more-positive-about-foreigners.

19. Cas Mudde, *The Far Right Today* (Cambridge: Polity Press, 2019), 177–78.

20. Nathaniel Rakich, "How Arizona Became a Swing State," *FiveThirtyEight*, June 29, 2020, https://fivethirtyeight.com/features/how-arizona-became-a-swing-state/.

21. Sheri Berman, "The Specter Haunting Europe: The Lost Left," *Journal of Democracy* 27, no. 4 (2016): 69–76.

22. Sheri Berman, "Populism Is a Symptom Rather Than a Cause: Democratic Disconnect, the Decline of the Center-Left, and the Rise of Populism in Western Europe," *Polity* 51, no. 4 (2019): 654–67.

23. Pontus Odmalm and Tim Bale, "Immigration into the Mainstream: Conflicting Ideological Streams, Strategic Reasoning, and Party Competition," *Acta Politica* 50, no. 4 (2015): 365–78.

24. Ezra Klein, "David Shor Is Telling Democrats What They Don't Want to Hear," *New York Times*, October 8, 2021, https://www.nytimes.com/2021/10/08/opinion/democrats-david-shor-education-polarization.html.

25. Anthony Giddens, *The Third Way: The Renewal of Social Democracy* (New York: Wiley, 2013).

26. Deborah Stone, *Policy Paradox: The Art of Political Decision Making*, 2nd ed. (New York: Norton, 1997), 2.

27. Nate Cohn and Kevin Quealy, "How US Public Opinion Has Moved on Black Lives Matter," *New York Times*, June 10, 2020.

28. Eric Van Rythoven, "A Feeling of Unease: Distance, Emotion, and Securitizing Indigenous Protest in Canada," *International Political Sociology* 15 no. 2 (2021): 251–71.

29. On the "Muslim ban," see Clara Eroukhmanoff, " 'It's Not a Muslim Ban!' Indirect Speech Acts and the Securitisation of Islam in the United States Post-9/11," *Global Discourse* 8, no. 1 (2018): 5–25.

30. Philip Bump, "Analysis: Most Americans Oppose the Wall—and Oppose Ending the Shutdown by Funding It," *Washington Post*, January 16, 2019, https://www.washingtonpost.com/politics/2019/01/16/most-americans-oppose-wall-and-oppose-ending-shutdown-by-funding-it/.

31. Jack Herrera, "Did Democrats Support Border Barriers Before Trump Took Office?," *Pacific Standard*, January 9, 2019, https://psmag.com/news/did-democrats-support-border-barriers-before-trump-took-office.

32. Greene Sterling and Joffe-Block, *Driving While Brown*.

33. Walter J. Nicholls, *The DREAMers: How the Undocumented Youth Movement Transformed the Immigrant Rights Debate* (Stanford, CA: Stanford University Press, 2013); Walter J. Nicholls and Tara Fiorito, "Dreamers Unbound: Immigrant Youth Mobilizing," *New Labor Forum* 24, no. 1 (2015): 86–92.

34. On abolishing ICE, see Dara Lind, "'Abolish ICE,' Explained," *Vox*, March 19, 2018, https://www.vox.com/policy-and-politics/2018/3/19/17116980/ice-abolish-immigration-arrest-deport; and for further information on this issue, see Elizabeth F. Cohen, *Illegal: How America's Lawless Immigration Regime Threatens Us All* (New York: Basic Books, 2020). On reaction to the Biden administration's policies, see, for instance, Katelyn Burns, "Biden Vows to Increase Refugee Cap After Criticism from Democrats," *Vox*, April 17, 2021, https://www.vox.com/2021/4/17/22389136/biden-will-increase-refugee-cap-criticism-from-democrats.

35. Gary P. Freeman, "National Models, Policy Types, and the Politics of Immigration in Liberal Democracies," *West European Politics* 29, no. 2 (2006): 228.

36. Henrik Bech Seeberg, "How Stable Is Political Parties' Issue Ownership? A Cross-Time, Cross-National Analysis," *Political Studies* 65, no. 2 (2017): 475–92.

37. Katy Brown, Aurelien Mondon, and Aaron Winter, "The Far Right, the Mainstream, and Mainstreaming: Towards a Heuristic Framework," *Journal of Political Ideologies*, early online, 2021, https://doi.org/10.1080/13569317.2021.1949829.

38. Fernanda Santos, "Sheriff Joe Arpaio Loses Bid for 7th Term in Arizona," *New York Times*, November 9, 2016, https://www.nytimes.com/2016/11/09/us/joe-arpaio-arizona-sheriff.html.

39. Mudde, *The Far Right Today*; Aurelien Mondon and Aaron Winter, *Reactionary Democracy: How Racism and the Populist Far Right Became Mainstream* (London: Verso, 2020).

40. Leila Hadj Abdou, Tim Bale, and Andrew Peter Geddes, "Centre-Right Parties and Immigration in an Era of Politicisation," *Journal of Ethnic and Migration Studies*, early online, 2021, https://www.tandfonline.com/doi/full/10.1080/1369183X.2020.1853901.

41. Daniel Ziblatt, *Conservative Parties and the Birth of Democracy* (Cambridge: Cambridge University Press, 2017).

42. Tim Bale, "Turning Round the Telescope: Centre-Right Parties and Immigration and Integration Policy in Europe," *Journal of European Public Policy* 15, no. 3 (2008): 315–30.

43. Swen Hutter and Hanspeter Kriesi, "Politicising Immigration in Times of Crisis," *Journal of Ethnic and Migration Studies*, early online, 2021, https://www.tandfonline.com/doi/full/10.1080/1369183X.2020.1853902.

44. Gary P. Freeman, "Modes of Immigration Politics in Liberal Democratic States," *International Migration Review* 29, no. 4 (1995): 881–902.

45. For an exception, see Brian Budd, "The Populist Radical Right Goes Canadian: An Analysis of Kellie Leitch's Failed 2016–2017 Conservative Party of Canada Leadership Campaign," in *Populism and World Politics: Exploring Inter- and Transnational Dimensions*, ed. Frank Stengel, David B. MacDonald, and Dirk Nabers (Basingstoke, U.K.: Palgrave Macmillan, 2019), 137–63.

46. Joost van Spanje, "Contagious Parties: Anti-immigration Parties and Their Impact on Other Parties' Immigration Stances in Contemporary Western Europe," *Party Politics* 16, no. 5 (2010): 563–86.

47. Julia Azari, "Weak Parties and Strong Partisanship Are a Bad Combination," *Vox*, November 3, 2016, https://www.vox.com/mischiefs-of-faction/2016/11/3/13512362/weak -parties-strong-partisanship-bad-combination; Andrew Gelman and Julia Azari, "19 Things We Learned from the 2016 Election," *Statistics and Public Policy* 4, no. 1 (2017): 1–2; Daniel Schlozman and Sam Rosenfeld, "The Hollow Parties," in *Can America Govern Itself?*, ed. Frances E. Lee and Nolan McCarty (Cambridge: Cambridge University Press, 2019), 120–54.

48. Bale, "Turning Round the Telescope."

49. Freeman, "Modes of Immigration Politics in Liberal Democratic States"; Freeman, "National Models, Policy Types, and the Politics of Immigration in Liberal Democracies."

50. "The Business World Hasn't Quite Grappled with Protesters Storming the U.S. Capitol," *Marketplace*, National Public Radio, January 7, 2021, https://www.marketplace.org /2021/01/06/the-business-world-hasnt-quite-grappled-with-protesters-storming-the -u-s-capitol/.

51. Matt McDonald, "Contesting Border Security: Emancipation and Asylum in the Australian Context," in *Contesting Security: Strategies and Logics*, ed. Thierry Balzacq (Abingdon, U.K.: Routledge, 2015), 154–68. See also Megan Specia, "Australians Protest Five Years of Offshore Detention Policy," *New York Times*, July 23, 2018, https://www .nytimes.com/2018/07/21/world/australia/australia-refugee-policy-protest.html.

52. George Packer, "The Demise of the Moderate Republican," *New Yorker*, November 5, 2018, https://www.newyorker.com/magazine/2018/11/12/the-demise-of-the-moderate -republican; Shawn Donnan, "Republicans Join Criticism of Trump Immigration Policy," *Financial Times*, June 17, 2018, https://www.ft.com/content/0126001e-7240-11e8 -aa31-31da4279a601.

53. Christopher Hare, Keith T. Poole, and Howard Rosenthal, "Polarization in Congress Has Risen Sharply. Where Is It Going Next?," *Monkey Cage* (*Washington Post* blog), February 13, 2014, https://www.washingtonpost.com/news/monkey-cage/wp/2014/02/13 /polarization-in-congress-has-risen-sharply-where-is-it-going-next/.

54. Pew Research Center, "The Partisan Divide on Political Values Grows Even Wider," October 5, 2017, http://www.people-press.org/2017/10/05/the-partisan-divide-on -political-values-grows-even-wider/.

55. Logan Dancey and Geoffrey Sheagley, "Partisanship and Perceptions of Party-Line Voting in Congress," *Political Research Quarterly* 71, no. 1 (2018): 32–45.

56. See, for instance, Joshua Kurlantzick, "So You Thought the Global Populist Wave Was Ebbing? Think Again," *Washington Post*, February 16, 2018, https://www.washingtonpost .com/news/democracy-post/wp/2018/02/16/so-you-thought-the-global-populist-wave -was-ebbing-think-again/?noredirect=on&utm_term=.082e9ceb4428; Jon Henley, "How Populism Swept Through Europe Over 20 Years," *Guardian*, November 20, 2018, http:// www.theguardian.com/world/ng-interactive/2018/nov/20/how-populism-emerged-as -electoral-force-in-europe; and Ian Bremmer, "Populism Goes Global: Why We Need to Brace Ourselves for the Wave to Come," *Time*, May 11, 2017, http://time.com/4775441/the -wave-to-come/.

57. Peter Bucchianeri, "Party Competition and Coalitional Stability: Evidence from American Local Government," *American Political Science Review* 114, no. 4 (2020): 1055–70.

58. Katherine Benton-Cohen, "Lead, Follow, or Get Out of the Way? Arizona History and the Nation," *Journal of Arizona History* 61, no. 3 (2020): 667–92; Gambino and Singh, "The Arizona County That Could Decide the Future of Trump—and America."

59. Jennifer Medina and Hank Stephenson, "Democrats Made Inroads in Arizona. But It's a Deeply Divided Place," *New York Times*, November 29, 2020, https://www.nytimes.com/2020/11/29/us/politics/democrats-made-inroads-in-arizona-but-its-a-deeply-divided-place.html.

60. Fernanda Echavarri, "Maricopa County Was the Epicenter of the Anti-immigrant Movement. It Just Handed Arizona to Biden," *Mother Jones*, November 13, 2020, https://www.motherjones.com/politics/2020/11/arizona-biden-trump-maricopa-county-joe-arpaio/.

61. Aída Chávez, "If Arizona Goes Blue, Look to Joe Arpaio—and the Latinos Who Organized Against Him," *Intercept*, November 2, 2020, https://theintercept.com/2020/11/02/arizona-latino-voters-joe-arpaio/.

62. Jennifer Medina, "The Arizona G.O.P. Is Sticking with Trumpism, Whether Arizona Republicans Like It or Not," *New York Times*, January 19, 2021, https://www.nytimes.com/2021/01/19/us/politics/arizona-republicans-trump.html; Sam Levine and Oliver Milman, "Arizona Republican 'Audit' Finds Even Bigger Lead for Biden in 2020 Election," *Guardian*, September 24, 2021, https://www.theguardian.com/us-news/2021/sep/24/republican-audit-arizona-bigger-lead-biden.

63. Mark Brodie, "Ducey, 25 Other GOP Governors Call For Meeting About Border with Biden," *Fronteras*, KJZZ, Phoenix, September 22, 2021, https://fronterasdesk.org/content/1718857/ducey-25-other-gop-governors-call-meeting-about-border-biden; Maria Polletta, "Sanctuary Cities Ban: Why Gov. Ducey Backed Off Plan for State Constitution," *Arizona Republic*, February 22, 2020.

64. Jeremy Duda, "'Unstoppable' Kari Lake? Former News Anchor Has Trump's Endorsement and Is Packing Them in a Year before the 2022 Election," *Tucson Weekly*, October 12, 2021, https://www.tucsonweekly.com/TheRange/archives/2021/10/12/unstoppable-kari-lake-former-news-anchor-has-trumps-endorsement-and-is-packing-them-in-a-year-before-the-2022-election.

65. Laura Gómez, "Voters Will Have Opportunity to Repeal In-State Tuition Ban for Undocumented Students," *Arizona Mirror*, May 11, 2021.

66. Fernanda Santos, "Joe Arpaio's Surprising Legacy in Arizona," *Politico*, November 10, 2019, https://politi.co/34M8eBx.

67. Tamsin Mcmahon, "Biden's Path to Victory Ran Through Suburbs Much Like Those of Arizona," *Globe and Mail*, November 9, 2020, https://www.theglobeandmail.com/world/article-bidens-path-to-victory-ran-through-suburbs-much-like-those-of-phoenix/.

68. Rakich, "How Arizona Became a Swing State."

APPENDIX: METHODOLOGY

1. Derek Beach and Rasmus Brun Pedersen, *Process-Tracing Methods: Foundations and Guidelines* (Ann Arbor: University of Michigan Press, 2013), 18–21.

2. Beach and Pedersen, *Process-Tracing Methods*, 19.

3. Tulia G. Falleti and Julia F. Lynch, "Context and Causal Mechanisms in Political Analysis," *Comparative Political Studies* 42, no. 9 (2009): 1147.

4. Charles Tilly, "Mechanisms in Political Processes," *Annual Review of Political Science* 4, no. 1 (2001): 26.

5. Tulia G. Falleti, "Process Tracing of Extensive and Intensive Processes," *New Political Economy* 21, no. 5 (2016): 455–62.

6. Stefano Guzzini, "Securitization as a Causal Mechanism," *Security Dialogue* 42, nos. 4–5 (2011): 335–36.

7. Corey Robinson, "Tracing and Explaining Securitization: Social Mechanisms, Process Tracing, and the Securitization of Irregular Migration," *Security Dialogue* 48, no. 6 (2017): 505–23.

8. Falleti, "Process Tracing of Extensive and Intensive Processes."

9. Alexander L. George and Andrew Bennett, *Case Studies and Theory Development in the Social Sciences* (Cambridge, MA: MIT Press, 2005), 207.

10. Beach and Pedersen, *Process-Tracing Methods*, 19.

11. John Gerring, "What Is a Case Study and What Is It Good For?," *American Political Science Review* 98, no. 2 (2004): 346.

12. Jonathon W. Moses and Torbjørn L. Knutsen, *Ways of Knowing: Competing Methodologies in Social and Political Research* (Basingstoke, U.K.: Palgrave Macmillan, 2007), 319–21; Bent Flyvbjerg, "Five Misunderstandings About Case-Study Research," *Qualitative Inquiry* 12, no. 2 (2006): 219–45.

13. Dietrich Rueschemeyer, "Can One or a Few Cases Yield Theoretical Gains?," in *Comparative Historical Analysis in the Social Sciences*, ed. James Mahoney and Dietrich Rueschemeyer (Cambridge: Cambridge University Press, 2003), 349–50; Kathleen M. Eisenhardt and Melissa E. Graebner, "Theory Building from Cases: Opportunities and Challenges," *Academy of Management Journal* 50, no. 1 (2007): 25–32.

14. Thierry Balzacq, "Enquiries Into Methods: A New Framework for Securitization Analysis," in *Securitization Theory: How Security Problems Emerge and Dissolve*, ed. Thierry Balzacq (London: Routledge, 2011), 50.

15. Flyvbjerg, "Five Misunderstandings about Case-Study Research"; Gerring, "What Is a Case Study and What Is It Good For?," 343.

16. Marc Geddes, "The Explanatory Potential of 'Dilemmas': Bridging Practices and Power to Understand Political Change in Interpretive Political Science," *Political Studies Review* 17, no. 3 (2019): 239–54.

17. Jeffrey T. Checkel, "Tracing Causal Mechanisms," *International Studies Review* 8, no. 2 (2006): 362–70.

18. Balzacq, "Enquiries Into Methods," 46.

19.   Robinson, "Tracing and Explaining Securitization," 509.

20.   Ann Swidler, "The Concept of Rationality in the Work of Max Weber," *Sociological Inquiry* 43, no. 1 (1973): 35–42; Rogers Brubaker, *The Limits of Rationality: An Essay on the Social and Moral Thought of Max Weber* (London: Allen and Unwin, 1984).

21.   Jeffrey T. Checkel, "Process Tracing," in *Qualitative Methods in International Relations: A Pluralist Guide*, ed. Audie Klotz and Deepa Prakash (New York: Palgrave Macmillan, 2008), 114–27.

22.   Georgios Karyotis, "Securitization of Migration in Greece: Process, Motives, and Implications," *International Political Sociology* 6, no. 4 (2012): 400.

23.   Balzacq, "Enquiries Into Methods," 48.

24.   Gabriel A. Almond and Stephen J. Genco, "Clouds, Clocks, and the Study of Politics," *World Politics* 29, no. 4 (1977): 489–522.

25.   Mark Bevir and R. A. W. Rhodes, *Governance Stories* (London: Routledge, 2006), 4.

26.   Valerie M. Hudson, "Foreign Policy Analysis: Actor-Specific Theory and the Ground of International Relations," *Foreign Policy Analysis* 1, no. 1 (2005): 2.

27.   Juliet Kaarbo, "A Foreign Policy Analysis Perspective on the Domestic Politics Turn in IR Theory," *International Studies Review* 17, no. 2 (2015): 190.

28.   Mark Bevir and R. A. W. Rhodes, *The State as Cultural Practice* (Oxford: Oxford University Press, 2010); see also Felix Ciută, "Security and the Problem of Context: A Hermeneutical Critique of Securitisation Theory," *Review of International Studies* 35, no. 2 (2009): 301–26.

29.   Bevir and Rhodes, *Governance Stories*, 26.

30.   Falleti, "Process Tracing of Extensive and Intensive Processes," 457.

31.   Bevir and Rhodes, *Governance Stories*, 26–28.

32.   Hayden White, *The Content of the Form: Narrative Discourse and Historical Representation* (Baltimore: Johns Hopkins University Press, 1987), 5.

33.   An example of secondary literature that provides new policy information is Judith A. Greene, "Local Democracy on ICE: The Arizona Laboratory," in *Outside Justice: Immigration and the Criminalizing Impact of Changing Policy and Practice*, ed. David C. Brotherton, Daniel L. Stageman, and Shirley P. Leyro (New York: Springer, 2013), 23–44.

34.   Darren G. Lilleker, "Interviewing the Political Elite: Navigating a Potential Minefield," *Politics* 23, no. 3 (2003): 208.

35.   George and Bennett, *Case Studies and Theory Development in the Social Sciences*, 6.

36.   David Knoke, "Networks of Elite Structure and Decision Making," *Sociological Methods and Research* 22, no. 1 (1993): 23–45.

37.   David Richards, "Elite Interviewing: Approaches and Pitfalls," *Politics* 16, no. 3 (1996): 199–204.

38.   Charles Morrissey, "On Oral History Interviewing," in Lewis Anthony Dexter, *Elite and Specialized Interviewing*, new ed. (Colchester, U.K.: ECPR Press, 2006), 98.

39.   Hank C. Jenkins-Smith and Paul A. Sabatier, "Measuring Longitudinal Change in Elite Beliefs Using Content Analysis of Public Documents," in *Policy Change and Learning:*

An Advocacy Coalition Approach, ed. Paul A. Sabatier and Hank C. Jenkins-Smith (Boulder, CO: Westview Press, 1993), 237–56.

40. Glenn A. Bowen, "Document Analysis as a Qualitative Research Method," *Qualitative Research Journal* 9, no. 2 (2009): 32.

41. Richard Freeman and Jo Maybin, "Documents, Practices, and Policy," *Evidence and Policy* 7, no. 2 (2011): 155–70.

42. A. Cochrane, "Illusions of Power: Interviewing Local Elites," *Environment and Planning A* 30, no. 12 (1998): 2130.

43. David Block, "Problematizing Interview Data: Voices in the Mind's Machine?," *TESOL Quarterly* 34, no. 4 (2000): 757–63.

44. Norman W. H. Blaikie, "A Critique of the Use of Triangulation in Social Research," *Quality and Quantity* 25, no. 2 (1991): 115–36.

45. Oisín Tansey, "Process Tracing and Elite Interviewing: A Case for Non-probability Sampling," *PS: Political Science and Politics* 40, no. 4 (2007): 766–67.

46. Dexter, *Elite and Specialized Interviewing*, 19, 28.

47. Beth L. Leech, "Asking Questions: Techniques for Semistructured Interviews," *PS: Political Science and Politics* 35, no. 4 (2002): 665–68.

48. Tansey, "Process Tracing and Elite Interviewing."

49. Knoke, "Networks of Elite Structure and Decision Making."

50. Glenn Beamer, "Elite Interviews and State Politics Research," *State Politics and Policy Quarterly* 2, no. 1 (2002): 86–96.

51. Philip H. J. Davies, "Spies as Informants: Triangulation and the Interpretation of Elite Interview Data in the Study of the Intelligence and Security Services," *Politics* 21, no. 1 (2001): 73–80.

52. Falleti, "Process Tracing of Extensive and Intensive Processes."

INDEX

GPSR Authorized Representative: Easy Access System Europe, Mustamäe tee
50, 10621 Tallinn, Estonia, gpsr.requests@easproject.com

www.ingramcontent.com/pod-product-compliance
Lightning Source LLC
Chambersburg PA
CBHW022137020426
42334CB00015B/938